FASHION FORECASTING

FASHION FORECASTING

Evelyn L. Brannon
Auburn University

FAIRCHILD PUBLICATIONS, INC.
New York

Executive Editor: Olga Kontzias
Editorial Assistant: Beth Applebome
Production Editor: Joann Muscolo
Copy Editor: Donna Frassetto
Art Director: Mary Siener
Production Manager: Priscilla Taguer

Cover Desig: Nataliya Burshman
Cover Illustration: Jane Sterrett
First Printing © 2001
Copyright © 2000 Fairchild Publications, Inc.

Library of Congress Catalog Card Number: 00-30207

ISBN: 1-56367-206-5

GST R 133004424

Printed in the United States of America

CONTENTS

Preface xii

Chapter 1 | The Fashion Forecasting Process 1

OBJECTIVES 1

TREND CHASERS—WHO, WHAT, WHERE, WHEN, WHY, AND HOW 2

Defining Fashion 4

Fashion Trends 6

Fashion at the End of the 20th Century 10

FASHION FORECASTING 20

Forecasting Specialties 21

Forecasting Defined 24

Forecasting in the Textile and Apparel Industries 27

KEY TERMS AND CONCEPTS 31

DISCUSSION QUESTIONS 31

ADDITIONAL FORECASTING ACTIVITIES 32

Part One | FORECASTING FRAMEWORKS

Chapter 2 | Introducing Innovation 37

OBJECTIVES 37

DIFFUSION OF INNOVATION 38

Characteristics of an Innovation 40

The Consumer Adoption Process 41

Fashion Change Agents 44

Fashions, Fads, and Classics 52

Forecaster's Toolbox: Visualizing the Diffusion Process 56

CONSUMER SEGMENTATION 60

Generational Cohorts 61

Lifestyle Segments 63

Life Stages 64

Forecaster's Toolbox: Visualizing Target Markets 66

DISCOVERING THE ZEITGEIST 67

Nystrom's Framework for Observing the *Zeitgeist* 68

Forecaster's Toolbox: Seeing the Big Picture 70

Key Terms and Concepts 71

DISCUSSION QUESTIONS 71

ADDITIONAL FORECASTING ACTIVITIES 72

Chapter 3

The Direction of Fashion Change 73

OBJECTIVES 73

FASHION MOVEMENT 74

THE DIRECTION OF FASHION CHANGE 75

Trickle-Down Theory 75

Trickle-Across Theory 83

Trickle-Up Theory 88

Directional Theories of Fashion Change in Tandem 94

LONG WAVE PHENOMENON AND FASHION CYCLES 97

Recycling Fashion Ideas 98

Wave Dynamics 106

KEY TERMS AND CONCEPTS 110

DISCUSSION QUESTIONS 110

ADDITIONAL FORECASTING ACTIVITIES 110

RESOURCE POINTERS 111

Part Two	FASHION DYNAMICS

Chapter 4	Color Forecasting 115

OBJECTIVES 115

CASE: A COLORFUL SEASON 115

DIMENSIONS OF THE COLOR STORY 116

    Color in Marketing 118

    Consumers and the Psychology of Color 120

    The Language of Color 123

    Color Names 126

COLOR CYCLES 128

    Long Wave Cycles 129

    Color Cycles and Cultural Shifts 131

    Forecasting with Color Cycles 132

COLOR RESEARCH 133

    Color Relationships across Product Categories 133

    Sources for Color Ideas and Palettes 139

    Techniques of Trend Analysis and Synthesis 141

ORGANIZATIONS FOR PROFESSIONAL COLOR FORECASTERS 144

    Color Association of the United States (CAUS) 145

    Color Marketing Group (CMG) 147

COLOR PLANNING INSIDE THE TEXTILE AND APPAREL INDUSTRIES 148

    Forecasts at the Beginning of the Pipeline 149

    Apparel Manufacturer's In-House Forecast 150

    Forecasting at the End of the Pipeline 151

    Color Specification Systems 152

KEY TERMS AND CONCEPTS 154

CASE: A COLORFUL SEASON REVISITED 154

ADDITIONAL FORECASTING ACTIVITIES 155

RESOURCE POINTERS 156

PROFILE: LEATRICE EISEMAN 136

Chapter 5

Textile Development 157

OBJECTIVES 157

CASE: *TEXTILE TREND WATCH* 157

FASHION IN FIBER AND FABRIC 158

SOURCES OF INNOVATION IN TEXTILE DEVELOPMENT 161

    The Timing of Innovation 162

    Trade Organizations and Fabric Councils 167

RESEARCHING SEASONAL TRENDS 168

    Print Shows 171

    Fabric Fairs and Trade Shows 172

    Presentations 177

    Fabric Libraries 178

KEY TERMS AND CONCEPTS 178

CASE REVISITED: *TEXTILE TREND WATCH* 179

ADDITIONAL FORECASTING ACTIVITIES 179

RESOURCE POINTERS 180

PROFILE: JO COHEN, COTTON INCORPORATED 170

Chapter 6

The Look: Design Concepts and Style Directions 181

OBJECTIVES 181

CASE: FROM CATWALK TO MAIN STREET 181

TREND MULTIPLICATION 182

    The First Era of Modern Fashion 183

    The Second Era of Modern Fashion 184

    The Third Era of Modern Fashion 185

THE FASHION MAP 188

    Fashion Geography 189

    Collections on the Runway 193

    Fashion off the Runway 195

    Street Fashion 200

TREND IDENTIFICATION, ANALYSIS, AND SYNTHESIS 202

Visual Core Concepts 204

Different Designers with the Same Design Concept 209

Trend Dynamics: Label, Coattail, and Flow 212

Trend Analysis and Synthesis 213

KEY TERMS AND CONCEPTS 214

CASE REVISITED: FROM CATWALK TO MAIN STREET 214

ADDITIONAL FORECASTING ACTIVITIES 215

RESOURCE POINTERS 215

PROFILE: DAVID WOLFE 207

Part Three   # MARKETPLACE DYNAMICS

Chapter 7   # Consumer Research 219

OBJECTIVES 219

CASE: EXTENDING THE LINE 219

BUSINESS BEGINS AND ENDS WITH THE CONSUMER 220

Demand-Activated Product Development 220

Fashion Brands 222

Retail Formats 226

Mass Customization—The Next Big Thing? 231

LISTENING TO THE VOICE OF THE CONSUMER 234

Asking "What" and "Why" Questions 236

Asking "What" and "How Many" Questions 240

Demographics Revisited 245

Consumer Segmentation Revised 252

KEY TERMS AND CONCEPTS 254

CASE REVISITED: EXTENDING THE LINE 254

ADDITIONAL FORECASTING ACTIVITIES 255

RESOURCE POINTERS 255

PROFILE: DEEDEE GORDON, LAMBESIS 246

Chapter 8

Sales Forecasting 257

OBJECTIVES 257

CASE: DATA ON DEMAND 257

THE FUTURE—"REAL-TIME MARKETING" 258

SALES FORECASTING BASICS 260

SALES FORECASTING METHODS 261

Time-Series Forecasting 265

Correlation or Regression Techniques 266

Qualitative Techniques 268

Figuring Out Sales Forecasting 270

Blending Quantitative and Qualitative Techniques 272

SALES FORECASTING IN CONTEXT 273

The Product Life Cycle 273

The Business Cycle 275

DATA MINING—A STEP TOWARD "REAL-TIME MARKETING" 279

STRATEGIC DATA PARTNERSHIPS AND REAL-TIME MARKETING 283

Automated Replenishment Systems 284

Category Management 285

KEY TERMS AND CONCEPTS 286

CASE REVISITED: DATA ON DEMAND 286

ADDITIONAL FORECASTING ACTIVITIES 287

RESEARCH POINTERS 288

PROFILE: BRIAN TULLY, OXFORD INDUSTRIES 262

Chapter 9

Cultural Indicators 289

OBJECTIVES 289

CASE: THE FUTURE OF INFORMATION 289

NAVIGATING CHANGE 290

THE PROCESS OF LONG-TERM FORECASTING 291

IMPLICATIONS FOR THE TEXTILE AND APPAREL INDUSTRIES 303

THE LONG-TERM FORECASTER'S TOOLBOX 304

Research Strategy 1: Media Scan 305

Research Strategy 2: Interviewing 305

Research Strategy 3: Observation 307

Reviewing, Organizing, and Editing Trend Folders 308

Looking into the Future 311

KEY TERMS AND CONCEPTS 313

CASE REVISITED: THE FUTURE OF INFORMATION 313

ADDITIONAL FORECASTING ACTIVITIES 314

PROFILE: ICONOCULTURE, INC. 300

Part Four — FORECASTING AT WORK

Chapter 10 — The Future of Forecasting 317

OBJECTIVES 317

BALANCING ACT: THE EDGE OF CHAOS 318

Insights from Chaos Theory 319

Insight about Self-Organizing Systems 320

The Balancing Act: Anticipation and Improvisation 322

The Balancing Act: Multiple Time Horizons 327

FORECASTING TRAPS FOR THE UNWARY 328

Avoiding Traps in Forecasting Methods 331

Avoiding Traps in the Forecast 332

Avoiding Traps in Trend Analysis 333

Avoiding Traps As a Forecaster 335

FORECASTING AS A TEAM SPORT 335

Problems Inside and Outside the Box 336

Shared Information, Shared Forecasting 339

KEY TERMS AND CONCEPTS 342

DISCUSSION QUESTIONS 342

ADDITIONAL FORECASTING ACTIVITIES 343

Chapter 11

Windows on the Future: Media Scans and Competitive Analysis 345

OBJECTIVES 345

INFORMATION AS AN ASSET 346

PROBING THE FUTURE WITH MEDIA SCANS 347

The Basic Scan: National News Media 347

Tricks of the Trade: Technology Tools for Scanning 351

Individualized, Customized Scans 355

COMPETITIVE ADVANTAGE: MEDIA SCANS FOR MARKET INFORMATION 358

Question Forming and Information Gathering 361

Methods of Data Analysis 369

From Scanning to Implementation 371

KEY TERMS AND CONCEPTS 372

DISCUSSION QUESTIONS 373

ADDITIONAL FORECASTING ACTIVITIES 373

RESOURCE POINTERS 374

Chapter 12

Presenting the Forecast 375

OBJECTIVES 375

PRESENTATION DESIGN AS A CREATIVE PROCESS 376

Data Gathering and Pattern Recognition 377

Transforming Data into Information and Knowledge 378

TREND REPORTING 381

Trend Map 383

Trend Boards 385

PRESENTATION TECHNIQUES 391

Speaking about Fashion 391

New Presentation Tools 396

KEY TERMS AND CONCEPTS 397

DISCUSSION QUESTIONS 397

ADDITIONAL FORECASTING ACTIVITIES 398

Appendix 399

Glossary 405

Bibliography 418

Index 434

PREFACE

The idea for this book developed from experiences consulting with textile and apparel companies, attending seminars by nationally known forecasters, and interviewing industry executives who use forecasting in their decision making. It became clear that the shift to more time-based strategies of competition was making forecasting ever more important in decision making. By anticipating trends, aligning product development with consumer preferences, and facilitating the timely arrival of products in the marketplace, forecasting creates competitive advantage for companies.

The National Textile Center (NTC), a consortium of universities, was created to focus research efforts on increasing the competitive advantage of the U.S. textile and apparel industries within a global economy. In the first round of proposals, the NTC funded a project on the design of a computer-integrated forecasting workstation. As head of that research team, I had the opportunity to delve into the various forecasting disciplines, the way they interrelate, and the technology that could import forecasting information to the desk of executives in the industry. The research involved interviews with product developers, management information specialists for manufacturers and retail chains, and forecasters. When the project began, building a forecasting workstation required a customized computer dedicated solely to the search, capture, analysis, and presentation of forecasting information. By the time the project concluded, advances in computer technology and the World Wide Web made it possible to do the same functions on any networked computer. This book derives from that research effort.

Observation of forecasting practices in the industry made it clear that the traditional role of forecasting as input for planning was expanding. Forecasting from color directions to cultural indicators, sales forecasting to consumer research, was essential as decision support. Naturally executives need familiarity with the forecasting disciplines associated with their direct decision responsibilities. As the industry continues to emphasize partnering between companies in the supply chain and working on teams within companies, executives need an understanding of the full spectrum of forecasting practices. The purpose of this book is to introduce each of the forecasting disciplines used by executives in the textile and apparel industries and to show how they can be integrated to support decisions on a timeline from short-term, tactical decisions to long-term strategic ones.

The most valuable currencies in today's competitive climate are information and learning. Executives' decisions are enhanced in an information-rich environment because forecasting begins with data. Information technology makes finding data easier, but without the ability to sift, frame, and integrate the information, no learning can take place. This book explains not only information gathering but also the process of organizing and analyzing the data, and synthesizing it into actionable forecasts.

This book is intended for students in forecasting and fashion analysis classes in two- and four-year colleges, universities, and technical institutes. The term "executive" is used throughout the book instead of "student" or "user" to recognize that students are executives-in-training—only a few steps from assuming decision-making responsibilities in the industry. Because decisions are seldom made with full knowledge of the outcome, every executive engages in some form of forecasting.

The backdrop to this book is the growing interest among companies for benchmarking, an approach to performance improvement that involves identifying the best practices in the industry and adapting them to a specific situation. The book provides extensive examples of forecasting practice in the industry and profiles of forecasting professionals. The goal of this book is to survey the best in forecasting practices in the textile and apparel industries and to provide the reader with the opportunity to rehearse these practices through case studies and forecasting activities.

The World Wide Web and fashion news via CD-ROM, video, and television have moved fashion forecasting outside the small coterie of fashion mavens who attend the runway shows. Today forecasting information is widely available. The book integrates traditional and new electronic approaches to the process of forecasting at each stage of research, organization, analysis, interpretation, and presentation. New computer-based tools and techniques take advantage of this new availability and are particularly applicable to the research and presentation phases. A section at the end of some chapters called Resource Pointers provides addresses for Web-based forecasting information. Chapter 11, "Windows on the Future," outlines the kind of environmental scanning and competitive analysis that brings forecasting right to the desktop of any executive and the benefits that it brings in terms of decision support. A Web site specifically designed to mirror that chapter provides readers with a menu approach to creating their own customized environmental scanning system for forecasting.

ORGANIZATION OF THE BOOK

The first chapter in the book defines fashion, trends, and forecasting and provides an overview of the forecasting process. The chapters in Part I, "Forecasting Frameworks," survey the theories of fashion change in the 20th century and examine their application to forecasting today. Part II, "Fashion Dynamics," then describes the process of discovering directional signals for color, textiles, and design concepts. This simultaneously collaborative and competitive process allows the segments of the textile and apparel supply chain to coordinate seasonal goods around looks that can be communicated to the customer through the press and stores. There is an adage that says, "Nothing will succeed in fashion if the public is not ready for it." Part III, "Marketplace Dynamics," explores the intersection between product, consumer behavior, and cultural change. The final part of the book, "Forecasting at Work," looks at the future of forecasting practice, the power of media scanning and competitive analysis in decision support, and the best approaches for presenting forecasting information.

For students studying forecasting at the freshman or sophomore level, an introduction to forecasting could include the first chapter with its overview of forecasting and the parts on fashion and marketplace dynamics. In this case, the forecasting frameworks chapters can serve as reference material for activities and projects and the final section as a resource for future classes. Students studying forecasting at the junior and senior level bring more experience to the class, and for them, an overview of the forecasting frameworks can provide the organizational structures they need to bring meaning and clarity to their observations of fashion change. Because the book is a handbook of forecasting practices, students can use the text as a reference for other classes in product development, merchandising, marketing, and promotion.

LEARNING FEATURES

Forecasting bridges the gap between ambiguous and confusing signs and actionable decisions. Nothing except a well-trained, sensitive, and flexible human mind can see the subtle patterns in information and integrate them into a plausible forecast. Professional forecasters do not proceed by rule of thumb or trial and error but by mastery of the theory and practice of the field. This book is designed to make forecasting techniques accessible with full consideration for the precision and validity of the forecast. Each chapter includes:

- Learning objectives to alert readers to the chapter content and potential outcomes that result from mastery of this material.
- Graphics and photographs to enhance the content, add visual interest, and supplement explanations in the text.

- Activities that reinforce the content of the chapter, allow readers to practice the techniques described, and build forecasting expertise.
- A list of key terms and concepts as a review of the chapter content, coordinated with an end-of-book glossary.
- Discussion questions to assist readers with reviewing and summarizing forecasting practices explained in the chapter.

The chapters dealing with forecasting disciplines (Parts II and III of the text) include two additional features. Each chapter is introduced with a case based on situations prevalent in the textile and apparel industries. The chapters conclude by revisiting the cases with discussion questions that encourage students to consider many possible approaches to resolving the issues raised in the case. These chapters also include a profile of a forecasting professional highlighting the real-world application of forecasting techniques. The appendix provides a list of agencies, consultants, trade associations, and other companies specializing in forecasting services. The extensive bibliography directs students' attention to sources of additional information about forecasting.

An Instructor's Manual is available to professors adopting the text. The Instructor's Manual shows how the book can be used in various classes depending on the focus of the course and time frame. It includes suggested solutions to the cases, test questions, and suggestions for video segments to provide visual interest to classroom presentations.

A Web site coordinated with the book provides teachers and students with a quick and easy way to launch their online research.

ACKNOWLEDGMENTS

The National Textile Center (NTC) has been a tremendous boon to textile and apparel researchers because it has funded both basic and applied research projects. The project on which this book is based was speculative when it began in 1992 because the computer hardware, software, and networks to accomplish the task were expensive and only beginning to be available to ordinary users. Since then, advances in computer technology and networking have made the tools accessible and affordable. My special thanks go to Joe Cunning, the Director of the NTC, for his encouragement and confidence in the project, and to Jerry Cogan of Milliken for his enthusiasm and support for the project while a member of the Technical Advisory Committee. Thanks also go to Carol Warfield, Director of the NTC, Department of Consumer Affairs, Auburn University, for facilitating the proposal process and the administration of the project. Don Duffield, Research Associate, provided invaluable technical assistance in designing computer systems and exploring software and networking solutions to satisfy the needs of the project.

I am appreciative to the Department of Consumer Affairs and the School of Human Sciences at Auburn University for granting a sabbatical leave during Spring quarter of 1998 so that the proposal for this book could be written and submitted. During the time I was away several faculty members—Robin Fellers, Lenda Jo Connell, Pamela V. Ulrich, Ann-Beth Presley, and Carol Warfield—assumed extra duties and I am grateful for their willingness to do so.

I am deeply indebted to Lenda Jo Anderson, Pam Ulrich, and Ann-Beth Presley for the teamwork and camaraderie we share while working on research projects and curriculum development as faculty members in apparel design, product development, and production. They, along with Sven Thomessen, Research Associate, have been my constant sounding boards, ad hoc reviewers, and support system during the writing of this book. Sven has been especially helpful in checking sections involving technology, economics, and theories related to complex systems.

Undergraduate students in classes on fashion analysis and forecasting, theories of fashion change, and apparel design have contributed greatly to this book by providing feedback on the content and by undertaking the activities as projects for class. Graduate students in consumer preference, research methods, and thesis research have also helped to clarify my thinking on forecasting and contributed to the book with their willingness to pursue forecasting-related research.

Forecasting professionals are busy people, but they made time in their schedules for interviews that found their way into this book. Special thanks go to Leatrice Eiseman, DeeDee Gordon, Jo Cohen, and Brian Tully.

When an author and editor agree to produce a book together, there are risks on both sides. I count myself very fortunate to have Karen Dubno and Joann Muscolo as editors for this book. Their professionalism and insightful suggestions have added greatly to the quality of the book. As an author I am grateful for the competence of the professional staff at Fairchild Books who transformed the stack of pages I sent into the book you hold.

A number of professors read drafts of manuscript chapters as part of a blind review process. Although their names are unknown to me, it was clear that they were a diverse group from two-year and four-year programs at colleges, universities, and technical institutes, who taught forecasting courses at all levels from freshman to graduate students. I have gratefully incorporated their suggestions into the final draft and I hope they will recognize the contribution they made to the quality of the content and organization of this book.

On a personal note, I must thank my mother, Mildred Brannon Vinson, for her unflagging support for me and for the project. I would also like to thank my family and friends for their patience and forbearance as I turned my attention away from shared activities to devote more and more time to the book. I hope they will see the result as worth the effort.

Evelyn L. Brannon

FASHION
FORECASTING

Chapter 1

THE FASHION FORECASTING PROCESS

"Peacock today, feather duster tomorrow."
—Lou Carnesecca

Objectives

- Understand the multifaceted character of fashion.

- Understand the characteristics of a trend.

- Analyze the trajectory of fashion change in the late 20th century and the implications for the 21st century.

- Understand the breadth and depth of the forecasting process.

- Identify the role of forecasting in the textile and apparel industries.

TREND CHASERS—WHO, WHAT, WHERE, WHEN, WHY, AND HOW

Meteorologists who study the formation and behavior of tornadoes are called storm chasers. They position themselves in the geographic location most likely to spawn these violent but short-lived weather events. Then, with skill, knowledge about storm behavior, perseverance, and a little luck, they locate and investigate the phenomenon. They transmit their findings to other meteorologists and, eventually, to the public.

Like the storm chasers, trend chasers locate the spawning ground of trends and use their skill and knowledge to identify emerging concepts. Trend chasers transmit their findings to other forecasters, product developers, marketers, and the press, setting off the chain reaction that people call fashion. The result is a continuous flow of products with new styling, novel decoration, and innovative uses.

Trend chasers work in many kinds of firms—for designers, advertising agencies, fiber producers, retail chains, and apparel brands. In each case the job is custom designed to the interests and needs of the firm.

- **Bonnie Young, Director of Global Sourcing and Inspiration, Donna Karan**

Young travels the world looking for shape, color, and detail to inspire Karan's clothing, jewelry, and home furnishings collections. She travels to Tibet, China, Mali, India, and other such locations with still and video cameras and the budget to buy what she sees. When she returns home, she produces a movie using the visuals and stocks her office with her finds, making it a design resource center for the company (Bowles, 1998).

- **Toni Strutz, Design and Product Development, Lee Jeans**

Strutz and the others on Lee's design and product development team track lifestyle trends and interpret them into jeanswear for each season. The evidence for a lifestyle trend for adventure travel and outdoor leisure surfaces in a drop in health club memberships and a rise in the popularity of mountain biking, rock climbing, and hiking. The team expresses that finding in natural colors, washed twills, functional details, and rugged fabrics. The evidence for a lifestyle trend toward nostalgia can be inferred from the popularity of the Volkswagen Beetle and the popularity of vintage clothing and furniture. The team expresses that finding in All-American styles and seventies' accessories ("Lee's lifestyle trends," 1999).

- **Irene Wilson, Vice President of Trend Forecasting and Consumer Behavior, Spiegel Catalog**

After some years of lackluster performance, Spiegel Catalog revamped by issuing offshoot catalogs catering to younger customers featuring clothes with a younger attitude. The new catalogs needed an exclusive mix of products with

FIGURE 1.1

Spiegel's Irene Wilson found new labels with a young attitude while doing fashion research in the Notting Hill section of London.

the kind of cachet that excites and attracts the fashion-forward customer. Wilson (Figure 1.1) found what she was looking for while doing fashion research in the Notting Hill section of London and signed exclusive deals with two labels, one making sportswear with sweatshirt material, the other featuring Asian-inspired styles (D'Innocenzio, 1998c).

• **Alex Bajrech, Fashion Director, Wet Seal, Inc.**

Bajrech's job is to predict what teens want to wear in time for his company to develop the product, produce it, and get it into its mall stores nationwide just as the trend starts its upswing. To do that Bajrech reads teen magazines, watches TV shows popular with teens, and follows the fast-paced music scene. He also stops kids on the street from New York to London to Tokyo to talk about what they are wearing and attends runway shows in the fashion capitals. Because his company's strategy is to limit the number of items it carries in any one look and to mark down slow sellers quickly, he visits Wet Seal stores around the country seeking feedback from store managers on what is selling and what is not. While in a mall, he checks out competitors' stores (Nelson, 1998).

• **Robyn Waters, Vice President of Trend Merchandising, Target**

Target, considered an upscale discounter, mixes hip design with value pricing, a combination that appeals to sophisticated shoppers. As Waters says, "It's a very real world. We're not talking 57th Street or couture ballgowns" (Seckler, 1998b). Before joining Target in 1993, Waters spent a decade in fashion and product development jobs for various department stores. Target created its unique niche by reinterpreting leading-edge trends for the budget customer through its own proprietary labels. The trend and product development team does research in the same European locales as department stores, but team members do not attend runway shows. When the team identifies fledgling fashion trends, it tests the styles in about 20 stores before rolling the look out across all Target stores a year later. In apparel and soft home goods, Target's assortment is 80 percent driven by the latest trends.

Whatever their title or hunting strategy, trend chasers enable companies to execute a strategy based on timing. Called **strategic windows,** this strategy involves timing the firm's product offerings to the customer's readiness and willingness to accept and adopt those products (Abell, 1978). Generating intelligence about future directions in the marketplace is a cornerstone of a **market orientation** with its core themes of customer focus, profitability, and coordinated marketing. Coordinated marketing means that responsibility for marketing is not solely vested in one department. Rather, many departments in the firm need access to **market intelligence**. That intelligence must combine an understanding of customers' needs and preferences along with data gathered in a variety of formal and informal ways—analysis of sales and customer databases, market research, observation, discussion with customers and industry partners, and many other complementary methods (Kohli & Jaworski, 1990). Knowing what intelligence to gather and how to analyze findings requires an understanding of the mechanisms of fashion.

Defining Fashion

In simplest terms, **fashion** is a style that is popular in the present or a set of trends that have been accepted by a wide audience. But fashion itself is far from simple. Fashion is a complex phenomenon from psychological, sociological, cultural, or commercial points of view.

Fashion As a Social and Psychological Response. Defining fashion means dealing with dualities because clothing simultaneously conceals and reveals the body and the self. Clothing choices express personal style and individuality but also serve to manipulate the public image to fit situations and the expectations of others. The engine of fashion is sparked by the dual goals of imitation and differentiation, of fitting in and standing out, of following the leader and being distinctive (Flugel, 1930; Simmel, 1904). Human ambivalence—conflicting and contradictory yearnings—finds an outlet in a capitalist marketplace as "appearance-modifying" goods. Through a process of negotiation between elements of the fashion industry and between the fashion industry and the consumer, ambiguous styles become accepted as fashionable (Kaiser, Naga-sawa, & Hutton, 1995). Duality exists even in the buying of fashion because the process is both cognitively challenging (as when people evaluate price and value) and emotionally arousing (as when people react positively or negatively to the symbolic meaning in the products) (Brannon, 1993).

Fashion As Popular Culture. Defining fashion means operating within the domain of popular culture. Unlike high culture (fine art, classical music, and great literature), popular culture often seems trivial and transient. Popular culture invites skepticism because it sometimes seems extreme and frivolous. For the same reasons, it is difficult to take fashion seriously. Fashion change is never entirely arbitrary, but ugly things are sometimes in vogue (Laver, 1937; Simmel, 1904). When a journalist writes about "fashion follies" and lists fashion's failed trial balloons, the whole enterprise takes on a slightly silly de-meanor (Colman, 1998). When a fashion commentator likens himself to the kid in the story "The Emperor's New Clothes" because he wants to stand up in fashion shows and yell "The emperor is naked!," then even industry insid-ers are questioning fashion's direction (Wolfe, 1998). When the editor of a leading fashion magazine can find no defining look for the decade of the 1990s except for a "pervasive minimalism," then the news is out—the decade before the millenium was a tough one for fashion (Wintour, 1998).

Does that mean that fashion is disappearing as a cultural phenomenon? Is it a signal, not just of the end of fashion, but of fashion forecasting? Not at all! Most people invest their time, interest, and dollars in popular culture. The study of popular culture—the content and people's relationship to that con-tent—has attracted the attention of scientists and scholars. Some very serious anthropologists, psychologists, and sociologists have written about fashion and theorized about its mechanisms of change.

Fashion As Change. Defining fashion as change captures the charm of nov-elty, the responsiveness to the spirit of the times, and the pull of historical continuity (Blumer, 1969; Simmel, 1904). Fashion is not a phenomenon re-stricted to apparel. It is present in the design of automobiles and architecture, the shifting popularity of cuisine, the development of technology, and the buzzwords of business management strategies. One day people are driving metal boxes, the next, rounded metal eggs. One day few people are eating oatmeal, the next day almost everyone is because it has been declared a health food. Once no one decorated using the colors and crafts of the Southwest, then everyone did. Every few years a new management strategy is touted as a breakthrough only to be replaced by another one a few years later. The World Wide Web was once an information network for scientists, now it reaches into offices and homes everywhere. Understanding fashion helps explain how do these transformations happen.

Fashion As a Transfer of Meaning. Meaning exists in the cultural environment. Designers, marketers, and the press transfer the meaning to a consumer good and increase its visibility. The consumer fetches the meaning out of the marketplace in the form of goods and constructs his or her own personal world (McCracken, 1988b). Not all goods catch the attention of or find favor with consumers. Some meanings are rejected initially and are then taken up later. Some meanings are recycled over and over. Obsolescence is designed into the process. Fashion in its many guises plays a constant role in the evolving cultural environment. As Simmel said at the beginning of the 20th century: "The very character of fashion demands that it should be exercised at one time only by a portion of the given group, the great majority being merely on the road to adopting it" (Simmel, 1904, p. 138).

Fashion As an Economic Stimulus. More than an abstract concept, fashion is an economic entity. A wag writing in the *New Yorker* summed up the issue: "If clothes can not be relied on to wear out fast enough, something must be found that will wear out faster; that something is what we call fashion" (Gopnik, 1994). Planned obsolescence powers the economic engine of fashion. Wearing clothes until they wear out or wearing the secondhand clothes of more fickle buyers are acceptable strategies for dressing, but they omit the pleasure in new clothes and the novelty in new looks. Creating fashion goods requires the ability to mix aesthetic concerns and market mindfulness—that is, mass-produced fashion is the product of negotiation within and between the subworlds that make up the fashion industry (Davis, 1991).

Fashion and Gender Differences. Where apparel is concerned, men and women have not been playing on the same field. Beginning in the 19th century, men's clothing has exhibited greater uniformity and a lack of decorative elements. Men rejected the social distinctiveness of dress in favor of "occupational" clothing with similarity in cut, proportion, and design (Flugel, 1930). Women, in a relatively weaker social position than men, used fashion as a field where they could vent their "individual prominence" and "personal conspicuousness" (Simmel, 1904). By the 1930s, fashion commentators were seeing a change—the breakdown of social hierarchies and the "ever-increasing socialization of women" (Flugel, 1930; Laver, 1937). These commentators began asking if these changes in the lifestyles and economic status of women would lead to the same reduction in clothes competition that had occurred among men. Only time would tell.

Fashion Trends

An innovative look appears in the street, on the runway, or in the media thanks to a trendsetter's ability to go ahead of current fashion, ignoring trends and yet anticipating them (Furchgott, 1998). The look has the appeal

Trace the evolution of men's suits in the 20th century. Working within a narrow band of allowable fashion change, men's suits have still displayed the influence of fashion trends on silhouette, fabric, and details. Use **primary sources**—publications from the time when the clothing was new. Collect examples including photographs of celebrities, newspaper ads, and offerings in mail-order catalogs. Identify the aspects of the suit that vary across time. How much variation is there between extremes? Do any aspects vary together as a recognizable pattern? Observing the details in the evolution of men's suits helps sensitize the eye to subtle variations in styles.

Activity 1.1
Small Changes

of "newness" because it has been missing or scarce in the marketplace. A **trend** is characterized by a building awareness of this new look and an accelerating demand among consumers (Perna, 1987). A study of fashion change shows that new looks rarely come out of the blue. Instead, fashion is a logical evolution from a precursor, the next step in building on a successful trial balloon, a response to social change, or an expression of cultural drift.

Evolution of a Trend. Tracking trends is very much like watching weather patterns. A warm and a cool air mass collide, and the results may be a tornado and golfball-size hail or just rain and gusty winds. Lawrence Samuel, co-founder of the marketing consulting firm Iconoculture, Inc., spelled out the predictable and unpredictable stages in the **evolution of a trend** ("Will cigars," 1997). The three stages are:

- Fringe—a stage when an innovation arises and the trendiest consumers and entrepreneurial firms begin to participate.

- Trendy—a stage when awareness of the trend grows because early adopters join the innovators to increase the visibility of the trend and the most fashion-forward brands and retailers test the concept.

- Mainstream—a stage when more conservative consumers join in, visibility continues to increase, and corporations and brands capitalize on the growing demand.

Once a trend enters the **mainstream** one of several things might happen. The trend may fade away once most consumers have a chance to accept or reject it. If this happens over a short period of time and appeals to a small consumer audience, the trend is labeled a **fad**. If consumers buy into the trend for multiple purchases or replacement purchases, the look reaches a plateau level of acceptance and continues at that level. If a look or trend persists long enough, it becomes a **classic**—a look that is always available in some form, appropriate across many occasions, and acceptable to many consumer groups. Or, a trend fragments into microtrends. The microtrends may be countercultural twists on the trend, a reinvention, or a backlash—all create a new trend back at the fringe stage.

At any stage, a trend can meet resistance, merge with another trend, or be deflected in a way that changes the course of the trend. According to Neville Bean, a trend tracker and instructor at the Fashion Institute of Technology in New York, the trends for texture and shine that had been building for several seasons merged on the Spring runways in 1996 when shantung, a textured silk that had not been in the fashion picture for years, became a surprise hit. To Bean's practiced eye the merger was logical, the kind of change that people in the industry can see coming and learn to capitalize on (MacLaughlin, 1996).

Trend Movement. Tracking trend movement may require only a few points to plot a line and detect a direction. The trend may be moving up from the street through levels of consumers from the most avant-garde to the more mainstream or down from an extravagant one-of-a-kind couture creation worn by a celebrity to a knockoff at the local mall. Horizontal movement occurs when more and more people progressively adopt a style as that innovation diffuses through the market segments.

The cyclical nature of fashion can be seen in the recycling of fashion ideas—such as the return of khaki and World War II movies late in the 1990s. Fueled partly by nostalgia among generations old enough to remember and partly by the younger generation's desire to experience the music and fashions of another era, pop culture seems to circle back, picking up speed each time (Wolcott, 1998). Looking for these movements, placing observations within a theoretical framework, and visualizing the shape and direction of the change enables forecasters to predict fashion direction and the speed of change (see Chapters 2 and 3).

Trend Contagion. The transmission of trends has been likened to the spread of a virus. Malcolm Gladwell, a writer for the *New Yorker,* used this metaphor when he spoke to the International Design Conference about creating design trends that are "contagious"—spreading quickly through the consumer population to reach "epidemic" proportions. He urged manufacturers to aim for "sticky" looks with flu-like staying power because consumers do not want looks that quickly disappear (Feitelberg, 1998a).

Gladwell's comments parallel the concept of **memes**—self-replicating ideas or bits of behavior that move through time and space without continuing support from their original source (Gelb, 1997; Kauffman, 1995). Memes can be advertising slogans, catchy bits of dialogue from a TV show, or any concept that establishes its own repetition by appearing in many formats. The more copies of the meme, the more likely that it will replicate through time and space. A product, a look, or a brand can become a meme. The characteristics of a meme are very similar to a trend: novelty and vividness. A meme has one additional important characteristic: it must catch on in a way that favors the leaping of the meme from format to format at a rapid speed.

Trends must be visible to possible adopters in order to spread. Trends spread through **word-of-mouth** among personal networks when one person visually or verbally recommends a new fashion to friends and acquaintances. **Buzz**—defined as excitement about something new—is created when trends pass through media networks, moving from one format to another (from news magazines to talk shows, from the morning shows to late night). Receiving information on a trend in this way gives the consumer a feeling of being "in the know" because of insider information from the media elite (Marin & Van Boven, 1998). Buzz lifts whatever people in the media are currently talking about to a new level of awareness. The Internet speeds up the transmission of buzz by preempting traditional media—that is, by breaking news about celebrities, new products, new shopping venues, upcoming movies, and other such happenings before the items can appear in traditional channels (newspapers, magazines, television, radio, and movies). Public relations (PR) executives try to create buzz by planting information on the Internet and other "under the radar" kinds of campaigns. As consumers rely more and more on nontraditional channels for information, **hype**—the artificially generated PR form of buzz—becomes less influential and buzz more influential for trendsetters and early adopters.

Buzz certainly exists on the Internet as trends are transmitted globally in an instant through Web sites and e-mail. Building on that concept is a new form of marketing aimed at getting customers to try a software product, share it with the people they know, and thereby propagate the product on behalf of the company that created it. Called **viral marketing,** the process has been called a "highly infectious digital sneeze" (Sandberg, 1999).

Viral marketing as it applies to apparel means launching a product by stimulating the curiosity of the target audience with unbranded posters or cryptic messages on Web sites and by infiltrating underground clubs or placing ads in nonmainstream magazines. The target audience is young people who have grown up with traditional marketing and no longer want to be marketed to. Instead, they prefer to discover products through word-of-mouth. Companies see these consumers as culturally creative trend initiators. Levi's sub-brand, Red Line, and Lee's Dungarees were both successfully launched in this way (Ellis, 1999).

Trend Management. Consumers develop relationships with style, pro~~d~~ and brands based on habit, familiarity, and satisfaction. For a new tr~~e~~ succeed, it must often replace a current purchase pattern. Managers ~~a~~ both sides of the process—one set attempting to shore up the estab~~li~~ trend with new and improved versions, the other attempting to break th~~e~~

pattern and start a new one. In both cases, managers must be sensitive to consumer and media networks, understand how they work, and recognize when they must be stimulated to gain competitive advantage (Farrell, 1998).

Managerial decisions are affected by three classes of change:

- Short-term variations such as the path of trends as they emerge, evolve, and dissipate
- Cyclical variations, as when style features repeat over time in response to an underlying trend
- Long-term trends, when there are fundamental and continuous changes in the pattern of culture

Understanding how trends develop and move through society provides the perspective that managers need to shape the decision-making process.

Fashion at the End of the 20th Century

At the beginning of the 20th century, Simmel observed that "the more nervous the age, the more rapidly its fashions change" (Simmel, 1904, p.138). Fashion change did accelerate in the 20th century. Some observers trace the beginning of this acceleration to Dior's 1947 collection (Cardin & Charney, 1992). Until Dior's New Look, fashion change had been evolutionary, but as Dior introduced a new look each season—the H-line, the A-line—people came to expect seasonal newness. The rate of change increased from seasonal introductions to a rapid seasonless introduction of novelty. By the 1990s, the number of seasons had increased from four to six or more. What had once been a stately progress turned into a rout with one new fashion crowding on the heels of another before consumers had a chance to assimilate either. The appetite for newness saturated the 1990s—a very nervous age.

The signs were already there in the late 1980s. At a panel discussion sponsored by the Washington Fashion Group in 1988, fashion insiders debated the role of the apparel industry and the media in determining trends (Chute, 1988). The impetus for the meeting was the growing realization that designing and selling women's fashions had become increasingly difficult. One of the retailers cited "the aggressiveness of women of the baby boom generation" who "will not follow the lead of European designers." By the late eighties, such realizations were already more than a decade old. A women's magazine in 1971 declared in bold type: "Fashion is going out of fashion" ("Creative," 1971). The reasons listed included a rejection of the image of beautiful people who wear the latest thing in favor of an expanded definition of beauty and individuality—a shift from "what's in" to "what works," to "fashion without fuss." The catchwords for consumers were becoming comfort and convenience.

A decade and a half later, an apparel industry analyst reported that too much merchandise was pushed into the pipeline in 1985, 1986, and the first half of 1987. The industry had guessed wrong in fashion, pushing youthful fashions to customers looking for more conservative work clothes. Stores complained that designers and manufacturers had got all the signals wrong and failed to create trends that excited the consumer ("From stupidity," 1988). Beginning in August of 1987, the women's sportswear market collapsed. One of the culprits singled out for blame was the lack of fashion direction—"six different hem lengths and no real trends" ("1988: In retrospect," 1988). Companies that did follow a trend ran into trouble. Nicole Miller followed Christian Lacroix's leadership and brought back the miniskirt in a big way, but the reaction was too fast for the American customer (Friedman & Pogoda, 1990).

The cover of *Newsweek* in December of 1988 headlined a fashion revolt (Kantrowitz, Witherspoon, & King, 1988). The holiday season sales for that year were in a serious slump. After the boom years of the early and mid-1980s, fashion in the late 1980s was meeting price and style resistance. Consumers had gripes about the difference between runway images and the height and weight of the average American woman, the prices in relationship to the quality and workmanship of the clothes, the way clothing was sold, and the hype for styles that working women considered unwearable. Working women accounted for 70 percent of all women's apparel sales and spent most of their clothing budgets on work clothes. These women were not interested in trendy styles. The thing that was different about this sales slump compared to others was that it came at a time when the economy was generally good, but people were uneasy about rising prices and inflation. Some blamed designers for the outrages on the runways. Others blamed fashion reporting for pressuring designers to come up with something new each season. As David Wolfe, a professional fashion forecaster, explained in a letter responding to the *Newsweek* cover, "nobody much *ever* wore that [runway] stuff, but fashion has become a media spectator sport" (1989, p. 11).

The strict social rules governing fashion ended in the 1960s. Gone were the traditions of no white shoes after Labor Day, no patent leather in the winter, no suede in the summer, velvet and taffeta only between Thanksgiving and New Year's Eve, and shoes matching handbags. Instead fashion professionals and consumers relied on their eye for what looked right (Turk, 1989). Fashion designers, once considered dictators, now began serving a buffet of options. Rich floral prints, paisley, and plaid shared the designer runway with asceticism inspired by the plainness of the Middle Ages. Skirts were long or short; pants were long or cropped, wide or pencil tight. As Karl Lagerfeld said, "Legs are like arms, you don't want to wear long sleeves every day." While retailers were looking for clear-cut direction for their private-label lines, the runway went "rag-picking through the history." One designer explained the fashion future in terms of tribes with a designer for each tribe (Gross, 1988).

By 1990 recession and threat of a war with Iraq were making consumers conservative in their spending. Price was becoming more of an issue, and quality rather than status was being emphasized in advertising. Designers' signature collections were not doing as well because of high prices. As one retailer put it, "It's a good time to be in a business other than high fashion retailing" ("Stores lament," 1990). Then came a fashion debate about "tight versus loose," with fashion moving in two distinctly different directions (Figure 1.2). In the July couture shows, Versace was showing very short, very tight dresses with a sexy sensibility while Saint Laurent, Lagerfeld, and Armani were showing soft, loose silhouettes. The division held in the American designers' reactions to the Paris shows with some opting for "tight clothes to show off the American body," others edging toward comfort, and many combining the two with "tight under looser layers" ("Loose vs. tight," 1990). The "loose revolution" quickly moved to acceptance at the consumer level (Friedman, 1990). Retailers were keeping inventories low and talking about austerity in operational expenses, and manufacturers were sweetening deals to get merchandise into stores. A manufacturer at the bridge level pointed out that Paris was only one small aspect in the design of a line be-

FIGURE 1.2

Runway shows in 1990 showed fashion moving in two distinctly different directions. Some designers like Versace (right) showed short, tight dresses. Others like Saint Laurent (left) showed looser silhouettes.

cause, while couture needed a sensational new look every season, fashion in the bridge line did not change abruptly. An editorial in a trade paper underlined the need for a system that allowed designers and manufacturers to become more aware of consumer thinking (Gordon, Hartlein, Pogoda, & White, 1990; Moin, 1990).

In 1992 and 1993, designers sought inspiration in frugality and inspiration from monks' robes, the plain clothes of the Amish, and religious symbols (Spindler, 1993). Clothing went from unconstructed to deconstructed with raveled edges, opened seams, and hanging strings—one fashion article called it the look of the "repentant nineties" (Brantley, 1992). Where designer clothes in the fifties looked as finished on the inside as the outside, now clothes looked unfinished, ragged, wrinkled, and tattered on both sides. The distressed look had moved from sliced denim jeans to the Paris runways. The look bypassed the manufacturers and retailers and was knocked off by young consumers who wore flea market dresses wrinkled, turned T-shirts inside out, and cut edges with pinking shears (Betts, 1992).

Also in 1992 and 1993, the "grunge look" migrated from Seattle to the runways in collections by Marc Jacobs and Christian Francis Roth (Shupe, 1993). Grunge was a look, a type of rock-and-roll music, and an attitude—an unsexy, nonstyle featuring long hair, flannel shirts, and wool caps. Once the look was co-opted by designers, it became unhip to the bands that made it famous who scrambled to revise their look. "Hip-hop" looks—baggy cuts and bright colors—moved through the young urban male population in the same years. Both looks were replaced with work clothes and work boots (Patterson, 1993). For this fast-moving young customer group, a look successful enough to become mainstream loses its expressiveness.

Chains catering to the young consumer, such as Merry-Go-Round, did very well when there was a clear fashion direction but floundered when the signals became mixed (Strom, 1994). Founded in 1968, Merry-Go-Round sold prewashed jeans in the mid-1970s, sold a knockoff of the leather jacket Michael Jackson wore in the video "Beat It," and continued growing (eventually including 1,434 stores) by supplying the look of the moment to adolescents. A merchandising misstep—large inventories of hip-hop when teenagers wanted the lumberjack look—sent the company into bankruptcy.

Magazines can get caught on the wrong side of a trend, too. *Mademoiselle* magazine targets a "twenty-something" audience looking for cool fashions and help "getting a life." The magazine devotes a quarter of its pages to fashion, another quarter to beauty, and the rest is split between relationships, fitness, and entertainment. The magazine got caught in "grunge fever" when a new editor took over (Lockwood, 1996). When grunge was in full swing in late 1993, advertisers began to pull out of the magazine. Recovery involved hiring a new editor, redesign, and an aggressive campaign to win back readers and advertisers with a new direction.

At the same time, the buzzword for mainstream American fashion was "value," and the message was collections built of past winners (White, 1992). The shift to classics was said to reflect consumers' desire for security, seasonless clothing, and wardrobe building (Figure 1.3). An executive at Donna Karan explained that the idea reflected "many of the things a man takes for granted" in shopping, such as being able to replace a navy blazer with a navy blazer. Instead of designer creations, clothes from The Gap were on the cover of *Vogue*. Designers had to cope with a recessionary economy and obstinate consumers whose minds were on other things than fashion. A few designers were becoming celebrities by creating not just clothes but lifestyles, and by epitomizing those lifestyles in personal appearances, advertising, and promotion ("Designers," 1992).

A *Wall Street Journal* article in 1994 listed reasons women were not buying as many clothes (Duff, 1994). One problem was the predominance of

FIGURE 1.3

Classics reflected the consumer's desire for security, investment dressing, and wardrobe building blocks.

black. Customers liked it because it was "safe"—no worries about appropriateness or about matching colors—and black was so versatile that they did not need so many garments. Retailers and manufacturers grappled with giving people what they wanted and ended up with a sea of black and neutrals in the stores. The article stated flatly that "fads are passé" because women no longer wanted gimmicks. The constant experimentation with a floating hemline was cited as disillusioning women about the press and designers as style guides. Holly Brubach (1994) of *The New York Times* summed up the situation: "In fashion . . . we have witnessed the abdication of the experts. Everyone's opinion matters now, and no one's opinion matters any more than anyone else's."

"Casual Fridays" was a called a **megatrend** in corporate dressing—the kind of trend that influences many consumers and has a profound significance for business (Bragg, 1994). Companies started by baby boomers were always more likely to have a more casual dress code than those started by earlier generations. In more traditional firms, the dressing down trend at work began as a one-day-a-week relaxed dress code (Figure 1.4). Productivity and morale were lifted and managers and workers reported reduced tension and im-

FIGURE 1.4

Casual Friday reduced job stress and improved productivity in the workplace.

proved communication. A whole workforce had a new reason to shop as the question became, "What are you wearing to work today?" It became necessary for corporate executives to have two wardrobes, one for regular workdays and another for "casual Fridays" (Glusac, Brown, Emert, & Edelson, 1995). Most turned to classic separates to bridge the gap between suits and jeans. Many companies extended casual to everyday dress. Casual extended to more than apparel; it spread to home furnishings, entertaining, and exercise as casual living became a lifestyle (Weir, 1994).

Not everyone was happy with the changes. Retailers such as The Gap prospered on styles such as khaki pants, but manufacturers of suits, dress shirts, and ties fared much worse (Norris, 1994). Many designers and the fashion press were showing glamour with red lips and nails and stiletto heels. Tommy Hilfiger was quoted as saying that the trend toward casual was growing: "We're just at the beginning of the 'casualization' of the workplace. I see glamour as just an option" (Weir, 1994).

In February 1995, dressing down had reached epic proportions. A *Newsweek* cover story printed pictures of casually dressed prominent people from Elizabeth Taylor to Bill Clinton to Brad Pitt with the question: "You're going out in that?" and headlined the story "Have we become a nation of slobs?" (Adler, 1995). Advertising shifted to a lifestyle message that said, "Be yourself." As one ad exec put it, "What you're urging people to do is to revolt" (Ramey, 1995). Manufacturers and stores jumped on the bandwagon and overproduced casual looks, sometimes confusing corporate casual and weekend wear (D'Innocenzio, 1995). The result was "aggressive markdowns" to clear the merchandise.

Apparel prices were being pushed down by a change in consumers' value orientation and by a continuing oversupply of apparel in the marketplace in 1995. Consumers were not getting the same gratification from buying clothing as they did in the 1980s. Casual dressing had become the norm, and cheap was chic and coveted (Figure 1.5). Mass merchants such as Wal-Mart aggressively expanded their apparel departments, and shoppers in all demographic categories were shopping down market as often as up. There was industry talk about how to operate in a "zero-growth" environment. The fashion industry had disrupted its own fashion cycles by espousing "individual style." By agreeing that "anything goes" in terms of fashion and appropriateness, designers and the press had removed one of the principle drivers for updating wardrobes (Agins, 1995). Without new fashion direction, specialty chains were forced to compete on price with department stores and mass merchants. Analysts believed that consumers were now motivated primarily by price (Seckler, 1995). The price race pushed the industry toward partnerships between retailers and manufacturers who combined their expertise to remain competitive (Wilner, 1995).

In April 1995, the trade paper for women's apparel, *Women's Wear Daily (WWD),* headlined a front page story "Fashion Depression." A full-page pic-

FIGURE 1.5

Every day was dress-down day on college campuses from Los Angeles to Austin, Atlanta to New York City.

ture of Freud with the following quote illustrated the article: "The great question . . . which I have not been able to answer, despite my thirty years of research into the feminine soul, is 'What does a woman want?'" In June, the paper carried "A 12-Step Program to Revive Fashion" listing scapegoats such as "the bad economy, hesitant consumer, lack of newness, off-the-wall fashion, no direction, poor timing—and, of course, the weather." Studies showed that women were spending two-thirds less time in stores than they had in 1980. Shopping had turned into "drudgery" (64 percent of respondents) instead of a "favorite pastime" (only 6 percent). The prescription for recovery was to "take the lead." The article bemoaned the loss of "seasonal obsolescence" and complained that women were buying "more like men" by choosing classics that would not go out of style. The article explained that the industry had created its own problem by "trying to respond to what women 'really wanted,' but women did not know what they wanted, and the result was a change in buyer behavior." Except for Step 4, "Offer Newness," the other steps were industry-based adjustments in the way of doing business. Soon, reports from the European runways highlighted two choices: "refined style" in good taste or "deliberately provocative bad taste" ("The taste test," 1995). American runways showed the same split in sensibilities (Figure 1.6).

On the runways in 1996 the big news was the return of polyester in "fully authentic mass-production" styled looks from the 1970s (Mower, 1996). The designer of the moment was Miuccia Prada. The look was called bad taste but it signaled a move away from minimalist looks to a colorful "thrift-shop aesthetic" that Donatella Versace preferred to call "young taste." At "The Real Woman—Fall '96 Women's Wear Forecast," the message was clear—"real women want it all ... comfort, quality, value, versatility, functionality, splashes of color, trendy touches and a hint of sexiness" (Friedman, 1996b). Women were described as having adopted the European philosophy of buying fewer but better clothes and adopting a working uniform. Demographics showed that the working woman cohort was more racially mixed than past generations, and their choices reflected their cultural preferences. In mid-1996, the dressing down phenomenon coincided with the downsizing of American industry, depressing apparel sales and prices even further (D'Innocenzio, 1996). The industry segments benefiting from these pressures included

FIGURE 1.6

European and American runways showed two different styles, two different sensibilities in 1995. Ana Sui (right) epitomized the deliberately provocative, Oscar de la Renta (left) a more refined taste.

value-priced chains and brands targeting the "better" price points. Big brands were getting bigger to become **mega nichers**—super brands that captured more store space by combining a distinct image, consumer recognition, and expanding across product categories from apparel to furniture. Names that defined the "mega nicher" approach were Calvin Klein, Ralph Lauren, Donna Karan, Tommy Hilfiger, and Liz Claiborne ("Defining," 1996).

In 1997, a strong economy increased the lust in upper-strata social worlds for luxury goods including high-quality apparel, but there was still confusion over finding the right formula to fit consumers' needs (Friedman, 1997). Ready-to-wear companies were turning out an array of options with some results "stellar" and other "lackluster." In June, 1998, the stock market was high and retailers were making profits, but the fashion industry heavyweights at the second annual Fairchild CEO Summit were not satisfied (Moin & Socha, 1998). Research showed that almost half of those shopping for clothes did not buy because they could not find styles they liked (61 percent) or because clothes did not fit right (62 percent). Repeatedly emphasized was the challenge for the industry to motivate a "hardened, time-impoverished consumer to shop." Ralph Lauren pointed out in a keynote address that "no brand could be all things to all people" because "the market is more diverse than ever and defined by an anything goes approach to fashion." He suggested that the anything goes attitude made "people more receptive to new ideas." Industry trends highlighted at the conference were customized products, one-on-one marketing, and continuous consumer research.

Fashion watchers in the 1990s had witnessed a sea change. Miniskirts in the 1960s, bell-bottom jeans in the 1970s, and power-shoulder suits in the 1980s had given women a clear directional signal, and the desire to be "in" still motivated shopping (Pressler, 1995). A massive promotional push by designers, retailers, and the press failed to put grunge across. Extreme looks got the headlines and editorial coverage in magazines but did not ring up sales. Market segments fragmented, and a "counter-fashion ethic" emerged based on price, value, and a casual lifestyle. Cultural and structural changes in lifestyles compounded the impact of any fashion-related problems with merchandising and service. Catalog shopping came to the rescue of time-starved working women but accounted for a relatively small percentage of all clothing sales. But fashion had not disappeared. People still bought clothes, and they still bought newness. It was no longer enough to have a trend, it became important to have the right trend for the specific target audience.

Where would fashion go in the future? Longtime fashion commentator Bernadine Morris (1998) suggested that designers feeling nervous about the year 2000 had coped by shuffling through the decades of the 20th century from micromini skirts from the 1960s to capri pants of the 1950s. She asked, where are the experiments? Vionnet invented the bias cut in the 1930s. Fabrics stretch and computers can design prints. Shouldn't designers be discovering something new? She points out the dichotomy between the Paris runways focused on the avant-garde and American design focused on clothes that "don't get in your way." This emphasis on women's clothes as "wearable" echoes the goal of a man's suit—a smooth, layered garment, not tightly fitted, allowing unrestricted movement and a harmonious, body conscious form (Hollander, 1994). The modern men's suit began its evolution with a move away from decoration in the late 1780s during the post–French Revolution period. A split arose between the design and manufacturing modes of men's and women's clothing beginning about 1820. By the mid-1800s, the prototype of the modern men's suit—matching pieces, a sack coat, simple and undecorated, designed for ease and action—had evolved. Women's clothes continued as colorful, ornamented, and restrictive. Perhaps the years of the new millenium will see the reconciliation between the sexes on the question of fashion with men having more access to color, ornament, and self-expression and women less reliance on extraneous accessories, painful footwear, and constricting styles.

Activity 1.2 *Prescription for Recovery*	Locate the June 21, 1995, *WWD* story on "A 12-Step Program to Revive Fashion." Analyze the suggestions. Were any carried out? To what extent did these changes "revive fashion"? Are there any elements of the recovery program still left undone? Which points related to the way industry does business? Which to the fashion system? How do actions taken by the industry influence the dynamics of fashion?

FASHION FORECASTING

The tempo of innovations in all fields has increased phenomenally since the Industrial Revolution—new trends emerged, some established trends were interrupted, some accelerated. The Industrial Revolution was based on the invention of machines that could supplement or amplify manual work. The Information Revolution, powered in part by computer technology beginning in the late 1940s, had a similar effect on speeding up the emergence of innovations and accelerating change (Makridakis, 1990). Executives can do little to change an established trend. Forecasting allows them to prepare, adapt, and adjust their strategies to be in harmony with established trends (Modis, 1992).

The decade of the 1990s is instructive in terms of fashion forecasting. Some of the change that rocked the apparel business in the decade can be traced to cultural shifts such as women entering the workforce, becoming time pressured, and reprioritizing their interests; other changes to the values and preferences of the baby boom generation played out in consumer behavior. Social rules governing appropriate attire had begun breaking down in the late 1960s, but the process continued until casual looks became acceptable for almost all occasions. At times, economic bumps and international turmoil played a part in dampening apparel spending.

The industry, attempting to reactivate demand, speeded up the flow of "new looks" into mass fashion and offered "options" in the service of individuality. Increased coverage of "soft" news by the press drew attention to runway extremes and unleashed general criticism of the fashion system. Consumers became confused by mixed signals and disillusioned with the style guidance of designers, fashion journalists, and the stores, voting with their dollars to reject highly touted looks. Some consumers began to play it safe by choosing classic clothes in black and other basic colors. Even more disturbing for the industry was the finding by a research firm that the core market segment for apparel—women between 25 and 44—held back on buying clothes beginning in 1996 while diverting spending to travel, fitness, and other leisure activities ("NPD: Clothes buying," 1999).

With seasonal fashion dimming as a driver in refurbishing wardrobes, consumers concentrated on getting the best price, even if it meant waiting until markdowns. These changes boosted the success of some parts of the fashion industry. The Gap and activewear manufacturers soared on the casual trend and the relaxation of social regulations regarding appropriateness. The changes in consumer behavior and the effect of the economy on consumer confidence magnified any missteps by the fashion industry, leaving some to rethink, reorganize, and relaunch. All of these changes relate to some aspect of forecasting—style evolution, cultural change, consumer preference research, competitive analysis, and trend forecasting.

Forecasting professionals were very active during the decade of the 1990s as prominent advisors to the industry. Marketing consultants counseled giving women what they wanted, a strategy that led to the boom in selling fashion basics. When that boom was over, the consultants got some of the blame (Spindler, 1995). Critics pointed out that the bare-all slip dress could never have come from a focus group. *Melrose Place* revived the miniskirt success suit when some trend forecasters called the category dead. Consultants seemed to be missing the vital quality of novelty and vividness that makes fashion cool and hot at the same time. The forecaster walks the same difficult line as the designers, manufacturers, and retailers—the line between fashionable and functional, between too funky to be wearable and too boring to be fun.

Forecasting Specialties

Forecasting is more than just attending runway shows and picking out potential trends that can be knocked off at lower prices (although that is part of it). It is a process that spans shifts in color and styles, changes in lifestyles and buying patterns, and different ways of doing business. What appears to be near random activity is in fact a process of negotiation between the fashion industry and the consumer and between the various segments in the supply side chain.

While attention is showered on the most exciting and extreme runway fashions, the mechanisms of fashion change work in the background to create patterns familiar to the most experienced fashion watchers. One of these patterns is the pendulum swing. About the sportswear crash of 1987, a designer explained in a muddled metaphor: "The pendulum is swinging from one side to the other. People got interested in dressing a certain way. Everyone jumps on the bandwagon and there are too many people on the boat and the boat sinks" ("From stupidity," 1988). About the move to fashion basics, fashion journalist Suzy Menkes explained, "Everybody overdosed on fashion in the Eighties and it got too much for everybody. What we are experiencing is just the pendulum swinging back. We go through these cycles. It's very important to realize that anti-fashion is also fashion" ("Designers," 1992). Chapters 2 and 3 of this book provide a more complete inventory of the patterns that underlie fashion change.

Fashion Watchers. Some of fashion's trial balloons do turn into popular looks (Darnton, 1992). Montana's linebacker-wide shoulder pads looked strange on the runway of 1977. Jean Paul Gaultier's lingerie looks as outerwear were considered daring in the mid-1980s. Lacroix's mixed prints broke all the fashion rules in 1989. Long jackets such as tunics worn over leggings were audacious in the Chanel showings of 1990. All these styles were initially criticized harshly, but each eventually entered the fashion mainstream. It took only two years for the jock look of workout clothes to catch on. Presenting fashion on the runway and in the showrooms is the end point of a chain of decisions stretching back to selecting a color palette, choosing fabric, and determining the themes that guide product development. These themes are played out in the merchandising and marketing of the products to consumers.

Consumer Research and Sales Forecasting. The adoption process for fashion is really a dialogue between designers and manufacturers who propose looks and consumers who decide to adopt or reject those looks. As one forecaster put it, "Nothing will succeed in fashion if the public is not ready for it" (O'Neill, 1989).

Consumers born into a particular time develop a generational identity. As they move through the life cycle, this generational identity evolves. Groups of consumers who share preferences and demographic characteristics are called **cohorts**. These cohort groups are the basic unit of consumer research. Market segments can be broken down in many different ways—working women as a group can be categorized by occupation, age, marital status, number of children, and ethnicity, and these subgroups can be paired with apparel price points, brands, shopping behavior, and style preferences. Consumer research, including style testing, focus groups, surveys, and panel studies, allows executives to match their offerings to the mood and preferences of the target market.

Evaluation of **point-of-sale (POS) data** is only the starting point for today's sophisticated sales forecasting techniques. POS data tell the manufacturer and retailer what sold when and at what price. However, POS data cannot explain why or what consumer needs, wants, and desires went unmet by the available assortment. Together, sales forecasting and consumer research help executives develop their short-term forecast and support decision making in product development, merchandising, marketing, and promotion.

Cultural Indicators. The shift to a casual lifestyle and a consumer resistant to following trends are manifestations of deep cultural changes in society. The fashion story is part of larger shifts in the culture, including the fragmentation of the marketplace. Fashion forecasting requires a wide scan to encompass cultural, economic, and technology issues that have an impact on consumer preferences and spending. Some forecasters and forecasting firms focus on large-scale shifts in cultural indicators. These megatrends cross industry lines because they involve shifts in lifestyles, reflect changes in generational cohorts, or mirror cycles in the economy. Trends of this magnitude may be felt over the period of a decade from the first time that they surface to the time that they influence purchasing decisions on a mass scale. For the fashion industry and related categories such as interiors and automobiles, monitoring these cultural indicators is essential for strategic planning and for providing a backdrop for viewing short-term forecasts.

Competitive Analysis. Space in stores is finite. Apparel competes for consumers' attention and dollars with many other alternatives, including electronics and entertainment. To be competitive in such a business environment, companies must observe the plans and capabilities of competing firms through regular tracking of key information. Over time this effort allows a company to benchmark its activities against competitors and to develop what-if scenarios based on current information about competitor initiatives. Whether it is called competitive analysis, competitive information, or competitive intelligence, business survival and growth depend on using public sources to monitor the business activities of partners and competitors. New businesses depend on this kind of information in the start-up stage; established businesses use it to help them scout out new markets; and large corporations treat it as input for senior managers coordinating activities across markets and lines. Competitive analysis is a continuous, long-term project that uses many of the same research and analysis strategies as other forms of forecasting.

Integrated Forecasting. One problem with forecasting in the 1990s was that little effort or attention was given to integrating across forecasting specialties to generate a more multifaceted outlook. Integrated forecasting provides both a better general picture of developments and a more fine-grained interpretation. No organization should rely too heavily on a single forecasting discipline or on an individual forecaster for decision support.

The best forecasts blend quantitative and qualitative components, the wide view of cultural indicators and the close focus of sales forecasting, and short-range and long-range time scales. Interpretations must be keyed to specific consumer segments and a competitive niche. Strategies that work for teens experimenting with identity and style and those that work for more mainstream working women are very different. Change produces different effects according to the target consumer and the industry segment.

Intelligent use of forecasting keeps an executive from focusing narrowly on a specialty instead of how that specialty integrates with others in the decision-making chain. Integration of the forecasting function provides a combined forecast targeted to consumer preferences, a company's marketing niche, the competitive environment, and cultural shifts. Forecasts do not provide "the answer." Instead, forecasting opens a window on the possibilities and probabilities of the future.

<table>
<tr><td>*Activity 1.3*
Megatrends</td><td>Locate forecasts for the megatrends that will affect the future. Such forecasts are usually available in book form from well-known forecasters or summarized in newspaper and magazines articles. *American Demographics* magazine is an excellent source for this kind of information (www.demographics.com). How will these trends affect the apparel industry? Formulate two alternative futures—one as if the megatrend develops just as forecast, the other in which the megatrend happens, but to a lesser degree than forecast.</td></tr>
</table>

Forecasting Defined

Fashion forecasting has been compared to chasing the future with a butterfly net (Gardner, 1995). But spotting trends is not that difficult for people who immerse themselves in popular culture and trade news. Forecasters pluck emerging trends out of public information by becoming sensitive to directional signals that others miss. Faith Popcorn, one of the forecasters most often quoted in the media, calls this "brailing the culture"—looking for the new, the fresh, the innovative, and then analyzing the whys behind it (1991).

Forecasters vary in the methods they use, but all are looking for an apparatus that helps them predict the mood, behavior, and buying habits of the consumer. Because trends signal the emerging needs, wants, and aspirations of the consumer, canny manufacturers and retailers capitalize on their potential for turning a profit.

Forecasting is not magic practiced by a talented few with a gift of seeing the future. It is a creative process that can be understood, practiced, and applied by anyone who has been introduced to the tools. A professional does not proceed by rule of thumb or trial and error but by mastery of the theory and practice of the field. Forecasting provides a way for executives to expand their thinking about change, anticipate the future, and project the likely outcomes (Levenbach & Cleary, 1981).

Executives use forecasting as input for planning. Marketing managers position products in the marketplace using short- and long-term forecasts. Planners of competitive strategies use forecasting techniques to look at market share and the position of competitors in the marketplace. Product developers, merchandisers, and production managers use the short-term trend forecasts of color, textiles, and style direction to shape collections.

Visualization and Forecasting. In the narrowest sense, forecasting attempts to project past trends into the future. A trend is a transitory increase or decrease (Makridakis, 1990). Some trends have lasted for millennia—human population growth, for example. But all trends have the potential to eventually slow down and decline.

Visualization helps forecasters understand and communicate the movement of fashion and project future directions. Fashion trends are usually classified by duration and penetration, visualized as curves with time on the bottom axis and consumer adoption rates on the vertical axis (see Chapter 2 for details on this kind of analysis). In this way it is easy to show the difference between the shortest trends, called fads, and the longest, called classics (Figure 1.7).

In the same way, forecasters visualize fashion cycles and waves. **Cycles** have a fixed, regular periodicity. Economic and business cycles have been proposed but are considered controversial. Variations in the length and depth of "cycles" make the term a misnomer. No fixed, regularly recurring cycles have been identified and used to accurately predict the next cycle in business or fashion (the failure to identify a regular recurring fashion cycle is discussed in Chapter 3). Instead, it is more accurate to call recurring patterns a **long wave phenomenon** (Fischer, 1996). Long wave refers to any entity (e.g., prices or styles) with movement that rises and falls with differences in duration and magnitude, velocity, and momentum across periods. This wave model is reflective of movement in social spheres, including fashion.

Steps in Developing a Forecast. Forecasting consists of tools and techniques applied systematically. Just as important are human judgment and interpretation (Levenbach & Cleary, 1981). The steps in developing a forecast are:

Step 1: Identify the basic facts about past trends and forecasts.

Step 2: Determine the causes of change in the past.

Step 3: Determine the differences between past forecasts and actual behavior.

Step 4: Determine the factors likely to affect trends in the future.

cathy®   **by Cathy Guisewite**

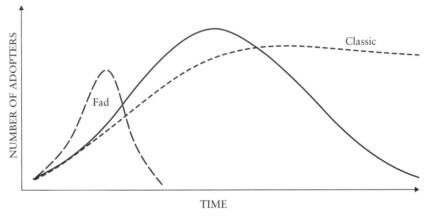

FIGURE 1.7

Short-lived fads versus classic clothes that stay in style for longer periods can be visualized by graphing their popularity and duration.

NUMBER OF ADOPTERS

Classic

Fad

TIME

Step 5: Apply forecasting tools and techniques, paying attention to issues of accuracy and reliability.

Step 6: Follow the forecast continually to determine reasons for significant deviations from expectations.

Step 7: Revise the forecast when necessary.

A trend forecast should identify the source, fundamental mechanism, direction, and tempo of the trend.

The most valuable currencies in today's competitive climate are information and learning. Information is a business asset that can be managed like any other. Executive decisions are enhanced in an information-rich environment. However, obtaining information is only the first step in the process of organizing, analyzing, understanding, and learning from it. Information is easy to find but difficult to sift, frame, and integrate so that learning can take place. Forecasting is the process that translates information into a form that allows learning to take place.

Forecasting in the Textile and Apparel Industries

Fashion and change are synonymous, and no publication on fashion goes to press without announcing some new trends. The forecaster stands in the middle of a constantly shifting fashion scene and translates ambiguous and conflicting signals to provide support for business decisions. Although they work with textile fabrications, colors, and styles, their real job is to predict the preferences of consumers in the future. Professional forecasters are employed by advertising agencies, consumer-product companies, trade groups, corporations along the textile/apparel pipeline, forecasting services, and as consultants. Forecasters work at all stages of the textile/apparel supply chain on timelines that vary from a few months in advance of the sales season to ten years ahead of it. Each type of forecast and timeline has its place in providing decision support for the executive. This book introduces the full range of forecasting professionals—those who report on innovations in fabrics, color forecasters, researchers who monitor the pulse of the consumer, others who watch the design laboratories of the couture and the streets, the retailer who tests a new retailing concept, and the fashion director who champions a new designer.

Every apparel executive in the fields of product development, merchandising, marketing, and promotion is also a forecaster because those executives make decisions about an uncertain future with incomplete information. In companies today, forecasting must be a team effort, with information shared between functional groups including design, merchandising, marketing, sales, and promotion, so that the right product gets produced and distributed at the right time to a target consumer. In the world of fashion, improving the success rate of new merchandise, line extensions, and retailing concepts by only a few percentage points more than justifies the investment of time and money in forecasting. Today's executive must be skilled in the use of an array of quantitative and qualitative forecasting methods that support the decision-making process.

Fashion forecasters share common ground: they believe that by keeping up with the media, analyzing shifts in the culture, interviewing consumers, and dissecting fashion change, they can spot trends before those trends take hold in the marketplace. By anticipating these changes, forecasters allow companies to position their products and fine-tune their marketing to take advantage of new opportunities. Major companies are becoming more and more dependent on this kind of forecasting because traditional forms of purely quantitative forecasting are less applicable to an increasingly volatile and fragmented marketplace. Two factors make forecasting more important today than ever before: the global nature of apparel production and marketing, and the shift to time-based strategies of competition. Forecasting creates competitive advantage by anticipating trends, aligning product development with consumer preferences, and facilitating the timely arrival of products in the marketplace.

Forecasters today integrate traditional and new electronic approaches to the process of forecasting at each stage of research, organization, analysis, interpretation, and presentation. The World Wide Web and fashion news via CD-ROM, video, and television have moved fashion forecasting outside the small coterie of fashion mavens who attend the runway shows. Now forecasting information is more widely available. New computer-based tools and techniques take advantage of this availability and are particularly applicable to the research and presentation phases.

Short-term forecasting is the process that begins two to three years before the arrival of merchandise in the retail store. This simultaneously collaborative and competitive process allows the segments of the textile/apparel pipeline to coordinate seasonal goods around looks that can be communicated to the customer through the press and stores. The process includes textile development, color forecasting, and style development as showcased in the international fashion shows and manufacturers' showrooms. These sources provide directional information necessary to the timely and successful introduction of seasonal fashion.

While comprehensive in the sense of seasonal fashion, these forecasting approaches must be augmented by continuous monitoring of the competitive situation and consideration of shifting cultural indicators that can influence the future. The two- to three-year timeline of short-term forecasting allows executives to take advantage of developments and position products in the marketplace. However, this timeline is not sufficient for decisions related to repositioning or extending product lines, initiating new businesses, reviving brand images, or planning new retail concepts. These decisions require other forecasting approaches with longer time horizons. **Long-term forecasting** can be more significant for an organization because it looks at social change and demographics. Demographic forecasts are among the most stable types of forecasts. Forecasting social change and technological developments is more difficult (Mahaffie, 1995).

Many people worry that they will not recognize a trend early enough to capitalize on it. Why spend the effort on trend spotting without the expectation of a payoff? Faith Popcorn (1991) says that a shift in lifestyle triggers trend cascades that take about ten years to work through the culture, affect related industries, and reach all market levels. Forecasters working in apparel fields need an early warning system so that trends can be fine-tuned for a specific product category and market segment. Although timing is important, trend information is useful wherever the trend is in its life cycle. Sometimes it is just as important to know when something is on its way out. If a fashion is nearing its termination point, that is a good time to survey the trendsetters to identify the next big thing. Together, short- and long-term forecasting approaches furnish the textile/apparel executive with access to information and the tools to shape it for decision support.

Forecasting in Apparel Planning and Scheduling. Short- and long-term forecasting has a different time horizon within the **manufacturing cycle** (Figure 1.8). The lynchpin in apparel planning and scheduling is the manufacturer (Michaud, 1989). The forecast is a rolling one that begins with a long-term forecast—in this context a forecast is usually for 12 months but can be as short as 6 months to as long as 18 months. The forecast is developed by the sales and merchandising managers using input from retailers, marketing representatives, sales history analysis (one to three years of data), and market research. This working, long-term forecast mirrors the manufacturer's business

FIGURE 1.8

Short- and long-term forecasting operate on different timelines depending on whether they refer to the overall marketplace or only to the manufacturing cycle for apparel.

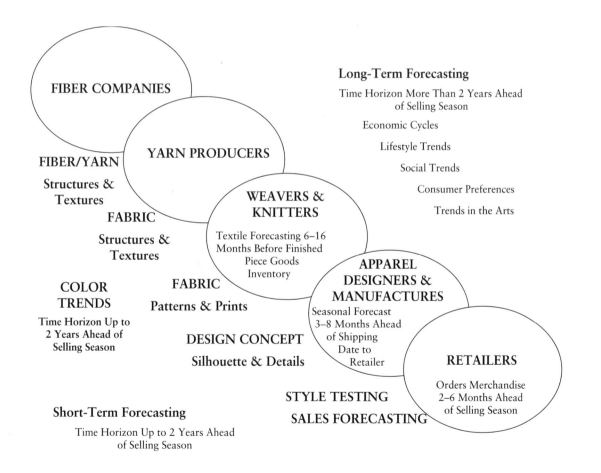

expectations in terms of lines and styles to be produced each month. The short-term forecast includes both basic and fashion goods detailed down to weekly production by style, color, and size. Proper forecasting assures the timely delivery of merchandise to the retailer.

The apparel manufacturer's long-term forecast traces the planning and scheduling process forward to the retailer because it is prepared before orders are received. Orders are shown as input to the short-term forecasts. The quality of the long-term forecast can be measured by comparing expected orders with orders received.

Tracing the planning and scheduling process backward, forecasts and orders feed back to the textile manufacturer. A process very similar to the one in apparel manufacturing occurs at the textile manufacturing level. The time period from initial forecast to delivery of finished piece goods to the apparel manufacturer is between 6 and 16 months. Tracing the process backward one more step leads to the yarn and fiber manufacturers, where a similar forecasting process takes place.

Industry fashion trends enter the model as input for the retailers' decisions and as part of planning at the other stages of apparel, textile, yarn, and fiber manufacturing. Color forecasting is typically done 20 to 24 months ahead of the target selling season. Textile development is typically done 12 to 24 months prior to the target selling season. International fabric fairs show new trends in fabrics one year ahead of the target selling season. All these forecasting activities are aimed at having the right product at the right time to meet customer demand.

Scouting for Fashion Trends. The segments of the fashion industry synthesize information into color and textile forecasts anchored by themes that reflect the spirit of the times. These forecasts serve to coordinate the supply chain for the product development process.

Many organizations and services are available to alert executives to industry fashion trends:

- To-the-trade-only shows showcase fabrics and prints for each season.
- Fashion-reporting services deliver news from the runway by subscription on the Web, on CD-ROMs, on video, or in print reports.
- Color forecasters present seminars at industry functions.
- Industry trade associations maintain fabric libraries for fashion research and present updates for apparel executives.
- The trade press covers industry events and reports forecasting information.

Members of product development teams, merchandisers, marketers, and retailers participate in events and read the trade press to gather trend information. Some team members are delegated specifically to scout for trend information and locate sources for the latest in fabrics, trims, and findings.

However, no organization can do all the scouting necessary to confirm fashion direction.

Most apparel companies subscribe to one or more services whose job it is to scout the market and report on developments. These services deliver trend information up to two years in advance of the selling season. Sometimes forecasting services are part of a buying office—either an independent organization or a division of a retailing corporation whose role is to scout the market and make merchandise recommendations to stores or chains. Sometimes the primary focus of a service is on developing seasonal trend forecasting reports. Some services specialize in providing information only in one format (e.g., video) or on a specialized topic (e.g., color). Because they serve as coordinating points for trend information, forecasting services exert a considerable trend-setting influence on the fashion industry (see the Appendix for a listing of these firms).

Using one of the search engines of the Web and the keywords "fashion" and "forecast," locate sites with forecasting information. How often are the sites updated? What organization or company sponsors each site? Bookmark the best of the sites and begin systematically to check these sites periodically for updates.

Activity 1.4
Surfing for
Forecasts

Key Terms and Concepts

Buzz	Long-Term Forecasting	
Classic	Long Wave Phenomenon	Point-of-Sale (POS) Data
Cohorts	Mainstream	Primary Sources
Cycles	Manufacturing Cycle	Short-Term Forecasting
Evolution of a Trend	Market Intelligence	Strategic Windows
Fad	Market Orientation	Trend
Fashion	Mega Nichers	Viral Marketing
Forecasting	Megatrend	Visualization
Hype	Memes	Word-of-Mouth

Discussion Questions

People often consider fashion as the trivial pursuits of a few people. Instead, fashion is a pervasive process in human culture that plays out in an infinite number of ways. The diversity produces many meanings for words such as fashion, trends, and forecasting. Executives in the apparel industry must be sensitive to the subtle significance of these meanings in order to successfully blend aesthetic concerns with market mindfulness. Use the following questions to summarize and review this chapter.

Defining fashion: What mechanisms in society power fashion behavior? What psychological traits of an individual power fashion behavior? How is meaning transferred in culture?

Defining trends: How do trends evolve and move in society? How have trends evolved to shape fashion at the end of the 20th century?

Defining forecasting: What is the role of forecasters inside corporations? What special forecasting disciplines apply to the apparel industry? Is there value to be derived from integrating forecasting disciplines within a company? What kinds of information are useful to forecasters and where do they find that information?

Additional Forecasting Activities

Rules for Appropriateness. What social rules governed fashion in previous decades? Collect oral histories from young adults, people in middle age, and older people. During what time period were they children, teens, and young adults? Ask them to recall things they were taught about appropriate dress. What rules did they have to follow on special occasions, on dates, going to school, starting work? When did they notice a relaxation of some of these rules? Should any of these social customs be revived? What would be the effect on the apparel industry?

Cover Stories. Track fashion evolution by looking at the covers of a fashion magazine over the past decade. Libraries often have bound volumes going back decades for the most popular and long-lived magazines. Because looking at all the covers would take too long, sample the issues by deciding which month or months to examine in each year. Then, systematically look at those covers. Imagine the editor and art director carefully considering the clothes, model, makeup, background color, and all the other elements making up the cover. The cover is the billboard for the magazine and has important implications for newsstand sales. How have cover design and content evolved over the decade? What directional signals for fashion change can you derive from this study? How are fashion magazines changing in the ways they showcase fashion?

Forecasting As a Career Path. Clip articles from trade and popular publications profiling forecasters in all the specialties. Note which work for companies or corporations and which work for consulting firms. Analyze the aspects that are common across all forecasting fields. What courses in your curriculum map to these competencies? Analyze the differences between the forecaster's focus and responsibilities depending on the product category, price point, and target market. What courses in your curriculum encourage the development of specialized knowledge useful in the forecasting process?

Part One

FORECASTING FRAMEWORKS

Chapter 2

INTRODUCING INNOVATION

Trends used to be wonderful because an idea rippled out, and out, and out, and eventually, everybody made a bit of money. Now a trend may have one or two ripples and die.
—David Wolfe (1999)

Objectives

- Identify diffusion of innovation as a framework for understanding and predicting fashion change.

- Identify the concept of *Zeitgeist*, or spirit of the times, as a framework for understanding and interpreting fashion change.

- Cultivate skills in analyzing current fashion within a theoretical framework.

- Increase awareness of visualization as a tool of analysis and communication.

DIFFUSION OF INNOVATION

Something new—an innovation—is proposed. It may appear in a hit movie, TV show, or music video and influence the buying decisions of millions. Or, it may emerge from the fashion runways as designers return to past fashion eras and spark retro revivals or try to create a modern look with no reference to past fashions. After the innovation arrives on the scene, individuals consider it for adoption. The cumulative effect of those decisions can be tracked in sales and visually on the street.

Sometimes innovation redefines what is appropriate as in the case of wearing lingerie as outerwear. At first the idea of uncovering bras, lacy teddies, and corsets was totally unacceptable. Then it became daring when rock music divas wore the look in music videos and on stage. Finally the style appeared in modified form in stores everywhere. Eventually echoes of the lingerie look were part of the woman executive's power suit—a lace-edged camisole showing at the neckline of her business suit. Then, fashion moved on and other options became "right" for pairing with business suits. But the lingerie look was

FIGURE 2.1

Innovation in details—a classic blazer silhouette but with extended sleeve length—plus innovation in coordinating pieces leads to a distinctive look.

extended with the introduction of the slip dress—a style that moved from models on the runway to the mall.

In fashion terms, the innovation may be the invention of a new fiber, a new finish for denim, introduction of an unusual color range, a modification in a silhouette or detail, a different way to wear an accessory, or a mood expressed in a distinctive style (Figure 2.1). Once introduced, it diffuses through the population as more and more consumers have a chance to either accept or reject it. This pattern of acceptance or rejection determines the innovation's life cycle. The **diffusion process** maps the response to the innovation over time.

The **diffusion curve** is an idealization of this process as proposed by Rogers in the early 1960s. He visualized diffusion of innovation as a bell-shaped curve where the far left-hand side represented early adopters and early diffusion of innovation, the center section, majority adoption, and the right-hand side, laggards (Figure 2.2). The shape, horizontal time axis, and vertical axis for number of adopters were retained as components of a visualization that came to express many aspects of diffusion.

The most critical stage of the diffusion process comes during the initial introduction. Without **innovators**—people who wear new fashions and expose others to the look—and without opinion leaders, who endorse a style to those who seek guidance, no diffusion will take place. For the forecaster, the diffusion model provides a framework for analyzing the movement of an innovation through a social system. The framework helps to answer questions about:

- The innovation—Why do some innovations diffuse more rapidly than others do? What characteristics of an innovation help or hinder its adoption?

- The **consumer adoption process**—What is the mental process used by individual consumers in deciding between adopting or failing to adopt an innovation?

- The diffusion process—How do innovations diffuse within a social system? What kind of consumer participates in each stage? What is the social process involved in transmitting fashion innovation?

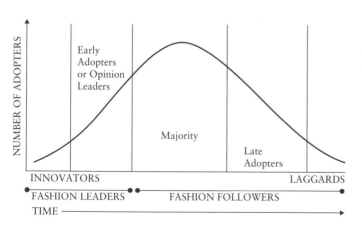

FIGURE 2.2

The diffusion curve is a visualization of the spread of innovation through a social system.

Characteristics of an Innovation

For something to function as an **innovation,** the consumer must perceive the newness or novelty of the proposed fashion—it must seem different when compared to what already exists in the wardrobe, across the social group, or in the market environment. This degree of difference from existing forms is the first identifying characteristic of an innovation.

Rogers (1983) identified characteristics that would help or hinder the adoption of an innovation.

- **Relative advantage** is the perception that the innovation is more satisfactory than items that already exist in the same class of products.
- **Compatibility** is an estimate of harmony between the innovation and the values and norms of potential adopters.
- **Complexity** is a gauge of the difficulty faced by a consumer in understanding and using the innovation.
- **Trialability** is an evaluation of the ease of testing out the innovation before making a decision.
- **Observability** is the degree of visibility afforded the innovation.

An innovation will be more readily accepted if it is conspicuous, clearly better than other alternatives, easy to understand, simple to try, and congruent with the value system of the consumer.

Marketing and merchandising focus on educating the consumer about an innovation and lowering barriers to its adoption. Spritzing consumers with fragrance as they enter a department store increases trialability, ads showing how to wear the latest accessory reduces complexity, the fashion show illustrating how to coordinate new items demonstrates compatibility. Many other marketing tactics are aimed at lowering the barriers to the adoption of a fashion innovation.

One other characteristic inhibits or encourages adoption of innovation—**perceived risk** (Robertson, Zielinski, & Ward, 1984). A consumer, when considering something new and novel, imagines beyond the purchase to the consequences (Venkatraman, 1991). The consequences may involve:

- **Economic risk**—the risk of performance problems after the purchase, the risk that the purchase price may reduce the ability to buy other products, and the risk that the price will fall after purchase.
- **Enjoyment risk**—the risk of becoming bored by the purchase or not liking it as much as expected.
- **Social risk**—the risk that the consumer's social group will not approve.

Lowering the perception of risk is a powerful element in encouraging the adoption of an innovation.

Forecaster's Toolbox: Sizing Up the Innovation. A forecaster uses the characteristics of an innovation to project potential acceptance. First, evaluate the ways in which the new innovation is better than other similar products (relative advantage). If the innovation is clearly superior to the product it will substitute for or replace, then acceptance is more likely. Then, evaluate the other characteristics for potential barriers to adoption. Can these barriers be reduced or removed through packaging, presentation, providing information, or demonstration? Can the visibility of the innovation be enhanced? What risks may inhibit the consumer's adoption of the innovation? Can the risks be eliminated, reduced, or downplayed? If the barriers to acceptance are low, it is likely that the innovation will enter the process more easily, diffuse more quickly, and be adopted by more consumers.

The Consumer Adoption Process

The diffusion curve is a visualization of group dynamics because it captures many individual decisions. In each individual case, a consumer decides to accept or reject a proposed innovation. The consumer's adoption process—the private decision—is performed with consideration of how the adoption will affect the way the consumer presents himself or herself to others and how others will react to the result. There are several versions of the steps in this mental process (Figure 2.3). The original formulation of the adoption process by Rogers (1962) included the stages of:

- Awareness—the stage at which a consumer first realizes that an innovation has been proposed.

- Interest—the period when the consumer seeks information about the innovation.

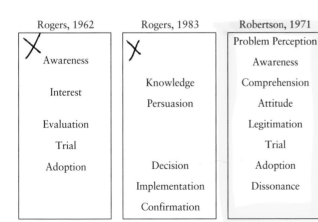

Rogers, 1962	Rogers, 1983	Robertson, 1971
		Problem Perception
Awareness		Awareness
	Knowledge	Comprehension
Interest	Persuasion	Attitude
		Legitimation
Evaluation		
Trial		Trial
Adoption	Decision	Adoption
	Implementation	Dissonance
	Confirmation	

FIGURE 2.3

A comparison of the steps proposed by different researchers for the consumer adoption process.

- Evaluation—the time required to evaluate the information and form an attitude toward the innovation.
- Trial—the testing of the innovation before adoption.
- Adoption or rejection of the innovation.

The most recent version of the process as outlined by Rogers (1983) included the following stages:

- Knowledge—a stage similar to awareness at which a consumer first learns of an innovation.
- Persuasion—the period when a consumer forms a favorable or an unfavorable attitude toward the innovation.
- Decision—the activities leading up to adoption or rejection.
- Implementation—actually using the innovation.
- Confirmation—the stage after adoption when a consumer seeks validation that the decision was correct.

Robertson (1971) proposed another model of the adoption process with the following stages:

- Problem perception—the time when a consumer recognizes a need for change.
- Awareness—the stage at which the consumer becomes aware of the innovation.
- Comprehension—the learning period during which the consumer explores the characteristics and function of the innovation.
- Attitude formation—the result of a period of evaluating the innovation.
- **Legitimation**—an optional stage during which the consumer seeks additional information about the innovation.
- Trial—the stage of trying on or experimenting with the innovation.
- Adoption—the ownership stage.
- **Dissonance**—a stage that occurs only when the consumer questions the adoption decision and seeks reassurance.

The Robertson model is less linear than the original Rogers model because it recognizes that consumers may skip steps, double back to an earlier stage, or reject the innovation at any point in the process.

The later Rogers version and the Robertson version both go beyond the adoption stage to what happens afterwards. This after-the-sale stage is crucial in determining consumer satisfaction and increasing the potential for repeat purchases. However, marketers and forecasters frequently ignore this crucial postpurchase evaluation.

Combining the models gives a view of the total process from initiation to purchase to postpurchase assessment. A consumer must first recognize a need—for something new or replacement when a possession reaches the end of its usefulness. In the awareness and interest stage, the consumer finds a possible solution in the marketing environment. By learning about the innovation, trying it, and evaluating it, the consumer forms a positive or negative attitude about the innovation. The consumer decides to buy or not buy the innovation. After purchase the consumer verifies the decision by seeking more information or reassurance from other people. Satisfaction or dissatisfaction with the decision affects the adoption process on future decisions.

One of the most critical stages in the adoption process is the learning phase (Wasson, 1968). If an innovation requires learning of a new habit pattern, that will slow down its adoption. If an innovative product merely replaces an old one and uses the same set of procedures, or even a simplified set, then it will gain ready acceptance. An innovation may trigger three kinds of learning: learning a new sequence, learning to perceive new benefits, or learning to perceive the consumer's role in the use of the product. The rare "overnight success" comes when the innovation fills a missing link in a system that has already been adopted. All other innovations must negotiate a learning phase.

For the forecaster, the model points out several opportunities. The process begins when a consumer becomes dissatisfied with the current situation. If a number of consumers feel the same dissatisfaction, the canny forecasters may pick up on that feeling and report it as a void in the market—an opportunity to solve the problem with a new product, process, or service.

The forecaster can trace consumer acceptance through the stages of awareness, exploration, and learning to gauge the eventual acceptance rate for the innovation. By monitoring consumers who discontinue the process or reject the innovation at an early stage, the forecaster can suggest ways to package or modify the innovation to overcome barriers to adoption. An early warning about the failure of an innovation to capture consumers can prevent losses by curtailing marketing efforts and by preventing overproduction of the item.

Keeping a journal is an excellent way to use personal introspection to gain insights on behavior. Ask yourself what is missing from your wardrobe or what possession would satisfy your heart's desire. The market proposes many innovations to answer your need or solve your problem. Keep a journal of the process of evaluating those options. Pay careful attention to your thoughts and feelings at each stage. Do you go through all the steps outlined in Figure 2.3? Which do you skip? At what points do you decide to continue or discontinue shopping? How do you feel at the point of purchase? How do you gauge satisfaction or dissatisfaction after the purchase? What impact will this purchase have on the next?

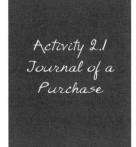

*Activity 2.1
Journal of a
Purchase*

Observing the end of the adoption process—the stages after adoption when the consumer evaluates the decision—often reveals a lack of satisfaction. Products rarely deliver the full set of tangible and intangible attributes sought by the consumer. This reality initiates a new cycle with the identification of a problem. The forecaster's function is to recognize the new problem, identify possible solutions, and report to clients on the new opportunity.

Fashion Change Agents

Rogers's (1962) original model shows a very small group of innovators who begin the diffusion process followed by a larger group of opinion leaders. Together these consumers are **change agents** and they perform several important roles in the spread of innovation in their social group:

- They communicate fashion trends visually and verbally.
- They are relatively more knowledgeable and interested in fashion compared to others in their group.
- They have the aesthetic taste and social sensitivity to assemble a stylish look (King & Ring, 1980).

When others recognize them for their abilities, they become **influentials**—group members who establish the standards of dress for others in the group. Change agents are effective because they represent the ideal within the social group.

According to Rogers's (1962) original formulation of the diffusion curve, innovators were expected to make up 2.5 percent of the total adopters, early adopters added an additional 13.5 percent. This model launched innumerable studies of the demographics and psychographics of innovators and opinion leaders, not only in the field of fashion but in all product categories and many kinds of social systems. Behling (1992) reviewed studies that had used Rogers's (1962) diffusion curve as a theoretical framework and where apparel was the product category. She concluded that the research had failed to confirm the subtle gradations of adoption outlined by Rogers. Part of the problem was attributed to the multiplicity of terms used—fashion innovators, fashion leaders, and early adopters—without clearly defining the similarities and differences between these terms. This lack of specificity means that the findings from such studies are interesting and provocative but not as useful as they might have been if the terms had been defined.

One thing is clear, fashion change agents are important to marketers because they control the diffusion of an innovation. The design director for Levi's women's wear jeans called this concept the "pyramid model." "Explorers" are the first to try new things, whether it is getting a tattoo or wearing something weird; "visibles" take the trend mainstream; and the trend reaches the "followers" about a year later (Ozzard, 1995). Whatever the groups are called—innovators or explorers; fashion leaders, opinion leaders, visibles, or influentials—they act in the early stages of adoption and lay the foundation for later mass acceptance of a trend.

Retailers play a role as change agents in fashion diffusion (Hirschman & Stampfl, 1980). Designers and manufacturers propose many more innovations in a season than can be merchandised in the retail space available. Retailers control the flow of innovation into the social system by selecting among the proposed innovations the ones that will appear in the stores. Some high-fashion stores and avant-garde boutiques are willing to present new fashion innovations based on their own judgment and clientele. They are analogous to the fashion innovators. Other more mainstream retailers are like opinion leaders because consumers turn to their assortment, sales associates, and visual merchandising for informed advice and fashion direction.

Innovators. Marketers usually identify innovators as people who buy new product innovations relatively earlier than others in their social group. In order to target such customers for product introductions, marketers need a profile of such early adopters. The usual profile is of a young, educated, affluent consumer who is very interested in the particular product category. But is there a personality trait that predisposes people to prefer new products? Innovativeness, the desire for new experiences, is such a trait (Hirschman, 1980). Personality traits affect general behaviors more than specific purchases, but they underlie the ways consumers approach, modify, simplify, and react to their marketing environment (Horton, 1979).

Innovative people can be segmented into three groups, each with a different profile (Venkatraman, 1991):

- Cognitive innovators prefer new mental experiences and enjoy novelty when associated with thinking and problem solving.
- Sensory innovators prefer experiences that stimulate the senses, have an easygoing attitude toward life, take risks, participate in pleasurable activities without thinking too much, and engage in dreaming and fantasy.
- Cognitive-sensory innovators prefer both cognitive and sensory experiences.

Fashion apparel has both cognitive and sensory components. Purely stylistic innovations such as a new silhouette, color, or detail make their appeal on sensory grounds (Figure 2.4). Innovativeness in clothing is related to enjoying dressing just for the positive feelings created and for the excitement of experimentation (Pasnak & Ayres, 1969). New fibers and finishes, new ways to wear accessories, and novel coordination strategies are more cognitively appealing as problem solvers.

Although all three types of innovative consumers buy new products and visit new retail stores earlier than other consumers, they vary in other ways.

Innovators respond early to the sensory appeal of new silhouettes, details, and style combinations, and they have the confidence to wear them ahead of others in their group.

Consumers who prefer new mental experiences monitor more mass media channels, attend more to ads, and do more exploratory shopping such as browsing window displays than other consumers. Sensory innovators prefer visual to verbal information, whereas cognitive innovators are the opposite (Venkatraman & Price, 1990).

Consumers who are first to make fashion purchases and wear new styles often pay a premium price. They are thought to be less price sensitive and more affluent that those who buy later in the season. Researchers found another factor that influences early sales—the degree of confidence the early shopper has in the economic conditions (Allenby, Jen, & Leone, 1996). By comparing sales data from five divisions of a retailer, researchers were able to show that consumer confidence about the future state of the economy was a strong predictor of preseason sales. The best predictor for in-season sales was the financial ability to purchase.

Discovering the factors that drive early sales of a fashion item are critical in business planning and forecasting. Early warning about the potential success or failure of a look, line, or stylistic innovation allows managers to adjust pricing and production schedules. (See Chapter 8, "Sales Forecasting," for a more extended discussion of consumer confidence and forecasting.)

Fashion Leaders. If innovators are change agents who first adopt a new fashion and make it visible within their social groups, how are fashion leaders described? Katz and Lazarsfeld (1955) sought to answer this question by interviewing women. If the women reported being asked for advice about clothes or believed they were more likely than others to be asked for advice, interviewees were classified as **fashion leaders.**

Katz and Lazarsfeld (1955) identified two kinds of fashion leaders, the glamorous woman who first displays expensive fashions and the woman who is influential face to face. When the characteristics of these self-identified fashion leaders were compared to others, the fashion leaders were found to be highly interested in fashion, sensitive to their impression on others, gregarious, and recognized as having qualities appropriate for leadership. The researchers found that single, unmarried women with a high interest in fashion had more opportunities for fashion leadership than women at other points in the life cycle. Unexpectedly, findings showed very little difference in the incidence of fashion leaders in different social classes. However, women in the lower class were more likely to seek leadership outside their class. Influence takes place mostly among women of similar circumstances and real-life groups—that is, in naturally occurring groups of friends, colleagues, neighbors, and acquaintances.

Almost 20 years later and with young, single women, Schrank (1973) confirmed the earlier findings about fashion leadership. She administered a fashion leadership scale and a clothing interest inventory to college women and interviewed them about 15 clothing or accessory items with varying degrees of diffusion. Respondents indicated which of the items they owned and when they had been purchased. Schrank found there was a significant relationship between fashion leadership and clothing interest and that fashion leadership is evenly distributed through all social classes.

If people have similar attitudes toward fashion, the difference between leaders and followers is a matter of intensity and speed of adaptation (Brenninkmeyer, 1963). In this view, fashion leaders are more susceptible to change and more interested in differentiating themselves from others. In terms of self-concept, fashion leaders consider themselves more excitable, indulgent, contemporary, formal, colorful, and vain that followers (Goldsmith, Flynn, & Moore, 1996). A fashion leader must be talented enough to sense the spirit of the times and anticipate change in tastes, self-confident enough to make her own fashion choices, and influential within her social group.

Leaders also differ from followers in terms of information seeking. Leaders and followers all use the same sources of fashion information, but leaders use a greater number of sources more frequently and more often preferred marketer-dominated sources—window and in-store displays, fashion magazines, and fashion shows (Polegato & Wall, 1980).

**Activity 2.2
Fashion
Measures**

Researchers have developed questionnaires that measure fashion leadership, fashion interest, and innovativeness. Take the measures yourself. What does your score indicate about you? Have others in your class take the measures but do not attach any names or numbers that identify individuals. Score the measures and report on the findings. What do the scores reveal? Measures such as these are the building blocks for consumer research on consumer behavior and fashion leadership.

Celebrities As Innovators and Influentials. **Popular culture** includes advertising, movies, television, music, magazines, and celebrity news. Popular culture serves as a source of new meanings and as a conduit to transmit those meanings to people (McCracken, 1988b). Slang expressions, lifestyles, sports and pastimes, personality and mood—popular culture is a visual dictionary of meanings. Mass media constantly revise the meanings of old goods and give meaning to new goods. In this way popular culture acts as innovator and as a **distant opinion leader** for consumer culture.

The connection between celebrities and products is not new. It began in the 1850s when Adah Isaacs Menken, a New York stage star, allowed Madame Marguerite to advertise that she was dressmaker for the star. Menken was compensated with a new wardrobe. Fifteen years later, Dr. Gouraud, a purveyor of cosmetics, not satisfied to link his products with the beauty of the Queen of Sheba and the wisdom of Solomon, pioneered celebrity endorsement with advertisements that featured testimonials from actresses and singers popular at the time (Banner, 1983). In 1927, the Thompson advertising agency launched a campaign in which Hollywood stars appeared to praise the skin care qualities of Lux soap (Fox, 1984). The practice of star endorsement was well established by the early 1940s.

The question of celebrity credibility was already a topic of concern in the 1920s. Starlet Constance Talmadge appeared as an endorser in eight ads for eight different products in a single national magazine in 1927—an early case of celebrity overexposure. By the 1950s, the public's attitude toward celebrity advertising had changed from one in which a celebrity could sell just about anything to a rejection of testimonials as insincere (Fox, 1984).

If consumers are suspicious of the motives of celebrity endorsers, how effective can they be? Advertising practitioners rely on a celebrity face to cut through the clutter of ad messages with the shock of recognition and expect the likability of the celebrity to transfer to the product. If consumers are skeptical of celebrity endorsements, how can celebrities function as opinion leaders? The relationship between viewer and celebrity is as psychologically complex as any other relationship.

Media performers create the illusion of interpersonal relationships with viewers. In today's media-rich environment relationships of this imaginary sort are intertwined with media experiences (Horton & Wohl, 1956). The real social world consists of the two or three hundred relatives, friends, and acquaintances a person actually knows. The artificial social world consists of celebrities and the characters they play. Although the relationship takes place in the imagination, people identify with celebrities and feel as if they know them (Caughey, 1978). Social behavior and consumer purchasing can be influenced by media personalities because they act as advisors, role models, and ego ideals (Figure 2.5).

For fashion, movies have been a great medium for showing clothes. Hollywood designers followed trends and set them—Marlon Brando in a white

FIGURE 2.5

Movies and the awards show and celebrity events associated with them are showcases for fashion because celebrities (Kate Winslet, right) function as advisors, role models, and ego ideas for consumers.

T-shirt for *The Wild Ones,* Joan Crawford's padded shoulders and tailored suits in the 1940s, John Travolta's wardrobe in *Saturday Night Fever* and *Urban Cowboy,* Jennifer Beals in a torn sweatshirt in *Flashdance,* Kate Winslett in fashions from 1912 in *Titanic.* Music stars showcased in music videos have been influential in setting and popularizing trends. Clothing styles worn by characters in television shows have excited demand for the same clothes in stores.

The consumption of fashion goods and intangible products such as fragrance is more involved than mere purchase behavior. Consumption is a cultural phenomenon and the designers, advertising executives, and fashion press participate in creating our cultural universe by connecting meaning to consumer goods. Consumers construct their personal worlds by choosing the products that have meaning for them (McCracken, 1988b). In this process, pop culture has both direct and indirect influence on the consumer's ideas about appropriateness, beauty, and fashion.

Activity 2.3
Star Map

Celebrities appeal to different groups of consumers. What movies, television shows, actors, bands, and singers are influential with the demographic group identified as "young adults"? Is there a difference between celebrities who are influential with fashion innovators, and those who influence fashion leaders and fashion followers? Map the celebrities most influential for each group and present your findings on a presentation board.

Fashion Followers. Fashion followers include both the majority adopters who swell the diffusion curve to its highest point and those who adopt after that. After the peak, the number of new adopters decreases until all people who are interested in the innovation have had the opportunity to possess it or at least try it.

If the innovation is a major trend affecting a large number of consumers over several seasons or even several years, manufacturers and retailers still have an opportunity for profit at the peak of adoption and as the innovation reaches the late adopters. If the trend is a short-lived fad, then the time scale is much shorter and the potential for profit is better for manufacturers and retailers participating in the early stages. For the forecaster, the waning of a trend signals the potential for adoption of a new innovation, one that probably already exists and is beginning its diffusion cycle.

Forecaster's Toolbox: Following the Leader
Monitoring Change Agents   By monitoring the acceptance of a given style by change agents, the forecaster has a window on the innovation's level of visibility and the likelihood it will be widely accepted. But change agents are not a stable

segment that can easily be targeted. A change agent may be influential regarding the performance of one role, in one product category such as activewear, or only at certain times, and a follower on other occasions (King & Ring, 1980).

Targeting Innovators   For forecasters and marketers, the segmentation of innovators provides a framework for planning advertising and promotional strategies (Figure 2.6). First, consider the demographic profile of people most likely to be attracted to the innovation. Then, consider the innovator types—cognitive, sensory, or combination—within that demographic group.

Innovator types interact with the characteristics of the innovation—relative advantage, compatibility, complexity, trialability, observability, and risk—to determine marketing strategies (Venkatraman, 1991). Relative advantage will be important to all consumers considering a new product but different innovator types will vary in other preferences.

Strategy for Cognitive Innovators Cognitive innovators are problem solvers who can figure out product complexity and analyze economic risk, but they are not risk takers. Because they closely monitor mass media and pay attention to advertising, the most effective strategy is to present ads that emphasize the relative advantage, provide the information for assessing economic risk, and reduce concerns about enjoyment risk.

Strategy for Sensory Innovators For sensory innovators, the most effective strategy is to reduce complexity and perception of risk although emphasizing the uniqueness of the product and the pleasures associated with it as a visual presentation.

Targeting Leaders   By positioning new fashion innovations as congruent with the fashion leader's self-concept, designers, manufacturers, retailers, and marketers can attract the attention of these important consumers. Although they may not be the very first to adopt the innovation, leaders are early adopters

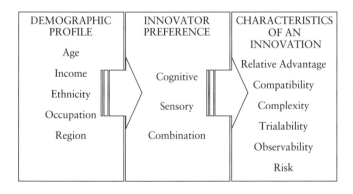

DEMOGRAPHIC PROFILE
Age
Income
Ethnicity
Occupation
Region

INNOVATOR PREFERENCE
Cognitive
Sensory
Combination

CHARACTERISTICS OF AN INNOVATION
Relative Advantage
Compatibility
Complexity
Trialability
Observability
Risk

FIGURE 2.6

Forecasters can use segmentation of innovators as a framework for determining marketing strategies.

who are very influential within their social groups. Followers do not monitor marketer-dominated information sources to the same degree as innovators and fashion leaders do. For the fashion follower, personal influence from a leader within the social group is much more compelling as an incentive to change.

Like individuals, social groups can act as fashion leaders. If a social group has a high proportion of leaders and frequent interaction with other groups, that group is more likely to export leadership to the other groups. Membership in one group may overlap another, allowing some individuals to serve as links between two or more cliques (Rogers, 1983). Understanding this between-group exchange suggests that adoption of an innovation will be enhanced if marketers target influential social groups and individuals who act as liaisons between groups.

The Forecaster's Observation Post   The idea that fashion leaders—influential individuals, social groups, and retailers—adopt an innovation and transmit it to others provides the forecaster with another observation target. The forecaster can monitor the second stage of the diffusion process by monitoring fashion leaders. The forecaster may choose to watch for fashion leadership in particular geographic markets where innovations are most likely to be introduced and then predict the potential diffusion to other locales with an estimate of the timing. Or, a forecaster may watch for fashion leadership in a particular market segment and predict the potential diffusion of an innovation within that segment and as a crossover innovation for other segments. Or, a forecaster may monitor the retailers who perform as change agents and estimate the path of an innovation from avant-garde retailers to more mainstream or mass market clients.

Mapping Celebrity-Consumer Interaction   The transfer of meaning from the cultural universe to the construction of an individual's lifestyle has implications for forecasting. Celebrities function as advisors, role models, and ego ideals on two levels—as themselves in interviews and editorial coverage, and as the fictional roles they play. For innovations in which celebrity leadership is a factor, the forecaster can map celebrity influence to the consumer segment most likely to be influenced. The visibility and desirability of the celebrity image may be a determining factor in the diffusion of some innovations.

Fashions, Fads, and Classics

The terms "fad" and "classic" are frequently used in discussing fashion, but do they have a precise meaning? Fads have been defined in different ways:

- As involving fewer people, of shorter duration, and more personal than other fashion changes (Sapir, 1931).
- As outside historical continuity—each springing up independently with no forerunner and no successor (Blumer, 1969).

- As satisfying only one main need, the need for a new experience, and having little value once the newness wears off (Wasson, 1968).

Fashions are themselves of short duration when compared to long-term social changes. Fads are fashions of even shorter duration. The difference between fads, fashions, and classics can be visualized using variations on the diffusion curve (see Figure 1.7 in the previous chapter). Classics are enduring styles that seem to reach a plateau of acceptance that endures for a long period of time.

Fashion and fads share many of the same characteristics. Meyersohn and Katz (1957) offer a comprehensive natural history of fads identifying these distinctive characteristics:

- Fads are typically confined to particular segments in society.

- Unlike new social movements that create a new social structure, fads move swiftly through a subgroup but leave the subgroup itself stable.

- Fads offer a simple substitution for some predecessor item.

- Fads are trivial, not in terms of the emotion or functional significance of the item, but in terms of its life expectancy—a fad is susceptible to being outmoded.

Meyersohn and Katz (1957) assert that fads are not born but rediscovered from a style that existed all along in the lives of some subgroup. Likely beginning points for fads include the upper classes and bohemians because these groups represent a special kind of laboratory where experimentation can take place without threatening society as a whole. Many other observers of fashion recognize the same source for fashion ideas—the elite and the outsiders.

Innovative ideas are discovered by fashion scouts and moved from source to marketplace by tastemakers. Scouts—journalists, fashion directors, forecasters, and merchants—have the ability to recognize and transmit fads from the subgroup to the mainstream because they have a unique understanding of both. Tastemakers—celebrities, models, fashion stylists, and fashion leaders—increase the visibility of the innovation and make it acceptable to more consumers.

Exporting a fad from the subgroup to a wider audience usually involves modifying the idea in ways that make it more acceptable to a broader audience. As a fad emerges from its cocoon in the subgroup, it undergoes developmental stages. First, the phenomenon is given a name, label, or slogan that becomes a popular identifier. Dior did not call his post–World War II rediscovery of close-fitting bodices, small waists, and full skirts "the New Look." A journalist in a review of the designer's collection used that term. The term stuck because it captured the spirit of that time, the radical change in silhouette that resonated with change in all aspects of life. With the **labeling** comes a surge in interest. Then a **coattail effect** begins when industry people recognize the potential of the fad and produce it and other allied products. **Flow** results when the fad passes from group to group across social boundary lines. If the innovation has broad appeal and staying power, the fad transforms into a fashion. With "the new look" this process took less than one year.

Two conditions signal the end stages:

- The fad loses its stylistic integrity as it flows through society.
- Feedback in terms of demand may stimulate a frenzied increase in production, leading to overproduction and rapid saturation of the market.

Another signal of the end of a fad is excess. Paul Poiret, a great couturier at the beginning of the 20th century and a master of fashion change, saw the role of a designer as providing unending novelty (Robinson, 1958). Poiret's credo was that "all fashions end in excess"—that is "a fashion can never retreat gradually in good order" but instead collapses. Eventually, the fad ages and departs the scene to be replaced by a successor.

Jumping on the bandwagon (or catching the coattail) of a fad is tricky, but there are some guidelines for this maneuver (Reynold, 1968). Greater staying power is achieved if the innovation meets a genuine need or function, is associated with other long-term trends and concurrent trends in other industries, is compatible with the values of society, and has high visibility. The problem for designers in assessing a fad is that they may see trends where none exist— that is, their point of view tends to exaggerate the importance of fads. The problem for managers is that they may delay to the point where they miss an opportunity to participate.

Purchase decisions are the result of an approach-avoidance reaction. When the buyer sees potential satisfaction of a need, want, or aspiration in the possession of a good, then the buyer makes the purchase. If the satisfaction sought is thwarted by price, by the effort of searching, or by some compromise in product design, then the purchase will not be made. Every purchase is a compromise between the attributes desired and the product that is offered.

The classic is a style that changes minimally over time. It remains within the acceptable range in terms of attributes offered and expenditure in terms of time and money. Classics represent midpoint compromises that deliver at least the core attributes desirable to the consumer (Wasson, 1968). Addition-

**Activity 2.4
Naming Names**

Labeling an innovation can mean the difference between rapid diffusion and failure to adopt the innovation. Forecasters are often part of the process of giving an innovation a label. A catchy name or slogan becomes part of the language and increases the visibility and desirability of a fashion product. Begin with the term "bikini" as an identifier for a two-piece swimsuit or "little black dress" for a simple, unadorned, basic black sheath. Look back in fashion history and research some of the fashion labels we take for granted. How did they originate? What effect did they have on the rate of acceptance? What labels are being applied to today's fashion innovations?

ally, classics appeal to a special kind of personality seeking to avoid extremes in styling.

Forecaster's Toolbox: The Future of Fads. Meyersohn and Katz (1957) suggest several approaches to assessing the life expectancy of fads:

- Look at the function the fad serves for the participants (e.g., using multiple expensive gold chains as a display of status, wearing strategically torn jeans to create a sexy look).
- Look at how the fad functions as a symbol for the spirit of the times (e.g., love beads in the 1970s, exaggerated wide shoulders in the 1980s, hiking boots as everyday footwear in the 1990s).
- Look at the fashion system—the network of designers, producers, distributors, and consumers that are involved in the flow of the fad across social groups.
- Look at the origin of the fad and the characteristics of the first innovators.
- Look at the barriers to acceptance and possible modifications as the fad shifts from fringe groups of consumers to more mainstream groups.

Reynold (1968) suggests analyzing the self-limiting aspects of the fad because they are more predictive than those that are merely visual and aesthetic. Begin by observing the direction of fashion movement and its speed. Predict how extreme the style must become before it is abandoned. Evaluate whether the excess is technological or functional and what modifications are possible and desirable to extend the life of the fad. This type of analysis can help forecasters estimate the tempo of the fad and its likely duration. The same general format can be used to assess more enduring fashion looks.

Information Cascades. Rarely do consumers make decisions in a situation in which all relevant information is available. Instead, most decisions are made based on incomplete information. Sometimes the information is difficult to access. At other times, too much information is available but it may be contradictory or confusing. In situations of information scarcity or information overload, individuals still make decisions. Imitating a fashion leader is a strategy frequently used in uncertain situations. Fashion followers presume that the fashion leader has more accurate and precise information (Bikchandani, Hirshleifer, & Welch, 1992).

When an innovation is introduced and a fashion leader acts to adopt or reject the innovation, frequently others imitate the action, beginning an **information cascade** of decisions. Information cascades can be positive, when all individuals adopt the innovation, or negative, when all individuals reject the innovation. If these important leaders do in fact have more accurate and precise information and make a good decision initially, then the information cascade will continue. However, if that initial decision was faulty, then the information cascade will be fragile and prone to fall apart. Additional information or a slight value change can shatter a cascade.

The idea of cascade reactions reinforces the disproportionate effect a few early individuals may have on the lifestyle of an innovation. These cascade reactions explain fads, booms and crashes, and other short-lived fluctuations that appear to be whimsical and without obvious external stimulus.

Forecaster's Toolbox: Visualizing the Diffusion Process

The visualization of diffusion in the Rogers model (1962) shows a **two-step flow** (Figure 2.7). The first step involves transmission of new ideas through the impersonal influence of mass media and marketer-based information to innovators and opinion leaders. The second step depends on the personal, face-to-face influence within social groups as new ideas move from fashion leaders to fashion followers.

An alternative diffusion model—the Bass model (1969)—makes this point even more explicitly. Instead of defining adopters only by the time period, the Bass model differentiates between the kinds of influence that most contribute to the decision. The visualization of the Bass model shows that most consumers at the beginning of the diffusion process adopt the innovation based

FIGURE 2.7

Diffusion occurs in a two-step flow from mostly mass media and marketer-based information to the innovators and opinion leaders and to fashion followers through personal influence.

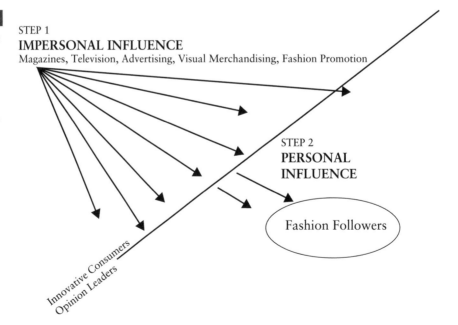

STEP 1
IMPERSONAL INFLUENCE
Magazines, Television, Advertising, Visual Merchandising, Fashion Promotion

STEP 2
PERSONAL INFLUENCE

Fashion Followers

Innovative Consumers
Opinion Leaders

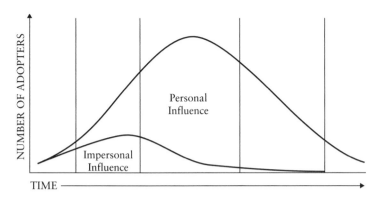

NUMBER OF ADOPTERS

Personal
Influence

Impersonal
Influence

TIME

FIGURE 2.8

The Bass model, an alternative diffusion model, shows that external, impersonal, and marketer-based influences are involved in the rate of adoption through the entire process rather than exclusively at the beginning as in the Rogers model.

on impersonal influences such as the mass media (Figure 2.8). Most subsequent adopters make the decision based on interpersonal influence. But some adopters, even at the later stages, rely mostly on external, impersonal influence.

The bell curve of the Rogers diffusion process can be redrafted into a cumulative form—the **S-curve**—which more clearly mirrors the growth phase of the product cycle (Brown, 1992). Using this visualization it is easy to see how an innovation could spread between social groups and market segments (Figure 2.9). For example, a series of S-curves could represent the spread of an innovation from a younger, hip, edgy consumer segment, to one that is more educated and affluent, and then to one that is older and more mainstream. Or, the series of S-curves could represent the transmission of the innovation from one company to another, each targeting a different consumer segment. At the first stage, when an innovative product is introduced, a company targeting early adopters sells it. If successful with that first audience, the innovation is picked up by a second company targeting the next group of adopters, and finally by a third company targeting the volume market. Visualization using the S-curve provides a complex understanding of the diffusion of innovation and a finer-grained framework for forecasting.

Modis (1992) suggests an even more intriguing elaboration on diffusion of innovation. He argues that the S-curve can be used to describe all forms of market growth. Then, he links a series of curves as Brown did. Finally, using data from a number of industries, he introduces the idea of chaos at the point where the curves overlap (Figure 2.10). In this visualization, the innovation is introduced and goes through the growth cycle until that market niche is filled. Then begins a period of chaos during which a new niche is identified. Once identified, another growth cycle begins, and so on.

The bell curve describes the process of diffusion within a social system. Its cumulative form, the S-curve, linked in sequence, shows the process of diffusion as it spreads from one social system or market segment to the next.

FIGURE 2.9

In the cumulative form, the bell curve becomes the S-curve. S-curves can be linked to visualize filling market niches segment by segment.

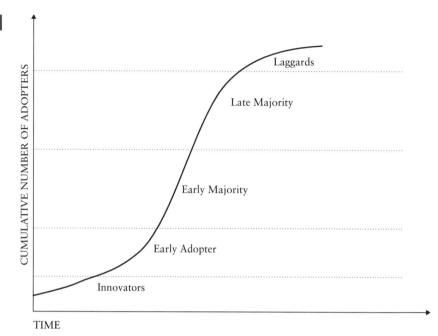

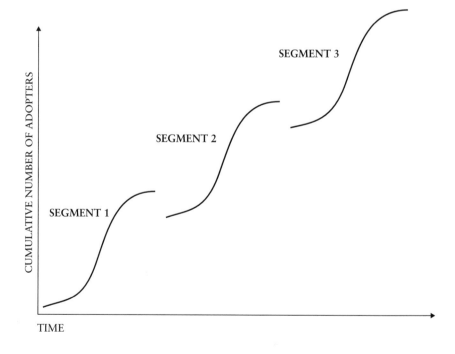

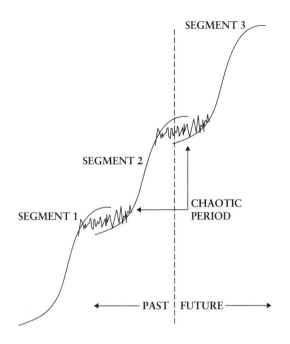

SEGMENT 3

SEGMENT 2

SEGMENT 1

CHAOTIC
PERIOD

◄——— PAST │ FUTURE ———►

FIGURE 2.10

As an innovation moves from one market niche to another, the period of instability during the change can be visualized as a period of chaos between periods of stable growth.

Failure to fill a niche in this progression signals the end of the innovation's life cycle. Success in filling the next niche indicates the potential for continued diffusion of the innovation to a wider audience. For the forecaster, this visualization holds out the tantalizing idea that such patterns of niche filling could be identified in sales data and be used to predict future patterns.

The chaotic phase between S-curves can be seen as a period during which the innovators in another social system experiment with the innovation. If innovators adopt the innovation into a new social system, the innovation is passed to the opinion leaders and continues until that niche is filled. The idea of a chaotic phase between growth cycles is intriguing because it raises the possibility that a chaotic phase is a precursor to a more stable and predictable growth curve. It is during a chaotic phase that the forecaster's job becomes important to a company. By evaluating the innovation's characteristics, possible barriers to consumer adoption, the influence of change agents, and any self-limiting factors, the forecaster helps a company anticipate the future spread of the innovation to other consumer groups and other markets.

Visualization provides the forecaster with a way to structure observations, determine potential markets for the innovation, and estimate the timing when the innovation will reach new consumer segments. Analysis of diffusion in terms of the curves allows the forecaster to take a snapshot of the current situation, **backcast** to explain the past events, and forecast future developments.

Activity 2.5
S-Curves Past,
Present, and
Future

Backcast an innovation using the linked diffusion curves as a visualization tool. Select a style or fashion item that is at a midpoint in its potential diffusion, perhaps a style that is currently being featured in fashion magazines. Trace it back to its origins. What was the first market niche it reached? Plot the timeline as it filled that niche. What was the next market niche? Continue until you bring the style or fashion item to its current market position. Using the S-curves, forecast its next market segment and the timing to fill that niche.

CONSUMER SEGMENTATION

The terms "consumer segment" and "target audience" have thus far been used in a general way to mean that certain people are more likely than others to adopt an innovation at a particular time in the diffusion process. For marketers, these terms have a more precise meaning. An editor describing the profile of the magazine's readers, advertising executives describing the consumers most likely to relate to an ad campaign, designers talking about the kind of person most likely to buy their collections—all these executives are describing the target audience. A **target audience** is that slice of the population most likely to be attracted to the tangible and intangible attributes of a product, company image, or service. Defining the target audience takes discipline. It is much easier to think that every person between the ages of 25 and 45 will want a particular product or identify with a certain image. However, attempting to hit a target audience that inclusive results in fuzzy, unfocused, generic products without differentiation from all similar products. Achieving **differentiation** means presenting a product in a way that highlights how it is different and better than other products of its type.

Traditionally a target audience would be defined as a segment of the population with certain demographic characteristics such as age, gender, ethnicity, and income—a **consumer segment**. Then, the marketing executive develops a **positioning** strategy (Ries & Trout, 1986), a unique marketing approach that:

- Appeals directly to that consumer segment.
- Differentiates the product from all others in the category.
- Positions the product in the minds of the consumers as desirable for purchase.

Segmentation strategies based on **demographics**—consumer characteristics such as age, gender, marital status, and occupation—are no longer effective because consumer attitudes and behavior are not driven primarily by demographics. Sometimes a product crosses boundaries by appealing to consumers in wide demographic categories but to only a small number of people overall—for example, technical fabrics for active sports crossing over into casual wear. Consumers can behave in unexpected ways—for example, when very affluent consumers combine luxury branded goods from specialty stores and basics from discount retailers. Some of today's consumers still ride the trend waves of fashion but others are decidedly antifashion in orientation. Shifts in consumer behavior mean that the traditional way of doing business whereby manufacturers propose new products, identify targets for those products through a segmentation study, and develop a positioning statement no longer work.

Psychographics—consumer psychology plus demographics—help identify a consumer segment by shared values, attitudes, preferences, and behaviors (Piirto, 1991). Psychographics evolved from groundwork laid in the late 1950s when characteristics such as personality traits, attitudes, and motives were used to identify consumer clusters. By the mid-1960s, nondemographic segmentation was becoming a keystone in marketing strategy. Today, marketers view the value system embedded in each individual—the consumer's culture—as having more impact than demographics.

The consumer's culture can overrule demographic classifications. High-income households (those with incomes of more than $60,000) consider brand quality to be more important than do consumers at lower income levels. Yet consumers of all income levels who tend to be trendsetters or opinion leaders show a far greater preference for quality than even high-income families (Kelly, 1994). Health-, fitness-, and nutrition-conscious consumers comprise a relatively small but influential segment of consumers in all demographic categories. Although they may be of different ages and come from various income ranges, they are more alike than different when it comes to choosing products that enhance and support their image of themselves as healthy and fit. Positioning becomes more actionable when it is built on both the "whos"—demographics—and the "whys"—psychographics—of consumer behavior (Rueff, 1991).

Generational Cohorts

Similarity in patterns of consumer behavior have been traced to **generational cohorts** who share the same age location in history and a collective mindset (Strauss & Howe, 1991). In this view, group membership is involuntary, permanent, and finite—all members from birth on always encounter the same events, moods, and trends at similar ages, giving each cohort a distinct biography and a peer personality. Individuals in the cohort may agree with the values and viewpoints of their generation or spend a lifetime battling against it; either way, membership in the cohort shapes their relationship to people and products. Using this typology, five generational cohorts are currently active consumers.

The G.I. Generation. Born between 1901 and 1924, the G.I. generation lived through the Great Depression in their youth and fought World War II (1941–1945) as young adults. Winning World War II defined the generation and gave them their name—G.I. for "government issue." Presidents Kennedy, Johnson, Nixon, Ford, Carter, and Bush were all members of this generation. This group's peer personality tends toward the characteristics that helped them meet the challenges of their times—confidence, conformity, and problem solving through teamwork.

The Silent Generation Born between 1925 and 1942, the silent generation came of age during the 1950s and fought in the Korean War (1950–1953). Although some presidential candidates came from this generation, no U.S. President from this time period has been elected. What did come from this period were beatniks and "rebels without a cause" such as James Dean, Elvis Presley, Clint Eastwood, and Barbra Streisand. People tended to marry young, and families formed during this generation averaged 3.3 children. Highly educated mothers who felt trapped in the family role were among the first to speak for Women's Liberation. The silent generation tended to be overshadowed by the larger and active G.I. generation and were more process oriented, more interested in the helping professions, and less decisive than the generation that proceeded it.

The Baby Boom Generation Born between 1943 and 1960, the children in this generation were the result of a post–World War II "baby boom." Boomers were the first TV generation and fought the first televised war, Vietnam. Instead of bonding to fight the war as the G.I. generation had, boomers bonded to protest the war and evading service. This is the generation of Youthquake, the Summer of Love, Woodstock, and Earth Day. They can be subdivided into an older cohort who were the flower children and hippies of the late 1960s and early 1970s and a younger cohort who became the yuppies (young urban professionals) of the early 1980s. G.I. and silent generation parents raised boomers in child-centered families. Their peer personality tends toward idealism, being together as individuals (rather than collectively as in the G.I. generation), and a willingness to trade economic gain for personal fulfillment.

The Thirteenth Generation, Generation X, or Babybusters Born between 1961 and 1981, this generation experienced a higher risk of being children of divorce (almost twice as often as boomers) and grew up as latchkey kids and as members of blended families due to remarriage. Boomers experienced the euphoria of Youthquake, but at the same age, generation X was labeled "slacker" for its pragmatic approach, sense of social distance, and falling expectations. The first computer generation, Gen X consumers are experienced, fond of popular culture, and cynical about media manipulation. These individuals seems to be searching for anchors with retro-revivals of proms and cocktail lounge music and a political conservatism that asks, "What's in it for me?" Unlike previous cohorts, Xers have not yet experienced a defining moment, and companies have fewer generation-specific images to use in wooing them (Rice, 1994).

Millennial Generation, Generation Y, or Echo Boomers Born between 1982 and the present, this generation's parents are mostly boomers. The size of this generation will swell to 72 million people, a large enough segment to influence politics, the economy, and cultural matters as their parents' generation did. They are already having an impact on popular culture with the launch of *Teen People* magazine and the popularity of TV shows and movies targeted to this group (Terrazas & Huang, 1998).

The apparel marketer must be savvy about targeting consumers by generational cohort. In men's wear, the tailored clothing industry may sell a navy blue blazer to the 45-year-old boomer and the 28-year-old Xer, but the styling will be different—metal buttons for the older customer and black or horn buttons for a downtown look for the younger customer (Musselman, 1997).

Use the generational names as keywords in a database search. What kinds of information are available on generational cohorts? Select one generation and collect several recent articles. Analyze how the observations in the articles relate to the design and sales of apparel products.	*Activity 2.6 Researching the Generations*

Lifestyle Segments

Psychographics was extended in the early 1970s by the introduction of research into lifestyles (Piirto, 1991). In that time, society was being remade by young people who dropped out rather than get married and start families and careers and by women who began choosing careers over traditional homemaker roles. Lifestyle research was an attempt to understand the changing social order. The framework for such studies is Attitudes, Interests, and Opinions (AIO)—How do consumers spend their time? What interests are important to them? How do they view themselves? What opinions do they hold about the world around them?

A typical lifestyle study will survey consumers and then sort them into defined categories providing the percentage each category represents in the population. A study by Arbitron NewMedia looked at the probable acceptance of interactive media using 2,136 completed mail surveys to identify eight distinct segments of U.S. consumers (Cleland, 1995), as follows:

- Settled Set (17%), who hold "old-fashioned family values" and are very brand loyal.

- Bystanders (16%), who lack preference for any activity and are the least confident of the segments.
- Family Focused (15%), who are home oriented and price conscious.
- Moral Americans (11%), who are concerned with personal security and are most often empty nesters.
- Sports Fanatics (11%), who are involved with sports and comfortable with technology.
- Savvy Sophisticates (11%), who are highly educated and information hungry.
- Diverse Strivers (5%), who are price conscious and goal oriented.
- Fast Laners (14%), who are entertainment focused and socially oriented.

The goal of the study was to pinpoint the prime drivers that guide people's consumption decisions. For shopping online, the Savvy Sophisticates are a clear target audience whereas Bystanders are not.

Today, lifestyle segments form a foundation concept for product development, marketing, and merchandising. A lifestyle message has become a key strategy for apparel brands. Vendor shops in department stores present the company's products as a recognizable, coordinated concept carried out in products, accessories, display fixtures, mannequins, construction materials, and ambiance ("One-stop shops," 1998). Consumers recognize products and presentation as belonging to their group and gravitate toward those brands.

Life Stages

Similarity in patterns of consumer behavior can be traced to the life stage of the consumer. Consumption priorities alter depending on the stage of life and the accompanying tasks and challenges. Using life stages as a framework, the forecaster can predict shifts in what consumers do with their discretionary dollars. Although boomers and Xers have very different attitudes and live in very different worlds, Xers are getting jobs, getting married, and starting families just as boomers were doing at about the same age.

In the late 1980s, an advertising agency used a panel study consisting of 2,100 adults who represented a statistical sample of the U.S. population. They gathered data on demographics, psychological variables, psychographic dimensions, life stage attitudes, attitudes toward products and brands, and media usage. The researchers avoided linking life stage solely with aging but looked instead at the combination of age, marital status, children, and whether one lived independently or with family. Most of the study was proprietary—kept confidential and used only with clients of the agency—but one set of findings was published. The study found five segments of singles (Levin, 1989; Piirto, 1991), as follows:

- Twenty-somethings who were living at home with their parents although going to school or working, and who spent money on fashion, entertainment, and nightlife.

- Slightly older twenty-somethings who had moved away from home, tended to be city dwellers, and were consumers of a broader spectrum of household goods.

- Forty-somethings who were divorced or separated and tended to be insecure, pessimistic, and difficult for marketers to target.

- Single parents—predominately women—who were often financially strapped and whose decisions tended to be dominated by their children.

- Senior singles with no children at home and spouses who had died but who were themselves healthy and health-conscious.

As this study indicates, a life stage is defined by events that change the way a person lives, such as moving away from home, marriage, childbearing, divorce, and the death of a spouse. These events occur partly in sync with maturation but cannot be characterized solely by arbitrary age categorization.

Lifestyle typologies work best in understanding younger markets because age, income, education, gender, and ethnicity correlate well with the psychological and sociological life stage. But lifestyle typologies are less useful with older groups because the psychological life stage and demographics have a less direct relationship. Instead of looking at the adult life stage from a sociological viewpoint of age, education, vocation, and family status, consider the psychological life stage of personality development. Adult life stages involve three kinds of consumption: possessions as signs of accomplishment and identity, the purchase of services rather than products, and the search for meaningful experiences (Wolfe, 1993).

Adults at every life stage blend all three kinds of consumption, but each life stage puts a different priority on the elements in the combination. A young couple starting life together and beginning careers will put emphasis on acquiring possessions and defining their image as individuals and as a family. Spending focuses on a car, a media center, a home, or an apartment with furnishings. Financial security dampens the need for acquiring possessions but fuels the satisfaction of personal, entertainment, and convenience needs through the purchase of services. Spending focuses on season tickets to the theater or sporting events, travel, restaurant meals, and professional services such as custom clothing, personal shoppers, lawn maintenance, and interior design services. With gratification of the needs for possessions and services, the consumer shifts emphasis to altruistic activities such as charity work or mentoring others, personally meaningful experiences, and life-enhancing pastimes.

The life stages represent consumption of different products and the pursuit of different kinds of experience. Although the stages are related to maturing, consumers at all ages participate in each kind of spending. Only the emphasis shifts and with it, the consumer's discretionary spending.

**Activity 2.7
Generations and
Life Stages**

Use the articles from Activity 2.6 to analyze the spending patterns for possessions as a sign of accomplishment and identity, the purchase of services, and the search for meaningful experiences for a generational cohort. Project spending for this generational cohort at the next life stage.

Forecaster's Toolbox: Visualizing Target Markets

Describing a "market of one"—one individual consumer—and a consumer segment is like describing a fractal. Fractal geometry is based on the unifying concept that self-similarity occurs regardless of changes in scale (Figure 2.11). The broken edges of a rock and the shape of the mountain it came from are similar in composition and fracture pattern even though the difference in scale is enormous. This insight has enabled scientists to understand and describe many phenomena in the natural world from the way a fern adds leaves to the shape of coastlines seen from space (Schroeder, 1991).

Consumer segmentation has the same underlying self-similarity because the pattern builds up from individuals with certain demographic and psycho-

FIGURE 2.11

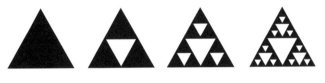

A fractal such as the Sierpinski gasket shows the growth pattern generated by self-similarity from a single shape to a three-dimensional version. In the same way, a single individual's demographic and psychographic profile can be aggregated with similar individuals to form consumer segments with certain degrees of self-similarity.

graphic characteristics, representatives of a certain lifestyle segment, and confronting a specific life stage. The individuals blend into groups and into larger consumer segments based on shared characteristics (Piirto, 1991). The consumer segmentation strategies for the 21st century reflect the new realities of consumer behavior—there is still an underlying similarity among consumers who gravitate to a particular style or image, but that similarity is complex and multifaceted. Forecasters use cohort membership, lifestyle, and life stage to project potential acceptance or rejection of trends and styles.

DISCOVERING THE ZEITGEIST *pronounced Teitgeists*

Fashion historians contend that fashion is a reflection of the times in which it is created and worn. Fashion responds to whatever is modern—that is, to the spirit of the times or the *Zeitgeist*. According to Blumer (1969), individuals in large numbers choose among competing styles those that "click" or connect with the spirit of the times. This collective selection forms a feedback loop between the fashion industry and the consumer, a feedback loop moderated by aesthetic trends and social-psychological processes. The problem with this concept in terms of forecasting is that it offers little advance warning of potential fashionability in proposed looks. The industry must wait until fashion demand converges on something symbolic of the times.

Another problem for forecasters is the difficulty in recognizing the spirit of the times while living in them. Retrospect allows the distinguishing characteristics of an era to become clear. Although there are some limits on newness in fashion—the shape of the human body, the cultural theme of the times, and the production technology available—there is still an enormous range of possibilities for experimentation. A fashion era can characterized by:

- A designer's signature style—Halston in the 1970s, Christian Lacroix in the 1980s.
- A style leader—Jacqueline Kennedy in the early 1960s.
- A fashion look—the flapper of the 1920s, Cardin's and Courrèges' space-age short white dresses and boots in the mid-1960s, the 1977 "Annie Hall" look.
- A bohemian element—the Beats, the Hippies, Rappers.
- A market segment—the middle class in the 1950s, the youth movement in the 1960s.
- A celebrity icon—Clara Bow, the It Girl of the 1920s; Madonna, the Material Girl of the 1980s.
- A model—Jean Shrimpton and Twiggy in the 1960s, Lauren Hutton and Christie Brinkley in the 1970s, the supermodels of the 1980s.
- A fiber or fabric—Chanel's jersey, the polyester of the 1970s, Lycra in the late 1990s.

The silhouette changes with the times but so does the figure underneath. The tall athletic Gibson girl gave way to the boyish flapper; the superfeminine sex goddess Marilyn Monroe was replaced by the reed-thin Flower Child, the waif was replaced by the powerful, toned physique of Lucy Lawless's television character, Xena: Warrior Princess. The ideals of beauty are just as malleable as the fashions (Danielson, 1989).

All cultural components respond to the spirit of the times. The power of the *Zeitgeist* is its ability to coordinate across product categories. Fashion and cuisine exhibit the same trends and cycles. The newest trend in cuisine was Tex-Mex in the mid-1980s, but that was replaced by Cajun only a few years later. Once all "fashionable" sandwiches were served on pita bread, a few years later it was the croissant, after that it was multigrain peasant-style bread. Fashion affects all product categories—food, sports, architecture, interiors, and automobiles. Soccer was once an obscure sport in the United States. Today it is an avid passion of many youngsters. Extreme sports were once the province of a small cadre of participants. Today they are covered on television sports channels and the functional clothing of participants has been adapted to mass fashion. Toys, avocations, pastimes, and play all respond to the same cultural currents that fashion does.

Media not only report on the culture, they are shaped by it. Watching network television was all important until the coming of cable, startup networks, the Web, video games, and computer games pushed the networks off the cultural front burner. Magazines that report on fashion are like any other product; they have a natural life cycle connected to the spirit of the times. Magazines reinvent or refresh their look and their focus in response to the spirit of the times. Often this process involves a change in editors. New editors replace old ones because they have a vision, one that is in touch with the times, and they can shape the magazine to reflect that.

Nystrom's Framework for Observing the Zeitgeist

What factors should the forecaster monitor? What external factors shape the spirit of the times? In 1928, Nystrom attempted to list factors that guide and influence the character and direction of fashion. His list still provides a framework for observing the formation of the *Zeitgeist*.

Dominating Events. Nystrom listed three kinds of dominating events: (1) significant occurrences such as war, the death of world leaders, and world fairs; (2) art vogues (the Russian Ballet and modern art in his day); and (3) accidental events (the discovery of the tomb of Tutankhamen in the 1920s). Historical examples such as the effect of pop, op, and psychedelic art on the fashions of the 1960s and 1970s extend Nystrom's analysis on the relationship between dress and art. Although world fairs no longer serve to set trends, other international events still pull in huge audiences. One such event is the Academy Awards ceremony with its celebrity fashion parade. Another is the influence of the Olympic Games on activewear for athletes and on casual wear for the mainstream consumer. An updated list of significant occurrences would include the end of the Cold War, the 1990s bull market on the stock exchange, Web culture, the Y2K Bug, and the millenium.

Dominating Ideals. Nystrom listed dominating ideals such as patriotism and the Greek ideal of classical beauty. An updated list would include ideals of multiculturalism, environmental and humanitarian issues, equality of men and women, and the connection between fitness, beauty, and youthfulness. Because of these ideals, headlines about the exploitation of workers in sweatshops where apparel is produced could have multiple effects on industry practices, pricing, and consumer perceptions. The ideal of a multicultural society is not new in the United States, but it is being reshaped by the changing demographics of color in the U.S. population. Census figures show the Hispanic and Asian populations growing much faster than the nation's population as a whole. Some cities such as Baltimore and Detroit are becoming predominately black, others such as San Antonio and Miami, predominately Hispanic. Asian influence is becoming stronger in cities such as Los Angeles, San Francisco, and New York. Because some of these cities are also important as style centers and as the starting point for trends, the impact on American fashion could be considerable. The ideal of fitness, beauty, and youthfulness is reflected in the sexy styles of some designers, the growing popularity of activewear styles, and concerns about the sun's effect on the aging of skin.

Dominating Social Groups. Nystrom identified the dominating social groups as those with wealth, power, and leadership positions. Although the groups themselves would have changed, the criteria still apply to today's culture. Today, the power of celebrities in popularizing fashion trends can hardly be overemphasized. In the mid-1980s, Cindy Lauper popularized a whimsical, colorful style in her music videos, a look that relied on the hip vintage clothing store Screaming Mimi's for inspiration. Her fashion influence was eclipsed by Madonna's sexy take on lingerie as outerwear in the late eighties and early nineties. In the mid-1990s, Courtney Love exerted significant influence on fashion trends as a rock diva and movie star as she switched from naughty baby doll looks to a hard-edged glamour (Horyn, 1997). Celebrities as presented through the multiple media channels—music videos, movies, TV series and interview programs, and photographs in magazines and newspapers—have become the highly visible and highly influential "new" elite.

Dominating Attitude. Nystrom's list must be extended to capture today's spirit of the times. Add to the list the dominating attitude of the times. The engine of fashion, the interplay between an individual's desire to fit in and to stand out, between imitation and differentiation, imprints the *Zeitgeist*

(Brenninkmeyer, 1963). When the desire for differentiation is the dominant attitude in an era, new fashions arise, the changes are revolutionary, and the pace of fashion change is swift. The flapper era and Youthquake in the 1960s are examples of eras when the dominant attitude was differentiation. When social conformity and imitation is the dominant attitude, fashion innovation slows down, the changes are evolutionary, and the pace of fashion slows down. The depressed 1930s and conforming 1950s are such eras.

Dominating Technology. Today more than ever, Nystrom's list must be expanded to include the dominating technology of the times. When he was writing in the late 1920s, the harnessing of the atom, the space race, the power of television, and advent of the computer were all in the future. Today, technology is deeply intertwined in everyday life, especially in the realms of communication, entertainment, and computers. Cell phones, portable music systems, and hand-held computers such as today's personal digital assistants (PDAs) may eventually give way to wearable computers—a development already being studied at the MIT Media Lab. Wearable technology—sometimes called cyberstyle or cyberpunk—may become the essential fashion accessory in the new millennium.

Technology not only imprints the *Zeitgeist*, it also imprints the production methods. Without computers and rapid worldwide communication, quick response strategies and global apparel production would not be possible. Instant information exchange, computer technology, robotics, and automation are driving the paradigms of production on a mass scale and production of customized products for a market of one (mass customization).

Together, the dominating events, ideals, social groups, attitudes, and technology exemplify and influence the spirit of the times. Together they illuminate the structure of society with fashion illustrating variations on the cultural theme (Brenninkmeyer, 1963).

| *Activity 2.8 Discovering the Zeitgeist* | Use Nystrom's framework to map the spirit of the times. Because each market segment will have its cultural identity within the larger cultural environment, try mapping the dominating events, ideals, social groups, attitude, and technology for your own generational cohort. Then analyze the difference between your map and that of other cohort groups. How important does an event have to be to affect multiple cohorts? What does this suggest in relationship to product development and marketing? How are such maps useful to forecasters? |

Forecaster's Toolbox: Seeing the Big Picture

Whereas others merely participate in fashion change, forecasters attempt to understand the process, trace the evolution, and recognize the patterns. To do this they must be participants, but they must also be spectators interpreting what they observe. The *Zeitgeist* is an expression of modernity, of the current state of culture, of the incipient and unarticulated tastes of the consuming public. Forecasters monitoring the *Zeitgeist* pay special attention to:

- Style interactions between apparel, cuisine, sports, architecture, interiors, automobiles, toys, avocations, pastimes, and play because all these fields respond to the same cultural currents.
- The content of media, the celebrities covered in the media, and the members of the press who decide what stories to cover.
- The events, ideals, social groups, attitudes, and technology that characterize the spirit of the times.

These cultural patterns define the present. Even slight shifts in these patterns act as directional signposts to the future.

Key Terms and Concepts

Backcast	Distant Opinion Leader	Observability
Change Agents	Economic Risk	Perceived Risk
Collective Selection	Enjoyment Risk	Popular Culture
Compatibility	Fashion Leaders	Positioning
Complexity	Flow	Psychographics
Consumer Adoption	Generational Cohorts	Relative Advantage
Process	Influentials	S-Curve
Consumer Segment	Information Cascades	Social Risk
Demographics	Innovation	Target Audience
Differentiation	Innovators	Trialability
Diffusion Curve	Labeling	Two-Step Flow
Diffusion Process	Legitimation	*Zeitgeist*
Dissonance		

Discussion Questions

Introducing a new product, ways to combine apparel pieces, or sensibility about clothing is an incredibly risky and complicated business. Consumers play many different roles and have many decision points in the process. Understanding how an innovation spreads provides a framework for forecasting because it suggests what to watch and where to do the observing. No innovation can succeed if it is incompatible with the spirit of the times—the *Zeitgeist*. Use the following questions to summarize and review this chapter.

Diffusion of innovation: What filters do forecasters use in evaluating the potential of an innovation based on its characteristics? How does the consumer adoption process interact with the characteristics of an innovation to produce an approach or avoidance behavior? What risks does a consumer face when deciding to adopt an innovation? What is the life cycle of a fad? How does that differ from the life cycle of a fashion or a classic? Who acts as fashion change agents? What is the role of a fashion change agent?

Consumer segmentation: What is the difference between target audience and consumer segment? How does a purchaser's generational membership define preferences? How does life stage influence the purchasing behavior of consumers?

The spirit of the times: Since it is difficult to recognize the spirit of the times while you are living them, how can forecasters sensitize themselves to cultural patterns? What product category interactions are indicative of the *Zeitgeist*?

Additional Forecasting Activities

Missing Links. Even with the abundance of apparel products in the market, consumers do not always find what they are looking for. Interview consumers from each generational segment—G.I., silents, boomers, Gen Xers, and millennium. What styles or features or characteristics are missing from the apparel marketplace? These voids in the market represent opportunities for extending diffusion of innovation to new consumer groups or creating new products.

Different Lifestyles Side by Side. Compare the lifestyle characteristics of the college community with towns nearby. Investigate lifestyle characteristics such as median age, income levels, educational attainment, size of families, and employment. Do a "walkaround survey" of the shops and the style and price range of merchandise in each town. Prepare guidelines for merchandise assortment based on lifestyle characteristics for each town.

Listening to Consumers. Convene a series of panel discussions with people at different life stages. Prepare a set of questions to find out about the priorities these consumer have for possessions, the purchase of services, and experiences. What are the implications for apparel companies based on your analysis of these discussions?

Mapping the Zeitgeist. It is difficult to recognize the spirit of the times as you are living through them. To sensitize yourself to this concept, map the *Zeitgeist* using the categories of dominating events, ideals, social groups, attitude, and technology for the decades from the 1920s to the 1990s. How do these categories define what is remembered about each decade?

Chapter 3

THE DIRECTION OF FASHION CHANGE

"The paradox of fashion is that everyone is trying at the same time to be like, and to be unlike, his fellow-men."
—J. C. Flugel (1930)

Objectives

- Identify the directional theories of fashion change—their source, basic tenets, and predictive power.

- Cultivate skills in analyzing current fashion within a theoretical framework.

- Increase awareness of visualization as a tool of analysis and communication.

FASHION MOVEMENT

Trend watching is an avocation enjoyed by many. Even a casual trend watcher will see discernable patterns. At some point in time, people begin to feel that wearing colorful clothes is unsophisticated and that black is "cool." Closets fill up with neutrals until, seemingly overnight, black looks drab and monotonous. A creative street fashion or a fashion runway fills up with pink and suddenly color seems fresh and inviting. Every aspect of fashion from color to the length of skirts, to the shape of the silhouette, to placement of pockets, is in constant motion.

Anyone can pick up on a trend when it lands in the mailbox trumpeted in magazine headlines complete with an eight-page photographic spread. For the fashion professional, recognizing a trend at that stage means that it is almost too late to use the information for competitive advantage. Instead, fashion executives look for competitive advantage by identifying trends early. To do that they must position themselves in the most likely spots to watch for emerging trends. With experience, a trend watcher becomes skilled at spotting the elusive and subtle shifts that signal fashion change.

Observation is not enough. If the trendwatcher is to take advantage, he or she needs a framework for explaining how the trend began and its likely path within a social system. The directional theories of fashion change make prediction easier by pointing to the likely starting points for a fashion trend, the expected direction that trend will take, and how long the trend will last.

Like fashion itself, the theories that explain fashion movement are constantly revised and refined. The fashion forecaster's toolbox contains all the explanations and recognized patterns that have explained past fashion and can be used to arrange and order current observations. Social scientists continue to seek better explanations and to suggest new theories of fashion change. The forecaster uses the theories by matching observations with the explanation that best fits, then projecting the next stage.

Visualizing the most likely pattern of change is a first step toward prediction. Abstracting a theory into a visual representation clarifies the situation and aids in analyzing what comes next. Visualizations—a layer cake with each layer representing a stratum of the marketplace or the formation of a fashion wave—help explain the concepts and communicate the logic of predictions to others.

Trendwatching executives move in the social world observing, categorizing what they see, and matching that to the preferences and behavior of consumers. These fashion professionals seem to make their decisions "from their gut" in a mysteriously intuitive process. Actually, that intuitive response is the result of a highly developed sensitivity to the social environment plus the almost instant application of one of the forecasting frameworks. Experience and application of the best explanations cannot guarantee success—the situation is too complex for absolute accuracy in prediction. However, preparation and practice can improve the odds for professional trend watchers.

THE DIRECTION OF FASHION CHANGE

The three directional theories of fashion change predict that fashion will either trickle down, trickle up, or trickle across consumer segments. Introduced at different times during the 20th century, these theories reflect not only a general understanding of fashion dynamics but also the specific marketplace conditions at the time they were proposed. Each theory has been criticized and revised since its introduction but remains a valuable guide in explaining fashion leadership and predicting fashion movement. The directional theories of fashion change help fashion professionals answer the questions, Where do fashion innovations begin? Who leads and who follows? How quickly will a fashion move through society? When will a style reach the end of its popularity?

Trickle-Down Theory

Imagine a fashion observer living at the turn of the 20th century. How would he or she explain fashion? Looking backward from that vantage point, the observer sees that in the past fashion was dictated by the nobility who were leaders in all areas of fashionable behavior by birthright, rank, and wealth. Fashion spread slowly downward through the class structure but never reached all levels. The lower classes did not have the income, access, nor the freedom to follow fashion's dictates. Looking around at his or her own time, the observer notices that fashion is still restricted to those at the top of the class structure—the rich and socially prominent. The Industrial Revolution has made possible the building of great fortunes and the display of wealth through fashionable possessions including homes, furnishings, art, and handcrafted fashion. This period, roughly 1900 to 1914, is know as *la Belle Époque* in France, the Edwardian period in England, and the Gilded Age in America. It was characterized by women wearing extravagant, elaborate fashions that required devotion, attention, and seriousness at both the acquisition stage and in wearing the clothes in everyday life.

Veblen (1899) was one such observer at the turn of the 20th century. He described the upper strata of the social system as the leisure class. Members of the leisure class displayed wealth in two distinctive ways, through **conspicuous leisure** and **conspicuous consumption**. A person who does not have to work for a living and participates in an extravagant lifestyle of travel, entertainment, and the pursuit of pleasure demonstrates conspicuous leisure. Philanthropy, art collecting, acquisition of homes and furnishings, and apparel with expensive modes of production and materials demonstrate conspicuous consumption. In both these modes, wealth serves as the background for the activities that were the hallmark of the times.

The Origins of the Theory. Explaining fashion movement in such an era is relatively easy: fashion moves downward from the elite class to the lower classes in stately and slow progression. But the explanation is not complete until it explains not only what happens but why. Simmel (1904), a sociologist, identified the engine of fashion change in the opposing human tendencies toward conformity and individuality. No aspect of life can satisfy the demands of these two opposing principles, but social life and fashion offer a perfect battleground where strivings for social adaptation and the need of differentiation can be played out.

The dual tendencies can be played out in individuals when one person's style is toward imitation and another's is toward differentiation. The imitator believes in social similarity, in acting like others. The individual seeking differentiation constantly experiments with the new, relying in large part on personal convictions. These dual drives can also be played out in social groups where fashion simultaneously functions as a means of class distinction and as a badge of group uniformity.

Simmel observed three stages, as follows: (1) the elite class differentiated itself through fashion, (2) the adjacent lower classes imitated the look, and (3) the elite class moved to adopt a new fashion in an attempt to maintain the differentiation. These stages played out in social forms, apparel, aesthetic judgement, and the whole style of human expression—a view that expands consideration of fashion change from simply apparel to a broader range of activities and behaviors. Simmel described the constant movement between the three stages as a game that "goes merrily on."

Because the motivation to fit in and stand out can never fully or finally be gratified, fashion change is inevitable for the individual and for the social group. Simmel explained that the distinctiveness afforded by newness in the early stages of a fashion is destroyed by its spread to imitators until the fashion wanes and dies. Simmel concluded that the charm of fashion lay in its novelty coupled with its transitory nature.

The views of Veblen and Simmel form the framework for the **trickle-down theory** of fashion change. The theory identified:

- The source of fashion ideas—designers who catered to wealthy clients with a taste for conspicuous consumption and the leisure to pursue fashion.
- The fashion leaders—those fashionable and highly visible individuals who served as models for the new looks.
- The direction of fashion change—downward from the elite class to the next adjacent class.
- The speed of change—regulated by the ability of the lower classes to see, obtain, and copy the fashion.
- The dynamics of change—the pursuit of the dual drives for differentiation and imitation.

Criticism and Revision of the Theory. Fashion observers in the latter half of the 20th century have criticized the trickle-down theory as being flawed.

The chief criticism is that the elite did not consistently set prevailing styles any time after the introduction of mass production and mass communication (Banner, 1983; Blumer, 1969; Lowe & Lowe, 1985). Another critic (McCracken, 1988a) points out that the theory oversimplifies the social system. Instead of just two or three layers with the elite at the top, the social system actually has many layers simultaneously engaged in differentiation and imitation.

The same critic questioned visualization of the process as trickle down because the impetus for change comes from the subordinate classes as they hunt for the **status markers** of the upper class. He proposed replacing trickle down with **chase and flight**—chase because fashion change was driven by the imitators who chased the status markers of the elite in a drive toward upward social mobility; flight because the elite responded to imitation by flying away toward new forms of differentiation. Although this new visualization neatly captures the dynamics of the process, the phrase did not catch on with fashion writers, who still use the earlier trickle-down image.

Along with the criticism came some proposed revisions to the theory. Behling (1985/1986) identified a new, highly visible upper class made up of those occupying power positions in business, politics, and media. As she points out, "they are Veblen's new conspicuous consumer . . . from whom, under particular circumstances, fashion trickles down." Simon-Miller (1985) pointed out that the fashionable elite in the later half of the 20th century practiced a kind of status denial—people with the wealth and status to wear anything they wished chose to dress down in jeans and drive Jeeps instead of Cadillacs. Instead of conspicuous consumption, this variation was called **reverse ostentation** or **conspicuous counterconsumption** but it served the same purpose, differentiation.

Dressing down by the fashionable elite became news in 1993 when fashion took a less ostentatious turn and logos and showy decoration were banished by designers who wanted to get down to the most basic elements of clothing (Brampton, 1993). At the same time magazines were asking celebrities, "How hard can it be to get jeans right?" as they lambasted their "style-free" dressing in shapeless T-shirts and denim, thrift shop finds, and "farm-wife dresses." As one actress put it, when you see people with real power dressing down, then it must be the thing to do. Media celebrities led the way in the antifashion, back-to-basics movement of the early and mid-1990s.

Interestingly, Simmel (1904) described the same phenomenon in his time. He characterized two distinctive fashion types:

- The fashion victims (whom he termed "dudes") in whom "the social demands of fashion appear exaggerated to such a degree that they completely assume an individualistic and peculiar character."

- The antifashion individual, whose "conscious neglect of fashion represents similar imitation, but under an inverse sign."

In both these types Simmel saw a commonality—both types are paying homage to the power of fashion, one in the form of exaggeration, the other, by consciously attempting to ignore it. Simmel said that both these types exhibit a "tendency toward individual conspicuousnes."

Kaiser (1990) suggested updating the theory by examining the underlying instabilities that exist in society. She identified the source of these instabilities in tensions among cultural categories, specifically in areas of gender, ethnicity, age, and attractiveness.

- Gender

Androgyny, **gender bending**, and **gender blending** have been potent sources for fashion change in the latter part of the 20th century. From the pants-wearing athleticism of Amelia Earhart in the 1930s to the gender ambiguity of RuPaul in the 1990s, the line between masculine and feminine in fashion has grown blurry.

- Ethnicity

While the debate about the salability of fashion magazines that feature African-American models as cover girls would seem to belong to another decade, it became a hot topic in 1997. At the same time, runways, advertising campaigns, and editorial pages of fashion magazines featured a wide range of ethnicity among the models.

- Age and Attractiveness

Only recently have models such as Lauren Hutton been able to extend modeling careers into middle age. With the aging of a large generational cohort, the baby boomers, definitions of attractiveness as they relate to age will be more open to redefinition than in previous decades

- Attractiveness

Women with exaggerated features and idiosyncratic styles who would not previously have been considered attractive enough for modeling assignments achieved prominence in the 1990s. Billed as edgy and modern, these models became symbols in a time of multiculturalism. Models and actresses were also breaking other stereotypes of attractiveness such as thinness.

Just as the instability of a more rigid class structure and the quest of lower classes for upward mobility led to the dynamics observed by Veblen and Simmel at the turn of the 20th century, cultural instabilities surrounding gender, ethnicity, age, and attractiveness fuel fashion change today. The areas of instability lead to different manifestations, but there remains a strong relationship to the dynamics described in the trickle-down theory of fashion change. Simmel's engine of fashion change—imitation and differentiation—is still at work at the turn of the 21st century as it was at the turn of the 20th century.

Forecaster's Toolbox: Theory in Action. Can the trickle-down theory of fashion movement be useful to a fashion forecaster today? People's motivations to participate in fashion remain essentially the same no matter the century. The trickle-down theory underscores the self-perpetuating cycle based on people's basic human tendencies toward imitation and differentiation. People still feel pressure to adapt to their place in society's structure and to the rules of their narrower circle while simultaneously seeking to affirm their individuality. And, the field of fashion is still an excellent battleground for these two opposing tendencies to be played out.

Status Symbols: "In" or "Out"?   Veblen's observations about the need that some people have for conspicuous consumption continues to be part of the fashion picture even if more prominent in some decades than in others. An article from *The Wall Street Journal* (Bird, 1995) provides the timeline: "Marketers spent millions in the 1980s pitching their products as badges of affluence for unapologetic yuppies. But by the early 1990s, as baby boomers aged and had children of their own, marketing experts predicted, family values would replace the quest for self gratification . . . . Even wealthy shoppers would choose Gap over Gucci and shun ostentatious brands like Rolex and Louis Vuitton." By the mid-1990s, conspicuous consumption was back in style and Simmel's ideas about differentiation could be seen in action when affluent consumers began treating themselves once again to easily recognizable status symbols.

The Shifting Power of Status Markers   The theory predicts status markers can lose power when they become too available to all consumers. Take, for example, the leather jacket, symbol of a cool, rebellious attitude and a rock-and-roll symbol for decades. As long as jackets were rare, hard to obtain, or costly, they retained their symbolic power. But when they became available at local malls or even discount stores for as little as $99, that killed the mystique (Agins, 1994a). Just as Simmel explained, status symbols are used to demarcate between those who are "in" and those who are "out." Once the symbols are readily available, the elite turns away to find another sign of differentiation. Or, as an editor of a rock magazine put it, "No self-respecting rocker would shop for leather at the Gap except maybe at gunpoint."

Quality Issues in Conspicuous Consumption   Nystrom (1928) constructed a business rule based on Veblen's ideas: " . . . to succeed as a fashion, [a style] must have qualities that advertise either conspicuous leisure or conspicuous consumption for the user." He also elaborated on the description of those exercising fashion leadership to include not only people with wealth and the power to use it, but also those who know how to use it artistically and recognize this artistic ability in others. These extensions of Veblen's ideas provide the fashion forecaster with more specification is applying the ideas of the trickle-down theory to observations of today's marketplace.

Fashion leadership is tied to more than price; it is about taste and quality. To most consumers, the $99 leather jacket is indistinguishable from the more expensive versions costing $500 or more. But to buyers with discriminating tastes, the $99 version is clearly made of cheaper leathers from pig and goat covered up with distressed finishes. For them, the symbol is meaningless unless connected to high quality materials and workmanship. Once the symbol is usurped by those without the ability to recognize the artistry, then the symbol becomes less appealing to the connoisseurs who were early adopters of the look (Agins, 1994a).

Groups Worth Watching   There are two problems for the fashion forecaster in applying the trickle-down theory to today's society: (1) the multiplication of layers in the social system since the theory was first proposed; and (2) the difficulty in identifying the elite. Simmel's formulation specified only two layers—an elite striving for differentiation, and a lower class imitating that elite. The 20th century has produced a rising standard of living for many more people and stratified society into many more status layers than in Simmel's day. Each of these layers undertakes fashion change for the purposes of imitation and differentiation (McCracken, 1988a). The result is a much more complex dynamic. The top layer is only concerned with differentiation, the bottom layer only with imitation, but the intermediate layers simultaneously imitate the layer above and seek differentiation from the layer below. McCracken sees this complexity as raising additional questions: Are some groups more imitative than others are? Are there aggressively imitative groups that move so fast that differentiation is not a concern? Are some groups more concerned with differentiation? Are some groups so concerned about differentiation that they create fashion rather than imitate a higher level group?

At first McCracken's questions seem to complicate the forecaster's job because it seems logical that a multilayered system requires more monitoring than a simpler one. However, identifying groups most likely to generate fashion change actually directs the forecaster's attention and narrows the job of monitoring the system. Because the forecaster cannot watch every layer, why not watch instead for instabilities where fashion activity is intense and fast paced?

Fast-Paced Differentiation   These groups are more likely to feed the system with fashion change because they are most concerned with using fashion for differentiation. They may be the elite, high status group in a particular stratum of the society or part of the new visible elite highlighted by media attention. As a group, these fashion innovators are likely to create ripples through surrounding groups, setting off a chain of fashion changes.

Take, for example, activity centered on South Beach, a neighborhood in Miami that became the playground for the new visible elite including designers, wealthy young people, and celebrities from the world of movies and music in the mid-1990s. The instabilities of gender, sexuality, ethnicity, and age were all apparent in the development of this geographic location that became associated with a freewheeling lifestyle. From that environment came a colorful, casual, and sexy fashion sensibility that, for a time, ruled the runways in Europe and America.

Aggressive Imitation Although some groups specialize in rapid style differentiation, feeding ideas into the fashion system, of equal interest to the fashion forecaster are the fast-moving imitative groups. Some teens and young adult groups imitate sports figures or other fashion icons, rapidly picking up on fashion looks or product identification and just as rapidly moving on to the next big thing. In such groups, fashion interest is high. Individuals are highly sensitive to the symbolic nuances of products, use them artistically, and recognize their artistic use by others. Groups that adopt these same looks after they have been discarded by the fast-moving imitative groups are much less likely to be as sensitive to the details.

Linking the Visible Elite to a Target Audience   Identifying the elite in today's society presents a problem. There is no longer a single source of fashion leadership even among the fashionable elite. Instead, there are many highly visible public figures, some using the strategy of conspicuous consumption, some using conspicuous counterconsumption. The fashion forecaster can use this phenomenon to advantage by linking particular celebrity cohorts with the audience most likely to admire their style and imitate at least some of their characteristics.

A few celebrities are perennial favorites appealing to a broad audience. Many are influential only for a short time, depending on their current roles or music videos. Some celebrities are influential only to a niche market that, while smaller, may be termed a desirable demographic. Teens and twenty-somethings are considered desirable demographics because they are in an acquisitive stage in life with discretionary dollars to spend. Today's fashion forecaster has to be canny about segmenting celebrity influence, monitoring it for fashion direction, and mapping its impact on consumers.

Applying the Theory in Today's Marketplace   The real predictive power in a theory derives from its ability to clearly establish the source, the mechanism, the tempo, and the direction of fashion change (Figure 3.1). The trickle-down theory provides the fashion forecaster with the tools of the trade—an early warning system for identifying the next new thing and a paradigm for mapping out the direction and speed of fashion change. The early warning system involves identifying and monitoring:

- The visible elite.
- The status markers most likely to be imitated.
- The consumer segments most likely to imitate.

FIGURE 3.1	DIRECTION	Downward from elite class to next adjacent class.

Trickle-down theory of fashion change.

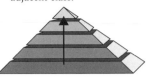

	TEMPO/SPEED	Depends on ability of lower class to see and copy.
	DYNAMICS	**DIFFERENTIATION**

	SOURCE OF FASHION IDEAS	Designers who propose innovation, elite as gatekeepers.
	SOURCE OF CHANGE	Imitators.

- The feeder groups for fashion ideas—that is, groups so concerned about differentiation that they create fashion rather than imitate a higher level group.
- The aggressively imitative groups moving so fast through looks that differentiation is not a concern because others often imitate these groups.

Step one is observation: identifying potential fashion change. Step two is analysis: mapping the potential change to consumer segments most likely to adapt the change to their own fashion purpose. The paradigm calls for imitation to begin in adjacent groups and spread from group to group. The speed of change can be inferred from the power of the elite and the desirability and visibility of the status marker to the imitating group.

Think about the power of star athletes in promoting shoes and the desirability of owning those shoes among young consumers. The combination of high visibility and a very desirable status marker leads to speedy diffusion. The trend ends when the fashion has moved from group to group until almost anyone who wants the product, has the product or a facsimile. In today's fast-paced marketplace, change becomes a constant. Celebrities, once famous, are eclipsed or replaced just as new status markers replace the original and begin trickling down.

The environment is a complex one but the trickle-down theory of fashion change helps the forecaster visualize the interactions. By tracking the new fashionable elite, feeder groups for fashion ideas, and aggressively imitative groups, the forecaster becomes sensitized to the ways fashion trickles down at the turn of the 21st century.

Identify a group that embodies the definitions of a new visible elite or a fast-moving social group with a penchant for differentiation or an aggressively imitative group. Use visuals and descriptive words to describe the group's current look. What consumer segments are most likely to imitate the group's taste? Use the visualization of the trickle-down theory of fashion change to predict the next stages of fashion change. Prepare a presentation board to communicate your prediction.

Activity 3.1
Group Identity

Trickle-Across Theory

Imagine a fashion observer in the early 1960s. How would he or she explain the fashion dynamics of the time? Nearly every characteristic of *la Belle Époque* had changed. Women gained the vote in 1920 and now have more access to education and the world of work than ever before. The United States fought two world wars, weathered the Depression in between, and fought to a standstill in the Korean conflict. At this time the United States is involved in a little war in a far-off place called Vietnam. Civil rights and integration are social issues being dealt with in the courts and in the streets. Mass communication has come of age. Television is a potent influence on the behavior of American consumers. The great development era of department stores has ended, but the stores and other retail outlets have expanded the fashion market. Mass production is in full flower and can provide fashion apparel at all price points.

For the first few years of the 1960s, the trickle-down theory of fashion change seemed as relevant as ever. John F. Kennedy was in the White House and his wife Jacqueline, born into the affluent upper class, was an international style setter. Jacqueline Kennedy wore clothing from American and European designers and her hairstyles, clothing, and accessories were widely copied by American women in all classes. With President Kennedy's assassination in late November, 1963, that era came to an end. Jacqueline Kennedy would continue to be a style setter, but not on the same scale as during those early White House years.

Looking backward at the previous decades, a fashion observer would remember that fashion in the 1920s through the 1950s had an authoritarian flavor—one or two looks were considered fashionable and all other looks were not. In the late 1950s, the youth culture began to be felt and the teenager had been discovered as a market segment. With the baby boom generation in the teen years, there was a shift away from traditional forms and establishment dictates. The original form of the trickle-down theory of fashion change did not provide sufficient explanations for the fashions of the 1960s. King (1963) said so in an article titled, "A Rebuttal to the 'Trickle Down' Theory." He argued that society had changed in profound ways including:

- The "leveling influences" that had changed the profile of the consumer market.
- The accelerating spread of fashion awareness brought on by mass media.
- The accelerated transitions from season to season, resulting in almost nonexistent time lags such as those required for imitation and differentiation under the trickle-down theory.

King contended that the trickle-down theory of fashion change did not help the sophisticated marketer understand fashion behavior in the 1960s. Instead, he proposed a rival theory, the **trickle-across theory** of fashion change (also called the **mass market** or **simultaneous adoption theory**). Simply stated, the theory holds that fashion information trickles across horizontally *within* social strata rather than vertically *across* strata (Figure 3.2). According to King, within a given fashion season consumers in all socioeconomic groups simultaneously have the freedom to select from a range of styles and this range is sufficient to satisfy personal taste. Rather than an elite introducing fashion ideas into society, King saw leadership within each social stratum and within each social group. In this view, personal influence plays the key role in the

FIGURE 3.2	DIRECTION	Horizontal across strata.
The trickle-across theory of fashion change.	TEMPO/SPEED	Rapid and simultaneous.
	DYNAMICS	

SOURCE OF FASHION IDEAS	Couture with selection by professional gatekeepers.
SOURCE OF CHANGE	Innovators and influentials in each market strata.

transmission of fashion information and two kinds of consumers are influential in popularizing new looks:

- The innovators—people who buy early, the earliest visual communicators of a season's styles.
- The influentials—those who are frequently asked for advice and define appropriate standards within their interpersonal networks.

Three factors were essential for the emergence of a mass market—mass production, mass communication, and a growing middle class. Mass communication—magazines, newspapers, television, and movies—made style information available to all simultaneously. Mass production made more looks available in any given season, offering the possibility of individual selection from among the many resources. Imitation and differentiation were still part of the dynamic because others would imitate innovators and influentials within their social strata and those fashion leaders would move to new looks.

Just as in the trickle-down theory of fashion change, designers play an important creative role. However, the gatekeepers had changed. **Gatekeepers** filter the many ideas proposed by designers and determine which will be disseminated widely and which will be discarded. In the trickle-down theory of fashion change, the gatekeepers were the fashionable and affluent elite who could afford the time and effort to view and select from the designers' collections. With mass media and mass production, a new set of gatekeepers rose to prominence—journalists, manufacturers, and retailers. The professional gatekeeper's job was to view the designers' collections and select the styles to be featured in the media and produced in mass quantities (Figure 3.3).

The efficiency of mass production now enabled fashion ideas to be "knocked off" at all market levels within the same season, but that was not a new idea. In 1931, *Life* reported on copies of the "Wally" dress, the $250 Mainbocher wedding ensemble worn by Mrs. Wallis Warfield Simpson when she married the Duke of Windsor (Figure 3.4). The dress appeared as a sketch in *Women's Wear Daily* on May 26 and by June 13 was available in the upscale Bonwit Teller store on New York's Fifth Avenue for $25. By early July it was featured in the window of a more moderately priced department store for $16.95. One week later, it was on the racks of a "cash-and-carry" store for $8.90 ("The descent," 1931).

By 1960, the **knockoff** had become the normal way to do business in the fashion industry. The practice began in earnest after World War II when discounters like Ohrbach's purchased couture models at a prearranged price and made line-for-line copies in the exact fabric, even advertising them with the name of the original couture house. The practice of copying became an entrenched convention within the industry. Communication and production technology continued to speed up the process until by the 1990s, manufacturers could preempt designers by making a sample of a dress shown on the runway overnight and deliver it to the stores ten days later, a feat that the de-

The press and merchants are the gate-keepers in a mass production fashion system because they decide which looks are made available to the public at all price points.

The "Wally" dress, a $250 Mainbocher design worn at her wedding by the Duchess of Windsor, was quickly knocked off at lower price points.

signers could not duplicate (Betts, 1994). Under these conditions, the trickle-across theory seems the ideal explanation of fashion change.

Criticism of the Theory. One tenet of the trickle-across theory is that the interlocking technologies of mass communication and mass production speeded up the process so much that time lags between introduction at the highest price points and availability at the lower price points practically disappeared. But, is that how the process actually plays out?

Behling (1985/1986) agrees with King that design piracy or knockoffs play an important part in today's fashion system. But she disagrees that this process occurs with the speed suggested by King's theory, which depends on fashion looks being simultaneously available at all levels of the marketplace. Instead, she identifies a time lag of at least a year between the time the style has been identified through a trickle-down process, is manufactured and stocked by the retailer, and becomes available for purchase by the majority of consumers.

Behling attributes some of this time lag to the unwillingness of consumers at all levels to adopt the new look. What may seem the inevitable next step in fashion change to fashion insiders may not be accepted readily in another social setting. It often takes time for the consumer to build a comfort level with a proposed fashion, taking into account the mores of a particular locality or social group. For example, models who wore actual lingerie slips as dresses introduced the slip dress of 1994. Picked up by designers as a trend, it traveled from the runways to the editorial pages of fashion magazines to stores and to the more avant-garde consumers (Betts, 1994). But, it continued to appear on the runways for several years as acceptance of the look grew across consumer segments.

Although it is undeniable that mass communication and mass production speeded up the process of moving fashion ideas from the runway to the store, Behling rightly points out exceptions to the functioning of the theory. Fashion change does not depend merely on mechanical and technological expertise. The speed of fashion change is regulated by the willingness of people to accept that change in numbers sufficient to made it profitable.

Forecaster's Toolbox: Theory in Action. The trickle-across theory of fashion change operates in an environment where designers propose fashion and gatekeepers such as journalists, manufacturers, and retailers determine which looks are reproduced in quantity at all price points. By providing a wide variety of looks at all price points simultaneously, the industry provides customers with the means to differentiate themselves from others through individual selection and the means to demonstrate group membership. Although the fashionable elite is still influential via mass communication, the key element in acceptance of a new look lies within the personal network through the personal influence of innovators and influentials.

The real predictive power in a theory derives from its ability to clearly establish the source, the mechanism, the tempo, and the direction of fashion change. As in the trickle-down theory, the trickle-across theory of fashion change provides the fashion forecaster with the tools of the trade—an early warning system for identifying the next new thing and a paradigm for mapping out the direction and speed of the fashion change. The early warning system involves monitoring the interaction of designers' introductions of fashion ideas; the response of journalists, manufacturers, and retailers; and the acceptance or rejection reaction of consumers in different market segments. By being sensitive to the time lag inherent in the consumer acceptance of a new fashion, the fashion forecaster can predict when different market segments are most likely to move from awareness of a proposed fashion to interest in that fashion, to trying the look on, to purchase (and repurchase).

Activity 3.2
Who Are the
Gatekeepers?

Learn the names and affiliations of the fashion executives who attend and the fashion press who cover the fashion shows. Each has an individual take on the world of fashion. These fashion insiders decide what looks are selected from the designers' collection to be disseminated more widely. Find out who they are by reading trade papers for reports on seasonal fashion shows. Collect clippings that feature quotes from these insiders describing their opinions. Watch fashion on television ("Style with Elsa Klench" on CNN, "Fashion File" and "VideoFashion" on E!, and "Fashion Television" on VH1). Who is interviewed? What point of view do they represent? Read the editor's letter in the front of fashion magazines for insight on how the press covers fashion. Develop an insider's map of the world of fashion and know the names and positions of the key players.

Trickle-Up Theory

Imagine a fashion observer in the late 1960s. How would he or she explain fashion change? This time the focus in not on the apparel industry as in the trickle-across theory, but on a new source of inspiration and fashion leadership. Youthquake is underway on both sides of the Atlantic as young people discover the expressive qualities of fashion. The symbol of the decade—the miniskirt—emerges at the midpoint of the sixties. It is a time when music, art, television variety shows, and movies all move to the youthful beat. The Beatles—John, Paul, George, and Ringo—revolutionize music, men's fashion, and the movies, along with the scruffier Rolling Stones. A new youthful sensibility emerges and is expressed in the hippie and the flower child looks. Women become more militant in their demands for equality and express their frustrations with social restrictions by burning bras and demonstrating in the streets. Long hair, bare feet, and nudity become socially acceptable. Unisex and ethnic looks are highly valued badges of changing attitudes. Adults, the former arbiters of fashion, now take their fashion cues from the young.

DIRECTION

Status markers trickle up from consumer stylists and subcultural groups.

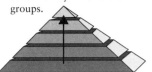

FIGURE 3.5

The trickle-up theory of fashion change

TEMPO/SPEED

Depends on the sensitivity of fashion gatekeepers and visibility of the subcultural groups.

DYNAMICS

Professional Gatekeepers   Designers   Fashion Leaders

Consumer
Stylists

SOURCE OF
FASHION IDEAS

Aestetic codes of subcultural groups.

SOURCE OF
CHANGE

Instabilities in age, gender, ethnicity, and appearance.

Against this backdrop, Field (1970) proposed a new theory of fashion change he called the **status float phenomenon** (now commonly known as the **trickle-up theory** of fashion change). According to this theory, higher status segments with more power imitated those with lower status—that is, status markers were floating up the status pyramid rather than trickling down or across it (Figure 3.5). To support this view, Field cited specific examples from the culture. Some of his examples sound quaint and condescending today but were relevant and groundbreaking at the time.

- **Black Is Beautiful**

"Negro" music and dance had a strong influence on popular culture, as did "Negro" speech on American slang. In relationship to fashion, Field pointed out the increasing use of "Negro" models, actors, and celebrities on television, in magazines and advertising, and as spokespersons for products aimed at a broad audience. "Afro prints" in fabrics were featured in fashion magazine editorial pages. The popularity of hairstyles associated with African Americans could be seen in the wigs that allowed anyone in society to emulate the styles. Field suggests that the channels of jazz and youth culture moved "Negro" fashion into the consciousness of a wider audience.

- **Youth Culture**

According to Field, extremes in fashion originally adopted by youth to express their rebellion against the older generation were adopted and worn by the middle aged. In a specific example, he cited the case of formerly ultraconservative automotive executives who were "sporting sideburns, square-toed buckled shoes, short, cuffless pants, wide, flashy polka-dot ties, sportcoats, colored shirts, and even sport shirts" by 1969. Field suggested that these executives were wearing fashions pioneered by the teenage and college-aged crowd.

- **Blue Collar Influence on White Collar Consumers**

Field saw the camping craze and the buying of pickup trucks by middle-class consumers as a case of typically blue-collar pursuits trickling up the status pyramid. Additionally he cited the use of garish male clothing and bright colors on automobiles as a shift from the conservative tastes of the upper class to the tastes of the lower class. He cited the adapting of work clothes—jackets, Levi's, boots, and the sleeveless undershirt—into more widely popular casual clothing styles for men as another case of status float.

- **The Sexual Revolution**

Women had freely borrowed from men's fashion at least since Chanel popularized the look in the 1920s. Field cites a reverse case of borrowing: by 1969, college men and entertainers had adopted the flare pants, a style originally worn by women earlier in the decade.

- **Style Leadership by Prostitutes**

Field cited the high heel, the use of rouge and lipstick, and women smoking cigarettes as examples of customs that originated in the subculture of prostitutes and spread over the decades to middle and upper class women.

Field concluded his article with a call for more research to document the extent of the status float phenomenon and its variations.

The trickle-up theory provides the cornerstone of today's view that street fashion is a laboratory for fashion change. The concept carries with it the essence of outsider sensibility. Simmel (1904) was aware of the connection between prostitutes and fashion except that he used the more refined term "demimonde" to refer to these fashion pioneers. He pointed out that an uprooted existence outside the bounds of acceptable society produced a "latent hatred against everything that has the sanctions of law" and that this hatred found expression in striving for new forms of appearance. It is this context of being dressed up, hanging out, and oozing attitude that finds expression in clothes, hairstyles, makeup, tattoos, body piercing, and accessories.

Today's fashion world takes the importance of street fashion for granted. Again, the motivation for differentiation drives **subcultures** where new looks are created. Members of these subcultures adopt specific aesthetic codes that differentiate them from other subcultures and from the mainstream (Blumberg, 1975). Imitation may occur between social groups but the importance of street fashion for the fashion industry is in the visual inspiration it provides for designers and other fashion gatekeepers such as journalists, stylists, and photographers.

Saint Laurent has been credited with reversing fashion's directional flow (Betts, 1994). He showed street-inspired trends on the runways as early as his 1960 collection for Dior. Later in the 1960s he was inspired by New York's army-surplus shops and by Paris's student protesters. It did not take other designers long to catch onto street fashion, the youthful club scene, vintage clothes, and flea market finds as the source for fashion change. Bicycle messengers, hip-hop homeboys, and gang members became **consumer stylists** whose looks and ideas were translated into $600 jeans, $55 cotton bandannas, and $150 tank tops (Gandee, 1993). Punk looks, dominatrix looks, and rapper styles all made appearances on runways during the mid-1990s.

Polhemus (1994) in his book, *Streetstyle: From Sidewalk to Catwalk*, traces the appeal of street-inspired fashion to the quest for authenticity (Figure 3.6). It represents hanging out on the wrong side of the tracks with "no-

FIGURE 3.6

In the 1990s, looks from the street influenced designers' take on fashion as in this poplin shirt and distressed chinos from the DKNY Pure line.

hopers [who] have none of those things that our society officially decrees to be important (money, prestige, success, fame)" and yet represent something real and genuine. Polhemus sees streetstyle garments as radiating the power of their associations. He traces the chain of events, beginning with a genuine streetstyle innovation that is picked up and popularized through a pop music video, through dissemination to street kids in other locales, until it finds its way into an upscale version in a designer's collection. He calls the process **bubble up**, the opposite of trickle-down fashion. The groups whose fashions are appropriated may react in an unexpected way: they may be insulted rather than flattered because the appropriation waters down the significance of the objects, robbing them of their power and magic as symbols of differentiation.

Forecaster's Toolbox: Today in Action. Forecasters applying the trickle-up theory of fashion change (Field calls it status float and Polhemus, bubble up) look to consumer stylists as the source of creativity, as naïve designers who propose new looks. Such people are not waiting on every street corner. Two sources serve as early warning signals for trickle-up fashion—the alternative fashion neighborhoods and the fashion scouts.

Fashion Neighborhoods   A conduit from street culture to the fashion system exists in almost all large cities—a neighborhood where young outsiders come to hang out, shop, and keep up with each other. The entrepreneurs and retailers who set up shop in these areas are the first to pick up on new trends because, in many cases, they participate directly in the social life and street culture their stores service. Often these colorful neighborhoods are a bit run-down and seedy, but they serve as a playground for free-spirited experimentation in lifestyles and dress. For the fashion forecaster, these neighborhoods offer the chance to see consumer stylists at work inventing the next new fashion.

Finding emerging trends means mounting an expedition to neighborhoods where young people congregate and observing people with an unconventional style of dress. When companies hire market research firms to scout fashion neighborhoods, the companies often interview people on the street, capturing on camera their views about life, favorite brands, favorite music and movies, and aspirations. A company that provides entry to street trends is Sputnik, a nationwide network of young correspondents armed with video cameras who track the youth lifestyle for companies such as Levi's (Lopiano-Misdom & DeLuca, 1997) (Figure 3.7). The interviews are edited into a series of montages to help companies better understand the consumer and the potential for translating the fashion for other consumers (Ozzard, 1995).

Fashion Scouts   Because forecasters cannot watch the globally diverse subcultures that may be the origin of an emerging fashion look, they must rely on scouting reports from other professionals. The cues may come from the cre-

FIGURE 3.7

Joanna De Luca and Janine Misdom are partners in Sputnik, a marketing and forecasting firm based in New York that specializes in researching trends among 16- to-29- year-old consumers.

ative director for a fashion-forward retailer, the pages of an avant-garde publication, the windows of a shop on the side street of a fashion center, the reports of a forecasting service, or the articles of a cultural journalist. These scouts patrol the edges of culture, recognizing the potential and power of a subcultural style and transmitting it into the fashion system.

The most famous example of the work of a cultural journalist leading to fashion change happened in the mid-1970s. A cultural journalist wrote an article on the dance club culture among young people in a lower class Brooklyn neighborhood for *New York Magazine*. The article became the seed for a script that metamorphosed into the movie *Saturday Night Fever* and provided visual inspiration for disco fashion (Aikman, 1997).

Cultural journalists and fashion writers go where trends are born and report about what they see. Tracking down shops with an outsider concept, such as Vexed Generation, tucked away up a staircase on a London street, is worth the trouble to uncover a potential trend. The theme of the shop is protective daywear, a fashion parody of police riot gear that includes cargo pants, high zip-up collars, and bags like those used by bicycle messengers. This utilitarian look is the uniform of choice for young people who are not satisfied with the status quo and who are "interested in anonymity and security" (Betts, 1998a).

Apparel companies even hire market research firms to perform the scouting function. Steven Rifkind runs an urban intelligence network of 80 kids working in street teams roaming the clubs, shops, and other spots in 28 cites. Their findings on style trends are reported back to companies such as Nike and Tommy Hilfiger (Levine, 1997).

Applying the Theory in Today's Marketplace   The real predictive power in a theory derives from its ability to clearly establish the source, the mechanism, the tempo, and the direction of fashion change. As with the trickle-down and trickle-across theories, the concept of time lag plays an important part in the dynamics of fashion as it trickles up from the street corner, to the runway, and then to Main Street. Looks developed as aesthetic codes for members of subcultural groups are usually too radical to be accepted instantly into mainstream fashion. It takes time for consumers' sensibilities to adjust to the proposed look and incorporate it into their own social setting. This time lag may be as short as a year or as long as several decades. The forecaster can estimate the path and time sequence by evaluating the degree of adjustment required, the visibility of the innovation to consumer segments, and the match between the symbolism of the look and the attitudes of the target consumers.

Activity 3.3
Scouting for
Change

Watch the fashion news for reports on fashion neighborhoods and subcultures feeding new looks into the fashion system. Use Web search engines such as Yahoo and Infoseek and the databases in libraries to locate newspaper and magazine articles by cultural journalists or fashion writers about avant-garde social behavior and radical lifestyles. When a source describes a look or uniform associated with the behavior or lifestyle, estimate the path and time lag for these edgy looks to be transmitted into the fashion system. What consumer group is most likely to first adopt this trend? (*Warning*: Avant-garde, radical, and edgy all signify cultural behavior beyond the boundaries of mainstream. To many people, the ideas, behavior, and dress of such groups can be shocking. Do not assume the role of scout on the cultural edge unless you can be an objective, detached observer.)

Directional Theories of Fashion Change in Tandem

A careful reading of the fashion theories reveals the interplay between the directional theories of fashion change. Simmel's article from 1904 contained the seeds not only of the trickle-down theory but pointed to the trickle-up theory through references to the conspicuously antifashion consumer and the demimonde as a source for fashion innovation. The instabilities of gender, ethnicity, age, and physical attractiveness that serve to update the trickle-down theory play an important part in the fashion statements of subcultural groups. A fashion forecaster's toolbox must come equipped with an understanding of how each theory represents a view of reality. But that is not enough. In a complex social system, it may take more than one theory to explain how a particular fashion moves from a starting point to widespread acceptance in everyday life.

A Model for Vertical Flow. Behling (1985/1986) saw common underlying themes in the two vertical theories of fashion—trickle down and trickle up— and sought to integrate them into a single predictive model. The model attempts to explain fashion change between 1920 and 1985 using the median age of the population and the economic health of the country as factors. When she arrays the decades on the horizontal axis and median age of the population in years on the vertical axis, a regular pattern appears (Figure 3.8). During time periods when the median age was low—the 1920s, and the mid-sixties to mid-seventies—fashion looks trickled up from youthful consumers to the market as a whole. During time periods when the median age was higher, fashion tended to trickle down from the older, wealthy, and influential strata. Behling's model shows a relationship between the median age of the population, fashion role models, and the direction of fashion flow. Events that can alter this directional flow are a depressed economy or curtailment of fashion by governmental decree, as in rationing.

This model can be applied to current demographic conditions. Because the median age is expected to rise as baby boomers enter middle age, the model suggests that fashion influence should trickle down from an older, affluent, and visible class at the turn of the millenium. After that, the large echo-boom generation will lower the median age which could reverse the direction of fashion change.

Time Lags and Idea Chains. The concept of time lags apparent in each of the directional theories of fashion change is an important issue in fashion forecasting. The technology of mass communication and mass production that makes possible the simultaneous adoption of a fashion across all market

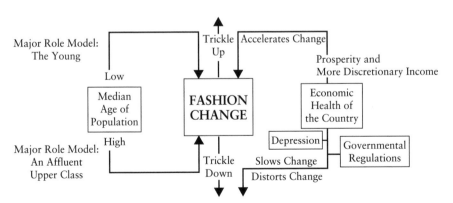

The direction of fashion change depends on several factors, namely, the median age of the population, the economic health of the country, and the presence or absence of government regulation (Behling, 1985/1986).

segments does not ensure such an outcome. Instead, the process often includes a time lag during which consumers become more aware, interested, and receptive to the new fashion—a trickle-down process. Street looks go through stages of modification that lead to wider acceptance.

Polhemus (1994) traces the path of the black leather motorcycle jacket from a functional beginning to a World War II designation of bravery and daring when worn by pilots, to a symbol of rebellious youth produced primarily by small, family-owned shops in off–Main Street locations in the late 1950s. Immortalized in the movie *The Wild One* by screen icon Marlon Brando, the garment was still not acceptable in Main Street society. Only gradually did the black leather motorcycle jacket become normal everyday wear through the seventies and eighties. Helping the look gain popularity was its adoption by a visible fashionable elite—rock musicians from Jim Morrison to Bruce Springsteen to George Michael. Fashion-forward designers known for street-inspired fashion, such as Katharine Hamnett and Jean-Paul Gaultier, first introduced the look to the runway. Designers such as Claude Montana, Thierry Mugler, and Gianni Versace further appropriated it into high fashion. In the designer version, the look was then available to professional gatekeepers for dissemination through mass media and mass production. In the history of this one style, all three directional theories of fashion change act at different stages. First the style moves from a street fashion for a particular subculture to diffusion among other outsider groups. Then it is adopted by the visible elite of rock musicians, appropriated by designers, and presented on the runway. Knockoffs make it available to all market segments. Mass communication aids its acceptance by mainstream consumers. At each stage there were opportunities for fashion forecasters to recognize and map the process.

In a 1992 *Newsweek* cover story (Alter, 1992) on the cultural elite, an accompanying graphic introduced the concept of an **idea chain**—a set of linked events that move a phenomenon from a subculture to mainstream. The subject of the magazine's exercise was rap music. The chain began in 1968 when a West Bronx disc jockey invented hip-hop. The style was elaborated on during the 1970s with the addition of break-dancing and the first small record labels specializing in this form of music. By 1981, the new-wave band Blondie had a rap song as a No. 1 hit. During the mid- and late 1980s, collegiate rappers, corporate record companies such as Columbia, and MTV took rap to the middle-class consumer. The 1990 film *House Party* further popularized the hip-hop idiom, and the sitcom *Fresh Prince of Bel Air* brought rap to weekly prime-time TV. No single event or influential celebrity or corporate sponsor was sufficient to move the idea along the chain. Instead, it took the entire chain of events played out over time.

In the same way, a single directional theory of fashion change is sufficient only to explain particular links in the chain, not the whole timeline as an idea moves from source to wide public acceptance. A forecaster in New York tuned into the right radio station in the late-1960s might have recognized rap music as a trend and begun considering the marketing potential. But there were other sightings throughout the 1970s and 1980s that offered the same opportunity to participate in the full-blown mass acceptance of the style in the early 1990s. At every stage, there were marketing opportunities for the music and for the fashion looks associated with it.

Select a fashion item—the T-shirt, denim jacket, stiletto heels, sneakers—and develop an idea chain. Show the origin of the item and trace its path into mainstream fashion. What celebrities, social movements, movies, music, or other cultural shifts were involved? Sources for this investigation include:

- Magazine articles on specific fashion items, because they often include a brief history of how the item evolved.
- Books on the history of fashion in the 20th century, because they often integrate the evolution of particular looks into a more complex timeline.

Find pictures to illustrate stages in the idea chain. Prepare a presentation board as a visualization of your findings.

*Activity 3.4
Idea Chains*

LONG WAVE PHENOMENON
AND FASHION CYCLES

Visualize the dynamics of fashion as waves striking a beach. Long before one wave has finished its course, new ones are being formed far out in the ocean. Each wave follows the others to shore, an occasional large wave with sets of smaller waves between (Brenninkmeyer, 1963). Each wave rolling toward shore has a curve, a crest, and a crash (Collins, 1974). The comparison can be taken further to explain the wave forms:

> *Some waves race headlong for a shallow beach, swell rapidly to a tremendous foaming top, then drop abruptly with a thud. Is this not precisely what happens with fads? But other waves move gradually upwards, curl over in a quiet, leisurely way, then break with little or no force. Is this not precisely the movement of sane, properly conceived style cycles? They are slow to develop, hold their own for a time, then subside rather than collapse. (p. 24)*

Imagine a forecaster standing on the beach and watching the formation of fashion waves. How far out can he or she see? What are the size and shapes of waves coming toward the beach? What is the underlying contour of the bottom and how does that influence the shape and speed of the waves? When will the waves arrive and with what force? If a forecaster can estimate these factors, then that gives a designer, manufacturer, or retailer a chance to capitalize on change. Part of that estimate involves recognizing **fashion cycles**— fashion ideas that return periodically to popularity.

Recycling Fashion Ideas

In the latter part of the 20th century, designers seemed to raid fashion's closet for inspiration. Fashions from every decade returned to the runways. Recycling fashion ideas is part of **historic continuity**—the steady evolution of clothing including the continual recurrence of symbolism, styles, and elements of decoration (Brenninkmeyer, 1963). When some element of style or decoration is neglected for a period, it is ripe for revival. Large pins on jackets had been out of fashion until the look from the 1940s was revived in 1991. Although never revived exactly in form or with the same companion elements or for the same use or occasion, the style is recognizably retro (from the prefix meaning backward). **Retro fashion** carries with it the nostalgia for other periods when that look was the prevailing fashion (Figure 3.9). Several theories of fashion change deal with the recurring nature of fashion.

The Theory of Shifting Erogenous Zones. One of the key characteristics of eveningwear in the 1930s was the bare back look. Laver (1973) noticed these sexy dresses and compared them to short skirts in the previous decade, when the emphasis was on the legs. From this and other examples he suggested that fashion changed systematically by covering one part of the body while uncovering another. As he explained, parts of the female body, which are exposed by a fashion, lose their erotic power to attract over time. When this happens, the fashion goes out of style. Another part of the body, one that has been hidden or de-emphasized during the previous period, becomes the focus of attention for the next fashion cycle. The newly emphasized part of the body becomes an **erogenous zone**. Any part of the female body may become the focus of erotic attention, and the erogenous zone is always shifting. Laver (1973, p. 383) said, "it is the business of fashion to pursue it, without ever catching up."

FIGURE 3.9

A platform shoe from the 1940s is mimicked yet enhanced in style for its 1970s counterpart.

Other scholars (Wilson, 1985) disputed Laver's theory of shifting erogenous zones by saying that it only applies to female fashion, that his examples can be explained in other ways, and that the meaning of any apparel item is too complex for so easy an interpretation. Although Laver's theory may not offer a sufficient explanation of fashion cycles, it does point to an important element of newness that can be part of fashion trends. Fashion does play an important part in seduction and attracting sexual attention. Even in the use of cosmetics the emphasis shifts—sometimes to the eyes, others times to the mouth or the cheeks. In the same way, different parts of the body are emphasized during different fashion eras.

In discussing the history of the bathing suit, historian Lena Lencek (1996) described changes in styles in terms of shifting erogenous zones. In the early part of the century bathing suits were very unrevealing; the only uncovered parts of the body were the ankles and wrists. By the 1920s, the bathing suit was beginning to shrink in size but the torso was still mostly covered, so the emphasis was on the legs and arms. Like the evening dresses of the thirties, the swimsuits of that era put emphasis on the bare back. New fabrics and bra technology made possible more structured suits in the 1940s and 1950s and the emphasis was on the bosom. When the bikini was introduced in the 1960s, emphasis shifted to the navel. Very revealing suits were seen on the beaches in Brazil and St. Tropez but arrived in other places with the fitness craze in the 1970s and 1980s. The new look emphased a part of the body that had not previously been visible—the toned and muscled upper thighs and hip, which were revealed by high-cut swimsuits. For the daring in the 1990s, thong suits bared a new part of the female body, the derriere. The changes in swimsuit styling through the decades are reminiscent of Laver's theory of shifting erogenous zones.

Forecaster's Toolbox: Theory in Action Although the theory of shifting erogenous zones may explain only a small percentage of fashion change, it is still a useful concept because fashion does move to uncover a portion of the anatomy not previously on view and to focus attention on that portion of the body. In the mid- and late 1990s, many tops, shirts, short jackets, pants, and skirts were designed to bare the toned midsection of women who worked out. A lifestyle change that favored the gym as a leisure activity and a redefinition of what is beautiful and desirable—a toned and flat stomach—was mirrored in fashion. Laver's theory helps explain the underlying mechanism that makes revealing or emphasizing one part of the body over all others seem new. It also explains how, after a time, the look no longer has the same effect. When this occurs, designers change the silhouette, the cut, the fit, the detail, and the emphasis to create a new fashion look.

Retro and Vintage Fashion. When people look back at fashions recently past, they find them at best amusing, at worst distasteful. As Laver (1973) put it:

Most women . . . will give as their opinion that the fashions of yesterday were indeed ridiculous, and that the fashions of the present day are both beautiful and practical. Women were probably always of this opinion, and all that can be said about it is that it is a complete delusion (p. 381).

Laver did more than just notice this trait; he established a timeline of acceptability (Figure 3.10). Looking backward, fashions closest to the present he said look dowdy. He developed a stepwise rehabilitation of a look, from frumpy and ridiculous for recently past fashion to beautiful for fashion 150 years in the past. On a somewhat shorter timeline, he suggested that innovative looks being introduced into the fashion mix were likely to be considered audacious and brazen. Only as they moved closer to full acceptance were they deemed appropriate attire. Laver called this trick of seeing current fashion as exemplary when compared to past and future fashions the gap in appreciation and suggested that it exists in all matters of taste.

As a style or look or lifestyle moves further into the past, it becomes a candidate for revival because the perception of it changes. Fashion change is often the result of revising an obsolete style or reinventing an outdated trend. A celebrity (e.g., Sinatra), a group (e.g., the Beats, the Rat Pack, the Brat Pack), a product (e.g., Birkenstocks and Hush Puppies), or a look is so "out" that it becomes "in" again.

Forecaster's Toolbox: Theory in Action   Laver's ideas about recycling fashion provide a timeline forecasters can use in gauging probable reactions to fashion revivals. But not everything gets revived. Hats, announced again and again as returning to the fashion picture, never became as ubiquitous as they were in the 1920s through the 1950s. Even in the midst of a seventies revival, some of that decade's hot design names—Halston, Fiorucci, and Sergio Valente—had difficulty making a comeback owing to rocky relaunches, the retail bureaucracy, and uncertain design direction (D'Innocenzio, 1998b). Whatever is selected for revival tends to be something nostalgic or a campy novelty or some guilty pleasure that is currently forbidden.

The 1950s were first revived in the early 1970s ("Back to the 50s," 1972), about on time by Laver's timeline. Not revived were the political upheavals, bomb tests, and civil rights issues that had plagued the decade. Instead the re-

FIGURE 3.10

Laver's "gap in appreciation" can be visualized as the period during which fashion looks from the past are rehabilitated prior to revival or a period of conversion as consumers become more comfortable with an innovative look.

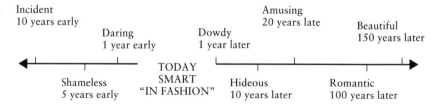

vival concentrated on the fun of Hula-Hoops, rock 'n' roll, early Elvis, and the return to classic looks in fashion. Bits and pieces of the 1950s continue to be revived. In their turn, the 1970s were revived in the 1990s. According to Laver's timeline, this occurred when the fashions of the 1970s could be defined as amusing. At the end of the 1990s, it was possible to sample many eras from super-wide bell-bottoms reminiscent of the 1970s to clam-diggers and capri pants, signature looks for the late 1950s (Figure 3.11).

Like the 1950s styles, some looks are constantly recycled. Men's wear looks for women first made an appearance when Coco Chanel began borrowing tweeds from the closet of her aristocratic English lover. From the mid-1940s to mid-1950s (Figure 3.12), high school girls appropriated blazers, crewneck sweaters, Oxford shirts, and blue jeans from brothers and boyfriends as their casual uniform (Feitelberg, 1996). Diane Keaton's "Annie Hall" look of 1977 had the same borrowed-from-boys élan.

FIGURE 3.11

At the end of the 1990s, fashion from many fashions eras coexisted such as the bell-bottom jeans of the 1970s and the capri pants of the 1950s.

High school girls from the mid-1940s to the mid-1950s appropriated looks from the closets of their brothers and boyfriends and made the looks their own.

According to Anna Wintour (1998a), editor of *Vogue*, "other than a pervasive minimalism, there has been no definitive look for the decade" of the 1990s. But there have been waves of revivals of past fashion eras—revivals of the tailored suits of the 1940s, the club scene of the 1950s, the psychedelic 1960s, the bell-bottoms and platform shoes of the 1970s, and hints of the extravagant, colorful, affluent 1980s.

Secondhand shops catering to models, celebrities, stylists, and designers have provided inspiration for many of the revivals. Living the retro lifestyle is the focus of an online magazine where vintage-period enthusiasts can find fashion information on eveningwear in the twenties, sources for reproduction items from the film *Titanic*, and directions on setting up an authentic 1950s cocktail bar, including glassware and bar accessories (Erlichman, 1998). Two leading men's wear firms were among the most prominent bidders at the auction of the Duke of Windsor's apparel (Vasilopoulos, 1998). Auctions of movie clothes, designer fashions, and the personal wardrobes of style leaders like Jacqueline Kennedy, Princess Diana, and the Duke and Duchess of Windsor often spark a revival of corresponding clothing and accessory styles (Figure 3.13).

FIGURE 3.13

The rooms at Sotheby's in New York were the site of an auction of the Duke of Windsor's apparel that brought in $773,145. Men's wear houses Kiton and Brioni were prominent bidders in the auction.

Prices at fashion auctions and secondhand shops echo Laver's idea of a gap in appreciation. Caroline Reynolds Milbank, a fashion historian and consultant to an auction house, says that prices depend on the age of the item (Browne, 1994): "It takes a while for people to get far enough away. Clothes from the '50s and '60s will sell for three to four thousand dollars. The '70s are at a tenth of these prices." Like the theory of erogenous zones, Laver's timeline of acceptability explains only one aspect of fashion change, but even a partial explanation can represent potential profits for a forecaster and his or her clients.

What fashion is poised for revival? What fashion from the later half of the 20th century will become collectable? Which designer's work or celebrity's clothing is likely to bring high prices in future fashion auctions? What effect does an interest in vintage fashion have on design evolution? Explore these kinds of questions by:

- Shopping secondhand shops to analyze differences in prices between styles and decades.
- Visiting vintage clothing sites on the Web (see the Resource Pointers section at the end of the chapter).
- Visiting Web sites on retro lifestyles (like retroactive.com).
- Using databases searches to locate articles on fashion auctions.

*Activity 3.5
Venture into
Vintage*

The Pendulum of Fashion. Just as a pendulum in a grandfather's clock swings back and forth keeping time, so the pendulum of fashion swings from a point of exaggeration and then moves in the opposite direction (Robinson, 1975). In this kind of fashion cycle, a trend terminates when all possibilities have been exhausted (Blumer, 1969). When short skirts get as short as possible, then the pendulum swings toward longer skirts. When the fit gets too body conscious and cannot fit any tighter, the pendulum swings toward looser cuts. When black dominates the market for a time, brighter or lighter colors move in to relieve the gloom.

In an idealized version of this kind of cycle, a fashion look would evolve to a point of exaggeration in one direction, move toward the opposite direction, pause at the compromise point on a classic form, and then swing in the opposite direction (Figure 3.14). Such cycles can be traced in historic fashion (Young, 1937), but modern fashion tends to take a more abrupt path between extremes.

Hemline changes epitomize this kind of fashion cycle. The thigh-high miniskirt, which dates from about 1965, was new to fashion and lifted all skirts to the knee or just above it by the early 1970s. Attempts to lower hemlines by the introduction of midi (midcalf length) and maxi (floor length) were unsuccessful. But skirts did eventually come down. Change in the opposite direction marked 1989 when, after seasons of knee-length or below-knee-length skirts, designers reintroduced short skirts. The quick change alienated working women who refused to buy. Retailers were left with stock to mark down and the press reported the short skirts as a failed trend. But, skirt lengths did rise in the early 1990s and the fashion-forward customer did wear miniskirts again and, eventually, microminis. By 1997, short skirts had gotten very short. Then designers found a way to go even shorter by adding slits. But by the Fall of 1998, Kal Ruttenstein, senior vice president of fashion direction at Bloomingdale's, thought that short skirts looked stale. Runways for the Fall 1998 season showed floor-sweeping long looks (Schiro, 1998).

Sudden hemline changes and retailing of multiple lengths tends to cause trouble for retailers and consumers. In seasons when designers introduce the

---

FIGURE 3.14

The pendulum swing of fashion can be visualized as moving from a point of exaggeration in one direction toward the opposite direction. The midpoint represents the classic form as a compromise between the two extremes.

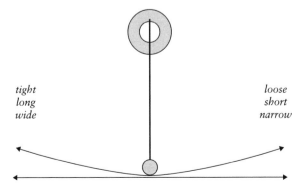

tight   loose
long   short
wide   narrow

opposite to prevailing fashion, retailers tend to hedge their bets by presenting multiple messages, letting the consumer decide the issue (Figure 3.15). Consumers are often confused and baffled by the necessity of learning how to coordinate the new length with coats, shoes, and other components of the look (D'Innocenzio, 1998a).

While modern fashion does not follow the idealized pendulum swing between extreme points, the cycle does manifest itself in fashion change. In the Fall of 1994, *The New York Times* carried a story about a conspiracy to "haul fashion away from a look that wasn't selling clothes or makeup"—the waif look, grunge, and minimalist fashion—and replace it with the glamour look of earlier decades (Spindler, 1994). Anna Wintour, editor of *Vogue,* is credited with championing the move. Consumers had already rejected the waif look, and accessory designers, who are heavy advertisers in fashion magazines, were feeling the sales pinch caused by stark, minimalist layouts. The abrupt swing toward glamour looks left stores and designers playing catch-up. The too-plain look was replaced with sexy glamour looks featuring animal prints, sequins, and stiletto heels—a look that was just as irrelevant to most women as the look it replaced. Donna Karan summed up the situation when she said, "Fashion links onto something so hard and then generalizes it and exaggerates it and frightens the customer."

Forecaster's Toolbox: Theory in Action   The pendulum action can act on hemlines, fashion colors, looks, and even lifestyles. David Wolfe, creative director for the fashion trend forecasting division of the Donegar Group, invoked the pendulum swing to ask, "What comes after casual?" In a speech to

FIGURE 3.15

Hemlines from BCBG Max Azria, below-the-knee, Donna Karan at midcalf, and ankle-length from Ralph Lauren—all from the Fall 1998 showings.

the National Retail Federation (1998), Wolfe explained that today's customer is comfort driven but that comfortable does not mean sloppy. He had detected a trend back toward appropriateness but not back to uncomfortable formality. Describing the change he said, "Think of fashion as moving slowly from sloppy casual to dressed up. It's going to take a long time. What's in the middle? What fills the gap? Classics are as comfortable as casual wear but they are a bit more traditional, tend to look a little more polished. They are halfway between casual and formal." For fashion professionals and forecasters, the visualization of fashion's pendulum swing helps to define fashion direction and aids in predicting the next fashion change.

Activity 3.6 Pendulum Swings

Use five years of back issues of a fashion magazine to backcast the pendulum swings of fashion. To narrow the search, check only key issues for each year, the ones most likely to preview seasonal fashion. Look for a season where the fashion news was a tight fit. Then look backward to locate a season when the fashion news was loose, unconstructed looks. Or, look for a season featuring short skirts and look backward to a time when longer skirts or pants dominated the runways. Now look at the seasons in between the extremes. Or, consider the work of a particular designer over several years. Is there the same kind of shift in emphasis between extremes? This kind of analysis requires a kind of abstraction of a fashion message. In every season there will be some tight, some loose-fitting styles, and some variation in hem length. For this activity, look for the overall message or theme or newness expressed in the issue. Use the pendulum visualization to explain your findings.

Wave Dynamics

People look for patterns in everyday happenings such as the weather and the stock market. Why not look for cyclical patterns in fashion change? Is there an inner logic peculiar to fashion? Is some aspect of fashion immune to exogenous factors (external influences)? Is there a rhythm underlying the seemingly random fluctuations in fashion? A discernible pattern that recurs over time? Researchers in the 20th century searched for such a pattern (see Table 3.1). Such research tends to use similar methods:

Step 1: Finding a suitable source for fashion images—fashion periodicals are frequently used.

Step 2: Because not all images can be included in the sample, develop a systematic way to decide which images will be excluded (e.g., images where the model is not pictured full length and facing forward).

Step 3: Standardize a set of measurements or observations to be taken on every image in the sample.

TABLE 3.1

Research on Fashion Cycles

Researcher	Time Period	Focus	Findings
Kroeber (1919)	1844–1919	Width and length of women's evening dresses.	Skirt length recurred every 35 years. Skirt width recurred every 100 years, 50 years for the transition from wide to narrow and 50 years for the transition back again.
Richardson & Kroeber (1940)	1605–1936	Width and length of women's evening dresses.	Skirts alternate from broad to narrow, from long to short with a regular cycle of 100 years.
Young (1937)	1760–1937	Style of skirts.	Cycle: back fullness to tubular to bell shape, each style ascending to dominance and evolving into the next cycle over 30 or 40 years.
Lowe & Lowe (1982, 1984, 1985)	1789–1980	Width and length of women's dresses.	Cycles expected to occur between 1937 to 1980 according to the Kroeber prediction did not occur. Instead there was increased variation within each year in terms of details of style.
Carman (1966)	1786–1965	Width and length of women's evening dresses.	Support for Young's identified cycles. Cyclical changes in waist and skirt dimensions. Periods when the cycles do not explain the changes observed—the decade of the 1860s, the decade of the 1920s and from 1935 to 1966.
Weeden (1977)	1920–1976	Width and length of women's day dresses.	Data indicated the fashion process was speeding up and no style dominated a period.
Belleau (1987)	1860–1980	Women's day dresses: skirt length, waist emphasis, silhouette, fit of the sleeve, bodice, and skirt.	Cyclical movement in skirt length and waist emphasis. Cyclical characteristics in silhouette shapes—back fullness, tubular, bell, and hourglass. Beginning about 1935 more than one silhouette co-existed in the same time period.
Lowe & Lowe (1990)	1789–1980	Width and length of women's evening dresses.	Failed to find accelerating change in fashion but they did find evidence of increased rates of within-year variation.

Step 4: Sample time as well as images by developing a systematic way to decide which issues of a periodical will be used and for what span of years (e.g., April and September issues from 1920 through 1990).

Step 5: Gather the data and analyze to reveal patterns of fashion change.

Researchers doing these rigorous **fashion counts** did find regularities and recurring patterns. Kroeber found evidence for a recurring pattern in skirt length of 35 years and skirt width every 100 years, 50 years for the pendulum swing from wide to narrow and 50 years for the swing back to wide. Young found a recurring pattern between back fullness, tubular, and bell-shaped skirts with steady evolution between the styles of 30 to 40 years. But these findings all apply to fashion before 1935.

The long-term cycles identified by Kroeber and Young and verified by other researchers are of little use to forecasters because the cultural institutions that created them no longer exist. Changes in women's status, the development of the automobile, and drastic shifts in culture terminated such cycles. Instead of slow evolution in styles, after 1935 there were increasing numbers of different styles available in the market at any given time (Belleau, 1987; Carman, 1966). More consumers became involved in being fashionable in their styles of life because of increasing levels of income, education, and leisure. With mass production, designers shifted from selling to individuals to selling to professional buyers representing large-scale retailers. Mass media increased coverage of the role of celebrities and their part in setting fashion. These cultural and industry changes meant that style options were more numerous and changed more frequently after 1935.

Still, researchers are fascinated by the idea of discovering evidence of long-term cyclic fashion change. Robinson (1975) was interested in economic cycles and saw potential in Kroeber's findings. He decided to do his own research to see if men were just as prone to following fashion as women. He analyzed the styles of men's whiskers—sideburns, sideburns with moustache, moustache alone, beard, and no facial hair—between 1842 and 1972. He found a wave of beard wearing started about the beginning of the study and disappeared around 1940. The moustache began a sharp rise in popularity in 1870 but bottomed out in 1970. He also found a long-term cyclic wave for men wearing some form of whiskers rising between 1842 and 1885 and declining until 1970. He also charted the swings in automobile styles between 1927 and 1974. He found that inch by inch the car roof had come down, necessitating numerous and costly redesigning as if "fashion were a heavy hammer, pounding the car body ever flatter" (p. 125). He concluded that there is a master force that he called "the style of life" that acts like Adam Smith's "invisible hand" in economics to guide fashion change. He concluded that long-term fashion cycles involve so many years that they are outside the influence of external events such as wars, technological innovation, and economics shifts.

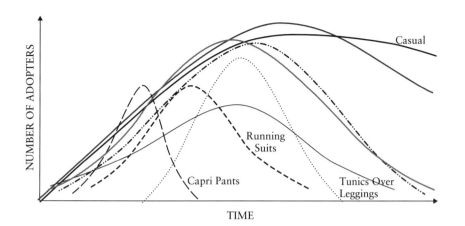

Casual

Running
Suits

Capri Pants

Tunics Over
Leggings

NUMBER OF ADOPTERS

TIME

FIGURE 3.16

The long wave change toward casual attire is made up of many other trends of shorter duration and different levels of acceptance.

The search for long wave cycles in fashion change is fueled by the desire to improve the accuracy in predictions. The idea is that just as long-term trends in lifestyles exist, so does an underlying logic in fashion evolution. In this view, seasonal fluctuations are the visible short-run phenomenon that moves fashion along from a precursor style, to the current look, and beyond. But these jumps and starts are part of a larger wave of change (Figure 3.16). With new computer technology, improved research facilities, and new methods, it may be possible for researchers today to carry on this line of research. Computer software now exists to search large databases of numbers for patterns that are not discernible to humans. Perhaps these new research tools hold the opportunity to study the multiplicity of looks after 1935 and discover more evidence of long-term cycles in fashion.

Forecaster's Toolbox: Theory in Action. Robinson's master force, style of life, can be a useful concept for product planners who need to forecast long-range change. He advised them to seek revelations among the most outrageous minority forms of conventional taste. These harbingers of change should be taken seriously when a few thousand consumers have bought into the form. Both the long- and short-term prognosticator should consider not only what the professionals are doing but also what the amateurs in a field are doing. The amateurs, enthusiasts, hobbyists, and buffs are often a compass for coming fashions in terms of dress and home décor. Producers no longer dictate fashion direction and consumers themselves often point the way to the next big thing, but only if a product planner is attuned to the signal. Finally, Robinson suggested that even the long fashion cycles are bounded by extremes, and a 50-year design shift is accomplished with an average yearly adjustment of 2 percent. This small incremental change gives the product planner a chance to decide what the consumer will want next year and ten years from then.

Androgyny
Bubble Up
Chase and Flight
Conspicuous
    Consumption
Conspicuous
    Counterconsumption
Conspicuous Leisure
Consumer Stylists
Erogenous Zone

Fashion Counts
Fashion Cycles
Gatekeepers
Gender Bending
Gender Blending
Historic Continuity
Idea Chain
Knockoff
Mass Market Theory
Retro-Fashion

Reverse Ostentation
Simultaneous Adoption
    Theory
Status Float Phenomenon
Status Markers
Subcultures
Trickle-Across Theory
Trickle-Down Theory
Trickle-Up Theory

Discussion Questions

Direction of fashion change: How does the trickle-down theory explain fashion movement today? Who is the visible fashionable elite today? Who are the people who exercise fashion leadership through their ability to use fashion artistically to create a style? How does the trickle-across theory explain fashion movement today? What happens to fashion in the long run if the knockoff is the usual way of doing business? How does the trickle-up theory explain fashion movement today? Do the sources for trends today parallel those identified by Field in 1970? Why are there time lags in fashion change?

Fashion cycles: What two frameworks deal with recycling fashion ideas? What is the difference between the pendulum effect of fashion in the first part of the 20th century and the later half? How can long-term cycles act like an "invisible hand," guiding fashion change? How useful are long-term cycles to a fashion forecaster?

Additional Forecasting Activities

Conspicuous Examples. Make a visual dictionary of examples of (1) conspicuous leisure, (2) conspicuous consumption, and (3) reverse ostentation or conspicuous counterconsumption. Use as a timeline the entire 20th century or the decade of the 1990s. Project these concepts into the 21st century. How will they be expressed in the future? Will one be more dominant that the others?

Classic Compromises. Study classics like the blazer, pleated skirts, trousers, five-pocket jeans, and the sheath dress as representations of midpoint compromises in the fashion pendulum. Using the fashion pendulum visualization, illustrate the extreme versions of the style. Analyze the cycle length between fashion extremes and the classic midpoint. Predict the future of these classic styles. Will they continue basically unchanged? What elaboration and details are likely to be grafted onto these classics to create the perception of newness?

Taste in Transition. Find pictures of fashion looks along Laver's timeline of acceptability. Make a flash card of each look—the characteristic look from five years ago, from 20 years ago, and so on. Then find pictures of fashion forward styles and make flash cards of each. Use the flash cards to test Laver's theory. Show the cards in random order to people who vary in age, income, and clothing preferences. Ask each person to look at the cards and then choose an adjective from Laver's list to describe the styles. Write down the descriptors used for each card. Does your research confirm or disconfirm Laver's theory?

Resource Pointers

Vintage clothing sites on the Web, many with links to other sites, including those that deal with retro lifestyles:

- www.pieceunique.com
- www.ballyhoovintage.com
- www.vintagevixen.com
- www.corneliapowell.com

Part Two

FASHION DYNAMICS

Winter
Garden

frost   _swan_   _fog_

dew

toothstone

trellis

silverbirch

fawn

A harmonious mix of warm and cool delicate opaques. Fragile, veiled and barely perceptible faux whites. A frozen landscape of precious icicles and frosted fruit. The family of pales are recreated as new neutrals.

Chapter 4

COLOR FORECASTING

> *"People do color forecasting: professionals merely notice it."*
> *—Santana (1994)*

Objectives

- Appreciate color as a marketing tool.

- Understand the process of forecasting color, taking into account color evolution, social and economic trends, consumer preferences, and other influences.

- Recognize color forecasting as a coordinating factor in the apparel supply chain from fiber producer to retailer.

- Become aware of the techniques forecasters use to synthesize color direction from cues, signs, hints, and traces in the cultural environment.

CASE: A COLORFUL SEASON

Whitney is design director for a large manufacturer of knit shirts—mainly T-shirts and polo shirts for both men and women. As design director, Whitney coordinates the efforts of the design staff for several lines. One of her most important functions is as a color forecaster because newness and fashion for basic products are tied to color. As the company's fashion forecaster, she scouts trade shows in the United States and Europe and participates in the professional color forecasting organizations. The company also subscribes to several color forecasting services.

For Whitney, the color forecast begins when she prepares for a brainstorming meeting with the other forecasters at an international meeting of color professionals. Each participant creates a concept board proposing a direction for colors that will dominate women's fashion two years in the future. Together the group will reach consensus on about 25 colors that will be reported to all members of the organization, their companies or clients, and the media.

When Whitney returns to her company, she will synthesize all the information she has gathered, analyze color directions as they apply to her company's line and target consumer, and develop the color story for each of the company's lines. This chapter provides information on the skills, techniques, and approach that Whitney will use in developing her forecast.

DIMENSIONS OF THE COLOR STORY

Color decisions begin early in the product development cycle. For designers a new collection begins with the selection of a **color palette**. From that first step, it will be from six months to nearly one year before those colors appear as a coordinated collection on the runway or in the showroom. The initial decision is critical to success because the eight to ten selected colors signal the personality of the collection. The **color story** (Figure 4.1) will be combined into prints, yarn-dyed fabrics, and solids and coordinated across jackets, tops,

FIGURE 4.1

The seasonal color story will be translated into prints, yarn-dyed fabrics, and solids and coordinated across jackets, tops, skirts, pants, and dresses into a collection with perhaps 200 separate pieces.

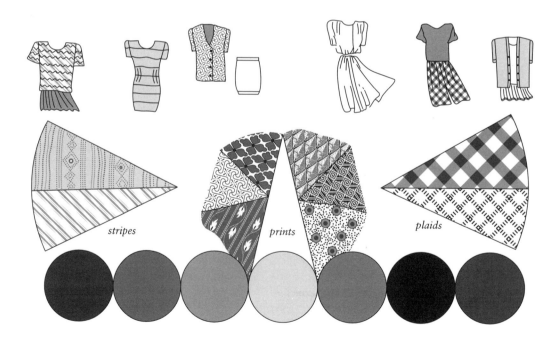

stripes   prints   plaids

skirts, pants, and dresses into a collection with perhaps 200 separate pieces (Allen, 1985).

Stimulating sales is the driving force behind color forecasting. Color grabs customers' attention, makes an emotional connection, and leads them to the product. Even when the basic product stays the same, changing the color gives a sense of something new. Color consultants help companies decide on the right color story to sell the product. Some consultants specialize in advising on color. Others develop color forecasts as part of their overall product development function. Some large companies have departments dedicated to setting color directions for multiple lines. Professional color organizations bring together experts to collaborate on forecasts for industries such as women's wear, men's wear, children's wear, and residential and nonresidential interiors.

Forecasting for the American consumer began in 1915 with the founding of the Textile Color Card Association of America, predecessor to today's **Color Association of the United States (CAUS)**. Begun by a group of manufacturers and retailers trying to keep up with the changing tastes of a consumer-oriented economy, the organization used textile industry specialists to select fashion shades that would be popular in the future. The first forecast was issued for Fall 1917—40 colors presented on cards with custom-dyed silk and wool swatches. The focus of the forecast was women's apparel with basic colors and fashion shades that might build volume sales in the future (Hope & Walch, 1990).

By the 1950s, Dayton's Department Store had a small staff watching trends and translating them into apparel (and later home furnishings) to be sold exclusively in their store (Lamb, 1997). The idea of forecasting trends in the marketplace boomed in the years after World War II. Trend merchandising entered the mass market in the early 1980s when trends became a coordinating factor for full product lines that extended beyond a single merchandise category (Nichols, 1996). Today, trend merchandising and color forecasting are an integral part of product development for both hard and soft goods.

Color forecasters work 18 to 24 months in advance of the season to provide input for the designer's decisions. To work so far ahead, color experts must combine knowledge of color theories and human behavior with acute observational skills. They may spot new color directions at a trade show, on the fashion runway, or in the street. By synthesizing the mood of the times from all the diverse elements of the culture—the economic conditions; happenings in the fine arts; and music, movies, and TV shows that top the charts—color forecasters track trends and recognize new directions. Because color looks different depending on the fabric, color forecasters also stay up to date on new developments in fibers, yarns, and fabrications. To accomplish the task the forecaster needs a background in the industry, a network of contacts, and the financial backing to travel the globe attending relevant trade shows and shopping the locales where new ideas originate.

The financial backing comes from manufacturers and retailers who need lead time to develop products for the consumer. Clients for color forecasting services include companies in the apparel supply chain—fiber producers, mills that produce yarn and fabrics, manufacturers of branded merchandise, retailers with private-label operations, and manufacturers who produce apparel in great volume. These clients want to gauge the tastes and preferences of the consumer far in advance of the selling season. Designers of couture collections and the highest priced ready-to-wear are more likely to influence color directions rather that follow them. Even so, top designers also subscribe to color forecasting services as a gauge of mass taste (Lannon, 1988).

Some people claim that color forecasters dictate colors in the marketplace, but forecasters do not have that power. Color forecasters cannot just say that chartreuse will be the new fashion color. Instead, they have to consider the evolution of yellow-green over the previous seasons and figure out when the consumer will be ready for chartreuse. Only a few consumers are innovative enough to try new colors when they are first introduced. The rest become used to the color over time, perhaps first trying it out in a print or multicolored knit or in an inexpensive accessory or T-shirt. Color experts forecast when consumers are ready for the new color in certain product categories and price points. Their forecasts help manufacturers and retailers keep product lines fresh and new while avoiding lost sales caused by presenting products that the consumer is not ready to buy.

Although a conspiracy does not exist among color forecasters to dictate colors, color forecasters are in agreement the majority of the time. They attend the same fabric trade shows in Europe; shop the trendy boutiques and watch street fashion in Europe, Asia, and America; and track the same media. They are members of one or more color associations and collaborate with other members to develop industry color forecasts (Lannon, 1988). It is in the interest of the entire apparel supply chain to have some common ideas about color directions since color is rated as the most important aesthetic criteria in consumer preference (Eckman, Damhorst, & Kadolph, 1990). For specific clients, forecasters fine-tune general forecasts by selecting particular shades for the target market, product category, price point, and selling venue.

Color in Marketing

Marketing fashion means positioning the product in the marketplace. Color plays a major part in positioning apparel products by attracting attention, establishing the image of the product and the brand, and evoking symbolic associations. Marketers harness the psychological power of colors to communicate with consumers through advertising, brand logos, packaging, and product colors. A consumer's first impression of a new product is largely mediated by the color. Some fashion companies have signature color ranges—think of Calvin Klein's muted neutrals and Tommy Hilfiger's bold primary colors—but others follow seasonal color trends. The selling power of color can be traced to two intertwined sources—emotional imagery associated with various hues and the desire for individuality and personal expression through color selection.

A company's identity package often includes a color or color combination that is immediately recognizable to consumers. This company symbolism will appear in advertising and on logos and packaging. However, color is only one element in establishing this identity. Most people cannot remember a specific color for more than a few seconds or pick out a particular shade when presented with several alternatives. The identity of a company and its logo is achieved through the combination of color, typography, proportions, and contrasts. What seems to be a simple problem—pair the right color, one with the right associations, with the right product—is far from simple. Choosing colors to symbolize a company can be risky because color connotations can change with time—white lettering on black was considered elegant until used by supermarkets to advertise generic brands. The look later regained its cachet when it was used in high-fashion apparel advertising (Hope & Walch, 1990). The solution of this problem is increasingly important for multinational companies where instant recognition worldwide translates into profits. In a 1995 landmark decision, the Supreme Court held that color is such a potent brand identifier that a particular shade is a legally defensible trademark (Heath, 1997b).

Color also tends to identify the target market—for example, bold primaries for children's products and trendy or whimsical colors to appeal to teens. With influences from television, toy marketing, and computers, children's preferences tend toward bright colors that adults avoid. In the 1990s, children developed a love for neon colors, especially green and yellow (Heath, 1997b). This segmentation by color preferences makes it important for product developers and marketers to carefully observe the target market—watch consumers in their natural habitat, read what they read, listen to their music, watch their movies, and research their preferences.

Collect advertising that is aimed at different consumer segments—men, women, teens, children, both upscale and midmarket. Compare the colors used in the images, the apparel, and the logos. Red is used in the logo of several top apparel firms. How do the companies create a distinctive image while sharing this same color signature? Which colors appear across all segments? Which are restricted to a particular segment? How is color combined with other aesthetic considerations to create a brand identifier?

Activity 4.1
Color Image

Consumers and the Psychology of Color

The power of color comes from its symbolic meaning for people. Colors can represent experiences, emotions, status, and other types of information that are difficult to convey in written or spoken language. Color symbols enter language and appear in pictures and poetry as metaphors—for example, the connection between good fortune and gold at the end of the rainbow. Color communicates emotionally by calling up all kinds of associations of which people are only fleetingly aware. Some color symbols are part of a kind of primordial memory. Red signals arousal because it is associated with blood and fire—signals of danger. Even overlaid with the trappings of modern life, red still gets our attention by evoking ancient responses. Some color symbols have religious origins, such as the depiction of the Virgin Mary in blue as a symbol for truth and justice. Color can be used for sociological or political reasons as in tribal identification, gang colors, and soldiers' uniforms. Individual colors have symbolic meanings that evolve over time. The Green Man of Celtic mythology was the god of fertility; today we talk about a gardener with a green thumb. Red, the Christian symbol for suffering and regeneration, can be inverted and applied to a "scarlet" woman and the "red-light district" (Hope & Walch, 1990).

Human response to colors can be traced to physiological reactions. Warm colors are associated with activity, cool colors with passivity. Psychologists have recorded immediate and measurable reactions to color, but the total effect depends on the duration of the stimulus. Exposure to red initially results in arousal, but the effect dissipates with continuous exposure over time. Another aspect mitigating the psychological impact of color is the strength of the color—an electric green is more stimulating than a weak, dull red (Hope & Walch, 1990).

Besides human reaction to color, psychologists are interested in the formation of color preferences. In 1941, Eysenck published a study showing a consistent order of color preferences in adults: the first choice was blue, followed by red, green, purple, yellow, and orange. Later research and preference surveys have tended to support the finding of a universal scale of color with a possible biological basis (Porter, 1994). The Lüscher Color test, first published in 1948, links color preference and personality. In this test, the subject is asked to arrange color chips (8 in the short form, 43 in the full test) in order of preference. The results are interpreted using a key that considers both the meaning of the color and the order of its selection (Lüscher, 1969). These psychological explanations of color point to the power and impact of color, but they are not very helpful to the color forecaster in predicting the success or failure of specific color symbols.

Another approach is to trace the roots of color preference to cultural influence. Some color theorists argue that color transcends cultural and geographic boundaries. To back up this "universalist" view, studies have shown that black, white, and red evoke similar responses in many parts of the world. American researchers compared color words in 90 languages and discovered broad, consistent rules in the cultural evolution of color. They found that the most primitive cultures distinguish only between black and white; if a third color is used, it is always red; the next two colors are yellow and green; then blue is added, followed by all the subtler distinctions (Hope & Walch, 1990).

Color "relativists" argue for a local bias in the development of color terminology. They find that regional and environmental conditions play a major role, citing the observation that Eskimos have more words for white because it is so predominate in their world view (Hope & Walch, 1990). Polly Hope (1990), an artist and writer who travels the world in her work, has observed a similar phenomenon—colors as a representation of a country's personality. She finds a distinctive "color conception of a place" that results from the combination of the natural environment and the indigenous culture. As examples she cites the earth colors, silver, and turquoise of the American Southwest and the lapis blue, gray-green of cacti, and reds and yellows of folk costumes as symbolic of Mexico.

Some color associations combine the universalist and relativist view: blue as a protective color to ward off evil spirits can be found in cultures as disparate as the Middle East and Native Americans in the Southwest. With increasing global communication and trade, there will be an inevitable increase in the exchange of color concepts across territorial and cultural boundaries. The color forecaster must constantly investigate the cultural symbolism and the cross-cultural implications of color (Eiseman, 1997).

Surveys tend to support the idea that there is a relationship between color preference and ethnic identity or geographic region. In a study of color preference among 5,000 consumers, participants were asked to rate colors that best conveyed power. White consumers were more likely to select red, African Americans black, and Hispanics bright blue (Heath, 1997b). Color preferences may even be associated with cultural status—lower socioeconomic consumers tend to prefer simple colors that can be described in two words; higher income people prefer more complex colors (Kanner, 1989).

Color preferences can arise from personal experiences—for example, a person's positive or negative reaction to the colors parents chose for them as children. Color consultants cannot account for these individual differences. Instead they concentrate on broad cultural preferences. In surveys of color preferences among American consumers, mid-range blue is consistently selected as the favorite color (Heath, 1997a; Hope & Walch, 1990). However, even strong cultural preferences can be overtaken by the mood of the times. Green became important in all categories of products from T-shirts to automobiles to kitchen appliances when consumers became acutely aware of environmental issues in the early 1990s. Blue reasserted dominance by the 1997/1998 Roper/Pantone Consumer Color Preference Study when 35 percent of participants chose blue as their favorite color, and green fell to second place (Heath,

1997a). This swing in preference supports the view that there is a collective color preference underlying the surface of seasonal fashion change.

Fashion color symbols arise from cultural norms that have consistent meaning over time—red nails and red lips are powerful sexual signals in all decades beginning in the 1920s. When dye technology permitted making only a few colors, fashion colors persisted for decades and developed deep symbolic associations. Now it is possible to dye any color, and the multiplicity of colors leads to seasonal change and color meanings that are more ephemeral (Hope & Walch, 1990). In today's complex color landscape a single color can have multiple symbolic meanings. In a 1995 survey, the color black signified mystery to 30 percent and power to 27 percent of participants, 23 percent considered it masculine, 20 percent found it depressing, and 18 percent considered it a conservative color (Heath, 1997b). Some colors declassify a product, extending its appeal to a broad audience; others classify a product as belonging to a specific type of consumer or socioeconomic level (Kanner, 1989). Sensitivity to these multiple meanings enables the color forecaster to target the right colors to the right consumer segment.

As predictors of color preference, categories such as age, ethnicity, income, and gender play a part, but the preference segments are more complex than simple demographics. The Cooper Marketing Group (Heath, 1997b; Jacobs, 1994) now divides consumers into three categories: color forwards, color prudents, and color loyals. The color-forward consumer enjoys being the first to try a new color but may shop for color ideas at both discounters and upscale department stores. The color prudents are mainstream consumers and wait until a color has more widespread acceptance before buying it. The color loyals play it safe with color, sticking with classic blue or gray instead of choosing fashion colors. Categories like these mirror the bell curve of consumer acceptance from the relatively few innovators and early adopters through mass acceptance to the fashion laggards and apply it to acceptance of color (Figure 4.2). Such mental images can help color forecasters justify their color choices and clarify the fit between color selection, product category, and consumer target.

Activity 4.2
New Color
Search

Be a color-forward consumer. Shop upscale department stores, discounters, and all the retail levels in between looking for new colors that are just beginning to be introduced into the marketplace. Do the colors differ at the various retail levels? Are the new colors so simple that they can be described in two words or are they more complex? Can you trace any of these colors back to their cultural roots? Analyze the appeal of these new colors in terms of consumer preference categories like age, ethnicity, income, and gender. What is your prediction for the future popularity of these new colors?

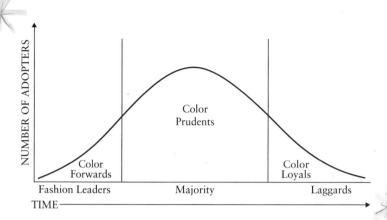

FIGURE 4.2

The Cooper Marketing Group (Heath, 1997; Jacobs, 1994) divides consumers into three categories— color forwards, color prudents, and color loyals. The definitions of these groups correspond to fashion leaders, majority, and laggard segments of a diffusion of innovation curve.

The Language of Color

The human eye can discern 350,000 colors, but the human memory for color is poor. Most people cannot remember a specific color for more than a few seconds (Hope & Walch, 1990). In everyday conversations about color, it is sufficient to refer to a few colors by name—red, yellow, green, blue, white, and black—and add a qualifier—light, dark, bright, and dull. Other terms in general usage in discussing color (*Designer's Guide to Color 2*, 1984) are those such as:

- "Concentrated" to refer to intense, strong colors.
- "Deep" to refer to rich, dark colors.
- "Subdued" for colors neutralized through the addition of black, white, gray, or color's complement.
- "Clear" for colors without any neutralizing mix, colors such as the basic colors of the color wheel.

General terms are not sufficient for communicating color information for design and manufacturing. Exact identification, matching, and reproduction of colors requires an effective system with colors arranged in sequential order and identified with numbers and letters. Such systems are based on the basic three characteristics of color—hue, saturation, and value (Figure 4.3). **Hue** refers to the color—each color system designates a set of basic colors. Varying the other two characteristics fills out the system. **Saturation** (also called **intensity** or **chroma**) refers to the strength or purity of the color and **value** to the lightness or darkness of the color. The term **tint** applies to any color when white is added. **Shade** refers to colors mixed with black. **Tone** describes a grayed color.

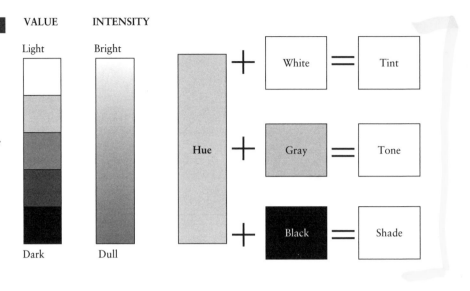

FIGURE 4.3

Color systems are based on the basic three characteristics of color—hue, saturation, and value—and how color can be mixed to produce tints, shades, and tones.

Color systems provide notation systems for the reproduction of colors and guidelines for harmonious color groupings. The **color wheel** (Figure 4.4) is the simplest version of such a system. The **primary colors** are yellow, red, and blue; **secondary colors** are mixed from two primaries (yellow + blue = green, yellow + red = orange, red + blue = violet). **Tertiary colors** are mixed from one primary color and one secondary color (yellow + green = yellow-green). Color combinations made from closely related colors adjacent on the color wheel are called **analogous**. Colors directly across from each other on the color wheel are termed **complementary**. When used in combination, complements intensify the impact of each other. Complex color combinations can be developed using sets of complementary colors (**double complements**) and variations (**split complements**). **Triads** are color combinations with three colors equally spaced on the color wheel—the primary triad is red, blue, and yellow; the secondary triad is orange, green, and violet. An infinite number of color combinations can be developed by varying the value and intensity of the colors (Davis, 1996).

Developing color stories means being able to select colors that share a common attribute so that they coordinate with each other. The temperature of color—either warm or cool—serves as the coordinating principle for such systems. The Color Key Program and the seasonal approach to personal color analysis provide consumers with guidance on color coordination.

• **Color Key Program**

Developed by Everrett Brown, the Color Key Program allows a person to coordinate paint colors and apparel. The program designates Color Key 1 for cool overtones and Color Key 2 for warm overtones and represents each key

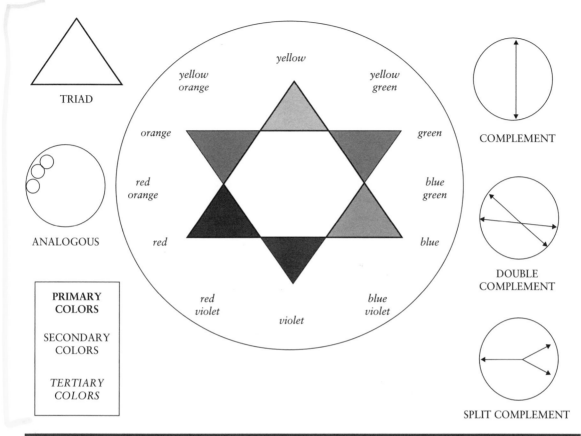

Color systems provide guidelines for harmonious color groupings. The color wheel is the simplest version of such a system. Color schemes are based on the position of colors on the color wheel.

in a fan of color chips. The basic idea is that people's personal coloring either has cool or warm overtones and they will look and feel better when surrounded by colors in the same key (Brown, 1994).

• **Seasonal Color Analysis**

In the 1980s, Gerrie Pinckney and Carole Jackson both wrote books elaborating on and popularizing the idea of a seasonal approach to personal color analysis. In this system, color groupings (Figure 4.5) relate to nature's four seasons—spring and autumn have a warm undertone, summer and winter have a cool undertone. The seasons are further defined by the saturation of the colors—spring and winter colors are clear, bright, and vivid; autumn and

| FIGURE 4.5 |

The seasonal approach to personal color analysis divided people into four groups depending on their coloring and suggested a set of colors most likely to flatter each. Colors for the four seasons varied in temperature (warm or cool) and in saturation (vivid or subdued).

	COOL	WARM
BRIGHT	Winter • Cool Undertone • Colors Clear & Bright	Spring • Warm Undertone • Colors Clear & Bright
LESS INTENSE	Summer • Cool Undertone • Colors Subdued	Autumn • Warm Undertone • Colors Subdued

summer are more subdued and less intense. The goal was to provide consumers with insight into the "right" colors to enhance their personal coloring and the "wrong" colors that should be avoided (Isbecque, 1990).

Color forecasters are trained experts who can look at colors, assess what they see, and express the qualities of each color in terms of hue, value, and saturation. They understand not only the individual colors but also the effect of colors in combination. Because research shows clear patterns of consumer preference linked to value, chroma, and color temperature, forecasters must also consider these relationships (Radeloff, 1991). With this expertise, the forecaster follows the subtle shifts in color trends, develops color stories for combining and coordinating colors, and predicts the significance of the colors for a product category.

Color Names

Changing the color of a product keeps the appeal of the new when the product itself does not change much. Think of the basic T-shirt presented anew each season in a range of fashion colors. Evocative color names boost marketing appeal and encourage the shopper to refresh his or her wardrobe. The color forecaster works in the two worlds of color naming—writing product specifications using the notation of particular color systems and color marketing using color names that coordinate with a theme (Figure 4.6).

Naming a color for marketing means drawing attention to its attributes by linking the color with the consumer's perceptions. Imagine a light brown "café au lait"—no two people would visualize it the same way. But the theme (a delicious and deluxe cup of coffee), the season (autumn), the color key (warm), the color family (brown), and the value of the color (light) all are conveyed by the color name. Even fashionability can be captured in the color

FIGURE 4.6

In color marketing, a color range is linked to a theme and each color is given a name evocative of that theme as a way to draw attention to the newness of the colors and stimulate consumer's interest in the colors.

name if it recalls cultural references. In the case of "café au lait," the reference is to coffee bars and gourmet coffee as high-fashion concepts—new a few seasons ago, they have now moved into the mainstream.

Naming colors takes imagination, sensitivity to fashion change across product categories, an understanding of the customer's perception of colors, and the insight to make connections between color and the product's end use. Naming colors may also take a stack of reference books! Color description moves from the universal color names (black, white, red, green) to adding qualifiers (light, dark, bright, dull) to "looks like" names. Most color names come from associations in the environment (Eiseman & Herbert, 1990):

- Natural phenomena: sky blue, sunshine, grass green, snow white.
- Flora: poppy red, moss green, mahogany, orchid.
- Fauna: flamingo pink, robin's egg blue, dove gray.
- Gemstones, minerals, and metals: amethyst, lapis, amber, slate gray, copper.
- Food and drink: caramel, apricot, champagne, burgundy.
- Spices: cinnamon, paprika, curry
- Dyes: indigo, cochineal.
- Building materials: brick, adobe, terra-cotta, bronze.
- Locations: Capri blue, Pompeian red.

Whatever the association, the goal is to depict a mood, paint a picture, and evoke fantasy in the mind of a consumer. Selling with color names dates back at least to the 1960s when green changed into avocado, olive, and lime (Wilke, 1995). Today, the color forecaster, the manufacturer, and the retailer routinely use color names to link fashion change to shifts in the culture—the earth tones of the late 1990s shifted to more celestial hues in anticipation of the millenium (Crispell, 1997).

Activity 4.3
Color Analysis

Look for color in the background of advertisements and fashion editorial spreads. Often these backgrounds provide a large sample of a fashion forward color. When you have a dozen or so colors, trade samples with other people to increase your color collection. When you have many colors to work with, create color swatches by cutting out each in a square, rectangle, circle, triangle, or diamond shape. Analyze your swatches using the language of color. Describe their hue, saturation, and value. Which are tints, shades, or tones? Describe their color temperature—warm or cool? How would they fit in the seasonal approach to personal color analysis? Arrange them according to the color wheel. What color combinations can you make? Try naming the colors using "looks like" names.

COLOR CYCLES

Color cycles refer to two phenomena: the periodic shifts in color preferences and the patterns of repetition in the popularity of colors. Both depend on the mechanism of boredom—people get tired of what they have and seek something new. New colors are introduced to the marketplace, available to consumers in product categories from fashion to interiors to automobiles. There is a lag time between the introduction of a new color or new color direction and its acceptance while people gain familiarity with the idea. Margaret Walch of the Color Association of the United States identified one such time lag—designer Stephen Sprouse introduced acid shades in the early 1980s but they were not included in the forecast until 1989 because some colors take longer to become trends. With acceptance, the color or color palette moves into the mainstream. In time, interest in the colors wane, and they are replaced by the next new thing. This mechanism means that colors have somewhat predictable lifecycles (Danger, 1968; Jack & Schiffer, 1948; Nichols, 1996). It also means that colors that were once popular can be repositioned in a future season—the harvest gold of the 1970s became the sunflower gold of the 1990s (Nichols, 1996).

Beginning with the first color forecast for women's apparel in 1917, the cycles in colors can be accurately charted (Hope & Walch, 1990; Porter, 1994).

That first forecast accurately identified the bright purples, greens, and blues, shown by avant-garde couture designer Paul Poiret, that would move into wider use. These colors were appropriated in the short dresses worn by 1920s flappers as a badge of rebellion against traditional women's roles. In the 1930s, Jean Harlow vamped in slinky white dresses for Hollywood films while those hit hard by the Depression preferred soil-resistant brown. In the late 1930s, Schiaparelli mixed art and fashion and introduced "shocking pink"—a radical repositioning of a traditionally pale color symbolizing sweetness and femininity. The years of World War II brought the withdrawal of dyes and pigments from consumer products.

After the war, pent-up demand for fashion was satisfied in the lavish use of fabrics and more vivid color palettes of the New Look by Dior. For less upscale consumers, the postwar period meant the practical, comfortable look of American fashion epitomized by Claire McCardell—bright-colored clothes, mix-and-match possibilities, and styles for a casual lifestyle. The stability of the Eisenhower era (1953–1961) was reflected in the popularity of pastels and American favorites, red and navy blue. With the 1960s came florescent, acid, and hot colors associated with the youth movement and psychedelic drug experiences. In the 1970s, hippies in denim became fascinated with the authenticity of the American Southwest, beginning the domination of earthy colors associated with the region.

The 1970s ended on a bright note influenced by the "punks" with their bold clothing statements and green and purple hair. The color explosion continued into the 1980s with an upscale pastel phase, the postmodern influence of Memphis designers on furnishings, and Nancy Reagan's signature red. Lacroix reintroduced Schiaparelli's pink as a fashion color, but because of the brights and neons of the 1960s, the color that had once been shocking was now perceived as a soft, bright color. Concerns about the environment made the 1990s the green decade, updating the color symbol for fertility from antiquity. Along with green came the "back to nature colors" of earthy browns and terra-cotta.

Long Wave Cycles

The recurrences of color themes can be traced not just in decades but in centuries. In the Victorian era, Owen Jones chose rich, bright, primary colors for London's Crystal Palace in 1851. He defended his choices saying that these same colors had been used in the architecture of the ancient Greeks. To some color historians, this comment illustrates the cycling of color through history, specifically the periodic return to primary hues. The cycle begins with bright, saturated, primary colors; this is followed by an exploration of mixed, less intense colors; then, it pauses in neutral until the rich, strong colors are rediscovered (Porter, 1994).

Researchers have confirmed a periodic swing (Figure 4.7) from high chroma colors, to "multicoloredness," to subdued colors, to earth tones, to **achromatic** colors (black, white, and gray), and back to high chroma colors. In the period between 1860 and the 1990s, there were four marked color cycles lasting between 15 and 25 five years (Darmstadt, 1982, 1985). Analyzing the color themes in a German home magazine, researchers confirmed the cyclical recurrence of collective color trends (Koppelmann & Kuthe, 1987; Oberascher, 1994). That cycle has been matched to color trends in recent decades (Barry, 1999), as follows:

- A high chroma phase (e.g., 1972–1974).
- A darkening phase (e.g., 1974–1976).
- Transition to autumnal colors in a brown phase (e.g., 1976–1979).
- Lightning of colors toward beige, off-white, and pastels (e.g., 1979–1981).
- An achromatic phase (e.g., 1984–1988)
- A chromatic phase combining black and white with primary colors (e.g., 1988–1991)
- A purple phase (e.g., 1992)
- A return to chromatic colors (e.g., beginning in 1991 and continuing).

Such long wave oscillations can be observed in color cycles through the decades of the 20th century.

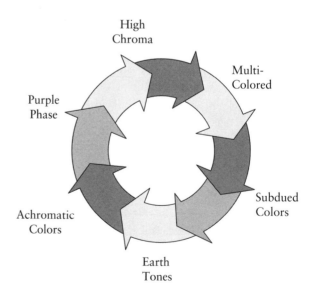

FIGURE 4.7

Researchers have confirmed a periodic swing from high chroma colors, to "multicoloredness," to subdued colors, to earth tones, to achromatic colors (black, white, and gray) and back to high chroma colors with purple signaling a new color cycle as an intermediary between achromatic and chromatic phases.

High Chroma

Multi-Colored

Purple Phase

Subdued Colors

Achromatic Colors

Earth Tones

Several forecasts in the late 1990s pick up on the diagnostic effect of purple. The idea is that a purple phase occurs between achromatic and chromatic phases and signals a new color cycle. David Wolfe, a trend forecaster for The Donegar Group, predicted the "end of the color blackout in fashion" at the National Retail Federation annual meeting in January 1998. He also predicted the beginning of a purple cycle that would continue for three to five years. In the 1997/1998 Roper/Pantone Consumer Color Preference Study, purple appeared as the third favorite color behind blue and green and ahead of red ("Results,"1997/1998). In forecasts for cosmetic colors for the Fall 1998 season purples and plums were the leading trend (Klepacki, 1998).

Color Cycles and Cultural Shifts

There are always subplots and digressions, eddies and currents in the season-to-season changes. Color cycles can be sparked by new technology. This happened about ten years after the opening of the Crystal Palace in the mid-1800s. One of the first synthetic dyes was introduced, a colorfast purple called *mauve* by the French. The color became the rage—Queen Victoria wore the color to the International Exhibition of 1862—and gave its name to the Mauve Decade. Other strong synthetic dyes for red and green soon followed, allowing for a strong color story in women's clothing. Something similar happened in the 1950s when the first affordable cotton reactive dye for turquoise led to a fad for the color and moved it from eveningwear into sportswear (Hope & Walch, 1990; Porter, 1994).

Economic conditions also perturb color cycles and start new ones. When recession or a steep drop in the stock market occurs, as it did in 1987, people's moods change and they curtail their spending habits. Japanese designers signaled the shift with ominous black clothing and an austere, minimalist look to begin the decade of the 1990s.

Color cycles can be associated with social change. A visible cycle was identified by June Roche, a corporate color analyst, in the mid-1980s—the shift between colors associated with femininity and those influenced by men's wear. She characterized the end of the 1970s as a dark men's wear phase with dusty colors that were called elegant, refined, and sophisticated. Use of these typical grayed European colors was new for American women's fashion but coincided with women's entry into fields such as finance, law, and medicine—fields formerly dominated by men. By the mid-1980s, those grayed colors looked dirty, and there was a shift to feminine colors. As a forecaster, Roche asked herself why the feminine colors were popular and how much longer that phase would last (Lannon, 1988). The shift between ultrafemininity and men's wear looks has been part of the fashion scene since Coco Chanel first introduced women to the concept of borrowing from men's closets in the 1920s.

Color cycles are also associated with nostalgic revivals of looks from previous decades (see Chapter 3). When the 1970s were revived in the mid-1990s, bright lime green came back with platform shoes, Brady Bunch reruns, and polyester. The color was not a literal lift from the 1970s, but that decade did provide a directional influence (Winter, 1996).

Forecasting with Color Cycles

When applying a color theory, the color forecaster has to take into account the consumer type and membership in a cultural group. Lifestyles, values, and attitudes all play a part in acceptance or rejection of collective color directions. Although mass media smoothes and integrates individual and cultural tendencies, differences between segments remain. Additionally, some consumers are early adopters of fashion change, whereas other more traditional consumers will adhere to traditional colors as color cycles come and go. Applying a color cycle theory takes insight and experience.

Complicating the process further, a color forecaster has more than one color cycle theory to consider. Using the idea that color cycles through all the phases from full primary hues to mixes to neutrals, the forecaster in the late 1990s would predict "a pause in neutral" prior to a rediscovery of full primary hues at the beginning of the new millenium (Porter, 1994). Everrett Brown, who introduced the Color Key Program for apparel and paint selection, identified a cycle of approximately seven years during which the pendulum swings between warm-toned and cool-toned colors (Brown, 1994). Using that theory, a color forecaster in the late 1990s would predict a shift from the orange-based earthy tones of 1998 to "more celestial colors" in cool tones for the turn of the millenium (Crispell, 1997). Which is correct? Perhaps both. Today's color forecasts offer a proliferation of shades, and the color forecaster's job is to match color with consumer segments.

Besides the cycles based on hue, intensity, and color temperature, there are other identifiable cycles. Some continuity is visible regardless of trends: nautical red, white, and blue appears in some form every spring; russets and tartan plaids every autumn (Wrack, 1994).

During the 20th century the consumer has undergone a color education that has changed visual perceptions. Still, the basic mechanism of color cycles serves the color forecaster well. A new color direction is usually introduced first by a high-profile industry and promoted as a theme. Based on mass marketing, other industries adapt the theme to fit their customers and promote the same set of colors. After a few years, the color direction becomes established; the consumer is ready for a change, and the cycle begins again. While a color trend remains in place, the theme used to promote it evolves—Southwestern colors transmute into a Mediterranean palette and then continue in an Adirondack lodge color story (Kinning, 1994). The colors themselves evolve from season to season. For the forecaster, it is important to monitor consumer response and work through the color families from level to level—from red to a rosy tone to a coral (Tunsky, 1994).

Research color cycles in the 20th century by comparing fashion magazines from each decade. Check the holdings of the library and locate a fashion magazine with copies going back at least four decades. To conduct fashion research, develop a systematic way to sample the fashion content:

- Choose a month—usually the early fall issues have the most pages of fashion.
- Choose a year early, in the middle, or late in the decade.

Activity 4.4
Cycling Around

To gather data, survey the issues in your sample looking for articles predicting color or giving advice on wearing color. Also observe the colors pictured in this issue. Make photocopies of the articles and a color photocopy of a characteristic page in each issue. Did you detect evidence of color cycles?

COLOR RESEARCH

Cycles in color preferences apply across product categories to both hard goods such as automobiles and appliances and soft goods such as apparel and household linens. The timelines differ for each industry because the consumer's replacement rates differ. Industrial products may lag two to five years behind fashion shades and require a shade modification, but if a color is popular in fashion, it is likely to end up on small appliances and other utilitarian products. People buy clothes more often than automobiles; they redecorate their image more often than their interior spaces. The colors for fashion can show a marked change every two years but the replacement cycle for interior design is between seven and twelve years (Linton, 1994).

Even to a color consultant specializing in a particular industry, the entire world of color choices is important. Clothing designers look for inspiration in the decorative arts: interior design, architecture, and furniture design. Home fashion designers look for inspiration from apparel and accessories. There is growing cross-pollination between industries regarding color evolution.

Color Relationships across Product Categories

Where does a color trend start? That is a controversial question, and the answer depends on whom you ask and in what decade. In the past, some experts claimed that new trends first show up in the array of colors offered by paint manufacturers (Danger, 1968). Others believed that trends started in the automotive industry because autos require a longer product development cycle (four to five years), and that industry is particularly sensitive to advances in color technologies (Reynold, 1968). Still others expect new color trends to originate in the area of interiors. Today most agree that color trends start with women's fashions (Birren, 1987; Hope & Walch, 1990). Whatever might have been the case in the past, Jean-Philippe Lenclos's (1994) international survey of color detected a fusing of color fashion across product categories in the mid-1970s. Until that time, color cycles had moved at different speeds in different industries. Subsequently, there was more unification of color trends across product categories.

Color in Cars. Buying a T-shirt or a pillow or a tube of lipstick may cost a few dollars; buying a car represents a major investment. Still, the power of color as a marketing tool applies across categories. Styling in cars follows the same societal trends as other products. The confident-looking 1980s cars had a straight-cut look that was replaced in the early 1990s by a sturdy, rounded, egg-shaped silhouette, a sensibility that matched an era nervous about economic conditions and environmental issues (Ward, 1992).

The range of color choices changes with the times, too. Henry Ford was quoted as saying that customers could buy a Model-T in any color they wanted "as long as it's black." In the color explosion of the mid-1950s, the Chrysler Corporation offered a choice of 58 exterior colors either alone or in 86 two-tone combinations. Today, we have more color choices than in the earliest era of the automobile but less than in the 1950s. Studies by DuPont between 1959 and 1971 showed fluctuations in some car colors, relatively stable popularity in others, and a link between popular clothing colors and automobile colors (Hope & Walch, 1990). By the mid-1990s, dark forest green was the most popular car color after an absence of 15 years, and purple was the new color trend (Lacina, 1996; Nichols, 1996).

Just as in fashion, color and price are linked. The color image must match the car image—a $50,000 car must look like money; what works for a Mercedes will not work for a sport utility vehicle. As paint technology continues to develop, colorists predict that postmillennium cars will feature copper, bronze, and pearlescent finishes that will reflect multiple shades, depending on the lighting (Heath, 1997b).

Color in Interiors. Trends in interior design are defined by a lifestyle concept and its associated colors—think of the long-running popularity of the country look and its evolving palette. Such concepts are said to last from 7 to 15 years (Lannon, 1988). Like the fashion industry, manufacturers and retailers work together closely on developing new looks and directions. Also like fashion, interior spaces reflect the personality and preferences of the individual owners, and color is a primary purchasing consideration. Because the investment in furnishings is generally more than in apparel, consumers feel more restraint in deciding on a change, and even when they decide to change, their choices tend to be rather conservative. Creative teams manage change by experimenting with style innovations and building on those with profit potential (Sykes, 1994).

Color in Cosmetics. Cosmetic colors are the most closely allied to fashion apparel. Fashion periods tend to take on an identifying image, and these changes are paralleled by cosmetics (Hope & Walch, 1990). When sliding-tube lipsticks appeared in the 1920s, the flapper had a convenient way to paint her lips bright red. In the 1930s, emphasis shifted to the eyes with the popularity of pale skin and unrouged cheeks. American actresses in the 1940s popularized the image of bright red lips again and added colored nails. The attention stayed on the mouth until the 1960s, when it shifted again to the eyes. Hippie looks in the 1970s shifted tastes toward the natural look and more beige and earth-toned cosmetic colors. Disco dancing sparked a glittery dress-up phase with eye shadows in metallic colors.

By the 1990s, cosmetic companies had begun to differentiate themselves based on their approach to color—some focusing on following the fashion colors of the runway, some on colors keyed to a person's skin, hair, and eye color (Wood, 1990). Major cosmetics companies selling in department stores usually have a core group of perennial sellers that stay in the line for years, a smaller group of colors that follow color trends, and seasonal promotion of a fashion color story (Sloan, 1988).

Also in the 1990s, professional makeup artists, models, and photographers began to have more influence on trends in cosmetics. Some makeup artists started cosmetic companies based on selling professional lines to the public (Edelson, 1991). In the Fall of 1998, Max Factor used a tie-in promotion with the blockbuster film *Titanic* and launched a Tina Earnshaw Color Collection named for the makeup artist who received an Oscar nomination for her work on the film (Klepacki, 1998).

Mass lines, those selling in discount stores and drugstores, may pursue a dual strategy: lagging slightly behind the color trends to attract less fashion-driven customers, and including extreme fashion shades for the fashion-forward customer seeking to satisfy the whim for a trendier image at a moderate price (Wood, 1990).

Cosmetics companies employ color marketers to chart the direction for their lines. These executives research color trends just as specialists in other product categories do: they travel, observe, sample popular culture, analyze trends in lifestyles, and track shifts in consumers' tastes. Their color forecast dovetails with the forecast in the apparel industry. In the Fall 1998 season, color cosmetics lines featured plums and purples—the same colors highlighted by David Wolfe in an apparel forecast for the National Retail Federation that same year (Klepacki, 1998). Such a strong purple message recalls the role of purple as an intermediary stage between achromatic and chromatic phases, signaling the beginning of a new color cycle.

Eiseman, Executive Director, Eiseman Center & Pantone Color Institute

man is a color specialist working with companies in helping them
st educated color choices for product development and corporate
She combines her background in psychology, fashion, and interior
tify and analyze color trends. As an authority, she has been quoted in
The Wall Street Journal, The New York Times, USA Today, and
many other publications. She authored the books *Alive with Color* (1985) and *Colors for Your Every Mood* (1999), and co-authored *The Pantone Book of Color* (1990) with Lawrence Herbert, president and CEO or Pantone, Inc. She is a member of The Fashion Group International, The American Society of Interior Designers, The Color Marketing Group Board of Directors, and the Color Association of the United States. Her favorite color is "purple with a warm red undertone" because it is "dynamic and magical—a fabulous color to combine with other hues" and also because it is "the color of creativity—something a color specialists needs a lot of!" ("Pantone," 1998, page 2).

Like musical talent, Ms. Eiseman believes some people are born with "a wonderful ability to become an interior designer or fashion designer or any area where color is inherent to the what they are doing" but that ability must be nurtured by interest and training. Other people with less inborn color ability can learn about color in the same way that people learn to play the piano—by taking lessons and playing for enjoyment. People can hone their color abilities by "reading more about it, observing more, and developing the nerve to venture forth, even if that means making some mistakes."

As an author of books on color selection, Ms. Eiseman avoids "dogmatic color systems because the psychological aspects of color is very important." Color preferences may be based on "a color remembered from childhood that is forever associated with happy thoughts or a special person or the wonderful affirmation of getting compliments when wearing a certain color." Color systems that rely only on consideration of complexion and eye color miss these important psychological factors, connections people make between certain colors and positive and negative thoughts. Ms. Eiseman's approach is to provide color guidelines as "a starting point" with the expectation that the consumer will look for a color with the same undertone, something that is similar but not exact.

According to Ms. Eiseman, a lifetime of associations plays into color preferences. When people over 50 look at yellow-green, "their mind immediately goes back to the 1960s with the acid greens and the 1970s with avocado green when that was all that was out there and it didn't make any difference whether the person liked the color or not. Young teens looks at strident yellow-green today and have no problem with the color at all because they don't remember the 1960s and

1970s, and they don't have the negative connotations with the color." Since "kids love to do things that tweak the adults" they are attracted to a neon version of yellow-green "because its so bright and strident and sort of in-your-face, and because Mom and Dad hate it." The reaction signals an important developmental stage when "kids break away from parents' influence and want to stand out, be different, and develop their own sense of color."

If color plays such an important psychological role, why is black so predominant in fashion? Ms. Eiseman sees this as more of a social outcome rather than a color choice: "I think that you see the pervasive use of black mostly in big cities to show that you are part of a knowledgeable group that wears black as a sort of a badge of honor. Even those who subscribe to black for the office workday probably introduce color on the weekends or when they exercise or in the evening when they put on their pajamas. I don't think there is anyone who could live all the time with black—black pajamas, black jeans, and T-shirt on the weekend. Like all trends, this phenomenon will pass because of the mindset of today's consumer. Long skirts and short skirts, full skirts and slim skirts, Lycra and loose—it's all out there and so is color selection. The human eye is always searching for novelty, its part of the human condition. We are all children in our psyches and we need the stimulation."

Flexibility in the use of color is a watchword for Ms. Eiseman who has spent time studying what she calls "crossover colors—these colors are prevalent in nature and can be used in many different ways." They include "all the basics like grays, taupes, aubergine, hunter greens, and navy blues which are always found in fashion because they combine so well with so many other colors and because our eyes are so accustomed to seeing them." Crossover colors tend to be "part of nature like blue skies." As she explains, "People don't think of sky blue as a neutral color or a basic color and yet blue in nature is backdrop to a beautiful day." The crossover list has expanded with the addition of the teal family of blue greens because they are a "kind of cusp between the blues and greens." This color family was "really discovered in the 1980s and people have learned to enjoy the color and find that it works with just about every other color in the spectrum."

Colors popular in one decade may fade away only to resurface later. Ms. Eiseman sees such a color cycle with green and its association with nature. "In the beginning of the 1990s interesting things were happening—reawakening to ecology, concern for the rainforest, worry about depleting resources, and a concern for preserving the earth. These issues first surfaced in the 1970s, subsided in the 1980s, and came back very strong in the early 1990s." Because people most associate the color green with nature, color forecasters "knew it was time for the greens to resurface—we hadn't seen them a lot during the 1980s but they were around a lot in the 1970s. With a 10 year rest, we were ready for green to be new again."

"Designers are responsible for creating the fashions and putting the colors on those fashions. They are the first ones to be influenced by color cycles because they are so tuned in to what's happening in the world, what's going on about them."

Forecasters, too, are looking "further into the future, not just tomorrow or even the next three to six months." To get this forward-looking perspective, Ms. Eiseman attends cutting edge trade shows "where you can see the colors that are being shown and projected for the future." But seeing colors is only the first step. "You have to know your audience. It could be that a color is going to be hot in Europe but if your demographics embrace a certain area of the country where that color has never done well, even if you think that ultimately the color will happen, it's a little too soon to try it. The bottom line is that you really have to know who your customer is." Cutting edge colors do "trickle down to the consumer level because the consumer is also looking at the media, new films, and art collections that are traveling around the country."

Membership in organizations for color professionals is another important part of Ms. Eiseman's work as a forecaster. The organizations become a meeting ground for color professionals from "various fields—cosmetics and fashion to automotive and plastics for the kitchen. The color pros discuss things that are happening in the world, the things they expect will be happening in the future, and develop a color palette approximately two years ahead of the current market." After returning to their jobs, the members "may or may not choose to embrace the colors in that palette but it helps them get a line on what others are doing in other industries and to create a connection between related industries." Ultimately, the connection between different industries "reduces confusion for the consumer shopping for related items because the color palettes are not terribly far apart."

Ms. Eiseman advises people interested in becoming color professionals to begin in retailing where they can "hear what consumers say at point of purchase and how they relate to the colors they are seeing." The retail store is also a good place to study displays because "many of the stores have very talented display people who are really tuned in to how to put colors together." Another training exercise is to be a "comparison shopper, going to Target as well as Bloomingdales—see the way that merchandise is presented, see some of the support materials like brochures and catalogs. Be a real user of everything that is out there. Most important—look at the big picture, not just a particular segment of fashion but other influences, the big films coming up, the television shows on the horizon, the technological breakthroughs, anything with a color connection. That is what color forecasters do."

Source of quotes unless cited in text, author interview with Leatrice Eiseman, May 6, 1999.

For more information, see the following:

Eiseman, Leatrice (1985). *Alive with color*. Washington, D.C.: Acropolis.

Eiseman, Leatirce (1999), *Colors for your every mood*. Sterling, VA: Capital.

Pantone Color Institute biographies. Pantone [WEB], 3 pp. Available: *www.pantone.com/bios.html* [1998, June 10].

Sources for Color Ideas and Palettes

Color forecasters are like finely calibrated instruments—they register subtle shifts in consumer preferences, sense when the time is right for a new direction, and pick up directional cues from myriad sources. Color forecasts reflect the mood of the times, both the present and the hints about the future. To forecast color direction the forecaster must constantly participate in the events that shape the cultural moment and monitor the running commentary of the media. Together the events and media shape the consumer's preferences and mood. Color stylists look for ideas on the East and West Coasts of the United States, in Europe, and in Asia. Colorists have an eye for the new, the novel, the unique, and the fresh combination. Sources include:

- Social, economic, and political issues significant enough to affect the thinking, mood, and actions of people.
- Magazines covering fashion, interiors, and entertainment, including those published in Europe.
- Newspapers, especially features on lifestyle, style, travel, entertainment, and business.
- Runways in the fashion capitals of Paris, Milan, London, and New York.
- Trade shows and exhibitions.
- The lifestyles of highly visible celebrities in entertainment and prominent role models from other fields.
- Color schemes featured in films, especially major films with exotic locales, set in stylish time periods, or featuring distinctive costuming.
- Styles worn by stars of popular television shows.
- The world of music through the club scene, music videos, dance crazes, and the style leadership of stars.
- Theater, especially productions in which the costuming, set design, or choreography are important elements.
- Travel destinations that merge new sights and experiences or involve new concepts in the hospitality industry.
- Street fashion in urban areas, districts associated with the arts, and emerging shopping scenes with small, unique, independent businesses.
- Flea markets in Paris and London and other inspiring open markets that reflect the character of a specific location and culture.
- Decorator houses and other showcases for trends in interior design and architecture.
- Museum shows focusing on artists, collections, archeological finds, photographers, or artisans, especially those with broad media coverage.

- Museum shows, auctions, and sales featuring vintage fashion and famous designers.
- Auctions, especially those featuring the possessions of famous people.
- Revival of interest in historic periods, especially the architecture, art, and signature looks of those eras.
- Fads and fashions in cuisine including shopping food markets for food products, produce, and flowers characteristic of the locale. ·
- Toys, games, and amusements for different age groups.
- New electronic gadgets, computer applications, and breakthrough technologies.
- Industrial design, graphic design, and package design because these fields often foreshadow new visual directions.

Consider it a strong directional signal when the same trend is visible during the same time period from multiple sources (Eiseman, 1994). In such cases style arbiters across industries reinforce the messages, widen the scope, and expand the coverage.

The color forecaster is always looking for clues to the next new color, the adaptation of basic colors, themes, and directions for color stories. There are some calendar dates that are especially important: the seasonal runway shows and key trade shows. An important trade show for color forecasters is **Première Vision,** an international textile industry fair, held annually in Paris. Fabric mills make presentations concerning the coming season, show organizers offer their own forecast, and color forecasts by European consultants are on display in the Hall of Prediction. This show is the crossroads for designers, manufacturers, and forecasters to see the latest in textile developments—a place for scouting and networking. Forecasters combine trips to the runway shows and fabric fairs with shopping the trendiest boutiques and watching street fashion.

The forecaster returns from trips with many new ideas, some of which have to be modified for the American market (Webb, 1994). In general, European colors are more complex, darker, and more neutral than the cleaner, brighter colors preferred by American consumers. Two organizing principles help to coordinate the new finds: the color cycle as it has evolved over the previous seasons, and the curve presenting diffusion of innovation across consumer segments (see Chapter 2). Usually the forecaster adds the new finds to an existing library of ideas. The editing process begins by pinning color samples to a board to study relationships and color groups. At first this process involves a free, open reaction to the colors. As the editing process continues, the forecaster consults the work of previous seasons to maintain the visual rhythm of color evolution. At some point in the process, the forecaster begins to define the themes and concepts that link the colors in a color story. In the final editing stage, the forecaster makes modifications and adjustments based on the clients' target consumer, product category, and price point. The final color board for the client provides overall color direction, color stories coordinated around visual themes, and specific color selection.

Find a bookstore with a large display of magazines covering many categories and special interests from cuisine to pets, from bodybuilding to art, from fashion to interiors. Seek out the newest titles and the most esoteric subjects. Using the magazines as a source, explore some of the topics listed as sources for color ideas and palettes. Discover one or more directions, themes, issues, or interests that will shape the fashion future. Report your findings on a presentation board.

Activity 4.5
Prospecting for
inspiration

Techniques of Trend Analysis and Synthesis

The methods used by the Nippon Color and Design Research Institute (NCD) illustrate the critical thinking process required to produce an accurate and justifiable forecast (Kobayashi, 1981). Their approach combines an understanding of the psychology of color and a sense of the spirit of the times. In their system, each color is assessed according to its position on three scales—warm to cool, soft to hard, and clear to grayish. These scales can be represented in a three-dimensional color space with individual colors occupying a unique location. Using this Color Image Scale (Figure 4.8) makes it easier to identify the similarities and contrasts between colors, their relative position to each other, and the color patterns or groupings.

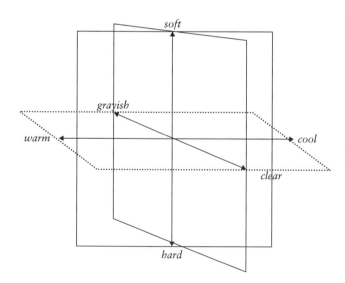

FIGURE 4.8

The Color Image Scale makes it easier to identify the similarities and contrasts between colors, their relative position to each other, and color patterns.

The method visualizes the colors of a season as pyramid. The broad base represents the colors that are resistant to change. The tip represents the fast-changing fashion colors. The middle represents those colors linked to the image and mood of the times—colors that may persist for two or three years until the attention of the culture moves on to other interests and concerns. Using this system it is possible to identify a range of colors from the basic ones accepted with no resistance, to the colors that symbolize the times, to the fashion-driven trend colors. Such a balanced method is like taking a snapshot of a color period. It allows the forecaster to create a color assortment for a range of products targeted to different segments along the fashion cycle (Linton, 1994).

For each season, forecasters at the Nippon Color and Design Institute (NCD) (1994) perform a step-by-step trend analysis.

Step 1: **Analysis of current trends** using information from newspapers, magazines, television, and other sources.

Step 2: **Analysis of current colors** in fashion across women's and men's apparel, interior design, and automobiles. Swatches of current colors are arrayed using the Color Image Scale to detect relationships.

Step 3: **Image analysis** across women's and men's apparel, interior design, and automobiles (sometimes including package design, corporate images, and environmental design). By collecting pictures of current images and arraying them using the categories of the Image Scale, common images emerge.

Step 4: **Synthesis of current and emerging lifestyle patterns.** Looking for agreement between the first three steps makes it possible to develop hypotheses about the direction lifestyles and consumer tastes are taking.

Step 5: **Discovering patterns in color preferences using consumer research methods.** Researchers use questionnaires and color-projection techniques (color-word associations) to explore the psychology of color and consumer preferences. Together with the other steps, this research allows the NCD to identify people's desired images and array them using the same categories as in the other steps.

Step 6: **Coordination of images, themes, and colors for the forecast.** A word or phrase and six to nine colors are identified to capture and communicate an image.

Consideration of political and economic conditions, special upcoming events, and cyclical changes are all part of the final NCD forecast. This comprehensive approach is effective in color planning, product development, marketing, and merchandising. The forecasts can be fine-tuned to identify the volume colors for mass marketing and fashion colors for other niches. The system allows the NCD and clients to compare past results and track shifts in color tastes across seasons.

Although other forecasters may not systematize their methods to the degree achieved by the NCD, their processes are similar. Forecasters (Szwarce, 1994) track the social, economic, and psychological influences on consumers and their reactions. They read all kinds of newspapers and magazines. They travel. They keep up with what is selling at retail. They attend trade fairs and fashion shows. They shop and watch people on the street. Wherever they are they collect clippings, color swatches, and take photos for inspiration. While preparing a forecast, they organize their observations on boards by product category and color family.

Forecasters work intuitively, discovering techniques that work, refining and reusing them. Some rely on their reading, observation, and networking. Others add qualitative research, including interviews and focus groups with potential customers.

Jean-Phillipe Lenclos (1994) of Atelier 3D Couleur in Paris developed a regular monitoring system. Each season he monitors color on billboards, at automobile shows, and window displays of selected fashion and furniture stores in Paris, London, Tokyo, and New York.

Irene Zessler (1994) of Peclers Paris begins by spontaneously buying yarns, ribbons, fabrics, books, and photos based on her experience as a designer. At brainstorming sessions, each stylist in the company brings ideas and inspiration. These sessions rationalize the process because they provide a forum for combining instincts, market knowledge, and a sense of fashion's evolution. The process culminates in a color range to guide the company's work with the textile industry and retail clients.

Forecasters may be asked to create a general forecast for an industry, for a product category, or for a more specific purpose identified by a particular client. Whatever the assignment, certain considerations must be factored into the forecast. When forecasting for clients, those considerations become more defined and specific. Forecasters consider the following (Eiseman, 1994; Verlodt, 1994a; Wrack, 1994):

- Product life cycle—some products remain stable, others are quick to change.
- Production cycle—some products can be manufactured with short turn-around times, others involve longer lead times.
- Product sensitivity to external influences such as changing demographics, geographic and cultural conditions, and prices of raw materials—factors affect all products but have more impact on some.
- Design-driven change—changes in silhouette, fit, pattern, and texture influence product categories differently.
- Product compatibility—how a product coordinates with other products.
- Sales history—top selling colors can be moved into related products.
- Competitors' color choices.

- Consumers' preferences, psychological relationship to colors, and economic status.
- Consumers' spending patterns and confidence in their economic situation.
- Climate in the regions where the product will be sold, bought, and used.

Taking all these considerations into account, the forecaster identifies stable, classic colors, fashion-driven colors, and new directional colors. For even the most stable colors the forecaster must calculate the exact shade (Hope & Walch, 1990). Does this season's black have a brown or blue undertone? Will the red be more orange or more blue? Should the peach be pink or coral?

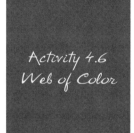

Activity 4.6
Web of Color

Search for color forecasts on the World Wide Web. Look at sites devoted to fashion, interiors, and automobiles. Sites often have a feature to keep you coming back for periodic updates. Some sites feature a single color and update this color monthly. Others are similar to magazines with new issues periodically. These magazine-like sites often have an archive of past issues. Be sure to check the archives for recent color forecasts or directional information. Look at sites that archive designers' runway presentations from past seasons. Set up a personal "bookmarks" list of color sites that you can check regularly to assist in developing color forecasts (see the Resource Pointers section at the end of the chapter for suggested Web sites).

ORGANIZATIONS FOR PROFESSIONAL COLOR FORECASTERS

Journalists looking for a good headline often call members of the professional color organizations the "color mafia." But the purpose of color forecasting is not to dictate but to discover and rediscover colors and relate them to lifestyles of the present and near future. Color forecasters come to the profession from many backgrounds—textile design, art history, product development, and others. Many work independently, consulting on a particular segment of the consumer market. A few consultants work across industry lines developing forecasts for both apparel and interiors. Some color forecasters work for industry trade associations like Cotton Incorporated or the American Wool Council. Others are employed by large fiber producers, fabric manufacturers, or apparel manufacturers. Organizations for color forecasters bring these professionals together to share ideas, inspiration, and resources. Such networking facilitates the overall goal of color forecasting: to establish future color directions for a given population, geographic location, and time as a way for industries in the supply chain to coordinate their efforts.

Color marketing intensified after World War II with the increase in demand and availability of consumer goods. Marketers realized that just as color sells apparel, it could be used to promote products across the spectrum of the marketplace. At the same time, the number of lines, size of assortments, and number of doors selling ready-to-wear was expanding. Color provided a way to satisfy many consumers with the same garment. The power of color as a marketing tool and increased demand meant that color forecasting assumed even greater economic significance. Today, the proliferation of colors, the advances in color technology, and increased demand by consumers for new colors has provided incentive for color forecasting.

By joining professional organizations, color forecasters continue to build their skills and expertise, benefit from the different viewpoints and keen vision of others, and promote professionalism of the field. There are professional organizations for color forecasters in many countries around the globe. These professional organizations restrict membership to those who focus on color exclusively or who meet specific membership criteria. The two leading professional color organizations in America are the Color Association of the United States (CAUS) and the **Color Marketing Group (CMG)**.

Color Association of the United States (CAUS)

The Color Association of the United States was founded in 1915 when textile companies decided to coordinate their colors after being cut off from Paris by the outbreak of World War I. Originally called the Textile Color Card Association of America (TCCA), they issued the first forecast in 1917, focusing on women's fashions. The forecast was aimed at designers and stylists and suggested color grouping just as today's forecasts do. As consumer-oriented marketing accelerated after World War II, more specialized forecasts were developed including:

- Man-made fibers in the 1950s.
- Men's wear in the 1960s.
- Home furnishings in the 1970s.
- Interior and environmental colors, children's wear, and activewear in the 1980s.

The association also publishes *The Standard Color Reference of America*, a book showing color standards for wool, cotton, and silk industries in United States. The original edition contained 106 shades, including those inspired by the colors of nature's flora and fauna, college and university colors, and U.S. Armed Forces shades on silk ribbons. Revised over ten editions, the number of colors has doubled (Hope & Walch, 1994).

Based in Manhattan, CAUS is a not-for-profit trade association. Members include corporations concerned with apparel, interiors and furnishings, paint, and automobiles plus designers from all those fields. The cost of membership—several hundred dollars—brings with it services. Members receive the forecast for one product category each season as a deck of silk-screened color cards, a monthly newsletter, invitations to seminars, consultations including having a collection critiqued, and access to the CAUS archives and research materials. The archive includes color swatches for every year in the association's history. CAUS has an internship program for college students (Malarcher, 1995).

CAUS members serve on committees specific to their interests and expertise. Once on a committee, the member may serve for many years, providing stability to the process, but there are small changes in the committee makeup over time. The Women's Committee meets two times each year for brainstorming sessions during which they select 25 to 42 colors for women's apparel to appear in the stores two years later (Figure 4.9). The members propose color directions by bringing presentation boards to the meeting. The presentation boards may show pictures of exotic travel locations, evocative images from historical sources, materials gleaned from nature such as bark or wood or stones, or color swatches. Over the course of the meeting, the members reach consensus on the forecast colors. The process is not mysterious but it does involve awareness of the mood of the times, preparation, and discussions where everybody contributes to defining the coming colors. Committees focusing on interiors, men's wear, children's wear, and other product categories follow a similar process when deciding by consensus on the forecast colors (Malarcher, 1995).

Color cards from the various committees may contain similar colors, but they are fine-tuned for a specific market. The classic navy may be light on the children's card, very blackened on the men's, closer to cobalt blue for interiors, and a more traditional shade for women's (Lannon, 1988). Subtle differences and color evolution are the tools of the color forecaster. Colors in combination

FIGURE 4.9

The Women's Forecasting Committee meets two times each year for brainstorming sessions to select 25 to 42 colors for women's apparel that will appear in the stores two years later. Photo courtesy of The Color Association of the US, New York City.

are important, too. If a certain red is in the forecast, its best complement in green must also be there (Malarcher, 1995). It is this level of sophistication and expertise in color that makes the professional's advice valuable.

Color Marketing Group (CMG)

The Color Marketing Group, an international nonprofit association based in the Washington, D.C., area, was formed in 1962 to provide advanced color information for industries from apparel to automobiles, from health care to corporate identity. Members' job titles range from designer, stylist, and product developer to marketing manager and merchandiser, and the companies they work for range from small independent studios to large corporations. The focus is on color as a marketing tool. Members share noncompetitive information about trends and forecasts because they see the process as translating into profitable business decisions for their companies. In addition to participating in expert panels and workshops, members receive four color palettes a year (the cost is much higher to nonmembers), a monthly newsletter, and access to the color library.

In the CMG, workshops are aimed at the interests and specialties of members (Jacobs, 1994; Verlodt, 1994b). The process begins with forecast workshops for over 40 product or end-use categories. The forecast workshops bring together an expert panel of members dealing with the same product category and whose work requires forecasting three or more years before the selling season.

The fashion industry panel meets in the winter and summer to develop the apparel palette. Eight weeks before the workshops members mail in color samples and their individual color directions forecast. Using these submissions as a starting point, participants negotiate to determine the set of forecast colors.

A representative from each expert panel participates in a final round of negotiations to determine CMG's palette of new colors for consumer (fashion, residential, communications, etc.) and commercial (retail, hospitality, health care) markets, including individual colors and color combinations.

For members whose forecast time frame is less than two years, there are different workshop formats than the experts' panel, including the following:

- Colors Current Workshops discuss colors that are or soon will be in the marketplace.
- Design Influences Workshops explore specific design trends as they relate to shifts in consumer demographics and the economy.
- Color Combinations Workshops explore combinations and blends of colors.
- Marketing Workshops look at issues related to market research.

The goal of forecast workshops is not to predict specific hues but to indicate color direction. According to the CMG, color direction is defined as an inclination, tendency, course, or trend. Members work year-round on committee assignments, but meeting schedules depend on the product category. The CMG tracks color by surveying its membership on the use of color in their industries and analyzes findings on an industry-by-industry basis. The result is a kind of continuing scorecard on color use across industries and product categories.

COLOR PLANNING INSIDE THE TEXTILE AND APPAREL INDUSTRIES

Large companies often have a division responsible for developing trend information on colors and styles and reporting to the other divisions involved in product development. Design groups or other executives may carry this responsibility in smaller firms. Wherever the function is located on the organizational chart, executives use forecasts in conjunction with company sales data (see Chapter 8) and in-house color tracking to prepare and present company-specific forecasts. The decision process factors together color forecasts, information about street fashion, fashion collections in the United States and Europe, and reports in trade publications and fashion magazines.

A design or marketing executive making decisions about color for a product category uses multiple forecasts. One or more will come from professional color organizations to which the executive belongs. Others may come from industry trade organizations. The executive probably subscribes to one or more additional color forecasting services. The availability of multiple forecasts is valuable not because forecasters usually disagree in any major way but because several forecasts tend to verify general color trends. In addition to the color forecasts, the executive will likely subscribe to the services of other forecasters who specialize in the fashion scene (see Chapter 6) or in discovering cultural trends (see Chapter 9).

This multiple forecast strategy applies within a company. Because the cost of membership in one of the professional organizations is substantial, a company may belong to more than one and send different executives to the meetings. In that way, the company benefits from having executives active in the workings of the organizations and obtains a multilens view of color evolution. When there is lag time between meetings such as sometimes occurs between the organizations in Europe and America, one company executive may participate in forecasting at the earlier meeting, and return to develop the seasonal **colorways**—color groups and combinations. Later, another company executive may participate in the sessions of another color organization sharing the gist of the company forecast with other professionals. In this way, color trends are often shared across national boundaries, organizations, and companies. Forecasters' palettes for a particular season rarely disagree in any major way even if the forecasts are developed independently—perhaps owing partly to the evolutionary nature of the task, partly to the the movement of the forecast through the supply chain (Webb, 1994)

Interpreting color forecasts is far from a straightforward task. All forecasts come with a disclaimer saying that they can be inaccurate. After all, a forecast is used when complete information is missing; it cannot be expected to predict the exact future. One complaint about color forecasts is that they include every color. Color forecasters reply that the forecasts indicate the general direction, not an actual color. They become useful only when executives consider color direction in terms of hue, value, and intensity and consider context and usage (Eiseman, 1994).

Even with several color forecasts in hand, the color planning decisions still remain with the executive. The executive edits the information in the forecast for the specifics of a product line targeted for a particular consumer segment. Upscale, sophisticated markets are likely to relate well to a more European color palette with its subtle, darker, and grayed look. A mass marketer chooses a more immediately understandable color palette that is brighter and more accessible to a broader market segment. For other lines, color decisions depend on the geography, climate, and preferences where the products will be sold or used. Tradition plays a key role in decision making—what is well-accepted in society as well as what is typical for a particular manufacturer (Stark & Johnson-Carroll, 1994). By having several forecasts, the executive sees the overall color direction and taps into the expertise of several forecasters when selecting the exact colors for a product line.

Forecasts at the Beginning of the Pipeline

Large chemical companies make dyes to sell down the pipeline where coloration actually takes place. More than 6,000 different synthetic dyes are known to exist, and the typical dye producer will offer about 600 in the company's palette. These companies need long lead times for production—typically four to nine months ahead of delivery to the dye house. These long lead times mean that the chemical company needs early warning about color demand so that it can provide the exact shades demanded by fashion. Often forecasting information makes it to the fabric producer but does not flow backward to the producers of the dye materials. Yet, when an order comes in for a particular blue, the company is expected to deliver dye for that exact color. In the past, meeting orders has meant holding high safety inventories in hopes of avoiding a stock-out situation (Dransfield, 1994).

Some dye-producing companies are setting up an early warning system by using fashion experts in Rome, London, Paris, and New York to predict color trends at a generic level—such as reds are going to be in, for example. These companies also need to know how dark the colors will be because very dark colors can take ten times more dye than pale shades. With this early warning system, a company can concentrate on 250 individual dyes to meet all color requirements for all types of fibers and provide desirable fastness properties. About 20 percent of key dyes are unique and cannot be mixed from other dyes; the rest can. For that large portion of mixable colors, the company depends on the art of the master blender. With the early warning system and partnerships with fabric producers and large textile retailers, the dye producer can be aware of the color forecast in time to meet the demand for fashion-driven colors (Dransfield, 1994).

Apparel Manufacturer's In-House Forecast

When a once-hot company runs into dropping sales figures, it seems shocking to point to color decisions. Yet that was the case with Eddie Bauer in 1998 when the CEO said that products in kiwi and orange were a major part of the company's problems. As the vice-president of merchandising explained: "Our heritage is classically based but when we saw the customer responding to color, we simply went too far."

Designers, stylists, and product developers apply forecasts to a line of merchandise specifically for the target customer. In selecting colors for a line in a given season, executives make an error if they are:

- Too brash, overreacting to the forecast by producing a line with fashion-forward colors that do not sell.
- Too conservative, ignoring the forecast in favor of playing it safe, missing out on hot new colors that catch on with the consumer.

In lines where economies of scale limit changes in silhouette, use of detail, and embellishment, color provides the visual power to attract customers.

Effective interpretation of the forecasts comes with experience managing color decisions from season to season. After several seasons of brights, the forecast shifts to newness in another color range as the color cycle continues. Brights will still appear in the forecast but will be less dominant than in the previous season. Brights that continue strong in sales figures may be modified to midtones as a transition, allowing the customer to use these new variations with the brights of the previous season (Calvert, 1994). It is never a good idea to leap from one distinct palette to another totally different one.

In the product development stage, executives must go beyond color direction to forecast the significance of the color story and the quality of the trend. Which colors are basic to the line? Which accent colors will signal fashionability and newness? Together with the marketers and merchandisers, they must decide specific colors for each item in the line, the coordination of those items within a group, and how many of each item to produce.

Forecasts arrive broken down into ranges of colors—darks, brights, midtones, pastels, and neutrals (Calvert, 1994). Each forecast may include as many as 50 colors. Women's wear has the widest spectrum of color among apparel products. If an executive works with four to six forecasts, that means finding the color undercurrents across 200 to 300 colors. Using these colors as a beginning point, the executive will develop five or six ranges of 12 to 20 colors as the in-house color range. Such a range of 75 to 100 colors allows for several in-store deliveries without repetition of the color. This color range will include long-selling colors, perhaps paired in a new color combination. It may recast classic color formulas like Spring's recurring red, white, and blue into a newer coral, beige, and teal. Perennial best-selling colors such as black, white, true red, navy, and ivory are so basic that they may not appear in any of the forecasts but still may be used in the line.

The in-house color range will be applied to fabrics in solid colors and to prints, plaids, and multicolor knit yarns. The newest colors are more likely to appear in these multihue formats or in separates that provide an accent to a group. To guide the product development stage and as a communication tool to the other functional groups in the company, the executive will present the in-house color range in the context of themes and imagery that relates to the target customer (see Chapter 12).

Forecasting at the End of the Pipeline

Retailers take a risk in selecting merchandise because they are predicting future consumer demand. By gathering information from a variety of sources, retailers seek to minimize risk (Kline & Wagner, 1994). Color is a very important part of merchandise selection. As one retailer put it (Noh, 1997): "After years of observing customers selecting one item over another I learned that color was their most important choice—often they selected a style that was not their favorite just because the color was right—but very rarely did they select a style or textile when the color was not what they wanted!"

Information is available for retailers through several channels. Small chains and independent stores use buying offices that provide forecasting information or subscribe to fashion forecasting services. Larger chains rely on their fashion director or corporate buyers who receive the forecast information and fashions subscriptions and disseminate the information to others in the organization. Trade publications such as *Women's Wear Daily* (*WWD*) for women's apparel and *Daily News Record* (*DNR*) for men's wear report on presentations by color consultants at conferences and trade shows. Consumer magazines and newspapers carry reports on color forecasting.

All this effort focuses on a single effect—consumers walking into a store receive a message about the color direction for the season. The merchandise shows the basic and fashion colors for apparel and accessories and the related colors in cosmetics. To be effective, the story must be read quickly and understood easily without verbal explanations. The message conveyed must satisfy many needs and wants—a new look, novel but not intimidating, the promise of complete makeovers, and carefully considered additions to existing wardrobes. As merchandise deliveries arrive over the selling season, the floor must continue to look coordinated even when groups from different delivery dates are hanging together. If the coordinating function of color forecasting has worked, colors on the selling floor show an underlying relationship that seems coherent and comprehensible.

Color Specification Systems

Achieving a coherent and comprehensible color story each season begins with the forecast and specification writing. Writing specifications is an essential part of turning ideas and concepts into products. In today's global trade arena, the same color may be fiber-dyed for blending into a sweater yarn, yarn-dyed for use in a plaid shirt, and fabric-dyed for a skirt, all in different countries, but all for the same apparel line (see Chapter 5). Yet the consumer expects that all the pieces will come together into a coordinated outfit. To satisfy the consumers' expectations, all levels of the supply chain have to communicate precisely and objectively about color.

Apparel product developers have several problems associated with color reproduction. It is difficult to accurately reproduce the same color on different surface textures. Perception of a color can be changed by the amount of the color used and by the colors surrounding it. In fabric dying, color can be affected by dye quality, mixing, and other manufacturing conditions. Because of the difficulty in exact matching, product developers balance that need against the economic necessity of achieving realistic price points.

Product developers try to resolve the various problems and challenges by writing color specifications in a color system, one that arranges color so that the color itself can be identified along with its value (darkness to lightness) and its intensity (bright to subdued). Color systems allow these values to be expressed in notation using a number or letter code. Various standardized systems have been developed, but no one system has been universally accepted (Hope & Walch, 1990).

A color forecast is delivered with a set of color cards, fabric swatches, or yarn samples. The designer working with the forecast can select colors for use in the product line and sometimes order additional samples of those colors. The designer needs a sample of the color to communicate the color specification to manufacturing. The designer sends a sample swatch of the color and a description of the color using the notation of a color system. The two most common systems used in the United States are (Hope & Walch, 1990):

- The **Munsell Color System,** which includes a color atlas, the *Munsell Book of Color* (1976), with about 1,600 chips arranged in equal steps of hue, value, and chroma (intensity or saturation) and a notation for each.

- The **PANTONE ® Professional Color System,** which includes a color atlas, *The Pantone Book of Color* (1990), with 1,225 colors identified by name and color code.

A color notation system may look incomprehensible at first glance but to color professionals the system becomes a precise language for color identification. For example, in the Munsell System of Color Notation ("Munsell web," 1998), hue, value, and chroma can describe any color. The Munsell system includes a series of 100 equally spaced hues. Numbers and letters designate each color. Value is designated on a continuum from zero for pure black to ten for pure white. Chroma indicates the degree of difference between a color and a neutral of the same value. The chroma scale starts at zero, but there is no arbitrary end to the scale—light reflecting materials extend to 20, florescent materials to 30. The complete Munsell notation is written symbolically: H(ue) V(alue)/C(hroma). For a vivid red, the notation would read 5R 6/14 (Figure 4.10). For finer definitions, decimals are used—5.3R 6.1/14.4.

The problem of color matching is made more complicated by the use of **computer-aided design (CAD)** and other computer-based functions. In the past, checking for accurate color reproduction has involved having a color stylist visit the manufacturing site to approve the colors or the exchange of color samples between design and manufacturing in a series of approval stages. With the advent of the Internet and companies' translation of the technology into their own Intranets (proprietary computer-based communication systems), the approval process is moving online. The problem comes in color matching—the on-screen color may or may not match the specified color because it has been altered by the hardware or software used to create it on the monitor. New software solutions are being developed to facilitate the designing and managing of colors on computers. These new solutions will increase the accuracy of color when viewed on the computer (Chirls, 1997).

The product developer uses the notation of a color system to write manufacturing specifications for the exact color of an item using the code to indicate the hue, value, and chroma.

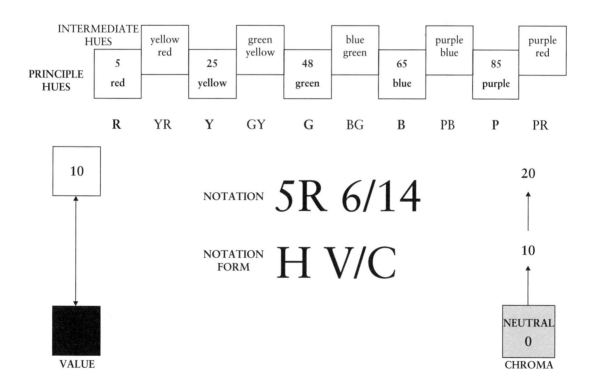

Locate the reference materials on either the Munsell or the Pantone system in the library. Using the color swatches from Activity 4.3, write the color specification notation for each color.

Key Terms and Concepts

Achromatic
Analogous
Chroma
Color Association of the
    United States (CAUS)
Color Cycles
Color Key Program
Color Marketing Group
    (CMG)
Color Palette
Color Story
Color Wheel

Colorways
Complementary
Computer-Aided Design
    (CAD)
Double Complements
Hue
Intensity
Munsell Color System
Pantone ® Professional
    Color System
Première Vision

Primary Colors
Saturation
Seasonal Color Analysis
Secondary Colors
Shade
Split Complements
Tertiary Colors
Tint
Tone
Triads
Value

Case: A Colorful Season Revisited

Whitney is creating a concept board suggesting the color direction two years in the future. First, she will present her board at a meeting of color forecasting professionals. After they brainstorm together, they will develop a consensus forecast that each can later use with clients. Use the following discussion questions to review and summarize this chapter as you follow Whitney's progress through this process.

Color ideas: *The first stage in color forecasting requires openness to inspiration from myriad sources. Review the list on sources for color ideas and palettes.*

- *Which sources on the list are most likely to be active and influential at this time?*

- *How can Whitney tap into these sources and gather color information as she travels? If she works from her home office?*

- *What color relationships across product categories will be important in guiding her during this first stage?*

Color cycles: *A forecaster must consider more than one kind of color cycle in making color directions understandable.*

- *What looks in current fashion will continue to evolve into the next few seasons? Are these looks part of fashion's historic continuity? How will they affect color evolution?*
- *What long wave oscillations will effect the next few seasons? Is the current cycle bright and saturated, multicolored, muted, earth tones, or neutral and achromatic? What comes next?*
- *Is there a cycle related to the influence of men's wear on women's clothes?*
- *Is there a color temperature cycle that will affect the next few seasons?*
- *Is there any new color technology that will influence change over the next few seasons?*

Color names and themes: Communicating color to the trade and to the consumer involves grouping colors around themes that are culturally and socially relevant to the times and naming colors within those themes.

- *What themes are emerging that would be appropriate for organizing the color story?*
- *What sources for color names seem most applicable to the forecast of colors two years from now?*
- *What elements should Whitney include on the board she takes to the meeting of her professional organization?*

Analysis and synthesis: When Whitney participates in the brainstorming session, she will be involved in a critical thinking process aimed at creating an accurate and justifiable forecast.

- *What techniques of analysis and synthesis will be in play during the session?*
- *When Whitney returns from the meeting and begins working with her clients, what technique of analysis and synthesis will she use?*

Additional Forecasting Activities

Contrast and Compare Forecasts. Collect color forecasts from several color forecasting services and industry trade groups for the same season (either the current forecast or one for a season just past). Compare and contrast color projections across the several forecasts. Are the color selections similar in terms of hue, value, and intensity? Are the themes, color names, and grouping of colors similar? How closely do the forecasts agree? Where do they diverge? Can the differences between the forecasts be explained by a different focus on product category or target market? Discuss how an executive would make decisions about a product line using these several forecasts.

Backcast Color Innovations. Pick a color once considered fashion-forward that is now mainstream (e.g., chartreuse, orange, or hot pink). Backcast the diffusion of this color innovation (backcasting is a method of tracing the development of fashion idea or trend backward to its origin point). Use the fashion and trade press as sources. Perform keyword searches in databases to locate references to this color. When is the earliest mention of this color entering the fashion forecast? What happened to advance the color's evolution? When did the color appear in mainstream collections? Has the color reached its popularity peak and begun to subside? What current fashion-forward color will replace it?

The Story of Black. Trace black as a fashion color. It has always had an important role in the fashion story. When did it dominate the marketplace? What factors were involved? Which designers became known for the dominant role of black in their collections? What associations make black so popular with consumers? How versatile is black in designs? Forecast the future of black as a fashion color and as a basic color.

Think Local Color. Develop a distinctive "color conception of a place" based on your area of the country. What combination of colors in the natural environment and colors associated with the history of the place symbolize the area's color personality? How are these colors present in the apparel, interiors, architecture, and art of the region? Create a collage expressing this "color conception of a place." Discuss the interaction between fashion colors proposed for national or international use and the distinctive colors of a region. How could local color preferences affect sales of apparel? Is color marketing becoming more or less responsive to local color preferences?

Resource Pointers

Web sites for professional color organizations:

- Color Association of the United States—www.colorassociation.com
- Color Marketing Group—www.colormarketing.org

Other Web sites with color forecasts:

- ApparelNews.net—www.apparelnews.net/archive
- Expofill—www.expofil.com
- International Fashion Fabric Exhibition—www.fabricshow.com.iff_whats new.html

Web site archiving designers' lines:

- First View—www.firstview.com

Web sites for color systems:

- The Munsell Color System—www.munsell.com
- The PANTONE ® Professional Color System—www.pantone.com

Chapter 5

TEXTILE DEVELOPMENT

"There's lots of experimentation with fabrics every season."
—Cynthia Rowley, Fall/Winter, 1998

Objectives

- Understand the fiber and fabric product development cycle in relationship to trend formation.

- Describe the sources of innovation in fiber and fabric product development.

- Understand the role of fiber and fabric trade organizations and fabric councils in disseminating trend information.

- Cultivate skills in researching trend formation in the fiber and fabric product development process.

CASE: TEXTILE TREND WATCH

Because businesses now exchange information over computer networks, small entrepreneurial firms in rural or suburban locations can do business with other companies around the world online. This is especially the case when part of the product mix is information itself. Kim is a fabric designer with a small state-of-the-art studio located on an upper floor of a commercial building on the high street of a small town in England. She is considering branching out to include forecasting services as part of her business plan.

Kim and her staff use computer-aided design (CAD) to create fabric designs for clients and transmit their designs electronically. The studio's clients are American corporations who produce fabrics in the United States and in the Far East. To keep current on trends in fabric design, Kim travels to all the European yarn and fabric shows. To guide the work of the studio, Kim develops concept boards using photographs from magazines, swatches of developmental fabrics collected at the trade shows, and other inspiring bits and pieces. For any particular season, Kim develops four or five concept boards, each coordinated around a theme that captures the newness emerging among resources in Europe.

Kim started her business right after design school by working as a free-lancer for one company—a contact she made while attending a trade show in Paris. She built the business by adding one or two clients a year and the staff needed to handle that volume of business. With all the news about marketplace turbulence and company mergers and acquisitions, Kim has begun to question the wisdom of depending on a few big clients for business survival. She recently attended a workshop for entrepreneurs in design fields where participants were urged to inventory the attributes of their companies that could be marketed along with design products. Kim realized that her clients value the immediate update information she provides on design directions—information she conveys casually in e-mail correspondence with them.

Putting together her concerns about the business, the marketing suggestions from the seminar, and her access to timely information, Kim decides to diversify her client list and promote her service by launching an electronic newsletter called Textile Trend Watch. *Kim plans to report on trends developing in European textile design, project those trends for the U.S. market, and show how the design work from her studio reflects those trends. For the first six months, the electronic newsletter will be sent free to a list of U.S. firms Kim found in an industry directory. After six months, the newsletter will convert to a by-subscription-only format, but one article and one concept board will be featured each month on a free Web site. In this way, Kim plans to develop a new profit center for the company while promoting her existing design business.*

To attract a loyal repeat readership, the newsletter must be authoritative and filled with leading-edge information conveyed in an interesting, time efficient format. This chapter provides a framework for the kind of information Kim will be gathering and reporting.

FASHION IN FIBER AND FABRIC

Seeing fashion is not enough. As people walk down the aisles of a store or move among the clothing racks, they reach out to caress the shoulder of a jacket or squeeze the sleeve of a sweater. This "petting" behavior shows the power of touch to connect consumers to textile products (Gladwell, 1996). Fabrics range from slick surfaces like leather and futuristic plastic to softer surfaces like cashmere, from flat weaves to heavy textures like bouclé, from the solid structure of flannel to the web-like open structure of crochet. Clothing has been called "the second skin" in recognition of its intimate connection with people's physical and psychological comfort (Horn, 1965). So, it is not surprising that news about which fabrics are "in" or "out" plays such a prominent role in forecasting fashion.

Reporting on fashion trends is incomplete without reporting on "newness" in fabrics and trims (Holch, 1998b). Newness can come from:

- The introduction of a new fiber with a unique set of properties.
- The blending of several fibers to create a different set of attributes.
- Finishing the fabric in a way that changes the surface or adds functionality.
- Creating a surface texture such as puckered effects, grid-patterns woven into the fabric, or beads applied to the surface.
- Coloring the fabric using the latest technology.
- Reviving a handcrafted look.
- Introducing a historical or ethnic source to inspire the texture, structure, or print motif.
- Returning to luxury fabrics after seasons of a more casual approach, such as the revival of cashmere in the late 1990s.
- Manipulating fabric by folding, tucking, quilting, and other ways that add volume and dimension.
- Using fabric in an unexpected way counter to rules of appropriateness, such as gray flannel for eveningwear and velvet for daytime.
- Substituting unexpected materials such as high-tech neoprene for fabric in apparel and accessories.

Newness is a fleeting thing for textile makers. Technology makes it faster to knock off textile products. Companies who want to compete on the basis of original design have to turn out designs quickly because their specialness is quickly diluted by copies (Malone, 1999).

In some fashion seasons, fabrics serve as background and the news is in the way they are cut or colored. Other seasons feature a strong fabric story—the shine of silk, the cling of matte jersey, the stretch of spandex, the texture of tweed. Sometimes the focus is on clean-cut minimalism and other times on a strong trim story—the femininity of lace, the handcrafted look of crochet, or the accent of beading. Seasons go by when few prints are featured and then painterly prints, romantic florals, or bold geometrics take center stage.

Trends in fabric move in the same currents that shape and reshape fashion. Even something as basic as fiber experiences waxing and waning periods of popularity. Natural fibers once shunned because of the care requirements and their wrinkled, rumpled appearance were lifted by the same wave that heightened the popularity of casual wear. Polyester, a popular fiber choice in the

FIGURE 5.1

FIGURE 5.1

In the mid-1990s, designers rediscovered polyester dubbing it "modern." This casual shirt and pants combination offers a dressy yet comfortable impression.

1970s, became unfashionable in the 1980s but rebounded in the mid-1990s as designers like Betsy Johnson, Mary McFadden, and Norma Kamali (Figure 5.1) rediscovered its performance qualities and dubbed it "modern" (Holch & McNamara, 1995). At the same time that fashion promotes new fibers and fabrics, it also acts to modify basics. The popularity of casual looks encouraged denim manufacturers to create lighter weight denim better suited than basic denim weights to mixing and matching with other fabrics (Chirls, 1998a). Denim itself is prone to cycles of extreme popularity and then eclipse. In 1999, denim was stronger that it had been in ten years, partly because it fit the differing tastes and lifestyles of teens and their parents, and partly because denim was reinvented as fashionable by designers (Schiro, 1999). Tom Ford of Gucci got lots of press when he showed a neo-hippie version of ripped and beaded jeans decorated with feathers in 1999.

Changes in cultural indicators reverberate in fashion choices. When the economy is strong and consumers feel confident, these factors combine to favor upscale clothes in luxury fabrics like wool. Increased interest in women's wool knitwear boosted demand from 19 million pounds in 1992 to 33 million pounds in 1998 (Chirls, 1998a). Deep concerns about the environment coincided with the development of ecologically friendly fibers such as organically grown, naturally colored cottons and lyocell, a biodegradable fiber manufactured from a renewable source (wood pulp) in a process during which the chemicals are recovered and recycled. Interest in the environment also reverberated in styling when garments with the appearance of being in their "natural state" became fashionable. That meant that color variations previously unacceptable were now in demand.

SOURCES OF INNOVATION
IN TEXTILE DEVELOPMENT

Designers choose fabrics very early in the product development cycle because the attributes of the fabrics are linked to the silhouette and mood of the collection. Some designers have a signature fabric that they constantly use season after season, such as Geoffrey Beene's jersey or Giorgio Armani's wools. Other designers use different fabrics from group to group, season to season. A few designers such as Issey Miyake, Muccia Prada, and Jil Sander become known for their experiments with fabrications—experiments that influence other designers in their selection and use of fabrics.

Just as fashion capitols—London, Milan, Paris, and New York—become identified with a certain approach or aesthetic, so certain parts of the world are known for the fabrics they produce. Designers in all the fashion capitols rely on the artistry of Italian fabrics, especially wools, in each season's collections. The link between fabric development and the fashion runway has proven advantageous for Italian spinners, dyers, and weavers who have a 200-year history of small family firms dotting the Italian landscape in linked networks ("Business," 1998). American manufacturers cannot match the Italians in the quality and craftsmanship of wools, but American manufacturers have the lead when it comes to developing synthetic fibers.

High-tech fabrics with novel properties are beginning to move from sports gear and rugged adventure wear to high fashion and street wear. Known as **technical fabrics** or **performance fabrics**, these fabrics can cost up to 30 percent more than nontechnical ones but deliver engineered characteristics. One of the first breakthrough fabrics was DuPont's Lycra spandex, now a regular component of jeans and sexy dresses. Although the roots of the technical fabrics are in survival gear and high-performance sports equipment, the new fabrications are specifically styled for the fashion market, and companies such as Polo, Nautica, and Jones New York are using and promoting these modern fabrics (Chirls, 1998c).

Activity 5.1
Fabrics for the
New Millennium

Do a keyword search of online sites and databases of trade publications and fashion magazines using the terms "technical" and "performance fabrics." Look for breaking news on textiles in trade sources such as *Textile World, Women's Wear Daily (WWD), Daily News Record (DNR)*, and *Bobbin Magazine*. What cultural shifts favor the development and use of technical and performance fabrics for streetwear? What novel properties will be in demand in the years to come? Will the engineered properties of these new high-tech fibers replace the popularity of natural fibers? Which technical and performance fabrics currently used primarily for active sports, safety equipment, or adventure sports are likely to make the jump to streetwear?

The Timing of Innovation

There are three general categories of fiber:

- **Natural fibers** that originate from animals (alpaca, angora, camel's hair, cashmere, mohair, silk, vicuna, wool) or plants (cotton, linen, and hemp).

- **Man-made fibers** manufactured from chemicals (acrylic, spandex, nylon, polyester, and polyolefin).

- **Manufactured fibers** chemically engineered from biological raw material such as wood pulp (rayon, lyocell, and acetate).

In the past, the development cycle for fabrics depended on such things as the growing season for cotton or the shearing season for wool. With the advent of man-made and manufactured fibers that can be produced at any time, these earlier seasonal considerations became less important. In today's market the most important consideration is the consumer's willingness to buy, a period that now closely coincides with the use of the apparel. To meet this "in-season" buying trend, merchandising is moving toward continuous delivery of new product throughout the season to keep the selling floor interesting and inviting for purchasers. Stretching back from each apparel purchase is a chain of production that extends to the production of the fiber.

The scheduling of textile development is a critical factor in the introduction of fashion products. The time involved depends on the source of the fiber and the production stages between raw material and final fabric. When production is located offshore, the production cycle involves longer lead times to accommodate transportation from factory to distribution points. The product development process for catalog merchandise and for certain product categories, such as sweaters, starts earlier than for other merchandise sold in retail stores.

The **supply chain** begins with the fiber which is processed into yarn, then into fabric, and ends with fabric finishing, including dyeing and printing. Vertically integrated firms control all aspects of the supply chain from yarn to fabric to finishing to apparel. Other firms form strategic alliances between segments of the chain to cooperate in product development, cut lead times, consolidate purchasing, and control inventories. Integrating the supply chain in this way allows companies to plan a 12-month flow of goods. Because today's fashion picture favors a variety of goods at all price points, the emphasis is on value-added fabrics—fabrics with special appearance or performance characteristics that will command premier prices over basic fabrics in the marketplace (Chirls, 1998b).

At each stage in the supply chain innovation is possible. Fiber producers and mills start projecting fabric trends at least 16 months ahead of the selling season. Fabric, like apparel, itself goes through stages of development, introduction, selection, and ordering. In the case of fibers and fabric, the customers are apparel design teams who select the fabrics they will use in creating their seasonal collections.

Innovation in Fibers

Natural Fibers   Natural fibers have been used for apparel across the millennia but today's textile technology continues to refine and expand their properties and uses ("Fibers," 1998). Cotton is moving into high-performance fabrics for activewear because of mechanical and chemical finishing and blending with other fibers. Treatment of linen yarn is increasing its use in knits and weaving techniques, finishes, and blends which has helped reduce wrinkling. New ways of controlling wool's shrinking and felting properties are making it more useful in knitwear and safe for machine washing and drying.

Man-made and Manufactured Fibers   Developing new fibers and variations on existing fibers takes a huge research effort and years of work before the innovation is ready for marketing. When new fibers are developed, the U.S. Federal Trade Commission (FTC) designates them with a **generic name** (e.g., nylon, polyester, spandex, and lyocell). Companies that produce and promote the fibers add a trademarked **brand name** (e.g., DuPont's brand name for polyester is Dacron, Hoechst-Celanese's brand name for polyester is Trivera). To be in compliance with the Textile Fibers Products Identification Act, clothing must be labeled with the generic name of the fibers by percentage composition.

While development of a new fiber is rare, newness in fiber comes about in other ways. The basic properties of a man-made or manufactured generic fiber can be altered chemically and physically to obtain different looks and properties. When a variation is distinctive enough, the company will give it a specialty brand name and promote its special properties as a mimic for a natural fiber or because of some other performance advantage. Performance fabrics feature a special attribute such as the ability to regulate body temperature. Newness in this area comes from making once industrial high-tech applications suitable for apparel.

Innovation in Yarns. Innovation in yarn production focuses on developing products with the fiber blends, finishes, and properties that meet consumer needs. Often innovation comes from exploiting the capabilities of weaving looms and knitting machines. Yarn production techniques create differences in:

- **Texture**—the surface variations from hard and slick to soft and fuzzy, from dull and matte to shimmering highlights to shiny metallic.
- **Hand**—the way finished fabric feels when handled, and properties such as its ability to recover when stretched or compressed.
- **Drape**—the way the finished fabric hangs on the body, whether it stands away from the body or clings to the curves.

Each natural fiber—silk, cotton, wool, and linen—involves a unique process to turn fiber into yarn. In contrast, the man-made fibers begin as solid chips or pellets that are liquefied and extruded through a spinneret. Holes in the spinneret can be engineered to vary in size and shape, and these differences alter the properties of the fiber. **Microfibers** are produced when the holes in the spinneret are very small and produce a fiber that is finer that than even the finest natural fiber silk. Generally, these small, fine microfibers make fabrics that are softer and drapier than the same construction in traditional fibers.

Man-made and manufactured fibers are produced as **filaments**—continuous strands. Man-made fibers can also be textured to create crimp, loop, curl, or coil to increase the bulk, loft, or elasticity of the fiber. They can be spun into yarn in filament form or cut into short lengths that mirror the natural fibers (called **staple length**).

During the spinning process, fibers can be blended together to make the yarn. Blending natural and man-made fibers offers many possibilities for innovation as the **blend** also carries the properties of the original fibers but in a new combination. Blending wool with silk, viscose, nylon, ramie, or linen translates the fiber known for warmth into a sheer or lightweight fabric suitable for spring fashions (Holch, 1997). Tencel, a trademarked brand of the lyocell fiber, blended with linen retains linen's esthetic but adds a softer hand to the fabric (Holch, 1996b).

Innovation in Fabric Structure. Fabrics used in apparel products are either knitted or woven from natural, man-made, or blended yarns. **Weaving** is defined as the interlacing of yarns at right angles. The order of interlacing produces patterns called weaves and each weave has its own characteristics and properties. In **knitting,** yarns are looped together in successive rows—a process that gives more natural stretch to the fabric, although the actual result depends on the fiber content of the yarn and the yarn construction. Variations in the weave or knitting pattern coupled with variations in the fiber content and yarn construction lead to an infinite universe of innovation in fabric structure.

Bonding, crocheting, felting, knotting, and laminating make other fabric structures. Called **novelty fabrics,** such fabrics often appear as accents in a fashion season.

Innovation in Dyeing Fabric. Color can be added at any stage in fabric production—to the fiber, yarn, or fabric or to the finished garment. In a process specific to man-made fibers called **solution dyeing,** the color is added to the liquefied fiber before it is extruded as a filament. Man-made and natural fibers in staple lengths can be dyed as loose fibers before being processed into yarn. Yarn can be colored after production—a method frequently used in the production of woven stripes, plaids, and check fabrics. The fabric can be dyed after weaving in a process called **piece dyeing**—an inexpensive method used most frequently for solid colors. If the fabric is made from two different fibers, it is possible to produce a two-color fabric by adding dyes that are reactive with each fiber to a single dye bath—an inexpensive method called **cross dyeing.** The color can even be applied after the fabric has been made into garments. **Garment dyeing** is used when an apparel manufacturer is trying to match items by dyeing them together. Garment dyeing is also used when an apparel manufacturer wants to manufacture the apparel but conduct consumer testing on colors before committing to delivery. These variations in the dying process allow manufacturers to choose the one best suited for their situation and to provide many variations in the effects achieved. Reports on new looks in fabrics frequently include a reference to the way the color was applied or to the effect created.

Innovation in Fabric Finishing. Finishing is used to manipulate the appearance characteristics, performance, or hand of a fabric. **Fabric finishing** may involve:

- A mechanical process such as passing the fabric between rollers with heat and pressure to create an overall glaze or abrading the surface with brushes for a suede-like look.
- A chemical process that changes the surface of the fibers.
- An applied finish that changes the properties of the fabric, such as increasing water repellency.

Finishing techniques allow a fabric to take on many possible looks and properties but it also increases the price from 10 cents to 50 cents a yard (Chirls, 1996b).

Take a basic fabric such as denim—the original fabrication was 100 percent cotton, 14-ounce indigo denim. Breaking in a pair of jeans could take countless wearings and washings. Consumers took finishing into their own hands in the 1970s soaking jeans in bleach to create a softer, lighter version. Sometimes these do-it-yourself projects resulted in unintended holes in the fabric when the jeans were left in too long or when the concentration of bleach was too strong. Today's controlled finishing processes with stones and enzymes, sandblasting, and abrading mean that new jeans have a well-worn feeling and holes only when that is the intended effect ("Beyond blue," 1998). Cotton Incorporated included 64 different finished-denim fabrics in its 1998 swatch book of new fabrics, including versions of enzyme wash, enzyme and stone wash, and enzyme and bleach wash (Maycumber, 1998).

Innovation in Fabric Design. Fabric designers work with color, texture, and light to produce an infinite variety of effects. They manipulate the weave or knitting pattern, surface texture of fabrics, and the color or design printed on the fabric. Fashion seasons (and even eras) are characterized by fabric design. In some seasons, solid colors predominate; in others, texture is the fashion story. Some seasons feature mostly plaids and geometrics; in others, prints become important.

Printed fabrics are particularly prone to **boom and bust cycles**—seasons (or even years) when fashion uses few prints alternate with those in which prints are the fashion emphasis (Chirls, 1996a). Of all print categories, florals are the most consistently popular.

Innovation in Trims and Findings. **Trims** refer to all the items used to embellish and finish a garment. While some are functional—buttons, buckles, belts—they also serve a decorative purpose. Others are purely decorative such as ribbons, appliqué, beading, binding, and lace. Fashion trends in trim can be a very visible seasonal direction. In the mid-1990s, lace moved into streetwear and innovations included metallic laces, unusual geometric patterns, and edgy-looking laminated lace (Holch, 1996a).

Functional items such as elastic, interfacing, thread, and zippers are called **findings**. Even findings can become decorative and trendy at times—for example, when zippers in contrasting colors became a decorative focus in activewear.

Color trends impact trims and findings. If silver is "in," then trims and findings will feature this color look. Novelty looks in trim are volatile but, as with prints, floral motifs are always popular. Once sold in a basic color assortment, the trend today is toward custom color matching of trim to apparel ("Brimming," 1998).

Collect reports on runway shows for a particular season from either trade publications or fashion magazines. Glean all the news about fabric and trim from each article and compile a profile of the important fabric news for that season. Repeating the process over several seasons will reveal directional trends for fibers, fabrics, and trims.

Activity 5.2
Fabrics in the News

Trade Organizations and Fabric Councils

Producers of both natural and man-made fibers band together in **trade organizations** and fabric councils to promote use of their fiber. These groups provide:

- Forecasting information about new developments in fiber and fabric.
- Public relations support for their industry.
- Facilitated fabric sourcing by linking fabric manufacturers using their fiber with apparel manufacturers.

In addition, some trade organizations and fabric councils sponsor research and fabric development activities. One, the Mohair Council, the promotional arm for U.S. mohair growers, went even further when it began creating, sourcing, and selling sweaters under the Dove Creek label (Holch, 1998b).

One of the most active trade organizations is Cotton Incorporated, the research and marketing arm for U.S. growers of upland cotton and U.S. importers of cotton products representing more than 300 cotton mills, knitters, and converters. Over the past few decades consumers have favored cotton for its comfort factor. Cotton's market share in apparel and home furnishings (by fabric weight, excluding floor coverings) had risen to 59 percent in 1997. Once a fiber reaches this level of market share, growth slows. To reach and maintain that level requires a commitment to be competitive—a commitment that includes aggressively promoting the fiber and its uses and supporting research activities to produce new fabric developments ("Cotton Incorporated," 1998).

There is similar promotion and research support for other fibers. The U.S. arm of the International Wool Secretariat, the Wool Bureau, develops new looks for wool and new wool blend fabrics. Man-made fiber manufacturers perform the same functions for their trademarked brands and are members of trade organizations such as the Acrylic Council and the Polyester Council.

Contact the trade organizations or visit their Web sites to obtain lists, descriptions, and (if possible) samples of **developmental fabrics**—the newly developed innovations that provide special characteristics or properties. Brainstorm possible product categories for these fabrics. What traditional fabrics will these new developmental fabrics replace? What traditional fabrics will be enhanced by pairing them with these developmental fabrics? What consumer audience is likely to see the value-added benefits in these developmental fabrics and be willing to pay more for those benefits?

Activity 5.3
The Leading Edge
of Fibers and
Fabrics

RESEARCHING SEASONAL TRENDS

Fabric trends emerge before fashion trends because reviewing and selecting fabrics is one of the initial stages of product development (Figure 5.2). Trends based on textile development follow a diffusion of innovation pattern (see Chapter 2): they are introduced, adopted, and experimented with by more avant-garde designers, then move into more widespread usage, and, finally, cross boundaries into different product categories and different price points.

Fiber producers, yarn and fabric manufacturers, and industry trade organizations play an important role in the diffusion process by informing apparel executives about new innovations in fibers and fabrics. They disseminate information by:

- Participating in yarn and fabric trade shows.
- Presenting seasonal trend forecasts with themes tied to specific developments in fiber, yarn, fabric, or finishing.
- Providing designers and product developers with samples of fabrics for in-house presentations, swatching designs, and writing specifications.
- Providing samples to **fabric libraries** where designers and product developers come to research fabrications and source fabrics from many manufacturers.

These same companies and organizations work with designers and fabric sourcing specialists to research the potential for new fabrics, including development of **concept garments** (sample garments made to show the potential of the fabrics in apparel). The presentations and consulting activities are designed to help sell more fabric and fiber (Musselman, 1998).

Apparel executives research seasonal trends by attending fairs and trade shows, hearing presentations by companies or trade organizations, visiting fabric libraries, and reading reports in trade publications. Fabrics exhibited at fairs and trade shows are designed for the selling season one year ahead.

FIGURE 5.2

Attendees at fabric shows look through fabric swatches seeking emerging trends and new resources.

Walking one of these shows gives forecasters and apparel executives an overview of the direction fashion is heading in terms of color, texture, and pattern on fabric. The foremost show for trends is Première Vision, the largest and most comprehensive for Western Europe. Apparel executives who do not travel to the European shows attend smaller shows in New York or Los Angeles. Trend presentations by marketing managers of fiber and fabric manufacturers and industry trade organizations provide a more edited source of information on fabric development. Another way to trace fabric development is in trade publications because they report on the European and American fabric fairs and trade shows and many of the presentations by trade organizations and companies.

Jo Cohen, Associate Director, THE COTTONWORKS® Fabric Library, Cotton Incorporated

Jo Cohen (Fig. 5.3) travels throughout the world researching and presenting fabric trends at industry trade shows. In her position, Ms. Cohen is responsible for supervising an extensive research program that leads to forecasts for fabric, color, and silhouette trends for THE COTTONWORKS® Fabric Library, which has more than 8,000 designer, manufacturer, and retail clients worldwide. Based at Cotton Incorporated's U.S. marketing headquarters in New York, Ms. Cohen oversees fabric sourcing services on the Internet and resource centers showcasing fabrics from 300 mills, knitters, and converters at the company's domestic and international offices. Prior to joining Cotton Incorporated in 1990, Ms. Cohen worked in the corporate buying office for Macy's (now Federated) private label collections where she worked on men's wear lines.

Ms. Cohen thinks of THE COTTONWORKS® Fabric Library as a "one-stop shopping center for clients" because services combine seasonal forecasts and fabric sourcing. Designers and product developers come in looking for a specific fabric classification but often "end up looking through all the display panels, sometimes because they are cross-referencing sources, but often because they become interested in looking at the range available."

In researching the forecasts, Cotton Incorporated staffers "do an enormous amount of research around the world, traveling to Europe, the Far East, and Latin America" where the company has satellite offices. According to Ms. Cohen, this network of offices "aids in terms of feeding information into the company" on a continuing basis. The company covers all the usual fashion venues but is always on the lookout for "new areas in terms of cotton and cotton-rich fabrics like Monterey, Mexico—a very high-end city, quite different from Mexico City, that has become much more fashion forward." Still, Ms. Cohen expects to "always look to couture and high-end designers in Europe, America, and the Far East for cutting-edge fashion because they use a lot of beautiful cottons and cotton blends in their lines."

Cotton Incorporated's fabric development team at its Raleigh, North Carolina, Research Center, focuses on creating new fabric ideas for weaves, blends, finishes, and coatings for use in both apparel and home markets. Swatches of these fabrics are available in THE COTTONWORKS® Fabric Library. "If a client likes one of the fabrics, they can obtain a swatch with all the technical information, and then they can bring it to their mill for production." Or, because the mills get the swatches and technical information from the fabric development team, the new fabrics may appear as swatches from that mill on the display boards. Either way, the work of the fabric development team in Raleigh and the forecasters in New York complements each other. As Ms. Cohen puts it, "Research and development does not claim to be forecasters in terms of fashion colors and silhouettes, they look to us for that, but we look to them for fabric development and technical information."

Ms. Cohen views forecasting as providing leading-edge information so that "designers, manufacturers, and retailers can reflect and react to" the trends. "The youth market has been an enormous influence on fashion in general, in terms of performance fabrics, and in performance-type outfits such as heavier denim and extra knee pads for inline skating. An offbeat kind of look comes from the youth market—a look seen in the most recent designers' collections which are reflecting this sort of youthful casualness." In terms of trends, Ms. Cohen looks for "something that is important to the consumer, something that is going to be wearable for more than the elite." Such trends may be "relatively short or not depending on whether the consumer picks them up." She uses khaki as an example: "It is not new. It started off as a color, not even referencing a type of fabrication or construction. But today everyone says they need a pair of khakis. They have become staples but also a trend because they represent a lifestyle. Khaki today can be trousers, a suit, or a dress. That's the type of trend/lifestyle that is important now."

Because Ms. Cohen often presents the forecast for audiences, she has definite ideas on this part of her job. She feels "that it is very important to have a theme to tie things together like a story—there has to be a beginning, a middle, and an end. And, you need to end on a high note to capture you audience's attention." The theme may be based on the season, on a trend, or on a lifestyle. "Lifestyle may differ a bit from season to season but there is going to be a theme that has appropriate elements for each person—you need to cater to that." For Ms. Cohen comfort in front of an audience comes from "knowing the material backwards and forwards, inside and out." That way, if someone interrupts with a question, the presenter "can just answer, recap the information just covered, and continue."

Ms. Cohen's advice to people interested in forecasting is to consider one or more internships. "No matter how much a person learns in school, how much they desire to go into the forecasting business, they need hand-on experience working for different companies. The corporate setting is so different—just answering the telephone, working with colleagues that are older, learning from mentors. Internships in special events, forecasting, or PR can all lead to forecasting."

Source: A telephone interview with Jo Cohen, June 9, 1999.

Print Shows

Directional trends for prints are first evident at shows of original artwork from studios specializing in fabric design. The artwork can inspire prints, embroidery, cutout designs, or beading (Figure 5.3). Held about 15 months ahead of the selling season, these shows are shopped by retailers with private label businesses, designers, and converters. **Converters** specialize in sourcing base fabrics and using contractors to dye, print, and finish them for apparel manufacturers unable to meet large minimum orders or who require short lead times. Buyers at the print shows such as Imprints NY and Printsource represent many product categories from scarves to children's wear, dresses to

Jo Cohen, Associate Director, THE COTTONWORKS® Fabric Library, travels the world researching color trends that she shares with industry executives at trade shows and at the Cotton Incorporated headquarters in New York.

lingerie. The shows provide a place to look for trends in color and pattern and an opportunity to buy the original artwork for prints that will add a distinctive look to their company's collection.

Identifying trends in prints involves looking for similarities across a season's offerings. For the forecaster, these similarities are likely to occur in the color combination, style of the print, and finished effect. Trends are frequently expressed in terms of:

- Overall style—folkloric, botanical, or romantic.
- Interpretation—realistic, stylized, abstract, or geometric.
- Scale—small-scale versus large-scale motifs.
- Figure/ground relationships—patterns with a lot of background showing versus more crowded patterns.
- Reference to art styles such as Art Deco.
- Allusions to artistic effects such as watercolor, pointillism, or collage.
- Complexity—simple versus complicated looks.
- Cultural reference—Asian-inspired or African motifs.
- Historical reference—revival of prints from earlier decades.
- Color story—tropical, sherbet colors, or brights with neutral grounds.
- Motifs—golf, seashells, or animal prints.

Fabric Fairs and Trade Shows

Color and fabric trends are the first building blocks for a fashion trend at the twice-yearly fabric fairs and trade shows. Many innovations may be proposed at the yarn and fabric shows but only a few will coalesce into the trend story for a designer's collection or for the fashion season overall. Trade shows and fairs in Europe and the United States help to coordinate the efforts for the supply chain by concentrating fabrics from many different mills in one location to be viewed in a short time span. Attendees include:

- Executives in charge of fabric development and purchasing for big-volume apparel manufacturers who are looking for new sources of innovative fabrics.
- Designers looking for inspiration for their next collection.
- Forecasters looking for clues to the direction fashion will take in upcoming seasons.
- The fashion press.

Apparel executives use these shows to detect developing trends, to identify new resources, for **sampling** (ordering a minimum amount of fabric as a trial order), and to place production orders for fabrics.

At the fairs and trade shows, participants also attend seminars and presentations on developing trends in color, fabrics, and fashion presented by forecasters and consultants. Some shows include a display of trend colors and invite participants to clip samples to take with them.

Because costs in terms of time and money prohibit attending all shows and fairs, executives, designers, and forecasters must decide which are most productive. Some choose to attend one show that is the most comprehensive. Others visit one show for Spring and another for Fall collections (Mazzaraco, 1990). For exhibitors, the show is not only about writing orders on-site but also for attracting buyers to the company's showrooms to write production orders for large quantities.

Dates for the shows are always controversial with sponsors, exhibitors, and attendees. A show too far ahead of the season results in very little business and poor attendance. A show too late in the season risks the same result because apparel companies have already placed their fabric orders. A calendar listing show dates is published in trade publications. The calendar allows executives and forecasters to plan which shows to attend for timely trend information. Changes in traditional show dates are usually covered in the trade press. Such changes are likely to increase as the industry continues to adjust the product development schedule in response to the consumer preference for buying in season and the demands of doing business in a global marketplace.

Each show fills a niche in the fashion picture and targets a specific audience with directional information. Two other shifts in the way the industry works are having an impact on the shows:

- Companies are placing final orders at the last possible date when they feel more confident about style trends.
- Companies are moving away from two seasons a year to more continuous delivery of product to retailers.

These two trends may eventually lead to show sponsors moving from the traditional two shows per year to a more frequent show schedule.

Yarn Shows. Yarn shows provide an overview of the newest fiber blends and finishes designed to deliver improved performance and new textures for innovative styling.

Expofil, a European yarn fair based in Paris, is the earliest view of new products and trends for the selling season 15 months ahead. Held biannually in June for Fall/Winter and in December for Spring/Summer, this show draws exhibitors from Western Europe (primarily from France, Italy, Germany, and the United Kingdom) and includes fiber producers and yarn producers for knitting and weaving. The emphasis at the show is not on basic yarns but on products that push the envelope (Figure 5.4). Attendees receive a color, fabric, and trend forecast developed in consultation with other trade fairs, fiber producers, fiber promotion associations, and forecasting services such as Trends Union and PromoStyl, plus a 15-minute video presentation by a forward-thinking designer. The seminar program includes presentations on trends in the markets region by region, with emphasis on knitwear and detailed evaluation of consumer segments.

FIGURE 5.4

Visitors to Expofil look over knit swatches in the trend display area of the show.

Pitti Filati, a showcase for Italian spinners of natural yarns and blends, is held in July and January in Florence. A preview fabric show called PreTex gives attendees the chance to see a small collection of fabrics three months ahead of the main slate of fabric shows.

Yarn Fair International, a show organized by the National Knitwear and Sportswear Association, is held in August and February in New York City. The Yarn Fair International is particularly important for American buyers who do not attend Pitti Filati. Exhibitors represent knit design collections and they show sweater swatches with innovative styling, fiber content, and texture. Ready-to-wear designers buy the swatches as inspiration for their own collections (Holch & Chirls, 1998).

European Shows. The most comprehensive and influential show in Europe is Première Vision held in Paris. Fabric fairs in Italy are smaller and each show has its own identity and target audience.

Première Vision (translates as First Look) features over 500 exhibitors representing over 800 Western European weavers and knitters from Italy to Northern Ireland in categories from better to couture fabrics. Held twice yearly in March and October in Paris, Première Vision draws over 45,000 attendees from over 100 countries. Première Vision features a color forecast developed for each show and exhibitors send samples corresponding to those colors for exhibit during the show.

Ideabiella focuses on upscale men's wear fabrics in wool and other natural fibers including cashmere, silk, and mohair. Held in Cernobbio, Italy, exhibitors present Fall fabrics at the September show and Spring fabrics at the March show, one year ahead of the selling season.

Ideacomo features high-end textiles for women's wear in natural and synthetic fibers from the producers of the Como region of Italy, a textile-producing region that traces its roots back to the 1550s. The area is the biggest importer of raw silk, mostly from China, and the biggest client for Como's silks is the United States. Held in Cernobbio, Italy, the shows feature Fall fabrics in September and Spring fabrics in March.

Moda-In is a middle-market fair featuring bridge fabrics and accessories for men's and women's wear in both natural and synthetic fibers. Fabrics are shown in specialized areas: shirting, leisure and sportswear, patterned fabrics, and trimming. Each area features a trend section. The trend sections are combined for presentations following the fair in London, New York, Paris, and Frankfurt.

Pratoexpo is also a middle-market fair featuring bridge fabrics for men's and women's wear in both natural and synthetic fabrics. The show is held in Florence near Italy's largest textile region, Prato. The Prato region traces its history in textile production back to the 13th century and has traditionally been known for wool. Visitors today will see a shift toward innovative woolen blends. Like the other Italian shows, Fall fabrics are shown in September, Spring fabrics in March.

Interstoff Frankfurt, once a powerhouse show, had to refocus its appeal in 1999 by looking for other fabric fairs with synergies to boost attendance. The April 1999 show combined with Techtextil, a biannual fair for technical textiles and nonwovens, to appeal to makers of active sportswear. Held in October and April in Frankfurt, Germany, Interstoff plans other moves to augment its European exhibitor base.

Fabric Fairs in the United States. Fabric fairs in the United States provide an opportunity for forecasters and executives to see fabrics from European and American fabric manufacturers. Each show has its own focus and presents a different facet of the apparel business.

European Textile Selection Show (ETS) features fabric for men's and women's wear in New York about ten days after the close of Première Vision in Paris. Exhibitors come primarily from five countries—Italy, France, Spain, Portugal, and Austria. Held in March and October, the ETS Show features fabrics ranging from top-of-the-range couture fabrics to sportswear, activewear, shirtings, silky fabrics, laces, and embroideries. Because of the timing of the show, most manufacturers have already selected fabrics for their lines but the show offers the opportunity to fill in gaps or add special fabrics.

International Fashion Fabric Exhibition (IFFE) features over 600 exhibitors in fabric, trim, computer-aided design/computer-aided manufacturing (CAD/CAM), and financial services and hosts over 12,000 attendees. Held in October and April in New York, IFFE includes mills at a variety of price points and fabrics from basics to novelty fabrics. The show has become a key exhibit for CAD and CAM systems and services. The show allows manufacturers specializing in supplying stores with the latest trendy merchandise to locate domestic sourcing so they can have the piece goods within weeks and merchandise into the stores in one or two months.

Los Angeles International Textile Show features over 300 exhibitors representing 600 lines in fabrics, trims, and findings and attracts about 6,000 attendees. Held biannually in April and October, the show comes after Première Vision and other fabric fairs so many large-volume manufactures have already made their selections. Still, California-based companies such as Levi-Strauss, Mossimo, and Karen Kane attend the show along with smaller manufacturers who work closer to the selling season. Because California has long been know for creativity and as an origin point for trends, forecasters and East Coast textile and apparel executives make this show a destination.

Activity 5.4 Backcast Trend Movement	Collect trade press reports on the print, yarn, and fabric fairs for a given season. Compare trend information to the collections—designer, bridge, and other categories—from the corresponding season. Which trends identified in the early shows can be identified in the collections? Which failed to materialize? Does coverage of the collections provide clues as to why some trends succeeded and others did not?

Presentations

Mills manufacturing couture fabrics show their fabric collections to designers like Vera Wang or Richard Tyler in the designer's showroom or studio (Holch, 1998a). At lower price points, design executives attend "show and tell" presentations structured around trend stories (Figure 5.5). Each trend story projects a look, mood, and lifestyle across a group of fabrics and illustrates the connection with photos from European runways, sample garments, and concept fabrics. Trend stories often include references to historical or ethnic sources of inspiration. The presentations may concentrate solely on fabric developments or merge fabric developments with color, fashion, and print forecasts. Presentations are sponsored by:

- Fiber producers such as DuPont, Solutia (a company spin-off of Monsanto), Hoechst Celanese, and Wellman.
- Fabric manufacturers.
- Industry trade associations—Cotton Incorporated, the Wool Bureau, or the National Knitwear & Sportswear Association.
- Forecasting services.

European forecasting services such as Trends Union and PromoStyl often bring the same presentations that they developed for European fabric fairs to New York a few weeks later. No matter the sponsor, the presentations are open to the trade only, and usually require an invitation to attend.

FIGURE 5.5

Seasonal innovations are presented to design and product development executives organized around the themes that characterize the season.

Collect reports on trend stories presented by fiber producers, fabric manufacturers, trade organizations, and forecasting services for a given season using trade publications and Web sites. The trend stories will have different names but there will be correspondence between the various forecasts. Identify the distinctive themes presented for this season. Relate these themes to product categories, consumer segments, and price points.

Fabric Libraries

Fabric libraries are collections of fabric swatches and trim samples representing the scope available for a specific upcoming season. The fabrics are usually arranged on large display boards according to styling and intended end use (tops, bottoms, shirting, etc.). Each sample is referenced with detailed information on fiber content, weight, color range, and fabric manufacturer. Some fabric libraries are maintained by trade organizations and represent the current fabrics from many mills and converters. Because swatches are updated seasonally, these fabric libraries are helpful when apparel design teams are looking for inspiration or for locating new fabric sources.

Some design consultants, museums, fashion schools, and designers maintain fabric libraries of historical fabrics, embroideries, and trims. Because mills often collect swatches of their fabrics for a given season on a card, poster, or in a book, these collections become a record of fashion trends for that time. These swatch collections are now avidly collected because of their value in charting style changes and because they represent a resource for today's designers seeking inspiration.

Key Terms and Concepts

Blend	Findings	Piece Dyeing
Boom And Bust Cycles	Garment Dyeing	Sampling
Brand Name	Generic Name	Solution Dyeing
Concept Garments	Hand	Staple Length
Converters	Knitting	Supply Chain
Cross Dyeing	Man-Made Fibers	Technical Fabrics
Developmental Fabrics	Manufactured Fibers	Texture
Drape	Microfibers	Trade Organizations
Fabric Finishing	Natural Fibers	Trims
Fabric Libraries	Novelty Fabrics	Weaving
Filament	Performance Fabrics	

Case Revisited: Textile Trend Watch

Kim plans to expand her textile design firm by providing an electronic newsletter reporting on design directions emerging in Europe and projecting them for the U.S. market. Kim faces many challenges to becoming a new source for forecasting information. Information is not free—it costs time, money, and effort to gather. Kim already attends some of the fabric fairs and presentations and subscribes to trade publications. Other information can be gathered through subscriptions to trade publications and online. Discuss the potential for Kim's idea as a way to review and summa-rize this chapter. The following questions provide a starting point for the discussion.

Sources of forecasting information: What kinds of information on textile de-velopment are available? How often should her newsletter be updated? Kim regularly attends European trade shows but how will she gather information that will help her project her findings for the U.S. market? What kind of arti-cles should the newsletter include?

Target audience (potential readers for the newsletter): What information will clients in the United States find useful and intriguing? Should Kim focus on particular product categories, on price points, or be more comprehensive in her reporting?

Cost/benefit analysis: Which trade shows are absolutely key for Kim's new forecasting business? What information can be gathered online or through trade publications? What would Kim's yearly travel schedule and budget (air-fares, lodging, and other expenses) be to gather the kind of information she needs for the newsletter? To cover these expenses, approximately how many clients will she need and how much will she charge for a subscription to her newsletter? (Hint: Costs for gathering the forecasting information can be re-couped either by charging a high subscription rate to a few clients or lower subscription rates to a wider audience.) Consider both covering costs and making a profit on the newsletter.

Additional Forecasting Activities

Enhancing Everyday Performance. Convene a panel of merchandisers repre-senting the stores specializing in active and adventure sports apparel and equipment. Interview them regarding trends in technical and performance fabrics. What sports and activities seem to be gaining in popularity? What features do consumers most request? What feedback do they hear from con-sumers on the technical and performance fabrics? What trends do they see in the development of apparel for this target audience?

Checking Out a Fabric Library. Contact a fiber, yarn, fabric, or apparel manufacturer in your area and ask if they have a fabric library or an archive of their products over the past few years. Request the opportunity to study this collection to discover the directional trends in this product category.

Going to a Fabric Fair Online. Use search engines on the Web to locate fabric fairs and resources in countries other than those in Western Europe and the United States. Asia, India, and South and Central America are all potential sites for innovation in textile development.

Resource Pointers

Check Web sites for fabric and color forecasts and trade show schedules:

- Fabric and Textile Organizations—www.handilinks.com
- Cotton Incorporated—www.cottoninc.com
- Made in Italy Online—www.made-in-italy.com
- Première Vision—www.premierevision.fr
- Expofil—www.expofil.com/trends
- International Fashion Fabric Exhibition (IFFE)—www.fabricshow.com
- Textile Association of Los Angeles—www.textileassociation.org
- Textile Web—www.textileweb.com

Chapter 6

THE LOOK: DESIGN CONCEPTS AND STYLE DIRECTIONS

"The couturier does not create fashion, he interprets it."
—Yves Saint Laurent

Objectives

- Recognize the origin points of attributes that shape today's information environment.

- Examine the concept of style tribes as an organizing principle.

- Appreciate the skills and abilities required of forecasters.

- Understand the fashion calendar and the interactions that create directional information.

- Develop skills in identifying trends, analyzing visual and symbolic core concepts, and synthesizing directional information for clients.

- Develop skills in researching trends.

CASE: FROM CATWALK TO MAIN STREET

Karla began her career in retailing where her flair for fashion led to a position as fashion director for a 16-store chain in the midwestern United States. The stores target young women with trendy, fashion-forward apparel presented in a lifestyle concept that covers categories from prom dresses to casual, weekend clothes. As Fashion Director, Karla's function is to translate the season's fashion story into one specifically targeted to her store's customers, location, and price points.

Karla begins by gathering information about trends originating on the runways, showrooms, and streets. She attends seasonal shows at the Apparel Mart in her part of the country, always looking for new resources to set her stores apart from others in the same market. She also attends trade shows in New York and Los Angeles and researches fashion trends in Europe one or two times each year. From these activities and sources, Karla develops a seasonal fashion story for the target market served by the chain. She synthesizes all the emerging trends into an overall fashion story, seasonal theme, and merchandising direction for the stores. She communicates her findings to the buyers and other executives in the corporate offices in a seminar using slides of runway shows, store windows, and street fashion. The fashion story is also available to the chain's executives on the company's Intranet—a proprietary network using Internet technology. She repeats the seminars for sales associates at each store in the chain at the beginning of the new season just as the new merchandise begins to arrive in the stores.

Karla's role expanded when the chain decided to launch a private-label line. The goal was to make the selling floor distinctive with fashion products not available at any other stores. The chain contracted with a product development company that would handle all the design and production of the products. Karla became the fashion link between the two companies. Now on her trips in the United States and Europe, she looks for fashion ideas that can be adapted for the private-label line.

This chapter covers the research and decision-making process Karla uses in developing the fashion story and customizing it for her chain.

TREND MULTIPLICATION

In his book *The Empire of Fashion*, Lipovetsky (1994) identified three modern eras in fashion. The first began in the 1860s when the first couturier, Charles Frederick Worth, set up a fashion house in Paris, began showing designs prepared in advance, changed styles frequently, and employed models to show the clothes to clients. The second began in the 1960s with the ready-to-wear revolution. While the earlier system continued, mass production and mass media reconfigured the structure. With the rise of mass production and mass media, being "in fashion" became possible and desirable for more and more people. The third era, beginning in the late 1980s, was characterized by:

- Extreme diversity from one designer to another.
- The proliferation in the number of acceptable looks.
- Increased autonomy among consumers.

- A feminist movement that promoted functional, less restrictive, and more comfortable apparel.
- The disappearance of clear-cut differences between what was outdated and in fashion.

The dating of the three eras is arbitrary. The system in each era survived into the succeeding era and the seeds of the new era already existed in the old. Still, Lipovetsky's divisions are a convenient way to view change. Organizing observations into a timeline and characterizing each segment allows the observer to see the shape of change, and the antecedents and consequences of change become more apparent.

The First Era of Modern Fashion

During the first hundred years of modern fashion (from the 1860s to the 1960s), Paris was known as the center of innovation and set the annual trends followed by the rest of the world. Organized fashion shows on fixed dates began after World War I, an innovation that coincided with France's need for fashion as an export and the influx of professional buyers from the United States and other countries in Europe. The professional buyers, through a fee arrangement with the designers, acquired models for manufacturing at lower prices in their own countries.

The absolute dictatorship of fashion by Paris was undermined in the 1920s. Early in the decade Chanel popularized "the poor look" of simple dresses, jersey suits, sweaters, cloche hats, and pants. Patou introduced the sportswear approach to fashion which he described as follows: "I have aimed at making [my clothes] pleasant to the eye and allowing absolute liberty of movement." These looks replaced the elaborate fashions and constricting stays that kept women sedentary with a new aesthetic ideal for the modern woman—slim, active, athletic. Chanel's "poor look" and Patou's sportswear were also much easier to imitate, thereby opening up fashionability to more consumers.

Daytime dress became more comfortable and functional, but evening fashion continued to be the epitome of seductive femininity. This fracturing of looks played out in ever more varied forms. A woman could choose to be a sexy woman, a "schoolgirl" in black dress with white collar and cuffs, a professional woman in a tailored suit, or a sporty woman in trousers and a sweater set. After the 1920s, the unity of a single fashion message disappeared and disparate and sometimes antagonistic looks shared the stage. Fashion gained transformative power as it became possible to manipulate appearance to express self, personality, and individuality—to change the way a woman saw herself and how other people saw her. Instead of issuing strict injunctions, fashion began to offer a diversified set of options inviting the consumer to choose.

<table>
<tr><td>

Activity 6.1
Business
Breakthroughs
and Classic
Designers

</td><td>

Investigate the design and marketing of fashion by influential designers like Paul Poiret, Fortuny, Patou, Chanel, and Schiaparelli to discover practices that were revolutionary in their time but are now commonplace ways of doing business. What revolutionary ways of doing business today will become accepted practice in the future?

</td></tr>
</table>

The Second Era of Modern Fashion

The ready-to-wear revolution coincided with a tilt toward youthfulness and novelty as ideals. A two-tiered fashion system emerged with couture focused on masterpieces of execution and ready-to-wear focused on improving manufacturing technology and trend-driven merchandising. Pierre Cardin showed a ready-to-wear line at the department store Preintemps in 1959, opened the first ready-to-wear department in 1963, and was the first to sign licensing agreements with ready-to-wear manufacturers. In 1966, Yves Saint Laurent created the first ready-to-wear line conceived on its own terms and not as an adaptation of haute couture. Emerging new designers like Mary Quant focused primarily on ready-to-wear. During this second era, designers became brand names for a constellation of products from apparel to fragrance, accessories to home decor.

The emergence of youth as an ideal brought with it new emphasis on the values of individual expression, spontaneity, and the humor of stylistic collages and juxtapositions. Good taste and the distinctions of class were identified with the "old" order. The cult of youth became intrinsically linked with the cult of the body. Instead of following the latest fashion dictates closely, the consumer became more autonomous. "In" was not defined by aspirations for status or social position but by being "in the know." Clothes could be casual as long as they conveyed a youthful, liberated, and individualized image.

<table>
<tr><td>

Activity 6.2
Good Taste/Bad
Taste

</td><td>

Go back to original sources published during the Youthquake in the mid-1960s—books of advice on how to dress, magazine articles, and newspaper articles. A debate raged between the adults of the era and young people. Read about what was considered "good" and "bad" taste at the time. Parallel this earlier debate with criticism of fashion looks from today's subcultural groups.

</td></tr>
</table>

The Third Era of Modern Fashion

The defining characteristics of the third era of modern fashion are diversity in acceptable looks and a blurring of the line between what is "in" and "out" of fashion. Today, all styles are legitimate—pared down modernism and sexy vamp looks, short and long, tight and loose, "down-and-out" distressed fabrics and refined chic, sneakers and stilettos. During the first two eras of modern fashion, following trends as defined by designers, the press, and merchants was important in presenting an appropriate image to the world. In the third era of modern fashion, a broad range of alternative looks became acceptable and people became less inclined to define appropriate in any definite terms.

The seeds of the current era of fashion can be seen in the 1920s when fashion began to fracture into multiple looks and in the 1960s when individualism and consumer autonomy encouraged a proliferation of fashion alternatives. Gone were the days of unitary trends passed from haute couture to the rest of the world. Instead the fashion world fragmented into multiple trends from multiple centers of creation and popularized by mass media. During the two earlier eras of modern fashion, the distinction between "in" and "out" of fashion was preserved. The loss of this distinction can be seen as a shift between fashion—the following of an accepted norm that fluctuates over time—and style—the pursuit of a personal, individualistic look outside of time-based oscillations (Polhemus, 1996).

The growing autonomy of the consumer and the rejection of fashions touted by designers and the press mean that today, few new styles achieve quick adoption. The pressure for instant assimilation has disappeared. For consumers the concepts of being "trendy" (i.e., following trends) and being a fashion victim fused (Polhemus, 1996). The wish to avoid both designations has driven consumers toward individualized selection and mixing of influences. The result of these forces is that while the pace of fashion introduction and the translation of styles into all price points has speeded up, the speed of adoption has slowed down (Lipovetsky, 1994). Instead of following fashion dictates and trends, consumers filter from the many options those that fit their individual aesthetic. Ironic mixtures of styles and influences define today's fashion. There is no longer a fashion, there are fashions.

Style Tribes. Substituting for the distinction between "in" and "out" in the third era of modern fashion is the distinction of "belonging to" a group, a cluster of like-minded and like-living people. Adopting an appearance style is a marker of membership in a **style tribe** (Polhemus, 1996). Such groups find a defining style in the look of a particular fashion era or evolve a look that reflects their own interests and tastes (Figure 6.1). Obvious historical examples of style tribes are hippies of the 1970s who dressed to convey their unmateri-

The Goth look began among teens as a marker if membership in a style tribe but it was picked up by designers and manufacturers and shown at trade shows as a fashion-forward trend.

alistic value system (Wintour, 1998b). Although the appearance style of this group has blurred into a stereotype, there were actually separate style tribes within the hippie look, including the flower child, African-influenced styles, groups with a political agenda, and others.

A more current example of style tribes is the popularity of wearing logo emblazoned clothing identifying a person as an "RL," "CK," or "DKNY" kind of person. Other current examples of style tribes can be found in the subcultural groups that give rise to street fashion, or the style tribes and sub-tribes in a U.S. high school who signal who they are and who their friends are by wearing a kind of cultural uniform, a uniform that identifies them as Goths, Rebels, Skateboarders, or Preps (Sullivan, 1998).

But the phenomenon is not confined to subcultural groups. A version of the same phenomenon is at work when high school and college students can identify different social clusters on campus by cues in what they wear. People in technological or creative fields often evolve a "uniform" look, even down to the preferred brand names for each item. Occupational clusters, groups sharing a special interest from stock car racing to birdwatching, cliques with the same taste in fashion and décor—all of these and many more are style tribes.

Designers act as style tribe leaders when they present a signature style that appeals to consumers who share that aesthetic and not to others. A casual fashion observer can tell the difference between an Armani and a Gucci ensemble. Even when the visual style of a designer is definite and defined, that designer is likely to pursue style variations within a collection. Sometimes a consumer completely identifies with one designer over all others. If a woman identifies with more than one designer, she is likely to partition her patronage by lifestyle—for example, Armani for daywear, Gucci for club wear.

Designers such as Calvin Klein, Donna Karan, Nicole Miller, and others have a signature style. Different facets of that style are presented in different brand tiers within the designer's company. The overall signature or one of the facets appeals to a particular style tribe. Other designers such as Anna Sui compete with subcultural groups in their zeal to freely mix ethnic and technology-inspired garb. Sui's term for her approach is "urban tribalism"—echoing the idea of style tribes (White, 1997).

Conduct visual research on the style tribes on your campus or in your town. Take candid snapshots of groups of people on the street. How many style tribes can you identify? Do not settle for a superficial reading of the cues. Look for differences in the fine details of footwear, logos, fabrications, straps, and toggles.	*Activity 6.3 Style Tribes on Campus*

The Role of the Forecaster. The proliferation of trends in this third era of modern fashion creates a more cluttered information environment for today's fashion forecaster. Because consumers' decisions are less restricted by social rules, buying behavior is more difficult to predict. In this third era of modern fashion, a "triple logic" is in effect (Lipovetsky, 1994):

- The logic of aesthetics.
- The logic of industrial clothing manufacturing.
- The logic of consumers acting on individual taste.

It is the fashion forecaster's job to sort out the workings of this triple logic. The forecaster appreciates and understands the aesthetics demonstrated in designers' collections. While appreciating the art, the forecaster edits away the theatrical trappings to discover the wearable clothes underneath. Wearable relates both to the industrial logic of being reproduced at lower price points and satisfying the needs of consumers' lifestyles. Clothes that are wearable for one consumer are impossible for another. The forecaster's understanding of aesthetics, manufacturing, and wearable from the consumer's point of view leads to an actionable forecast.

Fashion forecasting requires three competencies:

- Proficiency in researching fashion developments using the tools of environmental scanning.
- The ability to identify the visual and symbolic core concepts within and across collections.
- The expertise to analyze the match between fashion developments and the marketplace and to synthesize an actionable forecast for a client.

Information is gathered in the research phase from many sources, among them, attending fashion shows and trade events and gleaning fashion news from print, broadcasting, and online channels. These sources are sifted for core concepts or trends. Trends can be defined as similarities across information sources. Next, trends are analyzed to determine the potential match with consumer profiles. The consumer profile must go beyond demographics (e.g., age, gender, income level, occupational title) to the subtle differences in personal philosophy as expressed in lifestyle, group membership, preferences, and taste (Polhemus, 1996). Finally, the elements are assembled into an actionable forecast by product category, price point, and retail concept.

**Activity 6.4
Editing the
Avant-Garde**

Using television shows that report on fashion, videotape two or three of the most avant-garde collections from couture and ready-to-wear (see the Resource Pointers at the end of this chapter for suggestions). Watch them several times, mentally stripping away the theatrical trappings. Are there wearable clothes underneath? What styles from these avant-garde collections could meet the "industrial logic" of being reproduced at lower price points for consumers? What types of consumers are likely to relate to the aesthetics of these fashion looks?

THE FASHION MAP

As fashion insiders, forecasters have a mental map of the marketplace—the locations where innovations are likely to be glimpsed early, the supply chain of the textile/apparel industry, and the retail conduit to consumers. Fashion insiders also have another mental map—the map of seasons and shows. When consumers shop for winter coats or summer swimsuits, fashion insiders are seasons ahead in their thinking. Forecasters use these mental maps to organize their observation of directional information. Because innovations rarely apply to the entire marketplace, information must be tagged for the appropriate price point, category, and classification. In this way, forecasters turn random bits of data into useful information for decision support.

Fashion Geography

Fashion leadership in no longer exclusively a French commodity. Today, the fashion world is global with design centers in many countries. However, some design centers have special cachet. They are made distinctive by their design heritage and by the aesthetic that they represent (Hastreiter, 1997).

- **French Luxe**

In the first half of the 20th century, fashion spoke only French. The first years of the century, *la Belle Époque,* represents the high water mark for class-conscious extravagance with ribbons, laces, flowers, feathers, and jewels. This focus on artistry and workmanship has continued as a tradition of French fashion. Today many non-French designers choose to show in Paris. With the Chambre Syndicale, French fashion's governing board, and support from the French government, designers made Paris the fashion capital for luxury.

- **American Sportswear**

While the Nazis occupied Paris during World War II, American fashion came into its own as the center of sportswear design (Brubach, 1998; Tapert, 1998). Sportswear presented an alternative tradition by substituting practicality, casual comfort, and dash for virtuoso cut, custom fabrics, and embellishment. French fashion traces its roots to haute couture, one-of-a-kind showpieces made by skilled dressmakers for a particular client. American sportswear has its roots in mass-produced clothes like jeans and off-the-peg clothes from the department store. Whereas French couture focused on artistry, American sportswear focused on the changing lifestyles of women. Claire McCardell, an American designer of the 1940s, is credited with offering women a more casual, active, and less constricted view of what a modern woman should wear. Today, American sportswear is a paradigm—luxurious without being ostentatious, styled for women who want clothes that make sense. This paradigm has spread around the world as casual, sporty, unconstructed separates. American sportswear designers now head several influential fashion houses in Paris and Italy.

- **British Edge**

The high point for British influence on fashion came in the 1960s when young people exploded the repressive English class system bent on self-expression in music and clothing. This was the first wave of street fashion to make its way into mainstream fashion. Mods and Carnaby Street, Mary Quant and Biba (a boutique showcase for young fashion) still echo in today's fashion world. British fashion tends to take center stage when the accent is on youthful fashion and translation of street fashion.

- **Italian Ease**

The tradition of fine Italian fabrics transmuted into the high quality luxury of the 1970s. Working from a base of world class textiles and manufacturing, designers such as Giorgio Armani, Gianni Versace, and Missoni moved to center stage. The Italian look has always been a blend between quality and design—softer, more textured, and less hard-edged than French fashion.

• Japanese Cut

The radical modernism of the Japanese designers such as Issay Miyake, Rei Kawakubo, and Yohji Yamamoto emerged in the 1980s offering a sculptural alternative to the heavy French structures and the softer Italian styles. The Japanese designers relied on high-tech fabrics and finishes and unusual cuts and wrapping effects. Their innovations sparked the movement toward deconstruction and minimalism that continued to influence fashion in the 1990s.

• Belgian Individuality

Ann Demeulemeester, Martin Margiela, Dries Van Noten, and, more recently, Veronique Branquinho all trace their fashion roots to Antwerp. The first of the Belgian designers came to prominence in the 1980s. Their work is defined by structure and tailoring in a deconstructivist mode—a look that became very influential in the 1990s.

While some of the traditional roots of fashion are still visible in the collections shown in Paris, London, Milan, and New York, the design world is much more complex these days (Foley, 1998). English designers Galliano, McQueen, and McCartney are based in Paris at the head of venerable fashion houses of Dior, Givenchy, and Chloé. An American designer, Tom Ford, revived the Italian house of Gucci. American designers heading Paris houses include Oscar de la Renta (Lanvin couture), Marc Jacobs (Louis Vuitton), and Michael Kors (Céline). With new designers emerging, designers changing houses, and designers creating their own lines plus lines for other houses, the forecaster must revise the fashion map every season.

Activity 6.5
Fashion Capitals

Videotape segments on each of the fashion capitals—Paris, Milan, London, and New York—from coverage on television (see Resource Pointers). Does each fashion capital have its own style niche? What designers epitomize each fashion capital? Which designers are outside the tradition of each fashion capital? What are the aesthetic commonalities between designers of the same nationality—American, French, Italian, British, Belgian, German, and Japanese? What cultural factors contribute to these commonalities?

Fashion Weeks. **Fashion weeks** consist of fashion shows in each of the four fashion capitals—New York, London, Milan, and Paris. If a magazine editor, fashion director, or forecaster set out to cover the collections in a single season, he or she would see over 200 shows in four cities—some for commercial lines that insiders think should be seen in the showroom, not on the catwalk (Tilberis, 1998). The difficult and fascinating job of covering the shows means assessing these shows and identifying trends emerging from the multitude of images (Figure 6.2).

FIGURE 6.2

*Covering fashion
weeks means seeing
over 200 shows in
the four fashion capi-
tals and identifying
trends emerging from
the multitude of im-
ages. Bernard Arnault,
chief executive of
LVMH (Moët-
Hennessey-Louis
Vuitton SA) in atten-
dance at a European
event.*

In addition to the designers who stage runway shows, other designers participate in trade shows or showroom events. Satellite trade shows for accessories are set to precede, coincide, or follow each fashion week. Paris features
a particularly crowded schedule of showings and trade shows. Each trade
show in each city fills a niche and targets specific retailers. For example, the
Paris trade show, Atmosphère, features designers who are fashion forward
and directional and targets retailers with smaller fashion boutiques. For designers, showing in this trade show is often a stepping stone to international
import markets. Merchants and journalists must find time in a hectic schedule
of runway shows to also cover the trade shows.

When they are not covering runway shows or trade shows, attendees shop
for trends:

- In designer's boutiques, department stores, and international chains.
- In hip neighborhoods with a lively street scene—cafés, clubs, and small
  shops (Figure 6.3).
- In shops known for emerging young designers and thrift store finds.

This exhausting round of 18-hour days takes its toll on attendees. Most report
going into training in preparation for this biannual burst of focused action.

The Schedule. Traditionally, the designer ready-to-wear collections started
each season with London, then Milan, Paris, and, finally, New York. The
Milan and Paris shows came in October for Spring looks and March for
Fall/Winter looks. New York designers did not show until early November

FIGURE 6.3

Small market streets are transformed into hip promenades when designer shops, boutiques, cafés, and bars move into their Paris neighborhood.

(Spring/Summer) and early April (Fall/Winter). This arrangement tended to support the perception that trends started in Europe and that American designers were less creative "stylists" following rather than creating trends. The advantage to this calendar was that it gave American designers extra weeks to harmonize their collections with the looks that were drawing raves at the earlier shows. The disadvantage was that journalists and merchants had seen all the season's trends before viewing the New York shows ("Calvin," 1998).

In 1998, the fashion calendar was flipped around when a breakaway group—Helmut Lang, Calvin Klein, Donna Karan, and a few other designers—shifted their runway dates in New York to show ahead of Europe. The rest of the New York designers showed in the usual time slot after the European shows, making the schedule much longer than usual. While moving the shows was controversial, some journalists and merchants supported the idea. For merchants, writing orders at the earlier dates meant earlier deliveries to stores.

A consensus developed that the Fall 1999 shows would be moved to February for all American designers. And, in another groundbreaking decision, both men's wear and women's wear shows were presented. With more designers showing both a men's wear and a women's wear line and more interaction between the two categories in terms of trends, the change made for a focused message.

For merchants and journalists, the new dates created scheduling dilemmas. However, the benefits of the new schedule—the chance for American designers to boost New York's status as a fashion capital and capture retail dollars first—proved compelling.

One outcome of the changes in the traditional schedule was a closer coordination between organizers in Paris and Milan. Paris also made changes in the format for their shows to allow more designers—especially new French designers—to present their lines. The schedule for shows in the fashion capitals will continue to be a controversial issue because the dates must accommodate the requirements of designers, who need time to develop their lines; the merchants, who must place orders; and the press, who must photograph and present the fashion news to the public. The fallout from decisions about timing reverberates down the supply chain to manufacturers of fibers, fabrics, trims, and findings.

Collections on the Runway

Designer Ready-to-Wear. While not as costly as couture ($1,500 to $5,000 for a jacket), **designer ready-to-wear** is still expensive, luxurious, and beautifully executed (Figure 6.4). Whereas a couture outfit may be made only once or, at most, a few times, designer ready-to-wear is reproduced in the hundreds or thousands. Two times a year, ready-to-wear designers show their collections to celebrity clients, merchants from major stores, and the press in New York, Paris, Milan, and London. The designers walk a fine line between playing it safe and getting little press coverage and going over the top with offbeat looks that fail in the stores. Designers in this category get lots of press coverage and their successes and failures are recorded on the scorecard kept by the press.

Some collections leap forward into the fashion future sending sci-fi looks or suits suitable for space travel down the runway. Others collections work and re-work a concept season after season or refine favorite themes over and over. Trends reported in the press often begin here when editors notice underlying similarities across designers' collections, when a designer presents an outstanding collection with a unifying theme, or when an item stars in many shows and becomes newsworthy (e.g., transparent fabrics, slip dresses, or floor-sweeping skirts).

Press reports often identify a "must-have" item or detail that emerged from the seasonal shows. These elements will quickly trickle down to lines at lower price points. Designers often complain that before they can manufacture their

September 4-7, 1998
Spring/Summer Collections 99, Paris expo, Porte de Versailles. Paris.

In Paris, fashion is capital

Prêt à Porter Paris is the only major international event for women's ready-to-wear and fashion accessories.
Each season, over 900 fashion houses meet 45,000 buyers from across the globe.
1,400 journalists cover the event in the general and trade press.
Prêt à Porter Paris is also the best way to preview the season's main styles and latest trends.
In order to set off to their advantage the different brands and collections and help buyers make their choices, Prêt à Porter Paris has created 15 different sectors of fashion.

lines, companies at lower price points have already knocked off their innovations. When Gucci's creative director Tom Ford destroyed jeans at $3,800 a pair to create a "bohemian look," denim companies followed his lead. Consumer response was strong. According to one retailer: "As soon as it hit the magazines, kids saw it, and bought the junior and contemporary knockoffs" (Socha & Lee, 1999).

Couture. Haute couture shows after designer ready-to-wear for the same selling season—January for Spring and July for Fall/Winter collections. Because haute **couture** is made-to-order for specific clients, it does not require the lead-time for manufacturing that ready-to-wear clothes do.

Haute couture has been called irrelevant because with prices beginning at $12,000, the number of clients has dwindled to an estimated 2,000 women worldwide. The number of couture houses dwindled from 37 to 19 when designer ready-to-wear exploded in 1967. Industry insiders know that ready-to-wear is where the money is made on fashion. Interest in couture revived in the mid-1990s with the arrival from London of John Galliano at Dior and Alexander McQueen at Givenchy. At about the same time a new concept called "demi-couture" was introduced. **Demi-couture** takes many forms, but the idea is to mix ready-to-wear and made-to-order pieces (Menkes, 1996).

In one version, Donnatella Versace selected 15 looks from her couture collection and produced two models of each to be sold through the company's ready-to-wear boutiques. In another version, couture skills and embellishment are lavished on a jacket, but it is paired with a machine-made skirt from the designer's ready-to-wear collection. In a third version, designers known for their ready-to-wear collections, such as Prada, add made-to-measure clothes but without the numerous fittings required by traditional couture. In these ways, the difference between couture and the most expensive ready-to-wear are narrowing (Raper, 1998).

Yet the fashion world still goes to Paris because, for designers, Paris couture is the Fashion Olympics with the highest standards of competition (Tilberis, 1995). Most observers do not understand the rules and technicalities of the haute couture. There are two competitive arenas—the fantasy of the runway epitomized by Galliano at Dior and McQueen at Givenchy, and the invisible but essential superb execution of tailoring and dressmaking, intricate cuts, and embellishment with beading and embroidery. There is no comparable level of accomplishment in American fashion, but American customers are among the loyal clients of couture.

The couture loses money, but owners feel that costs are justified given the promotional boost the attention brings to fragrance, licensed lines, and ready-to-wear. Because it can be experimental, couture is directional for fashion themes, references to designers and eras of the fashion past, ethnic influences, silhouettes, fabrics, and colors. Ideas introduced in couture may show up later in ready-to-wear collections.

Using trade publications and fashion magazines, examine the couture season one, three, and five years ago. Compare these seasons with today's trends in designer ready-to-wear and bridge. How is the inspiration and experimentation in couture translated into later collections?	*Activity 6.6 Couture in Review*

Fashion Off the Runway

Showrooms. When a forecaster, magazine editor, or retail buyer talks about scouting the market, he or she often means visiting the **showrooms** of designers, manufacturers, and entrepreneurs in the Fashion Center (also known as the Garment District) of New York City (Figure 6.5). Here is the highest concentration and greatest diversification of apparel resources. Open on weekdays throughout the year, the Fashion Center allows a fashion professional to discover new trends and new resources. Not only a district for seeing apparel lines, the businesses run the gamut from agents for European fabric houses to suppliers for trimmings, belts, buttons, and other findings.

FIGURE 6.5

For forecasters, scouting the market means visiting the showrooms of designers and manufacturers in the Fashion Center (also known as the Garment District) of New York City.

Boutiques. Emerging designers newly graduated from school or from apprenticeship as an assistant to a well-known designer need a retail showcase. They find it by opening small boutiques in fashion's capital cities. These shops are usually found in arty, edgy, fashion-forward enclaves clustered with the boutiques of other designers, vintage apparel stores, bars, and restaurants. One example is a shop called Shop in London's Soho. The owners launched a line of tops and a jewelry line that has found favor with U.S. specialty store buyers. As one put it: "When I'm in London, I always go to Shop [because] it's very of-the-moment" (Fallon, 1998).

New designers also find a showcase in multibrand specialty stores, with a reputation for discovering design talent. In the specialty stores, the fashion is often mixed with an in-store café, gallery space for art, objects, fashion, and accessories in a unique retail concept (Raper & Weisman, 1998). One such shop in Paris is Colette on the chic Rue St. Honoré (Figure 6.6). Here the owner presents a carefully edited selection of miniature phones, toys, beauty products, jewelry and accessories, and clothes by designers such as Narciso Rodriguez, Daryl K, and Antonio Berardi. The store also features art exhibits, magazines and books, and a café (Jackson, 1998). A rival with a sensibility closer to street fashion is L'Epicerie, which also crosses fashion and art. The clothes range from Japanese utilitarian to limited-edition pieces by young designers.

FIGURE 6.6

The Colette store on Rue St. Honoré in Paris draws editors and buyers with its combination of a café, exhibition space, and leading-edge fashion and accessories.

Boutiques and specialty stores such as these are frequented not only by customers but also by the fashion press and forecasters. The visual presentation, product mix, and styles are directional for trend spotters.

Trade Shows. Almost every week of the year somewhere in the world there is an apparel trade show. There are trade shows for:

- All categories of apparel—women's, men's, and children's.
- Categories of accessories.

- Niche and specialty categories such as ecologically conscious vendors.
- Private-label manufacturers.
- Special sizes—plus sizes and petites.

Trade shows are centered on selling fashion but they also showcase new design talent and identify trends for specific product categories, price points, and target audiences. Seminars at the shows provide a venue for networking among apparel executives and for discussion of issues that have an impact on the apparel industry.

In Europe, an important German trade show producer has two women's wear shows each season—CPD (Collections Premieren Dusseldorf), a key German trend and buying fair with international exhibitors from over 50 countries and buyers from even more (Figure 6.7). CPD is a season opener, more about information gathering than about writing orders. Many exhibitors show standardized products, but there is always news on new companies, fashion-forward lines, and brands that have revamped their approach (Drier, 1998).

A group of New York trade shows coincides with the line releases by manufacturers—January (Summer), late-February to early-March (early Fall merchandise known as Fall I), late-March to early April (fall merchandise known as Fall II), August (Holiday and/or Resort), November (Spring merchandise). These shows (e.g., StyleWorks, Fashion Coterie, and New York Premier Collections) allow buyers from around the country to see a wide range of lines. The trade shows feature name designers' lines, lines by young designers, and international contingents.

FIGURE 6.7

The CPD fair in Dusseldorf, Germany, is just one of the international trade shows where manufacturers mount presentations of their brands and forecasters scout for fashion direction.

The shows are especially important for independent stores because they offer a chance to see many lines and select merchandise that differentiates the independents from the large department store chains. Buyers use the New York trade shows to place orders for immediate delivery and to order for the upcoming season. For many buyers, the shows offer a chance to crystallize trends into specific lines and items customized for their location and customer. For buyers and forecasters, the trade shows offer a way to get an overview of seasonal trends in a more convenient and concentrated way than the alternative, canvassing individual showrooms.

Regional Markets. Serving the same purpose for buyers who do not come to New York are the **regional markets** around the country in Atlanta, Dallas, Chicago, San Francisco, Los Angeles, Denver, Miami, and other regional centers. Regional market centers lease space to manufacturers and sales representatives who carry multiple lines in permanent showrooms and for seasonal shows.

Planned to make buying easier and more convenient for smaller department stores and specialty stores, these marts have evolved as sites where merchandise aligns closely with the needs and preferences of different regions. Manufacturers use regional markets to test the direction of lines and to test the market response to items. Entrepreneurs in the middle price points often begin by showing at regional marts to test the viability of their design direction. Forecasters and buyers for large department store chains use regional markets to explore local market trends that may not show up in national buying patterns.

In addition to the well-known designers and apparel manufacturers showing at regional markets, such shows provide a showcase for designers working far from the runways on the fringes of the market. One such trendsetting concentration for contemporary clothing is in Southern California. Working outside the fashion establishment, these designers specialize in the California look—body conscious and active looks that display a gym-toned young body, ethnic-inspired looks, and ironic combinations (things not usually thought to be compatible like luxurious casual clothes and casual workwear inspired by workers in Silicon Valley). The result is inexpensive contemporary clothing, sophisticated junior wear, and more directional clothes than traditional bridge and career clothes lines. Aimed at independent stores making "smallish buys," these lines epitomize trends toward seasonless fabrics and a casual lifestyle (Steinhauer, 1998a).

Regional markets and trade shows usually encourage and accommodate the attendance of fashion students. Attend a market or trade show and focus on small manufacturers, emerging design firms, and avant-garde fashion. Report on the potential for these companies and designers to reach larger markets and appeal to broader audiences.	*Activity 6.7 The Market for Fashion*

Street Fashion

Street fashion is synonymous with youthful experimentation. Consumers become fashion stylists when they take available clothing resources and mix, restyle, and customize items in individualistic and expressive ways. While innovative street looks sometimes influence designer collections, for some apparel categories—juniors, contemporary, and denim—virtually all trends derive from street looks. Street looks are influential for casual streetwear and directional for other age groups and categories (Figure 6.8).

To research these trends, companies send designers to locales expected to furnish inspiration. Two other sources for information on street fashion are forecasting firms and trade shows. Forecasting firms scout for images and supply companies with pictures and video. Trade shows bring together small firms with direct ties to street influences.

Cities identified as directional for youth-oriented fashion include the expected—Tokyo, London, and New York—and the unexpected—Reykjavik, Iceland (Socha, 1998c). Any city where the focal point for youth is on playful experimentation with fashion can provide trend information. Likely locales

FIGURE 6.8

Denim trends start with street looks.

feature small, local, nontraditional companies; vibrant street life centered on underground music culture, cafés, and clubs; and shops experimenting with new retail concepts. Shops in these neighborhoods tend to have a point of view—perfectly plain all-natural knits or bohemian classics or sturdy utilitarian clothes by designers that are not yet mainstream. The retail concepts mix apparel, decorative accessories for the home, and vintage finds in displays reflective of the tastes of the proprietor.

Flea markets offer hunting grounds for trends. The flea market aesthetic was a linchpin of 1990s style in fashion and home décor and offered inspiration to the runway designs of Jean-Paul Gaultier, Anna Sui, Todd Oldham, and Dominico Dolce and Stefano Gabbana (DeCaro, 1997). Entrepreneurs selling clothes at flea markets modify old garments for resale and feature items popular with consumer stylists. Shoppers at flea markets are likely to be more inventive in the ways they dress (Parr, 1998b).

Entrepreneurs who begin selling at flea markets may turn into proprietors of **vintage fashion** stores, presenting edited selections gleaned from charity thrift shops and rummage sales and targeted to youthful local shoppers (Figure 6.9). In San Francisco and Los Angeles, the vintage superstore Wasteland

FIGURE 6.9

The Candy Store is a vintage store in the East Village of New York City that features feminine looks like this wall of colorful slips.

"creams"(skims the topmost desirable vintage clothing available) using a buying team hired for their "hypersensitive trend-spotting radar" (Zimbalist, 1998b). In turn, designers such as Anna Sui and Jean Paul Gaultier and design teams from Donna Karan, rock stars, models, and actors shop the store.

Some influences from the street are translated directly into manufacturer's lines if the target consumer is likely to identify with source and readily adopt the innovation. But some influences from the street are too raw or too advanced to move directly into the mainstream. These influences instead trickle up from the street to mainstream in modified form over time. Or, street influence may have a more general effect in inspiring a shift in mood or emphasis.

Activity 6.8 Trends in Vintage	Find the vintage clothing stores in your area or seek out the vintage clothing collectors in your town. Interview the proprietors or collectors about the items that are being hotly collected. Ask them about categories that are emerging for collectors. Locate articles on vintage clothing and magazines that cover that marketplace. Prepare a presentation board or report on directions in vintage clothes and the effect that these directions will have on mainstream fashion.

TREND IDENTIFICATION, ANALYSIS, AND SYNTHESIS

Forecasters work for clients as consultants and within corporations. The Sears chain has a Product Development Trend Management group whose business is to make regular trips to Paris, London, and Milan to determine the trends that will pay off when translated into merchandise at the Sears price points. Their suggestions now have styles at the chain only one year behind the latest styles, as opposed to two or three years behind as in the past. The result has been substantial gains in apparel sales for the chain (Chambers & Davis, 1998).

The yearly agenda for a trend forecaster might look like this (Schwiss-Hankins, 1998):

- Trips to Europe to shop key cities, attend international trade shows, and purchase samples—two to four trips per year.
- Trips to trade shows in cities around the United States—six to eight per year.
- Trips to attend fabric previews and markets—two to four per year.
- Purchase trend predictions and color services—four to ten per year.
- Subscribe to fashion magazines and trade journals to stay up-to-date on trends and industry news.

- Attend presentations by fabric mills and other key suppliers.
- Attend meetings of professional organizations such as color forecasting groups.

The purpose of all this activity is to organize observations, present findings, and suggest ways to implement these ideas into merchandise targeted to the company's customer base. Executives attending the presentations represent three domains:

- Product developers who will create branded or private label lines for the company.
- Buyers who will select merchandise from national brands that address the trends.
- Marketing, promotion, and sales staff who will present the merchandise within the context of the trends to the customers.

The forecaster and the other executives sift through the information using a process called **abstracting** (Fiore & Kimle, 1997). The process consists of identifying underlying similarities (or differences) across products and design collections—that is, comparing individual elements and the interrelationships among those elements in an apparel ensemble and recognizing a similarity in other ensembles. The similarity may be based on visual or symbolic core concepts expressed in:

- The totality of the look—minimalist versus extravagant, feminine versus masculine, sexy versus refined.
- The theme or mood—survivalist versus gothic romanticism.
- A swing in fashion's pendulum—from flared to narrower legs, from functional to frilly.
- The proportions of the apparel pieces—hem length or in-seam length for pants, placement of the waistline, width or fullness of the garments.
- The silhouette—tubular shift, hourglass, blouson, wedge.
- Point of emphasis—shoulders, bust, waist, derriere, legs.
- The fit—body hugging, body skimming, body conscious, or loose.
- A specific detail—collar, pocket, lapel, waistband treatment, sleeve, or cuff.
- Exaggeration in the details.
- A specific trim—beading, embroidery, appliqué, lace, or cording.
- A specific finding—buttons, zipper, or snaps.
- A fabric type—woven or knit, napped or metallic.
- Fabric finishing—gradation in color dyeing, slashing, or abrading.
- A specific fabric—transparent fabrics, velvet, or jersey.
- A color story.

The trend may be reported within a product category—dresses or suits—or across categories. The trend may involve the growing strength of a category (e.g., office casual) or its eclipse.

The ability to recognize similarities between garments and between collections is useful in many fashion careers (Fiore & Kimle, 1997):

- Designers, product developers, and buyers abstract across the garments in a group and the groups in a collection so that a visual theme or aesthetic connects the items.

- Sales representatives and marketing executives abstract across the product line to recognize symbolic and visual core concepts that can be emphasized in selling the line.

- Fashion journalists abstract across multiple collections to identify patterns in the seasonal offerings and visual and symbolic core concepts that can be translated into editorial features.

- Forecasters abstract across multiple collections and across time to identify patterns that indicate fashion change and direction.

The forecaster must recognize the symbolic and visual core concepts and patterns as they emerge and when they enter eclipse. The forecaster puts these core concepts in perspective by considering fashion evolution and projecting the potential for continuation or termination in the future (see Chapters 2 and 3).

Visual Core Concepts

Designers are inspired by myriad influences from new fabrics to travel experiences, art movements to popular culture, street fashion to the spirit and style of a **muse**—a woman who embodies the ideal look for that designer. Identifying the **visual core concept** in an apparel ensemble, a group, a collection, or a season is more than just analyzing the tangible form. It involves active processing of the intangible attributes—references to past fashions or to ethnic costume, the sensuous or sexual connotations, and imaginative and expressive aspects. It is the juxtaposition of familiar symbols with the exotic ones that creates a *frission*—a thrill or quiver that signals something new and different (Craik, 1994)

- **Concepts Referencing the Past**
Vera Wang's favorite kind of research is buying vintage dresses and swatch books of rare fabrics and embroideries. She explains, "I find an idea, then I study it, evolve it . . . you always have to take it to another level" (Talley, 1998). She is one of many designers who are influenced by fashion from the distant and not so distant past.

- **Concepts Referencing Ethnic Sources**
Nicole Miller imitated the tiles of Morocco in burnout velvets and jacquards and Pamela Dennis, the jewel colors of Morocco. Ralph Lauren created a col-

lection of Masai-inspired looks. Badgley Mischka and Oscar de la Renta found inspiration in Russian imagery (Wilson & Friedman, 1998). Middle Eastern, Asian, Latin, and African cultures have been interpreted into fashion looks in the late 1990s as part of a multicultural trend. However, some of the results have been controversial with some critics seeing African regalia on white models as politically incorrect and on black models as patronizing. Critics locate the fault in a "detached view" that tries to "simulate" a look instead of integrating or synthesizing it into something "authentic" to its time and place (Spindler, 1997). Still, references to ethnic sources continue in collections as homage to the creativity of naïve artists and as shorthand for the symbolic values of naturalness and authenticity.

• Concepts Related to Sexuality

Fashion watchers have long identified the outsider sensibilities of prostitutes as a source of fashion innovation (Field, 1970; Simmel, 1904). Stiletto heels, the use of rouge and lipstick, red nail polish, and women smoking cigarettes all began in the subculture of prostitutes and spread to other classes. Expressions of sexuality go with the attitudes of living outside accepted norms and dressing the part with clothes, hairstyles, makeup, and accessories. The specifics are linked to the time—Carole Lombard in a white bias cut dress in the 1930s, or Kate Moss in a transparent slip dress in the 90s. Today's fashion picture includes all the symbols for seduction, including partial nudity, red lips and nails, stiletto heels, and the colors red and black.

• Concepts Referencing Sports

American sportswear grew out of fashions designed for an active lifestyle that included playing sports and being a spectator at sporting events. Today, all categories of sports from skateboarding to motorcross to extreme sports are referenced in collections for casual and streetwear. Famous brands have usurped many of the looks originated by small manufacturers of adventure gear as apparel for participants in active sports. Some consumers favor the authentic sports apparel that they use as multifunctional pieces for recreation and work. Other consumers are satisfied with the outdoor look in name-brand lines ("City slickers," 1998).

• Concepts Referencing Appropriateness

Sometimes referred to as "uptown chic" versus "downtown hip," the concept means that some styles mate with certain places and attitudes. An uptown girl wears a jacket, silk T-shirt, and carries a Hermès bag. A downtown girl wears black jeans, white cotton T-shirt, and technosneakers. Designers tend to relate to one sensibility or another.

• Avant-Garde Concepts

Labeled "artsy" by some, original, creative, individual, and surprising innovations are not usually praised or accepted. Avant-garde designers frequently have a point of view that comments on the issues of the day (Betts, 1998b). Few really avant-garde styles are sold or worn. However, these ideas sometimes have a long-lasting impact on fashion. Examples include Rudi Gernreich, Paco Rabanne, Courrèges, and Pierre Cardin in the mid-1960s and Japanese and Belgian designers today. Designers who work in the space between art and commerce appeal to the individualists and intellectuals among fashion insiders. Their appeal to a larger public is negligible. Their work often references architecture. Other style points include intricate draping, wrapping, and pleating, asymmetry, unconventional fastenings, and unusual fabrics.

• The Concept of Modernity

The term **modernity** refers to the aesthetic that emerged with technological innovations such as the automobile, telephone, plastics, synthetic dyes, and man-made fibers, and with mass media and entertainment such as the movies. Collections with modernity as a theme strenuously avoid any reference to past fashion. Instead, they focus on sleekness, banishment of frills, functional details, and performance and technical fabrics.

• The Concept of Postmodern

Postmodern culture is associated with an emerging global economy, fragmentation in society, extreme eclecticism in the use of signs and symbols, unease with the consequences of modernity, and fluidity in social identities. Collections with a postmodern inclination focus on mixing symbols from different cultures and times or on the protective function of clothing. As designer Jil Sander puts it: "We don't know what the future will bring. We're confused and almost feel lost in our mass consumer society with its global information system" (Cooper, 1998). The design response is to create clothing that is a mad mix of all that has gone before or that functions as a utilitarian personal habitat.

Semiotics is the science of analyzing culture as a system of signs—a system of shared cultural conventions. Forecasters, too, are readers of signs and interpreters of meaning. To recognize core concepts when they appear on the runway and in the street, a forecaster must be conversant with the visual sources and the symbolic meanings of fashion. That means understanding the meaning for the originators of the look and for those who appropriate the look for their own use. It is this deep understanding of signs and symbols and how they are used to create meaning that makes the forecast more accurate, meaningful, and actionable.

Activity 6.9 *Deconstructing a Designer's Core Concepts*	Select a designer and deconstruct the visual and symbolic core concepts in the most recent collections. Prepare a presentation board showing the original source referenced in the collection and the translation of that source by the designer. Compare to other designers referencing similar sources.

David Wolfe, Creative Director, D³
(Doneger Design Direction)

David Wolfe began his career in 1959 in Ohio but he soon became one of Europe's leading fashion illustrators with his work appearing in *British Vogue, The London Sunday Times, Women's Wear Daily,* and *L'Uomo Vogue.* He switched to the fashion forecasting industry in the late 1960s, was Creative Director of I. M. International in London for a decade, and later joined T.F.S. (The Fashion Service). He is currently the Creative Director of D³ (Doneger Design Direction), a color and fashion trend forecasting service. Wolfe has become a popular personality on television shows covering the fashion scene. Within the fashion industry he is known for his witty and astute take on fashion, an approach showcased in his "State of Style" presentations annually at the National Retail Federation convention in New York City.

D³ publishes forecasts for women's wear, men's wear, children's wear, and juniors. Unlike many forecasting services, D³ is based in a resident buying and fashion consulting office, the Doneger Group, who in turn advise over 800 domestic and international retailers on merchandising concepts, specific fashion trends, key items, and promotional opportunities. Fees for membership in the buying office and subscription to the forecasting service are separate. Subscribers to the forecasting service include manufacturers and retailers with private label programs who need directional information several seasons in advance or other retailers who use the information to prepare for the upcoming season in terms of in-store displays and themes that coordinate merchandise. Annual fees for the forecasting service range from $200 for a monthly newsletter to several thousand dollars for seasonal trend forecasts, reports from the international designer collections, and access to the sample and slide library.

Wolfe's perspective on fashion comes from observing change over time. He thinks fashion is changing more slowly now than it did when he began his career. According to Wolfe, the fashion business "was so easy then; it is so difficult now" because then "there were rules, it was organized, we had a consumer population who was obsessed and obedient—they're not even listening to us any more!" (1998). He sees style today in a holding pattern where most consumers, male and female, are content with the familiar.

While fashion booms in print with fashion magazines bulking up with advertising, most people ignore the fashion looks. Wolfe (1999) worries that fashion media is "being led astray by the cutting edge"—the ugly and shocking images on the runways and in fashion photography. While the media claim that such images are necessary to catch people's attention, Wolfe suggests that while people are noticing, they are "noticing in a negative way." He has been forecasting the end of this over-the-top, edgy approach for the last few years and continues to see a softening of the cutting edge.

Wolfe (1999) characterizes most of the Twentieth Century as about upward style mobility—"No matter where you were on the economic or social strata, you looked up, up, up." But a few decades ago fashion began to look downward to the street for inspiration. He even goes farther back in tracing the shift: "I think Levi Straus invented the garment that was the watershed turning point in fashion. He's responsible for the entire downward dressing spiral." According to Wolfe, the fashion industry "pretends it's a positive thing" but he "thinks we're close to the bottom" and may "start looking upward for fashion inspiration again"—away from the Courtney Love and more toward Martha Stewart. "I think *Martha Stewart Living* is closer to where we are going in fashion." Wolfe sees the Grunge look, an influence for about a decade, as a thing of the past.

For Wolfe (1998) the shift in the later half of the Twentieth Century toward an anything-goes-anywhere way of dressing had negative economic consequences for the fashion industry. As he puts it, "If we can redefine appropriate apparel for different occasions, different lives, different ages—we are going to sell a lot more. I think we are going to see people reestablishing some rules because it is too difficult to get dressed in the morning if you don't have rules. Rules make it easier, not harder." That doesn't mean that consumers will give up comfort and casual clothes but he thinks fashion is "starting to chart a trend toward dressing up again—back toward not uncomfortable formality but appropriateness."

Wolfe (1999) remembers when "black was the hot color—that was twenty years ago." He suggests that it is time to move on and that designers have finally gotten the message. Recovery from the "blackout" may require a "kind of twelve-step program, and maybe fashion is on step one, but will start stepping faster." One clue to this shift cited by Wolfe is the move toward color in interior decoration. "We're going to be able to stomp out black, maybe not once and for all, not for every occasion, but maybe now it can go back to being just the little black dress and not the big black wardrobe." He sees the challenge as re-educating the fashion industry and the consumer on the use of color: "We have an entire population of people-merchandisers, designers, retailers—whose entire careers have taken place during the decades of color deprivation. They don't know how to work with color—how to combine color, how to wear color, how to display, merchandise, ship, and distribute color." He expects color in the future to be truly unisex with color available not just for women, but also for men.

As for trends, Wolfe (1999) thinks they work differently now. When he started in the business, "all you had to do was pick out the right person to copy." In those times trends started as an idea "and it rippled out, and rippled out, and rippled out, and eventually everybody made a bit of money from it." Today he divides trends into "macro" and "micro" categories. "Macro trends are the big, big ideas that affect everybody, in every walk of life, in every price point, every gender—those are the big deals, the real trends." The micro trends are "those cute little ideas that fashion editors love, and fashion stylists love, and the display people love—because they are a great way to communicate excitement to each other in the fashion industry, to get our ideas across." Because of the short life span of these micro-trends, people in the industry can make "a little bit of money, intensely for a very, very, short period of time, but a nanosecond later, it's over."

Wolfe (1998) sees the world shrinking in terms of fashion inspiration as designers take a global trip. "Designers have always wandered the world and wherever they went on vacation became the collection. It's not quite that way anymore. Now it's everything—the entire world all at once." Wolfe (1999) also sees young designers looking to three designers of the past for inspiration—Madeline Vionnet, Claire McCardell, and Charles James. "The common denominator for all three is the fact that they worked with shape—a macro trend as far as fashion is concerned." He identifies another trend with roots in American sportswear ("the big gift America has given to the world")-a "strange hybrid that is becoming the new modern way of dressing that mixes traditional sportswear with active sportswear pieces and extreme sportswear pieces," a look called "casual fitness."

As a forecaster, Wolfe (1999) goes back to look at the forecasts he made a decade before to see how things actually worked out. He seems to have been right about the past decade: "At the beginning of the 1990s, I said the decade is going to be all about marketing, not about design at all." Looking forward Wolfe thinks the next decade will be all about technology and the way "it is going to change not just the world of fashion, the world of style, but our world in general." Technology will change what clothes are made from (like high performance fabrics), the way clothes are made (laser cutouts for decoration and fused seams rather than sewn), clothes themselves (pockets designed for take-along electronic gadgets), and the way the industry communicates with the customer (pinpointing individual customers with electronic messages about new merchandise).

Different Designers with the Same Design Concept

Designers are presumed to be creators and originators. Their goal is to build a recognized branded image that consumers identify with and feel loyal to. They work independently and cloak their collections in secrecy until they are revealed on the catwalk. How then do designers in a given season so often end up with a similar design concepts, themes, and moods for the season?

Zeitgeist. The usual answer to this question is *Zeitgeist*—the trend is in the air, it is part of the spirit of the times (see Chapter 2). Listen to designers talking in the same buzzwords about a given season's style, fabrics, and fit. When asked to explain the sudden appearance of capri-length pants in the Spring and Summer of 1998, designers claimed to have seen Italian women cutting off their husbands pants to make baggy capris, surfers wearing Jams on the street, hip young kids cutting their jeans right below the knee, and other directional sightings. Another way that trends become "air"-borne is through insider talk. Designers see the same fabrics from the same houses and trends in fabric lead to similar silhouettes (Zimbalist, 1998a).

Designers do inhabit the same cultural strata—read the same periodicals, attend the same parties, know many of the same people, and know which movies and plays are "hot" topics of conversation among the media elite. Because designers are experiencing the same cultural current, it is only natural that these influences will foreshadow fashion change and lead to some similarities in the collections.

Knockoffs. The designers' aesthetic is translated to lower price points in three ways:

- The **counterfeit**—a close copy passed off as authentic.
- The knockoff—a close copy of another company's original but one that does not carry the originator's label.
- An interpretation of the look.

The difference between a counterfeit and a knockoff may be difficult to distinguish in the marketplace but legally these cases are easier to decide. The difference between a knockoff and merely a garment inspired by the original is more difficult to determine in a legal sense—how much can be copied without crossing the line?

Copying is a deeply ingrained historical practice in the fashion industry. An article in the *Saturday Evening Post* from 1963 states flatly that design "piracy is not the exception in the industry, it dominates it" and illustrates the point with a running industry gag, "At least I changed the buttons" (Poling, 1963). However, more and more legal cases are being brought to protect ownership of the way a product looks or is presented under the definition of **trade dress,** a form of trademark infringement (Young, 1998). In these cases, the firm with an original design is attempting to prevent others from trading on its reputation, image, and customer's goodwill.

Even with increased suits for infringement of trade dress, there is so much copying in the fashion industry that it is difficult to tell which designer originates a look. Some designers, even those with big names, copy other designers (Agins, 1994b). Ralph Lauren was found guilty and fined by a French commercial court for "counterfeiting" a long, sleeveless tuxedo dress from Yves Saint Laurent's Fall 1992 couture collection (Betts, 1994; Ingrassia, 1994). Merchants attend runway shows and buy for their designer shops, but they also use what they learn to advantage in their private-label businesses.

Some manufacturers specialize in knockoffs—the translation of high-priced fashions into cheaper versions. The copying process that took weeks in the

1960s now takes days. Images move from the runway to the Internet in hours or into trade papers in one day. Manufacturers specializing in speed-to-market can have samples of runway styles in their showroom for sale to retailers within one week. Merchandise from these manufacturers hits the stores in a few months—often before the original designer's company can even ship its own runway version (Steinhauer, 1997).

The original designers' aesthetic remains to some extent when a look from a collection is knocked off. However, the translation into mass-produced clothing at different price points dilutes the look through the use of cheaper fabrics and less quality in the workmanship.

Designer's Designer. A few designers in each era are highly original talents who experiment with new design directions. Paul Poiret, Coco Chanel, Vionnet, Charles James, Christian Dior, Yves Saint Laurent, and Courrèges were such designers in their eras. Christian Lacroix's 1987 debut with his pouf skirts and mad mixes of color and pattern introduced something new and directional. The emergence of Japanese designers in the late 1980s played an influential role in setting the design agenda for the early 1990s. In the late 1990s Ann Demeulemeester, Martin Margiela, and Helmut Lang played this role. These are the designer's designers—the ones who influence other designers.

Today's version of the breed creates clothes appreciated by only the most intellectual of the fashion insiders, but they exert tremendous influence on other designers following their lead. David Wolfe (1997), a fashion forecaster and commentator, complained that the edgy "uniform" of sheer top, sexy slip-dress, bootleg pants, and thrift-shop-looking coats that overtook couture in the late 1990s was the result of the designer-following-the-designer mentality. This observation confirms that there are style tribes even among designers—designers doing their own versions of a shared aesthetic.

Trial Balloons. Each collection, each season is a learning experience for a designer. The designer sends out a collection and gets feedback from the press, the professional buyers, and the clients. Plans for the next collection mix design influences, the response to the designer's most recent collections, and the reaction of press and merchants to the most recent collections of other designers.

Couture designers are in the business of innovation but ideas evolve over time. Revolutionary revisions like Dior's New Look in 1947 and Courrèges' future-oriented modernism in the 1965 collection are rare. Instead, new fashions first make their appearance as trial balloons, as tentative explorations of a new direction or a new look. Designer Daryl Kerrigan claims to be the initiator of the capri trend of 1998 because she showed capris in 1993. She describes the evolution from a trial balloon to a trend (Zimbalist, 1998a): "People saw mine in the store, stylists pulled them into magazines, or took my idea and chopped the jeans for a shoot. The idea gets out there, and the many, many others follow suit."

Once an idea debuts, the designer more fully exploits the new approach in subsequent collections. Meanwhile, others have recognized the innovation, transposed it, developed variations, and amplified it. All these modifications are individual acts of creation based on that initial seed. Together they coalesce into a trend recognizable across collections in a given season. These similarities arise because designers must assert their individuality within the constraints of what their competitors are doing and the spirit of the times (Lipovetsky, 1994).

Trend Dynamics: Label, Coattail, and Flow

Of the many ideas on the runway, only a few are successful in attracting backing. In the first hundred years of modern fashion, this backing came from clients. Some fashion counts from that period show that only one-tenth of the designs were produced for clients (Lipovetsky, 1994). The rest were neglected, forgotten, and replaced by a new crop of proposed fashion ideas in the next season. The gatekeeper role initially played by clients was taken over by merchants and by the fashion press. Merchants decide which fashion ideas will be available to consumers, which will be made in small numbers and which in volume. The fashion press defines trends by deciding which of the many ideas on the runway will be promoted in the pages of trade publications and fashion magazines.

In the past, collections could be categorized as either "editorial" (providing a hook for telling a story or creating a fantasy) or "retail" (wearable, targeted for a consumer segment). Now the press and the merchants tend to be in sync on the looks that will be tested further in the marketplace (Socha, 1998b). Editors know that readers buy from the pages of the magazine and that everything shown must be available at retail. Both magazines and stores cover established designers and new talents. More than ever editors and store executives share information—key fashion stores invite editors to see what they are buying and creating in private label merchandise for a season, store fashion directors carefully analyze the press's approach. Designers have to be realistic about appealing to both the needs of retailers and the press.

Trends once identified must be given a name, label, or slogan that can be used as a popular identifier (Meyersohn & Katz, 1957). If the name is synchronous with the spirit of the times, original, and catchy, it will speed the trend on its way. With the labeling comes a surge in interest. This surge of interest catches the attention of people in the industry who recognize the potential of the trend and rush to produce it in their own lines. This phenomenon is called the coattail effect. Popular at first with a relatively small sphere of "fashionistas," the trend will pass from group to group across social boundaries of age, income, and lifestyle—a process called flow.

Using highlighter pens, identify labels attached to trends, apparel items, and fashion looks in a recent fashion magazine. Develop a dictionary of names, labels, or slogans associated with current fashion in a notebook. Jot down additional ones as you read fashion magazines from now on. Over time, this dictionary of fashion labels will chart the emergence, diffusion, dominance, and eclipse of fashion trends.

Activity 6.10
Charting Fashion
Labels

Trend Analysis and Synthesis

Many variations of apparel styles are available in the marketplace simultaneously. Almost all are "marked" with meaning. An unmarked apparel item is the most generic of its kind. Once color or styling is added, the apparel becomes a marker for some identity. Think of a white T-shirt. How many meanings can be attached to a simple white T-shirt depending on the way it is worn, its fit, what it is paired with, the occasion when it is worn? People are symbol users and apparel offers a stage for that ability.

Each person—female or male—must make decisions about what styles to pluck from the marketplace for personal use. These decisions include those about hair, cosmetics, clothing, and accessories. Being antifashion or no-fashion is as much a decision as being fashionable. People make these decisions every day when they dress. Because the decisions are based partly on demographics, lifestyle, and situation and partly on personality and taste, a certain consistency emerges for each individual—a personal signature style.

People in all likelihood are a member of a style tribe because of where they live, how they make a living, or how they choose to spend their leisure time. Groups evolve a way of dressing that signals the group's identity and aesthetic code.

Because there exists an almost infinite universe of style variations, the possibilities for individual expression and group identification are also infinite. Yet, people's styles can be classified into general categories. Combining styles under an umbrella definition makes it possible for designers to act as style tribe leaders, specialty stores to develop retail concepts that appeal to certain customers and not to others, and marketers to target a specific consumer audiences. Marketers call these classification schemes **consumer segmentation** (see Chapters 2 and 7).

Analysis and synthesis are the two faces of forecasting. In **analysis,** a phenomenon is dissected to achieve a more complete understanding of its components. **Synthesis** is a creative reintegration of the parts. In fashion forecasting that means:

• An accurate reading of the trend in all its subtle aspects.
• Matching the trend with the consumer profiles most likely to adopt it initially.

- Matching the trend with the product category, price point, and retail concept most likely to complement it.

Finally, the forecaster hypothesizes about what it will take to energize and accelerate the flow of the trend across consumer segments.

Key Terms and Concepts

Abstracting	Flow	Semiotics
Analysis	Haute Couture	Showrooms
Coattail effect	Labeling	Style Tribes
Consumer Segmentation	Modernity	Synthesis
Counterfeit	Muse	Trade Dress
Demi-Couture	Postmodern(ism)	Trade Shows
Designer Ready-to-Wear	Regional Markets	Vintage Fashion
Fashion Weeks	Runway Shows	

Case Revisited: From Catwalk to Main Street

As fashion director for a 16-store chain in the midwestern United States, Karla translates the seasonal fashion story into merchandise (purchased from manufacturer's lines and the chain's own private-label operation) targeted for a young, fashion-forward customer. Use the following questions to review and summarize Karla's approach.

Information gathering via travel: Karla does not have a large budget for travel but she can make one trip to Europe and two trips within the United States. When should she go? What should she plan to accomplish on these trips?

Information gathering on the desktop: To augment her travel, what subscriptions should Karla have? What part should TV play in her information gathering? How can she use the Internet in her information gathering?

Merchandising the store:

- *The stores need a constant influx of merchandise to keep the look fresh and exciting but the selling floor mustn't look disorganized. Can both requirements be met?*

- *The stores use a lifestyle concept carrying everything from casual clothes to prom dresses. How can Karla use trend merchandising in each of these categories?*

Additional Forecasting Activities

Location, Location, Location. Fashion forecasting services cover the season's styles and then prepare trend books for their clients. These trend books forecast fashion's general direction and make specific suggestion for target audiences. For a given selling season, develop a trend book specifically for your region of the United States.

Systematic Updates. Develop a "bookmark" list of Web sites related to fashion—sites on designers and their collections, online fashion magazines, sites promoting trade shows, and sites associated with fashion on television (see Research Pointers for suggestions). Group the sites according to when they are updated—daily, weekly, monthly. Monitor these sites for three months on a regular basis. Evaluate the costs in terms of time and the payoff in terms of increased knowledge of fashion and trend identification.

News on the Net. Identify one or more Internet newsgroups where fashion is discussed. Monitor the newsgroup for one month without participating in the discussion—a practice called "lurking" in Internet parlance. How would monitoring fashion newsgroups be helpful to product developers, marketers, and merchandisers? What would be the advantage of more active participation like proposing questions for discussion?

Resource Pointers

These sites on the Web show fashion-forward design:

- www.placedemode.com
- www.glitter.com
- www.firstview.com
- www.vogue.com

Fairchild Publications' Web site carries news from *WWD* (women's wear), *DNR* (men's wear), and other trade publications—www.fashioncentral.com

These sites feature online-only fashion magazines:

- www.lumiere.com
- www.hintmag.com

Fashion television Web sites:

- Fashion TV—www.citytv.com
- Style with Elsa Klench—www.cnn.com/STYLE

For industry calendars, check these sites:

- www.doneger.com/predoneger/6.0/calendar.asp
- www.7thonsixth.com

For vintage clothing sites, see Resource Pointers in Chapter 3.

MARKETPLACE DYNAMICS

Chapter 7

CONSUMER RESEARCH

"We are not a manufacturer of apparel. We are a company that learns what consumers want, then we produce it."
—Mackey McDonald, President and CEO of VF Corporation

Objectives

- Understand the relationships between consumer research and product development, brand awareness and loyalty, and retailing.

- Identify the connection between consumer research and forecasting.

- Examine the methods for answering questions about consumers' preferences for new products and marketing initiatives.

- Examine current views on demographics and consumer segmentation and their relationship to forecasting consumer demand.

CASE: EXTENDING THE LINE

John is a marketing executive with a successful men's wear designer line. The brand has an established name and a winning fashion concept that it wants to extend through a launch of a women's wear line—a much more volatile and risky market. The lure for such a strategy is the market potential, at least twice as big as men's wear. However, the risks are big, too. The women's wear market is more competitive and more trend driven than men's wear. Where four collections a year is customary in men's wear, women's wear requires six to eight. Costs for fabrics, sampling, models, and photographers are all higher. The formula for success in men's wear—high-quality tailoring and a rational, practical way of dressing—does not translate easily to the faster paced women's wear business. Although the quality and simplicity of the men's wear approach to dressing appeal to career women, women have more experience with change, newness, and self-expression in clothes.

Some men's wear designers—Tommy Hilfiger, Giorgio Armani, and Ralph Lauren—made the crossover, but even Hilfiger had difficulties initially. Another well-known company, Nautica, attempted to translate its bold colorful men's wear look to women's wear but ran into problems, partly because the line lacked focus. Introduced as a bridge line, the prices were scaled back to the better category after lackluster consumer response.

John's company plans to build the next big mega brand with multiple lines spanning the apparel market. The first step is an extension in women's wear. If the new line is to succeed, the company must learn about this new target audience, find out how to position its brand in this new market, and use the findings to project the company's future. The ideas and techniques discussed in this chapter show how companies investigate new market opportunities, research consumer preferences, and use consumer information to plot their future moves.

BUSINESS BEGINS AND ENDS WITH THE CONSUMER

Stages p. 42

The apparel supply chain has one purpose—to provide an appealing and desirable product to satisfy customer needs, wants, or aspirations. When successful, the connection results in a sale. Because this connection is the purpose of the process, every forecast begins with the customer—in observing the customer's adjustments to the marketplace and in the unexpected ways the customer adjusts the marketplace to his or her lifestyle and preferences. Consumer research figures importantly in decisions about product development, brand marketing, and retailing.

Demand-Activated Product Development

Product development had traditionally been production-driven—a "push" system because fiber, textile, apparel manufacturers, and retailers pushed product through the system toward the consumer. Consumers chose from the abundance of available product. To succeed, a company competed against the consumer's inhibitions to purchase and against other producers in the same category. Advances in production technology made it faster and more efficient to produce more products. The "push" system shaped retailing—new styles were introduced seasonally, selling first at full retail price, and then closed out in a flurry of markdowns at the end of the season. In this system consumers participated only when they made a selection and that decision was reported in the sales figures.

As apparel executives realized that shoppers were smarter, more demanding, and more independent than ever before, attention has shifted to a "pull" system—consumers' demands pull product through the fiber, textile, and apparel product development process and into retail stores. By the late 1980s, the apparel market was described as "consumer driven" in recognition of this principle. Manufacturers had to shift from products that can be made conveniently in volume to products shaped by consumer input. In such an environment, only a continuous flow of consumer information can shape product. Consumer research became a priority as a way to tap into shifting consumer preferences. Product development has become a team activity that assimilates the expertise of consumer researchers, marketers, merchandisers, and production people. Conducting studies, translating consumer input into specifications, and delivering product pretested with consumers became the new paradigm as talking to customers replaced trying to second-guess them.

Evolution toward a demand-activated system had four waves (Lewis, 1996a):

- **The First Wave: Building An Information Infrastructure**

The first wave began in the early 1980s when large companies began experimenting with information technologies and building the infrastructure for a "pull" system.

- **The Second Wave: Time Efficiencies and Inventory Reduction**

Quick Response (QR) initiatives characterized the second wave with emphasis on efficiencies, cost reduction, reduced cycle times, and inventory reduction through shared communication between firms in the supply chain.

- **The Third Wave: Focusing on the Consumer**

By the mid-1990s, leading companies were in the third wave, focusing on the consumer as the "center of the universe," partnering with other firms in the supply chain to deliver maximum response to consumer needs, and reaping the benefits in increased market share and profitability.

Together the second and third waves emphasized timely stocking of goods, a continuous flow of information, and accelerated schedules. During this phase, response time between an order to a manufacturer and delivery to a retailer's distribution center shrank from a few months in the 1970s to a few weeks in the 1990s. New team approaches required the breaking down of functional departments and the updating of computer networking capabilities within companies. Partnerships between textile producers, apparel manufacturers, and retailers created challenges. Harmonizing development schedules and facilitating the information flow between partners meant faster product development and manufacturing and continuous release of new product. The characteristics of the second and third waves highlight the need for reliable and valid forecasting of consumer demand.

- **The Fourth Wave: Markets of One**

The fourth wave is arriving as suppliers define "markets of one" and segmenting down to the individual level (Pine, Peppers, & Rogers, 1995). With this approach, supply chain partnerships deliver not just replenishment of desired products in a timely way but actually anticipate consumers' needs and develop new products to satisfy them.

The demand-activated "pull" approach places more emphasis on creating, producing, and delivering the right products for consumers. Yet, according to a 1988 *Newsweek* article, most companies in the apparel industry avoided market research, the traditional method of finding out about consumer preferences (Kantrowitz, Witherspoon, King, 1988). Ten years later, the same debate was still going on at Fairchild's CEO Summit. In a panel session, a market consultant argued that price was the ultimate issue for consumers and that retailers who were gaining market share were the ones offering lower prices. Paul Charron, chairman and chief executive officer of Liz Claiborne, argued that value was the issue and that delivering value "begins with an understanding of the consumer. Anybody not doing [consumer] research is headed down a real wrong road" (Lohrer, 1998).

The debate may continue but when the margin for error is narrow, the best forecast comes when manufacturers and retailers take the consumer's pulse throughout product development, marketing, and retailing. After all, the process of making and marketing apparel rightly begins and ends with the consumer. In the fourth wave, forecasting focuses on anticipating consumer needs and on testing new styles and products to meet those needs.

Fashion Brands

What's in a name? Whether the name belongs to a designer or is just a catchy word or phrase, brand names signal a level of fashion, taste, and style. In the fashion field, there are different kinds of brands. **Store brands** are products developed and merchandised through the company's own stores and the stores carry no other brands—Land's End, The Gap, Eddie Bauer, and Victoria's Secret. **Private-label brands** are brands owned by retailers and merchandised through that retailer's stores along with the brands of other companies—Arizona for J.C. Penney, Jaclyn Smith for Kmart (Figure 7.1). **National brands**—Liz Claiborne, Levi's, Nike—and **designer name brands**—Calvin Klein, Tommy Hilfiger, Nicole Miller—are developed by manufacturers, sold to retailers through the wholesale market, and carried by many

FIGURE 7.1

J.C. Penney's private-label brand for denim, Arizona, has the kind of high recognition and brand loyalty that once belonged only to national brands.

retailers who often compete in the same market area (Figure 7.2). These traditional definitions are being revised by new competitive strategies as national and designer name brands open freestanding retail stores and private label brands achieve the prominence of national brands.

Brands build customer loyalty by delivering excellent value no matter the price point—high, low, or medium. Value includes styling, durability, quality fabrics, and consistent fit. To the consumer, a brand name represents familiarity, consistency, and confidence in performance. In surveys, consumers report a willingness to pay more for brands they prefer because brands deliver more than nonbrands (Lewis, 1995). Because brand names are associated with so many desirable attributes, they also act to simplify purchase decisions, saving time and adding convenience to the shopping experience. Brand names when linked with lifestyle, self-expression, and aspirations epitomize intangibles that are desirable to the consumer. Market research firms explore this kind of

FIGURE 7.2

Department stores allocate more and more space to designer and national brands that are merchandised in boutiques such as this one for Ralph Lauren and Tommy Hilfiger.

connection when they ask teens to name the "coolest" brands, because the question taps into the emotional significance of wearing certain brands of clothing and footwear ("The cool ones," 1996).

Branding is a competitive strategy—a way of targeting customers with a coherent message. Building a brand requires substantial investment by a company, an investment that must pay off to justify supporting the brand with advertising and promotion. The payoff for brands meeting or exceeding consumers' expectations is **brand loyalty**—purchase and repurchase of the brand again and again (Friedman, 1996a). Consumer research tracks how much a brand is worth using surveys, panel studies, and focus group interviews.

Creating a distinct **brand image** means identifying a set of tangible and intangible characteristics across a collection or product line and promoting that image to customers (Carpenter, 1998). A relevant brand image begins with a vision that invites the consumer to enter a world, participate in a lifestyle, and express a certain style. Think of the consistent point of view carried across the products, visual merchandising, and advertising of designer Ralph Lauren. No matter the product category or price point, there is an unwavering brand identity that the consumer can read. Successful brands have high recognition and an emotional connection with consumers. To consumers, possessing the products is connected to identification with the brand image.

Once brand identity is defined, advertising and promotion become keys to building **brand recognition** and loyalty. Positioning means emphasizing the differences between a brand and its competitors (Ries & Trout, 1986). Promotion and advertising help consumers perceive the product and the experience of possessing that product. Advertising works two ways: it builds brand awareness over time and it grabs attention for a particular season, line, or item. The most successful apparel advertising campaigns today project an aspirational dream world and replay the imagery over and over—Hilfiger ads show the spirited, fun-loving American spirit; Donna Karan, the unfolding potential of women; Calvin Klein, the many sides of sensuality; and Ralph Lauren, the rewards of the good life (Parr, 1996). A brand definition that strikes a cord with the public and allows for consistent reinforcement through multiple messages lays the foundation for brand building.

Brand building also involves distinctive visual merchandising. Visibility is boosted for a brand when the product is showcased in an in-store shop. Also important is point-of-sale identification such as packaging, hangtags, and signage.

When successful, branding results in a consumer's identification of a brand name with a reputation for style and quality and a unique niche in the marketplace. But brand loyalty can be a fleeting thing. Every other year a market research company asks consumers which brands they are most likely to repurchase among 180 female apparel brands (Owens, 1998). Findings show dramatic fluctuations with brands once at the top of the list falling and new names rising. The results point up the fact that if a brand disappoints a consumer enough, the consumer will stop buying that brand and regaining that customer is very difficult. As the cost of getting a new customer is about six times that of keeping an existing customer happy and loyal, that alone justifies investment in supporting brands (Lewis, 1995).

Monitoring trends enables companies to regulate brand image and positioning to changing conditions and to innovate when new opportunities arise. One such innovation is the emergence of **mega nichers** and **3-D brands**—a strategy that requires multiple lines of coordinating products supporting the brand image (Figure 7.3).

In earlier eras Anne Klein, Yves Saint Laurent, and Pierre Cardin all licensed their names to other product lines. What is the difference between these brands and today's mega niche brands like Calvin Klein, Donna Karan, Ralph Lauren, and Tommy Hilfiger? A mega nicher is a powerful brand name with a generic image that taps into the consciousness of a broad consumer population and then extends out to fill more and more product niches with its branded merchandise (Ozzard & Seckler, 1996). Mega nichers may offer products at the designer, bridge, and better levels plus accessories, footwear, jeanswear, fragrance, hosiery, eyewear, activewear, intimate apparel, handbags, and leather goods. Some expand into additional niches such as children's wear, bed linens, and products for the home. Unlike earlier versions of

FIGURE 7.3

Mega nichers and 3-D brands use the brand extension strategy to offer co-ordinating products across many categories but with the same brand image.

this strategy, today designers exercise more control over the design, marketing, advertising, and distribution of products using their brand name. They tend to view these arrangements as collaborative partnerships rather than just revenue sources.

✦Brands that focus on a lifestyle concept and produce products in many categories have been called 3-D brands because the effect is a three-dimensional world defined by the brand image (Lewis, 1996b). Whether based on a designer's name, a retailer identity like The Gap, or an idealized lifestyle like Nautica, the success of a 3-D brand depends on an image people can buy into and express through possessing the products.

The forecasting challenge for a mega nicher or 3-D brand is determining how much core product to make and how to stay flexible enough to take advantage of a rising trend or a surprise bestseller. Follow up to both situations requires a strong infrastructure in sourcing, manufacturing, and distribution. Accurately forecasting the strength of a trend and market discipline helps avoid too many end-of-the-season markdowns.

Retail Formats

Department stores emerged as a retail concept at the turn of the 20th century from a neighborhood collection of independently owned shops. The department store format brought everything the customer wanted under one roof. The next shift occurred when the department store moved out of downtown locations and into malls. The mall can be viewed as a much bigger department store with specialty stores acting like departments in that larger store. When discount stores came along, they were not in a mall; instead they were their very own mini-malls. Department stores got into trouble in the mid-1990s because they did not see the emerging customer, a two-earner, educated, younger family who found department store shopping unappealing and too time consuming. Specialty stores pinpointed not only the kind of merchandise consumers wanted but also the kind of environment they wanted to purchase it in. Combining shopping and entertainment appealed to a consumer trying to get more out of every experience. But other retail concepts emerged to meet the new interests, needs, wants, and aspirations of consumers.

The Emergence of Catalogs. Catalogs came to the forefront in a time when busy customers wanted to be able to shop any time of the day or night. For the retailer, catalogs aimed at two audiences: current customers and potential customers. Catalogs can work as a brand builder, to generate store traffic, and as a profit center (Dean, 1998). The early flush of success in catalog retailing was tied to a specific consumer—consumers who were better educated, working in professional or managerial fields, earned more money, were more comfortable with technology, liked branded merchandise, and preferred traditional clothes as compared to the in-store customer (Braun, 1993). The chief reason people shop catalogs is convenience, but other reasons include access to special sizes and brand loyalty based on previous experience with the catalog's merchandise. Sales of women's apparel through catalogs grew 5 percent between 1993 and 1995, and increased to 14 percent in 1996 ("Courting and keeping," 1997). However, there were signs that the upward trend could not be sustained in a catalog-saturated environment.

Traditionally catalogs have reached the over-35 consumer pressed for time by multiple commitments to family and a career. Consumers in the younger demographic rarely purchased from catalogs. According to the Cotton Incorporated Lifestyle Monitor, only 19 percent of females 16 to 34 shop for clothing in catalogs whereas 23 percent of women 35 to 55 do ("Revamping mail order," 1998). Catalogers are targeting this younger demographic with creative catalog formats like the *A&F Quarterly,* a catalog that looks more like a magazine. Nordstrom's junior department, Brass Plum, has expanded into *BP Style,* a magazine/catalog targeted for young women. The publication includes features on singers and television stars along with sportswear and cosmetics that can be ordered through a toll-free number or by e-mail (Parr, 1998a).

Aside from sales, catalogs allow companies to build consumer databases showing who responded, what they bought, and where they live. Tracking returns helps identify consumer satisfaction with quality, fit, and fabrication. Databases derived from catalog sales have a much greater level of detail than that captured at point-of-sale in stores. Patterns in this data can be directional for deciding where to locate new stores as well as for targeting customers' style preferences.

The Emergence of TV Shopping. When store personnel became too busy or too unfriendly to interact with customers, the TV hosts and visiting designers took time to explain products in detail and to talk consumers through the purchase process. With department stores on the wane as destinations for shopping, a new shopping phenomenon arrived on the scene—TV shopping channels and infomercials. In 1993, TV shopping accounted for an estimated $3.2 billion in sales and was expected to bring in $20 to $100 billion by the year 2000 (D'Innocenzio, 1993).

Most prominent among the channels was QVC, targeting the over-35 consumer (Figure 7.4), but MTV Networks experimented with the format for younger consumer on a test program called The Goods and on its other channels, VH-1 and Nickelodeon (Edelson, 1994). However, after a year of hype, TV shopping as a format had to retrench (Fitzgerald, 1994). Announced plans by companies like Macy's, Spiegel, and Nordstrom were delayed or abandoned. A test channel, Catalog 1, a joint venture of Spiegel and Time Warner, never rolled out after the test. A-list designers, including Karl Lagerfeld, Calvin Klein, and Donna Karan, considered and then rejected the TV format of selling (Edelson, 1995). The key problem with TV shopping turned out to be time—presentation of merchandise on TV is linear, consumers must wait to see what is presented before they can buy. The advantage in TV shopping turned out to be the interactive buying environment between the personable hosts and shoppers on the phone. But for consumers with busy lifestyle, this form of shopping was not a match. QVC emerged as the major survivor of the many experiments with TV shopping.

The Emergence of Online Shopping. On the Internet, consumers find information, entertainment, and interactivity. Apparel sites on the Web can be viewed as another form of mail order catalog (Figure 7.5). Unlike catalogs, some Web sites use flashy innovations such as **virtual dressing rooms**—software that lets users try fabrics, patterns, and colors together while making mix-and-match decisions, sometimes on a computerized model that resembles the user in terms of shape and hair color (Crockett, 1998). Like catalogs, the

FIGURE 7.4

Many designers use TV shopping networks to sell their products to a mass audience.

FIGURE 7.5

Web sites such as fashionmall.com act like a collection of catalogs, giving consumers access to merchandise from many vendors.

consumer must risk buying without seeing the actual garment—return rates for apparel on the Internet are about the same as for catalogs, 10 to 20 percent or more. Other barriers include mediocre Web site design and consumer concerns about security and privacy (Moin, 1999).

Still, the Internet is a growing sales channel for apparel and lookers on the Web are sometimes converted into customers in stores. As the number of households with personal computers and access to the Web increases, so grows the interest in browsing for apparel in this venue. Online sales of apparel reached $530 million in 1998 and were expected to reach $1.3 billion in 1999. Estimates are that 41 percent of the U.S. households will have online access by 2002 (Seckler, 1999). The Web was originally male dominated, but by the end of the 1990s the gap was narrowing quickly. For instance, the Land's End Web site drew mostly male shoppers initially but that changed to an even split between males and females visiting the site ("Revamping mail order," 1998). The number of women Internet users is expected to grow dramatically with up to 40 million users by 2000.

Today, many apparel companies, designers, national retailers, fashion magazines, trade shows, and industry organizations have Web sites. Some provide information only; some are nothing more than catalogs transferred to cyberspace. Many allow the consumer to shop but not to buy. When the purchase decision is made, the Web site visitor is referred to a store or asked to call a toll-free number—a disruption of the transaction process. But some are beginning to take advantage of the interactive qualities of the Web, qualities that are not present in other nonstore alternatives. Once a customer fills out a survey on his or her preferences, an online retailer can send e-mail when new merchandise in the same category becomes available. In the future, such one-to-one marketing may include reminders for routine purchases (Seckler, 1998a).

Designers are finding a place on the Web ("Designer's customers," 1998). Norma Kamali invites customers to "shop like a celebrity" on her site as they view her latest designs in swim-, gym-, evening-, and sportswear. Clothing is sent to the customer's home or office against her uncharged credit card. Customers have 40 hours to ship back any clothing they do not wish to purchase. Kamali began the service for her on-the-go celebrity clients, but then extended it to her other customers because she sees convenience as the ultimate luxury.

There are virtual shopping malls that combine well-known fashion brands with newcomers and build site loyalty with trend information, fashion coverage, and links to other fashion cites. When fashionmall.com, a site that is half catalog and half fashion magazine, went online in July 1995, it logged about 100,000 hits per month; by 1997, it averaged 1.5 million per month ("Fashion on the Internet," 1997); by 1998, 12 million hits per month. As video and animation technology become more easily accessible on Web sites and download times are reduced, the use of the Web for shopping, fashion advice, and personal sourcing is likely to increase. For entrepreneurs and small apparel companies, the Web offers an extra advantage in visibility: a small company can look just as sophisticated and present a fashion image just as potent as that of a much bigger company.

Activity 7.1
Styles on the Net

Find five or more fashion retailers who have Web sites (see the Resource Pointers in this chapter for some suggested sites). Are the sites easy to understand and navigate? Do they allow purchase or do they direct the visitor to a store or phone number? How long does it take for the graphics to appear on the screen? Is there a way to send e-mail to the retailer if you have questions or comments? Is the design of the Web site congruent with the style of the clothes? Are the graphics clear enough to match catalog pictures? Discuss the advantages of e-commerce for the retailer. For the consumer. What barriers are there to the use of this technology for apparel?

The Role of the Forecaster. Because the marketplace is in a constant state of evolution, the seeds for the next innovation in shopping venue or shopping experience already exist. It is the forecaster's job to:

- Recognize shifts in retail formats, evaluate their potential impact, translate the potential to their clients, and assess problems and threats that may derail the innovation.

- Assist clients in repositioning their businesses to be more in tune with the changing marketplace.

- Assist entrepreneurs, small companies, and spin-off lines in finding the optimal entrance strategy into a business niche.

- Assist clients in matching consumer segments, products, and services.

Mass Customization – The Next Big Thing?

Mass production develops standardized products for a stable, homogeneous market where the goal is efficiencies of scale. If it is true that consumers want *what* they want, *when* they want it, the *way* they want it, then the time has come for mass customization. Mass customization is an alternative strategy to mass production's one-size-fits-all and couture's one-of-a-kind. The idea is to deliver a unique, personalized, or customized product on a mass basis at a cost competitive with mass production (Bathory-Kitsz, 1996). In **mass customization,** companies collaborate with customers to design a desirable product which is then constructed from a base of pre-engineered modules. In essence, mass customization reverses the traditional supply chain by making the consumer an integral part of the initial stages of product development.

Market turbulence signals the need to investigate alternative strategies to mass production. To measure market turbulence, Pine (1993) looked at demand factors such as market stability, rate of change, and market position and structural factors such as the intensity of competition, product differentiation, and the rate of technological change. Peavy (1996) studied market turbulence in the apparel industry and concluded that the level of market turbulence in the women's sportswear category justified consideration of mass customization as a strategy.

Mass customization takes advantage of the technological advances in manufacturing and communication to facilitate a one-to-one marketing strategy (Anderson, Brannon, Ulrich, & Marshall, 1998). A research team blended qualitative and quantitative research to synthesize a model of mass customization in the apparel industry (Figure 7.6):

- **Expanded Selection**

Instead of being restricted to the narrower selection of items displayed in stores and catalogs, the consumer would be able to view an entire line and make selections from this broader assortment.

- **Expanded Search**

In this approach, consumers would be able to use intelligent search capabilities to locate desired apparel items across brands. For example, a consumer could type in "red dress" and retrieve all available red dresses in the collections of 25 companies.

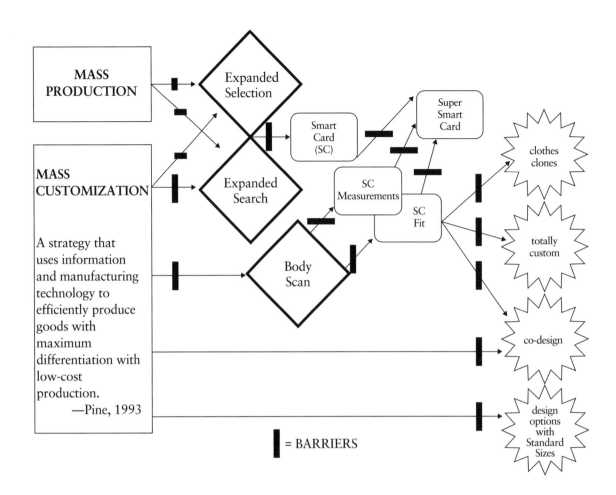

MASS PRODUCTION

MASS CUSTOMIZATION

A strategy that uses information and manufacturing technology to efficiently produce goods with maximum differentiation with low-cost production.
          —Pine, 1993

Expanded Selection

Expanded Search

Body Scan

Smart Card (SC)

SC Measurements

SC Fit

Super Smart Card

clothes clones

totally custom

co-design

design options with Standard Sizes

▮ = BARRIERS

FIGURE 7.6

A research team used surveys and focus group research to synthesize a model of mass customization options and to evaluate consumer reaction to the enabling technology.

• **The Smart Card**

The Smart Card looks like a credit card but has a different function. It stores the profile of a consumer, including measurement, fitting preferences, and other information in digital form. The card makes it convenient for consumers and companies to collaborate on customized products.

• **Body Scanning**

Three-dimensional body scanning is a method of taking a very complete set of measurements electronically. The consumer stands in a booth, a set of lines is projected onto the person's body, and a computer translates the body topography into a set of personalized accurate measurements. Having such accurate, individualized measurements on a Smart Card is one of the enabling technologies that will drive mass customization (Giannovario, 1998).

Consumer research (Anderson, Brannon, Ulrich, & Marshall, 1998) identi-fied four versions of mass customization that appeal to consumers:

- **Clothes Clones**

Consumers who have made a successful purchase would like to repeat that purchase in alternate colors and fabrics. Specifically, they want to buy ex-act copies of favorite items in their existing wardrobes—clothes clones—to save time shopping and reduce the risk of buying new items that provide less satisfaction.

- **Design Options**

Consumers create an individualized garment by choosing from standard com-ponents (collars, pockets, and trim) and several colors and fabrics offered on only a few items in each line. In this way consumers feel special, companies build consumer loyalty, and customization options are kept at a reasonable level in relation to costs (Zimmermann, 1998b).

- **Co-Design**

Consumers looking for the perfect suit, bathing suit, evening dress, or bridal attire may have the ideas but not the confidence or know-how to design their own. In this approach, the customer works with a design advisor (Co-Designer) using software templates to facilitate the process.

- **Totally Custom**

A few consumers would like to have all the customization options of fit, color, fabric, and styling—made-to-order clothing streamlined by the latest information and manufacturing technology.

Specialty retailers and entrepreneurs are already experimenting with mass customization options on the Internet (see Resource Pointers for sites). Mass customization will probably appeal most to consumers with a high level of interest in clothing and those with special needs. Mass cus-tomization was never envisioned as replacing mass production. Rather, the two will coexist and evolve with improvements in manufacturing and com-munication technologies.

Individually produced garments carry higher costs, but consumers are gen-erally willing to pay more for customization. Mass customization represents future opportunities for the apparel industry. However, there are obstacles: delays in the development of appropriate technological linkages or imaging systems, the capital investment required to implement the strategy, and the learning curve when companies and consumers encounter new ways of con-ducting business. However, the payoffs for mass customization include higher customer satisfaction, stronger loyalty to the brand, the ability to gather more information about the consumer, and the potential for better forecasting be-cause of the relationship between the core customer and the company (Zim-mermann, 1998b).

LISTENING TO THE VOICE OF THE CONSUMER

The opportunity to build consumer satisfaction comes with each occasion when the individual considers a purchase [Figure 7.7]. Satisfaction depends on how well manufacturers and retailers help consumers achieve an impact in real-world situations. To succeed, manufacturers and retailers must make the connection between the consumer, the product, and the situation clear. One approach is to bring the voice of the consumer into product development. The process begins with a series of questions:

- What creates customer acceptance?
- What are the consumer's expectations?
- Is the product competitive on desired attributes?
- Does the product surprise customers with exciting attributes?

FIGURE 7.7

The consumer juggles many factors when deciding whether to buy or not buy. The degree to which manufacturers' products meet expectations plays a major role in the decision.

When a company focuses on delivering quality, the effort is only worth-while in terms of sales and brand loyalty if consumers understand and appreciate the value-added attributes. The process continues with a series of questions about consumers' perception of quality:

- Does the product over- or under-deliver expected attributes?
- How will quality influence performance or appearance?
- Does the customer really appreciate the differences in quality?

Answers to these questions form a conceptual map that becomes the "voice of the customer" in product development. The voice of the customer is translated by a multifunction product development team into operational terms—specifications, process planning, process control (Nayak, 1991). Creating a knowledge base through years of systematic questioning cannot be undertaken without the commitment of senior management. But, such a knowledge base makes forecasting consumer acceptance more reliable and valid.

It sounds easy—just ask customers what they expect from products and have product developers write specifications to fit those responses. But a list of product attributes is not enough. Even with a list, it is a leap to assume that the more an attribute is present, the more satisfied the customer will be. When asked, consumers attempt to generate a rational, socially acceptable explanation for behavior or preferences (i.e., reading and following care labels, careful prepurchase searches for value) even when these behaviors are really a minor part of decision making. Some attributes are expected but do not significantly contribute to customer satisfaction (e.g., buttons are expected to stay on, seams are expected to hold together). Others are desirable and customers say they make an important contribution to satisfaction (i.e., ease of care, accurate labeling). Others, the unspoken motivators, are exciting attributes consumers do not expect but which increase customer satisfaction when they are present (e.g., design details for a "good" price, flattering colors, novelty embellishment) (Snyder, 1991). More important than a list of attributes is an understanding of the dynamics of consumer/product/brand interactions—the consumer of products is really a consumer of images, of products *as* image. The trick to anticipating consumer demand is discovering what "bonds" a consumer to a product (Pine, 1993).

The product may be right, but if the experience of buying it is not, then consumers will not buy. Recreational shopping—browsing and window-shopping, leisurely visits to the mall for fun—has been crowded out of the American schedule by other activities. Retail has polarized into the minimal-service, wide selection warehouse formats and the high end, entertainment format stores. Conventional department stores are left in the middle, competing without much differentiation on product, pricing, assortment, or service. Consumers are savvy about selecting a specific store to meet a precise need with convenience as important criteria. Consumers are also savvy about selecting the preferred experience—one that is functional, fulfills the need, and is value-oriented versus one that is creative, emotional, and "high touch," where the experience is more important than the price. Some consumers are mostly value-oriented shoppers and prefer low-price/low-service venues; some are mostly experience-oriented and prefer high-price/high-service stores. Some cross over, seeking a different retail experience depending on the product or situation. Retailers and the manufacturers who provide product to them are finding such polarity makes understanding the customer more difficult ("The polarity of retail," 1998).

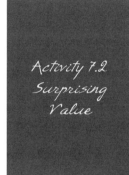

Activity 7.2
Surprising
Value

Select a fashion basic—jeans or khaki pants, T-shirt or turtleneck sweater. List the attributes that are most desirable for this product. List the checkpoints for quality in this category. Which attributes are expected in products at all price ranges? Which make an important contributor to satisfaction at point of purchase? Which make an important contribution to satisfaction in use? Compare three versions of this product, one from each of three retail stores or brands. Does any product in the category surprise customers with exciting attributes? Which products deliver more or less quality than expected? How likely is it that a customer will recognize and appreciate the differences in quality? Prepare a list of recommendation on desirable attributes and quality levels for product developers in this category.

Asking "What" and "Why" Questions

Instead of just asking consumers about products, begin by identifying the activities associated with the product. Where will the product be worn? How does it fit into that activity? What other products will be combined with it? Then, ask production people to discuss ways that present and future technology in fibers, fabrics, or manufacturing could add value to the product given the demands of the activity. Finally, ask the marketing people to discuss the likely competitive environment for the current or enhanced product. With this background information, the product development team can conduct research that reflects the world of the prospective buyers in ways that produces actionable information for designers and marketers (Fennel, 1991). **Focus groups** are frequently used to understand the relationship of a product or product category to a consumer segment. For a deeper understanding of the interplay between consumers' attitudes and their behavior, researchers use a lengthy one-on-one interview (called a **depth interview**). Attributes that bond a consumer are difficult to verbalize, so some researchers turn to observational techniques to unravel these connections.

Focus Group Research. Focus groups are a **qualitative** method of research based on informal, uncensored talk about products in an group interview setting. Focus groups are designed to help companies become more responsive to consumer needs and wants and, thus, more competitive. Successful focus group discussion elicits consumer perceptions, opinions, beliefs, and attitudes as they relate to the product. The intent of focus groups is to understand consumers by identifying the range of response, not to determine the incidence of that response in the population (Kreuger, 1988). The focus group researcher will use the interviews to identify all the reasons that motivate acceptance or rejection of a product. Then, the researcher can generalize from those ideas to the ideas in the population. But, the researcher will not be able to estimate how many people hold those views (McQuarrie & McIntyre, 1988).

The **focus group moderator** works with the company sponsoring the research to develop a set of questions to serve as a guide to the discussion. Focus group participants are recruited, usually by a market research firm that maintains a database of consumer contacts, and they often receive a monetary incentive for participation. Participants must meet a set of guidelines defined by the sponsoring company. Usually these guidelines involve age, gender, income level, and recent apparel purchase activity. A focus group interview consists of 8 to 12 participants who meet with the moderator in a specially designed room equipped with audio and video recording equipment. The participants are told that the session is being recorded for later analysis. Often the client views the sessions through a one-way mirror. The research may include multiple groups at different locations. Although it involves extra expense, some focus group research merits interviews in different parts of the country to determine if consumers hold different views depending on location.

Moderators need a way to break the ice so participants feel free to talk about feelings and experiences. Some groups begin with participants sharing stories about their latest shopping trip, the nicest sales associate they ever met, or describing their favorite outfit. Sometimes participants are asked to assemble a collage illustrating who they are or their relationship to the product and share it at the beginning of the session. Such activities help reduce a group's inhibitions about talking about feelings and lifestyle practices. As a catalyst to the discussion, the moderator often introduces a stimulus. The stimulus may be storyboards for ads, mock-ups of packaging, video clips of styles or shopping environments, or actual products. Reacting to these stimulus items organizes and directs the discussion in ways that elicit information of interest to the sponsor.

In focus group research, the best information related to consumer satisfaction comes not from asking consumers to describe the kinds of goods they want to buy but from asking instead about their experiences engaging in a consumption activity (i.e., shopping for gifts, buying and wearing career clothes). In analyzing focus group research, each element mentioned has equal status—the attribute mentioned more often is not more important than any of the others. The interviews offer the chance to collect both reactions to proposed products and information on the ways that consumers allocate resources, evaluate outcomes, and develop expectations. Using the context information—how people buy and use the goods—and the concrete personal and environmental elements present in the product talk generates a set of tangible and intangible product attributes that are important to consumers (Fennell, 1991).

Focus groups are not designed to seek consensus but to extract the maximum information from a group heterogeneous in many ways, except that participants come from a specific consumer segment based on age, gender, income level, and the recent purchase behavior. The analysis of the interview transcripts often leads to identification of naturally occurring subsegments that can be further researched in the quantitative phase.

Activity 7.3 *Ask the* *Moderator*	Invite a focus group moderator to class to share some experiences about interviewing people for clients. Ask for referrals from research firms, advertising agencies, or university departments where professors conduct marketing research.

Consumer Anthropology. Although focus groups are the most popular qualitative research approach to asking "what" and "why" questions, observation in natural settings is gaining in popularity (Kaufman, 1997). Traditional research helps companies understand motivators within a product category but not the more specific motivators to buy a particular brand. When people can not verbalize what they think, observing actual behavior provides rich data on the meanings attached to brand choice (Levin, 1992). A researcher at an advertising agency visited teens' bedrooms for a game company and videotaped consumers showing off their wardrobes for an apparel company. The goal of this form of research is to elicit true and honest responses by locating consumers in their natural habitat (Cuneo, 1994).

Some researchers rely on video to bring the consumer's behavior alive for companies. They may videotape consumers at the mall or at a bar after work, or they may use the video camera to capture interviews at schools or offices. Some researchers give the camera to consumers and ask them to create a videotape of their experiences with products. Observational research is useful in generating questions for survey research, capturing the language used by consumers to describe styles and shopping experiences, and providing insights for product development (Rickard, 1994).

Pioneering a field called retail anthropology, a company called Envirosell analyzes consumers' in-store shopping behavior using cameras that look like those used for security and "trackers"—researchers with clipboards who observe and note the time consumers spend in shopping activities. Using the trackers' notes and annotated tracking sheets, the company analyzes how much time a person spends looking at displays, scanning racks, or reading labels. Because the company has been conducting studies for years, researchers are able to trace shifts in consumer behavior, such as how much less time consumers are spending on each shopping trip (Gladwell, 1996).

In interview situations, psychologists and psychotherapists try to discover consumers' emotional and subconscious motivations behind consumption decisions. They use projective methods that allow people to reveal themselves in a nonthreatening way. For example, consumers may be asked to create a personality for a brand and then discuss how they feel about that brand and how the brand feels about them. The goal is to create a match between the product or brand and the personality of the consumer (Masterson, 1994).

Instead of shopping, become an observer in a store. Watch how consumers interact with their surroundings. Jot down a brief description of some of the consumers you are observing. Then note where they shop, how long they spend, whether they try on clothing or not, their interaction with sales associates, and whether they make a purchase. What can a forecaster learn from this kind of observation?

Activity 7.4
How People Shop

Relational Marketing. Companies communicate with consumers through different media. Each type of media serves a different purpose (Sloan, 1991):

- Preference media, such as advertising on TV and in print, attempts to win new users for a brand.

- Behavior media, such as promotions in stores or direct marketing, attempts to spur action in potential or infrequent users.

- Relationship media talks directly to the company's current, active customers.

Building a "learning relationship" with customers means building an ongoing, interactive connection that encourages collaboration on how to meet consumers' needs. As companies move toward mass customization—using production and information technology to deliver individually customized goods and services—companies also move toward one-to-one marketing, where customers' specific needs and preferences are the essential information that drives the system (Pine, Peppers, & Rogers, 1995).

In **relational marketing,** each company develops ways to interact directly with customers. When a denim and casual wear manufacturer was testing a line extension for large-sized women, they attached a consumer-response hangtag that asked questions such as "Pick the three most important factors that influenced the purchase of this garment" and "What problems have you experienced in shopping for casual sportswear?" They reported a 4 to 5 percent return of the cards (Ozzard, 1993). Levi Strauss developed mass-customized jeans by taking measurements in the store, having customers try on jeans to discover fit preferences, and using the results to produce and deliver individualized jeans to the customer.

Retailers are using relational marketing when they identify their best customers, offer them preferred customer cards, and promote the use of the cards with discounts on purchases. With the cards, companies can track purchases and discover consumer preferences. Some companies take it further and alert customers via e-mail, fax, or phone when something new in their preference range arrives or when a special promotional event is likely to be of interest.

A digital approach to relational marketing involves a company's Internet Web sites when the site is used to elicit consumers' opinions about styles and products. When Web site visitors register providing preference profiles, the company can target promotional information directly to them.

Some companies offer 800 numbers on which consumers can talk about products. Building direct-to-consumer relationships depends on multiple contacts and follow-up but marketers feel the effort is important to increase brand loyalty and as a way to justify premium prices. As one apparel executive put it, "Every customer we have is our focus group" (Socha, 1998a).

Activity 7.5 *Preferred* *Customers*	Locate a store in your area that issues preferred customer cards. Interview the store manager or the marketing director about the benefits to the consumer and to the company of using these cards. Is this form of relational marketing likely to expand in the future? Why or why not?

Asking "What" and "How Many" Questions

The qualitative phase of testing provides the product development team with data on the way consumers view and operate within their marketing environment. The **quantitative** phase centers on determining the incidence of those responses in the population. Traditionally, marketers have used large-scale surveys to provide answers about the size and preferences of consumer segments.

Research in Malls and Stores. Malls sometimes include a consumer research facility where studies are conducted for companies (Figure 7.8). The study sponsor identifies particular characteristics for participants, usually demographic categories such as gender, age, and income. Personnel from the research company intercept customers in the mall, ask them some preliminary questions to verify that they meet the sponsor's requirements, and invite them

FIGURE 7.8

The mall provides a researcher with the opportunity to observe consumer behavior. Some malls have an on-site research facility and recruit subjects from the shoppers in the mall, a technique called mall intercept.

to participate in a study. Participants are usually offered a small incentive like free lunch at one of the mall's restaurants or a gift. Customers who agree to participate are taken to the research facility where they may be interviewed, asked to provide opinions on products, or complete survey questionnaires. By conducting studies at mall-based consumer research facilities in different geographic areas, companies gain insight into consumer preferences and how they differ according to location.

One of the main drawbacks to **mall intercept research** is time. It may take several weeks to design the study, negotiate with the research sites, distribute the research materials, and run the studies. Suppose it takes a month before data are available; that time horizon may be too long in a fast-paced competitive environment. The quality of the data depends on the scrupulousness of the research facility in recruiting participants, administering the research, and analyzing the data. Because a research facility works for many companies, it must keep each sponsor's data confidential.

Some consumer research facilities in malls are equipped with computers that enable consumers to see products on the screen and indicate their views by touching the computer screen. Large chains that prefer having research facilities in their own stores at geographically dispersed sites also use this technology. At in-store testing facilities, participants are carefully screened as to demographic profiles. During the tests, participants sit in front of computer screens and are asked to indicate preferences related to color, price, purchase intent, and the retailer's image and advertising. Because the research can be designed and sent via satellite to the sites simultaneously, the company can quickly poll 300 to 400 consumers about products and shopping behavior. Results are available in days versus the traditional three to four weeks for mall intercept studies (Fisher, 1991; Tahmincioglu, 1990).

Because of the speed, this approach makes it possible to incorporate a research phase in the product development process. **Style testing**—pretesting styles with consumers—can aid in early identification of "winners" and "losers" (styles with such low consumer interest that they can be eliminated from further development). A fashion scout can see a new design in Europe, transmit the idea via color photo to corporate headquarters where a prototype design can be developed using computer-aided design, the design submitted to consumer testing at the company's sites, and results tabulated within 24 hours (Potts, 1990).

In a traditional **survey,** consumers answer questions posed by a researcher and may give responses that seem more socially acceptable than their actual behavior. Moving the research onto the computer as simulated shopping trips can help eliminate this bias because consumers are less likely to identify what is being tested (Rickard, 1993). On the computer, the participant navigates through several shopping trips, each of which includes different prices and products. During the simulated shopping trips consumers browse shelves, choose items by touching the screen, take a closer look at the item, and either "buy" the product or return it to the shelf. Computer simulation technology offers researchers another tool for discovering consumer preferences and projecting the potential market for products.

To be reliable as decision support, polling in malls and stores must involve:

- Careful selection criteria for participants so that people answering the questions represent a larger, identifiable population of potential buyers.
- Stimulus items as close as possible to what the consumer would see in an actual buying situation.
- Results that are integrated with other sources and with other research findings to become part of but not replace the executives decision process.

Activity 7.6
Become a Test
Subject

Locate a mall that includes a test facility by checking in the Yellow Pages under "market research." Visit the mall and you may see people with clipboards intercepting shoppers. If you fit the consumer profile for a study that day, you may be asked to participate. If visiting a test facility is not practical, volunteer to participate in a study on campus. Participating as a subject provides insight into all the things that can go right and wrong with a consumer study.

In-Store Testing. In surveys, a small sample of consumers are asked questions about their intention to purchase and the results are inferred to be representative of the actual behavior of a larger population. Such a leap of inference is not necessary when research is conducted in a natural in-store environment. Sales are a clear measure of behavior, whereas attitudes or intention to buy are not.

Product development often proceeds blindly without consumer feedback because planning for the new season is well advanced before the preceding season is even shipped, much less sold. Oxford Shirtings, a division of Oxford Industries, is a large manufacturer of private label men's woven sports and dress shirts. It formed a three-way partnership with J.C. Penney, a long-time retailer of their company's products, and the mill where the shirt fabrics were produced. The goal of the partners was to test fashion styles in stores in advance of bulk purchase decisions. Oxford merchandisers and Penney buyers discussed trends and style direction to determine which style concepts to test. Mill, manufacturer, and retailer collaborated on each stage of developing the product for testing. Using 50 test stores, the different fashion looks were evaluated for consumer acceptance of fabric and color. Feedback from the test enabled Penney buyers to refine their buys and provided Oxford Shirtings with valuable information about where to focus product development efforts (Skinner, 1993).

In-store research takes several forms:

- **Showcase and Laboratory Stores**

Some manufacturers operate specialty stores as laboratories to test the viability of new products (Gordon, 1990). Designers and manufacturers create **showcase or laboratory stores** that are museums to the product and offer a chance to present their entire line (Figure 7.9). While primarily a billboard for the brand and an educational environment for retailers on the latest in visual merchandising, the stores also serve a research purpose. The stores are a place for the manufacturer to gather intelligence about what consumers want, which products in the line are heating up and which cooling down, and which packaging and promotional initiatives are most effective (Fitzgerald, 1992).

- **Test Stores**

Specialty store chains selling store labels designate certain stores as test sites. Any store in the chain may be designated a test store for a particular time period. The test store is cleared of merchandise and reset with test merchandise. Then, business continues as usual—consumers are completely unaware that a test is underway.

- **Test Merchandise Groups**

A less extensive approach is to place test groups of merchandise in with ordinary merchandise. When product developers monitor sales information from

FIGURE 7.9

FIGURE 7.9

Showcase stores are museums to the product and offer a chance for designers to present their entire line. Here, the entrance to the Tommy Hilfiger shop in London features the women's and men's Red Label collection.

these test sites the company can fine-tune sales potential by optimizing the selling price and color assortment. They can also discover items that often are sold together as input for promotions and visual merchandising.

Activity 7.7 Showcase Stores

Look for a stand-alone store for a well-known brand—one where the entire line of that brand is presented without the distractions of other brands. Showcase stores are ususally located in large malls in urban areas or in shopping districts where the architecture and vibrant street life draw crowds. Shop the showcase store and compare the merchandise and presentation with the same brand in a department store. What merchandise is the same between the two stores? What merchandise is available only in the showcase store? List the ways this store could serve a research function.

Surveys and Panel Studies. A survey asks a set of questions to a group of people at one point in time. The purpose of a survey is to investigate consumer attitudes and opinions. Surveys are a relatively inexpensive way to tap into consumers' views on products, shopping habits, and information sources. However, there are drawbacks. Surveys are only a snapshot of a particular point in time and may not provide directional information in a fast-changing marketplace. Further, what consumers say in answer to survey questions and their actual behavior may be very different.

A **panel study** asks questions of a group of people over time in order to track changes in consumer attitudes and opinions. The Yankelovich Monitor has administered questions to large consumer panels for almost 30 years, seeking insight into the consumer values and attitudes that shape purchase decisions (Heath, 1996c). Other companies use panel studies to track purchases and planned purchases in various apparel categories as a means of diagnosing shifts in market share by company and retail channel ("Mass sees," 1997; "Tempting," 1997). A few firms specialize in panel research on specific consumer segments. The Zandl Group tracks the fast-moving teen consumers and their opinions about which brand makes the "coolest" clothing. The study indicates which brands are currently the coolest, which are gaining in the cool factor, and which brands are in decline ("Teen cool," 1997).

Even though surveys have significant drawbacks, the technique will continue to be a popular way to take a snapshot of current market conditions. The panel study, with its potential to track changes through time, provides more directional information for forecasting. Surveys, panel studies, and the statistical quantification they provide continue to be an important element in understanding consumer preferences and behavior.

Demographics Revisited

Geodemographics. **Geodemographics** links geography and demographics to show the clustering of similar people in a neighborhood (Riche, 1990). Census data on age, income, ethnicity, and other categories are "smoothed out" to create an identity, label, and affluence rating for a neighborhood. The resulting clusters are useful for pinpointing locations for new stores or malls, to target mailings of catalogs, and to reveal insights about consumer preferences. The fragmentation of markets in the 1980s means that products and services must be targeted not to a mass market but to submarkets identified by combinations of demographics and geography.

In the early 1970s, a college professor and entrepreneur used cluster analysis and census data to create zip code clusters (Weiss, 1988). The concept behind the analysis is that neighborhoods geographically separated may be more similar to each other than those nearby. For example, the demographic makeup of college towns and the preferences of the residents are similar no matter where in the country they are located. These college towns are more like each other than they are like other towns in their vicinity. Using this logic, the company Claritas merges U.S. Census data with credit card, mail-order sales, TV viewing, subscription, and other purchasing information to create PRIZM (Potential Rating Index by Zip Market)—a system sorting all the zip codes in the United States into neighborhood types. Each type can be

Profile

DeeDee Gordon, Director of Market Research and Product Development, Lambesis

DeeDee Gordon was only 18 years old when she opened a boutique in Boston called Placid Planet, a lifestyle destination for "cool kids" and the market researchers who track youth trends. Cool can't be manufactured, it can only be discovered—first by kids who do something no one else is doing, then by the market researchers who are cool enough to understand what they see. A job offer from Converse moved Ms. Gordon from retailer to shoe designer. She scored big right away by recognizing that the tube socks and shower sandals worn by teenage girls in Los Angeles as part of a Mexican gangster look could be translated into a thick-soled sneaker-sandal—a style that continues to be popular (Gladwell, 1997). As a shoe designer she was "unimpressed by the trend forecasts available to her and decided there had to be a new way." Ms. Gordon now works for the image and advertising agency Lambesis where she runs her own business unit as her staff of 40 keep tabs on cool kids in cities across America and abroad. She says it took three years to "prototype the system" she uses. She has worked on campaigns for Bebe, Skyy Vodka, and Airwalk. Her career parallels the rise of an industry based on knowing what kids are thinking, doing, and buying.

Ms. Gordon's focus is on developing a youth culture forecast based on a survey of 1,800 respondents in New York, Los Angeles, San Francisco, Seattle, Chicago, and Miami. In each city Ms. Gordon's team finds the most popular bars, clubs, and hangouts inviting kids to fill out questionnaires or sit for an interview. The team asks "questions about everything and everything is an open-ended question." Topics covered include: music, sports, fashion, advertising, aspirations, artistic endeavors—"the entire lifestyle." The questions use "language appropriate for the teen and it's not contrived—the last thing they want to hear is [the interviewer] calling something cool." Since the questions are posed by their peers, Ms. Gordon contends that interviewees "don't censor the material" and tend to reveal "what is really happening—drugs, sex, entertainment, and the real sites kids look at on the Internet." Both interviewer and interviewee are paid so "they have an incentive, they are selling their information, and they walk away with money in their pocket."

Data are gathered from trendsetters and the mainstream, both male and female across three age ranges—14- to 18-year old, 19- to 24-year old, and 25- to 30-year old. Based on these data, Ms. Gordon publishes her forecast, the *L Report*, four times a year for industry subscribers who pay $20,000 per year. The *L Report* includes one book for each city and a seventh book containing Ms. Gordon's overall trend analysis. International editions of the *L Report* covering youth culture in England and Japan were added in 1999.

What makes the *L Report* different is the coupling of the trendsetter and mainstream data. According to Ms. Gordon, mainstream interviewees' "answers are already out in the marketplace, on the cover of every magazine." Trendsetters are "more forward thinkers—people who are looking outside their own backyard for inspiration for a lifestyle, they are more inquisitive than others (buying magazines from Europe and Asia, staying on the Internet)." They don't care if their friends give it their stamp of approval." Instead, "they want to bring new information to the people they know." Such people are difficult to find but, once located, a trendsetter becomes a valuable informant because Ms. Gordon contends that "a trendsetter always stays a trendsetter—it's a frame of mind."

Ms. Gordon observes trendsetter data for her own work, allowing her to be anywhere from one to sometimes three years ahead of a trend. Interviews with trendsetters often turn up things Ms. Gordon and her team have not heard of before. When this happens "street teams of kids" are sent to locate and verify these findings. The mainstream data are "there mostly for the clients to be comfortable about and understand where things are going."

Unlike some other trend forecasters, Ms. Gordon carefully analyzes the results of questionnaires and interviews to increase the accuracy and precision of her findings. "Everything is backed up with data. It's not like we're pulling blanket statements out of the sky. We've got enough data from all over the world to back up everything we predict. Then, we use diffusion theory to explain how some people are more important than others in starting word of mouth." Ms. Gordon's purpose is to make trends "understandable to people who don't understand."

The *L Report* allows subscribers "to watch a trend start with trendsetters—people who are innovators—and move into the mainstream." According to Ms. Gordon, a "fad is a quick hit—in and out" whereas "a trend hits every part of the lifestyle." The pace appears to be picking up as Ms. Gordon observes that "earlier it took about a year-and-a-half to move to the mainstream, now it takes 3 to 5 months." Ms. Gordon reports seeing "differences in timing—New York, Miami, and Los Angeles will be more fashion-forward than Dallas." But, because of the Internet, trends spread faster—"all this information is going out in real time, it's going out all over the world, and people are able to communicate with each other and spread the word." Ms. Gordon also looks for movement of trends between age groups. She "watches the action of 19- to 24-year olds—"they are the most important decision makers. Their ideas 'trickle down' to 14- to 18-year olds who want to appear cooler and 'trickle up' to 25- to 30-year olds because they want to be younger."

Ms. Gordon's research efforts include teen panels of young people from around the world who are hired for one year to track and report on what is going on in their home country. Teen panel members have to be "very forward thinkers, very objective" (not biased toward any one thing). They are shown products, asked lifestyle questions, and tracked over time. Reports come in from the United States, Europe, Japan, Australia, China, and South America. As she explains, "Now we are finding places that are influencing the world, all over the world, in places where I never thought I'd have to look."

Ms. Gordon not only uses survey methods but also participant observation techniques as she shops in cities like London, Paris, Tokyo, Rome, and Milan. But she doesn't shop like other people would. Instead she "scans"—that is, she looks, tries on new styles, and buys two of things that illustrate where style is heading, one to show clients, one for her personal archive. She uses the items in her archive to illustrate "the actual innovation over a certain type of product from 10 years ago to now." She also clips and saves interesting visuals, a practice she has followed since high school. A staff member is now scanning her extensive collection onto a computer to create a CD-ROM library of visuals. As she puts it, "you can never have too many visuals."

As for working with clients, Ms. Gordon looks for "that one person with any company who has vision—that's the person who is going to hire someone like me." That person "understands that things are changing, is willing to keep an open mind and put aside everything he or she assumes is happening, and just take the data and information at face value."

Sources:

Gladwell, M. (1997, March 17). The coolhunt. *The New Yorker*, 78–88.

Author interview with Gordon, May 6, 1999.

Speech given by Gordon as the Grisham-Trentham Lecturer, Auburn University, May 6, 1999.

profiled by demographics, lifestyle, media usage, and preference for make of car, food, and other products. The data are updated each year (Levanas, 1998). A 35-year old professional who buys expensive suits, drives a Volvo, and buys fresh-ground coffee and olive oil is living in a "Kids & Cul-de-Sacs" neighborhood while an aging baby boomer who lives in the suburbs, drives a Mercedes, reads *Golf Digest,* and buys salt substitute is living in a "Cashmere & Country Club" neighborhood (Valle, 1994).

PRIZM was one of the first companies to make geodemographic information useful to marketing executives, but it has been joined by others so that today's executive can choose among firms. One of the key questions in using geodemographics is, how do you define a neighborhood—by zip code or by census track? Each company offers its own version of clustering and its own interpretation of the resulting clusters.

Today's executive is not restricted to buying geodemographic analysis from one of the research firms. The technology is now available on the executive's desktop. While the basic technology linking census data and mapping has been around since the 1960s, the software did not become available on the personal computer until the mid-1990s (Freed, 1994). At that time, companies began to sell the basic mapping software at a relatively low price, planning to make money by selling updated packages of geographic, economic, and demographic data. With the software in place, an analyst can map competitor locations, areas of dense population, neighborhoods with highest income, high-traffic roads, and other information to support strategic marketing decisions.

Geodemographics is useful to forecasters in pinpointing the markets where hot trends begin and mapping their potential diffusion. Geodemographics can identify the towns and neighborhoods that are teen-poor (under 4% of the population is aged 14 to 17) and those with higher concentrations for teens, areas that are attracting young adults, and those where boomers are migrating (Sutton, 1993). These patterns signal retail growth potential for some stores and product categories and a mismatch for others. Because the United States is heading for a more diverse population in the 21st century, one way to forecast the future is to identify and monitor locations where diversity already exists (Allen & Turner, 1990). Geodemographics allows forecasters to locate diverse neighborhoods where consumption patterns today may anticipate those that will develop in other locales as the future unfolds.

Demographics and Preferences. The traditional demographic variables of age, ethnicity, gender, and income are still helpful in visualizing consumer markets. But the concepts underlying these variables are more complex today.

Preferences and Age   After declining for 16 years, the teen population began to grow in 1992 and will continue to expand according to projections until 2010, when there will be 35 million teens or 10% of the population (Silverman, 1998b). Teens are still more likely than other age groups to follow trends and spend a disproportionate amount of their discretionary spending on fashion. Like teenagers of earlier generations, they are attracted to an air of irreverence in ads and authenticity in products. Growing up with computers and music videos creates a preference for fast-paced media that does not appeal to their parents' generation (Feitelberg, 1995). However, interest in clothing declines for both men and women in their 20s when their spending priorities shift to other categories and comfort becomes a priority over defining and expressing identity ("Standing out," 1998).

The problem for executives is to appeal to one age group without turning off another. Malls entice teens with lights, signs, video banks, and unisex stores designed to entertain (Parr, 1997). Yet an environment that appeals to teens and young adults can be stressful to people in their 40s and 50s (Figure 7.10). In 2000, there will be 35.7 million boomers aged 45 to 54 and that segment controls 50 percent of the discretionary income in the United States. Malls burst onto the retail scene when the baby boomers were teens and young adults. Now, this same consumer cohort is cutting the time they spend in malls and malls are struggling to attract consumers (Silverman, 1998a).

FIGURE 7.10

Mall environments that entice teens can be stressful for people in their 40s and 50s. Executives must decide how to attract one generational group without turning off another.

Change based on demographics accumulates slowly, and change in behavior that can be traced to marketing is incremental at best. Wolfe (1998) suggests that the adult median age plus or minus five years represents the psychological center of cultural change. As an example, he cites median age in the 1960s in the mid-30s and people in that age range such as Bob Dylan, Jane Fonda, and Abbie Hoffman, who inspired the boomers that followed to challenge the traditional path for young people. The change from traditional to nontraditional behavior seemed to happen overnight, but the foundations of that change had been laid by social innovators in the median age cohort that preceded it.

The median age in 1998 was almost 43 and would move upward to nearly 50 within 15 years. If the median age hypothesis is true, values held by those in the median age group are directional because group size reaches the critical mass necessary to set the agenda for society. Wolfe's idea mirrors the prediction pattern proposed by Behling (1985/1986) and discussed in Chapter 3—median age is linked to the directional flow of fashion, fashion trickles up when the median age is low and trickles down when the median age is high.

Preferences and Ethnicity   Ethnicity presents the same kind of complex puzzle as age. Hispanic, African-American, Asian, and other ethnic consumers wield considerable purchasing power and outspend white consumers in some apparel categories. However, research indicates that they are frequently dissatisfied with the retail selection. When given a choice between a clearly Anglo style and a more multiethnic image, ethnic consumers choose the multiethnic (Silverman, 1998c).

Ethnic consumers have distinctive characteristics and preference patterns. African-American women prefer to be slightly overdressed rather than underdressed (57 percent compared to 44 percent of all other women) and almost a third of all African-American women are classified as fashion innovators (only one-sixth of all other women are fashion innovators). Yet preferences vary among black women according to their cultural identification as American, Caribbean, or African ("Fashion noir," 1998).

It would be a mistake to classify all members of ethnic groups in a simplistic way that ignores diversity. Hispanic consumers from different countries of origin display different preference profiles. Asians from Japan, Korea, and China also differ in product preferences. Product developers, marketers, and forecasters must take such variations into account in explaining preference patterns and their effect on consumer demand.

Preferences and Gender Preferences based on gender develop very early in life, and by the age of five boys and girls assume different roles and choose products accordingly. By the time children become teens, the gender gap grows more obvious ("Bridging the gender gap," 1996). Many products are gender-specific in appeal, but some brands manage a unisex appeal although the products are usually modified to target the preferences of each gender. Girls are more likely to cross over to make a purchase on "boy's turf" than vice versa. Young women aged 16 to 19 enjoy defining their individuality through clothing, but young men of the same age tend to adopt a uniform approach that fits in with their friends ("Standing out," 1998).

Women on average earn less than men—71.4 cents for women to a dollar for men. But women influence 70 to 85 percent of all purchasing decisions and act as purchasing agent for their families. For marketers, targeting women in a generic or stereotypical way will not work anymore because women's lives are so varied today. For example, beginning in 1991, women outspent men on sports shoes and apparel. One marketer estimated eight different segments of women consumers based on income and lifestyle variables. Research on gender role shows that men have stayed the same but women have broadened their interests and their roles. Women have been in the forefront of the move away from dress-for-success strategies and toward more casual clothing at work or working from home. This shift has had a major effect on apparel sales (Lauerman, 1997).

Women of the boomer generation have set societal agendas throughout their life cycle, beginning with delaying marriage and childbearing in their 20s and embracing ardent careerism in their 20s, 30s, and 40s. The baby boom generation has a high level of educational attainment. As women of this generation enter their 50s, they may overturn traditional thinking about the way a mature consumer behaves. Consumers in the older age group are expected to be traditional in their values, brand loyal, and quality conscious rather than fashion conscious. Most marketers believe that boomer women will be much less predictable than those of earlier generations (Rock, 1995).

Preferences and Income   Middle- and upper-income shoppers are confirmed **cross-shoppers**—consumers who shop up and down the spectrum from discount stores to luxury lines at department stores (Steinhauer, 1998b). Of shoppers with household incomes of more than $70,000, 90 percent shop in discount stores, a percentage twice as large as five years ago. What began in the frugal early 1990s as a necessity persisted throughout the decade. Affluent consumers had not gotten cheaper—sales for luxury goods were still selling at high rates. But low-priced stores such as Target and Old Navy attracted the same crowd with stylish and basic products and quick and easy shopping formats. Trendspotters for stores up and down the spectrum attend the same trade shows around the world. Colors and style concepts show up at all levels at about the same time, even if the quality level differs. For the consumer, that means indulging in high-end items when quality and visibility are important and shopping at the lower end for everything else. Evidence of the cross-shopping consumer revised the price-value equation in a way that made simple segmentation by income less reliable.

Consumer Segmentation Revised

Consumer segmentation attempts to discriminate between types of consumers and to profile each type (see Chapter 2). Consumer segmentation is useful in researching target audiences for products, brands, and advertising or promotion campaigns. The critical issue is to decide what set of variables will yield the clearest and most accurate picture—demographics, psychographics, generational cohort, lifestyle, life stage, or geodemographics? Ideally, the marketing executive would have all available information, but because information is expensive, this is unlikely. Complicating the decisions further are fragmentation of markets and the seemingly contradictory behavior of today's consumer. Even if an executive has a large budget to buy research and information services, that information supports but does not replace decision making.

In earlier eras, it was sufficient to tell a consumer about a product or service and the benefits that would accrue from its use. Today, positioning is much more likely to include the experience associated with consumption of the product and to engage the consumer's imagination in linking product and benefits. Such appeals can reach across generational boundaries. For example, Dockers ads focus on the features and benefits of the product, avoiding any age reference. The product could appeal to twenty-somethings or to the mature customer's increasing girth. The mature buyer emerges from the experience with ego intact, perhaps with a change in brand if not in size (Silverman, 1998a).

Where consumer segmentation focuses on the type of consumer, **product segmentation** focuses on differences between brands on product-specific criteria. Product segmentation is used to research brand image, brand associations, and consumer perceptions of brand similarities at critical points in the purchase decision—before purchase, at the point of purchase, and in use. The research attempts to understand the decision rules consumers use in selecting one brand over another or deciding that one brand can substitute for another.

Both consumer segmentation and product segmentation are incomplete because in today's market, each consumer represents multiple segments. Blending the two approaches—a consumer selects a product for a particular use or occasion and may use a different set of criteria in making the same decision at another time—explains the independence and savvy of today's consumer.

Whether the goal is to define a market, create optimal strategies for existing brands, position brands and products, or identify gaps in the market for new product opportunities, the steps are the same:

- Define the situation using point-of-sale data and findings from past research efforts.
- Use qualitative and quantitative research to collect consumer-defined attributes of the product, the search and purchase experience, and the experience of using the product.
- Map the preference patterns using techniques such as cluster analysis.

The resulting "maps" of the market by consumer type and product category help marketers and forecasters identify the microsegments in the market that are directional for purchase patterns in the future. Being just ahead of these trends is an excellent place to be when making decisions about product development, marketing, and merchandising.

Locate a published report of a consumer segmentation study in marketing journals or apparel trade publications. Select a product category and analyze the connection between the types of people profiled in the study and that product category. Is the category likely to rise in popularity or fall? Is the market for the product category increasing or decreasing? Should the product category be repositioned to target a different consumer audience?

Activity 7.8
Research
Reports

Key Terms and Concepts

Brand Image
Brand Loyalty
Brand Recognition
Branding
Cross-Shoppers
Depth Interview
Designer Name Brands
Focus Group
Focus Group Moderator

Geodemographics
Mall Intercept Research
Mass Customization
Mega Nichers
National Brands
Panel Studies
Private-Label Brands
Product Segmentation
Qualitative Research

Quantitative Research
Relational Marketing
Showcase or Laboratory
   Stores
Store Brands
Style Testing
Survey Research
3-D Brands
Virtual Dressing Rooms

Case Revisited: Extending the Line

An established men's wear designer plans to introduce a women's wear line. The signature look of the line must be translated into new products for a new customer in a more volatile marketplace. John is the marketing executive in charge of researching the opportunities and the problems in extending the line. He needs many kinds of information on the preferences of the new female customer in order to project the company's future in this new endeavor. Use the following questions to review the chapter and summarize the route John might take to get the answers his company needs.

The conceptual map of consumer preferences: The company needs a picture of the potential match between the company's line and consumer expectations. What are the consumer's expectations for the brand? What are the most desirable attributes of products in this category? What exciting or surprising attributes of the product or brand will attract consumers initially? What attributes will turn consumers into brand loyal customers? How sensitive is this consumer segment to quality issues?

Research strategy: Initial answers to these questions may come from women who are already buying from the men's line. The next step is to map out a research plan to gather continuous information about consumers' wants and needs. How will information be gathered: In focus groups? By marketplace anthropologists, psychologists, and ethnographers using observational techniques? In mall intercept studies? Through relational marketing? Through surveys or panel studies?

Reducing risks: Before rolling out a complete line and placing full production orders, executives will need data on consumer reaction to proposed styles.

How will these tests be conducted: In-store testing? As stimulus items in focus groups? As images in a computer poll of consumers nationwide?

Identifying the consumer segment: *What must an apparel manufacturer understand about customers in order to meet their needs, wants, and expectation? Develop a checklist of the information needs of an apparel executive who must forecast directions in consumer preference patterns into the future.*

Additional Forecasting Activities

Consumers' Natural Habitat. Use a video camera to record observations about the style characteristics of various consumer segments in your town. Film at locations like the mall, downtown, and in the parking lot of discount or mass merchants. What value can observing consumers in their natural habitat have for product developers, marketers, and merchandisers?

How Do They Do That? Analyze how the mega niche and 3-D brands developed. Develop a corporate history for one of these companies. What were the turning points? What problems were overcome? What key strategies propelled the company to the next level? What part does consumer research play in product development, marketing, and retailing in mega-niche and 3-D brands?

Research on Your Own. Conduct your own consumer research on brand names. Ask 20 people to name three favorite brands in three categories of goods—jeans, intimate apparel, and shirts. Then, ask them to select which brand in each category they would "always" buy again. Compare across your sample: How many different brands were named? Was there one predominant brand in each category? How many types of brands are represented in the sample—store brands, private-label brands, national brands? Do your results support or dispute industry survey data that indicate consumers do not discriminate between the types of brands? Discuss the impact of your findings on the future direction of branded merchandise.

Resource Pointers

Online retail sites with consumer profiling and leading-edge interactive technologies:

- Bloomingdales—www.bloomingdales.com
- The Gap—www.gap.com

- Land's End—www.landsend.com
- Levi Strauss & Co—www.levi.com and www.docker.com
- Esprit—www.esprit.com

Web site for Envirosell, a behavioral market research and consulting company, featuring articles about the company and their methods—www.envirosell.com

Web sites related to mass customization:

- Squash Blossom (children's clothes)—www.squashblossom.com
- Arthur Gluck (custom-fit men's shirts)—www.shirtcreations.com
- IC3DJeans—www.IC3D.com

Chapter 8

SALES FORECASTING

> *"As a fashion and design house, we are automatically working many seasons ahead. We are continuously factoring changing economic conditions into our planning."*
> —Gabriella Forte, President and Chief Operation Officer, Calvin Klein Inc

Objectives

- Understand the role of sales forecasting in linking supply and demand.

- Identify the basic techniques of sales forecasting.

- Become aware of new developments in sales forecasting practices.

- Appreciate the link between computer technology and advances in sales forecasting practices.

CASE: DATA ON DEMAND

Patricia started as a manufacturer's representative calling on small accounts and regional chains. She was promoted last year to national sales manager for a manufacturer specializing in activewear. The company recently merged with a former rival to form a company with several brands—one at the better price point sold through specialty stores, two moderate lines targeted to department stores, and one line sold through mass marketers. With these brand tiers in place, the company is investigating new collaborative ventures with top retail accounts, including category management and automated replenishment.

After a decade with the company, Patricia has seen sales forecasting shift from the calculator to the computer. The computer on her desk gives her ac-

cess to the company's data warehouse with years of sales history available for analysis. During her rise through the company, Patricia has taken advantage of the company's liberal policy on professional development. As the technology changed, she attended seminars on forecasting software and other courses to update her skills. Patricia's analysis skills are important to success in her position, but just as important is her experience and knowledge of the market.

For about a month Patricia has been noticing a trend in the sales figures from the Northeast—sales are markedly higher for sportswear in brighter colors. Patricia knows that fashion is moving away from neutrals and toward a more colorful palette. Still, traditionally the Northeast is a region thought to favor a more traditional color range. She wonders: What is driving these sales in the Northeast region? This chapter will introduce some of the strategies and techniques Patricia uses to analyze this development and adjust the sales forecast.

THE FUTURE — "REAL-TIME MARKETING"

Imagine the typical day for a marketing executive in the 21st century. That is what apparel industry executives started doing in the latter part of the 20th century. Starting with emerging technologies such as computer networks, these industry futurists imagined that future marketing executives would work in shifts to cover the 24-hour business day (Smith, 1989). On each shift the marketer would actively process information about marketplace dynamics—consumer behavior and competitors' actions. Information would be updated continuously as sales happened around the world, were scanned in at the point of sale, tabulated, and transmitted to the marketer's desktop on secure communications networks. Watching a video display, the marketer would react quickly to weaknesses and opportunities visible in the stream of sales data by adjusting the flow of goods or making changes in promotions and pricing. In this scenario, marketers become information gladiators looking for competitive advantage and using computer-assisted techniques to evaluate, verify, and act on marketplace data. At the same time that futurists were visualizing the new business day, the textile and apparel industries were rapidly moving toward this ideal of instant response in an information-rich environment.

The first move was to retool the manufacturing process and shorten the product development cycle in an effort to make manufacturing fast enough to respond directly to demand—a strategy called **Quick Response** (Fisher, Hammond, Obermeyer, & Raman, 1994). Paralleling Quick Response (QR) was a strategy to reduce inventory costs called **Just In Time** (JIT), in which components of products arrive just as they are needed in the production process. If sales are concentrated seasonally, applying QR and JIT becomes more complex because manufacturers need high capacities to service demand at peak periods and must shrink production at other periods. Complicating matters even further, some suppliers of fabrics, trims, and findings (buttons, zippers, and other similar components) require long lead times.

The second move was to create an up-to-the-minute continuous flow of sales information by installing point-of-sale (POS) scanners in retail stores (Fisher et al., 1994). Although this seemed like a logical move toward real-time marketing, there were some unanticipated results. The availability of POS data made it possible to identify smaller market niches. Flexible manufacturing made it possible to produce smaller quantities of products efficiently enough to earn a profit. Together with global competition, faster product development, and attempts to give consumers exactly what they wanted, these forces unleashed a proliferation of products. So many new products meant that each one had a shorter lifetime. The result was that there was little or no sales history on which to base forecasts. POS data is **aggregated** (summarized and combined by categories) making it is even more difficult to forecast demand for the many individual products or stock-keeping units (SKUs).

Forecasting is relatively easy, straightforward, and accurate for products with long lifetimes and steady sales. However, the fashion apparel business is one of the most volatile because it creates products that are new, highly seasonal, or have short lifetimes. In such situations forecasts become increasingly inaccurate. Errors in sales forecasting result in two kinds of losses:

- **Markdowns,** when retailers have unwanted goods remaining at the end of a selling period, goods that must be sold, even at a loss.

- Lost sales on more popular items because of **stockouts** (merchandise not available in stock at the time when consumers request it).

Companies have been slow to recognize the changing marketplace environment and adapt forecasting practices to increasing uncertainty about product demand.

Sales forecasting has an impact on every apparel executive's work life whether that executive helps develop the analysis, reads and acts on the reports, or merely reacts to the result of over- or underestimating sales. For this reason, apparel executives need a basic understanding of the traditional approaches to sales forecasting and the leading-edge technologies making real-time marketing a reality in the apparel industry.

Invite retail executives from one or more stores to discuss markdowns and stockouts and their effect on sales revenues. Ask the executives to describe the differences in technology and sales reporting that existed early in their careers compared to today's situation.

Activity 8.1
Reports from the
Front Lines

SALES FORECASTING BASICS

Some people confuse the sales forecast with the sales plan (Mentzer & Bienstock, 1998). The **sales forecast** is a projection of expected demand given a set of environmental conditions. Quantitative and qualitative methods are used to develop the sales forecast. A **sales plan** is the managerial strategy designed to meet or exceed the sales forecast. The sales plan merely defines goals and provides motivation for sales levels that meet or exceed the base—the underlying sales forecast. Managers sometimes make the mistake of skipping or ignoring sales forecasting and set the sales plan goal at 5% or 10% higher than last year's sales. Unless environmental factors favor that increase—factors such as growth in the industry, market share, or consumer demand—no amount of motivation or promotion will make the sales plan happen. The measure of accuracy for the sales forecast is the difference between the forecast and what actually happens. The best way to improve forecasting accuracy is to review actual sales figures against the sales forecast for the same time period. Differences between the two must be explained in terms of variation in the environmental conditions or problems with assumptions underlying the forecast. In this way, executives build a better understanding of how environmental factors have an impact on sales.

Sales forecasts have a specific time horizon and are usually updated quarterly. Many executives in a firm need access to the sales forecast, including:

- Marketing managers planning promotion, pricing, and channel placement for individual products and product lines.
- Sales managers as input for the sales plan by geographic territory or sales force deployment.
- Financial managers projecting costs, profit levels, and capital needed to operate.
- Production managers planning and scheduling labor and equipment, and ordering raw materials.
- Distribution managers planning the logistics of getting products from production sites to retailing venues.

Sales forecasting requires access to three kinds of information. First, forecasters need internal data on sales volume and marketing actions such as changes in pricing, promotional efforts, or channels of distribution. Second, they need information on future plans for marketing and product distribution. Finally, they need external data relevant to their market and information on general economic, political, and cultural conditions.

The internal data allow the forecasters to group data in different ways to evaluate recent and past performance (Bolt, 1994). Some of the basic ways to group data for analysis are by:

- **Sales Volume**

Determine the relative contribution each product or product group makes to the company's revenue by comparing sales for that product or group to total sales volume.

- **Sales Volume by Geographic Area**

Break down sales by geographic area (such as by sales territories) and compare actual sales to potential sales given the demographics and retail climate in each area.

- **Sales Volume by Time Period**

Discover seasonal effects and the effect of price changes, promotions, and advertising on sales by comparing fluctuations in sales against a time scale.

- **Sales Volume by Sales Channel**

Discover which sales channels are most profitable by comparing sales performance by type of distribution and retail venue as a guide to increasing or decreasing reliance on each channel.

Viewing sales volume through these various lenses, the forecasters correlate the effect of past decisions on sales and market share.

The quality of the forecast depends on how precisely sales are tracked. Company executives decide whether to track sales by:

- Stock-keeping unit (individual products by color and size).

- Individual product.

- Product family (related items).

The company executives also decide how to aggregate sales data—daily, weekly, or monthly. Setting these levels for analysis depends on the prior experience of the company, the product profile, and the volatility of the marketplace.

The sales forecast is a projection of expectations given past performance and what is known about future marketing efforts. These projections will be inaccurate unless they are corrected to take into account external data such as the expectations for the economy and the effects of the product life cycle. Putting sales projections in context improves forecasting accuracy.

SALES FORECASTING METHODS

What does a company do with the POS data it collects in large-scale databases? To be meaningful, the data must be reduced to meaningful proportions using conceptual and statistical frameworks. Yet many managers have a limited background in sales forecasting and are daunted by the many statistical techniques that can be used. Selecting which techniques are appropriate for a

Brian Tully, Operations Manager, Lanier Clothes, Oxford Industries

Brian Tully began working for Oxford Industries in 1978, first in the shirt division, later in the tailored clothing division. He has worked in operations, customer service, and sales. As Operations Manager for Lanier Clothes, he oversees both branded and private label businesses in tailored clothing. His division was "more negatively impacted by the trend toward Casual Friday than any other division [in Oxford Industries]—some divisions were probably impacted favorably." With a diverse product line, "if something cycles down, chances are pretty good that another type of clothing is cycling up." Total sales for tailored clothing "has been pretty consistently a downward trend for the last 15 years with little blips here and there where it has gone back up." For Mr. Tully's division "the real key has been increasing market share every year." To do that the division has adopted a value-added strategy and has moved toward more branded lines. "Becoming more branded is definitely a strategy—it gives you a stronger identity in the marketplace."

Mr. Tully's experience means that he has been around for many changes in the way sales forecasting is done. He sees the biggest change as "the way technology allows people to do more—a function of being able to collect the data and format the data." Specifically, in the past executives "had less time to forecast because so much time was spent collecting the data." Now that it is easier to gather results, the emphasis has shifted from acquisition to more analysis. "Technology has been wonderful in giving us great tools to play 'what-if' with, but people have to understand the market and what the numbers should be. It takes a sense of the business (which you only get by time and involvement) to recognize when the numbers aren't right or when you want to look at them in a different way."

According to Mr. Tully, the forecasting process is "very interactive, very dynamic." The "starting point is historical data—how has [the company] done with this customer in the past, how has [the company] done with this style in the past." The account executive plays a dual role: the "primary responsibility is sales, but the secondary responsibility is providing information to help with forecasting." The account executive "looks at the historical data, incorporates that with input from the customer and what's going on with the customer base, and adjusts the numbers based on a qualitative judgement." The information is sent back to the corporate office for "more analysis and double checking for data integrity." At this stage the "forecast is at a pretty high level—customer, division, product, and season." The forecast is them submitted to a group of experts within the company—"upper management, people with many years of experience," who "look at the numbers and add a more qualitative or expert opinion." That opinion takes into account "consumer confidence, macroeconomics issues, what's happening in the marketplace, and what's happening with competitors." For example, suppose a particular forecast shows a 15% increase compared to the same period last year, the expert committee "decides whether it makes sense or is totally out of line."

The forecasting time horizon for apparel, no matter what kind of apparel, is by season "because there is a selling season and market weeks that correspond to that selling season." The number of seasons for a particular product can vary "from two season per year to up to six or more season per year." Forecasts are updated monthly in a process that takes "the seasonal nature of the business and overlays that with an annual budget process—a 12 month process." The apparel executive looks at a number of seasons at once with "different levels of granularity" in the forecasts. A forecast looking at a selling season farthest in the future will be "at a very high level" such as the total number of units for a particular season. The forecast of the closest season to the selling period will break the total units into product categories such as "how many suits, how many sportcoats and a breakdown by customer." For the next season the forecast shows a breakdown by style. For the current selling season, the company gets "point-of-sale history every week showing how you actually stand."

Even with all the technology available to forecasters today, Mr. Tully sees a critical missing element: "Nobody has found a way to measure lost sales." When a consumer enters a store looking for a specific color, product, or style and does not find it, that constitutes a lost sale. "Nowadays there's so much self-service that there's no way to capture the fact that the store just lost that sale. We can measure inventory turns, markdowns, and the price of promoting, but we are not very good at capturing lost sales." The one exception is in catalogs where "you had a request and couldn't fill it." Capturing lost sales would help forecasters "do a better job of getting the right stock-keeping units at the right place, at the right time." Not capturing those sales has "really hurt retail and that's hurt all the way down the line."

Mr. Tully sees sales forecasting as "becoming more and more important because of the way the business has gone global—lead times have gotten longer in spite of any efforts to shorten them. As a result, we are more dependent on forecasts." Oxford Industries is "looking at an integrated, uniform forecasting process and tools that could be used across divisions." Mr. Tully finds that "the tools have made quantum leaps in the last couple of years in terms of ease of use." Oxford Industries does "have a data warehouse in place—in some divisions more than others." Mr. Tully defines a data warehouse as "a multidimensional database that lets you look at the information in different ways." The data warehouse is "definitely helping forecasting from the standpoint of making it quicker and easier to get at things like historical bookings and shipping and compare them."

"New products are the toughest things to forecast," says Mr. Tully. "On fashion, it's really just a matter of looking at history. The only tool we have is what we have done in the past that is similar. Will the color behave like a similar fashion color in the same product? Will this new style behave like one in a similar rollout?

> If you can find something similar [to the new product], that can help, but you can still get burned in both directions." Whether forecasting for "a new product or a new target customer or a new channel of distribution, it is very difficult to forecast growth and the expert opinion becomes crucial." Additionally, when volatility is expected, the company tries "to set things up so you can respond quickly to changes—if things go one way or the other you are in a position to react quickly."
>
> "One of the keys to the future is getting everyone to share information so that we can shorten the pipeline—a situation where everybody wins, nobody loses." Along these lines, Mr. Tully sees "the burden of forecasting is being shifted further back in the supply chain." When that happens it "becomes even more critical to get point-of-sale data, get product into inventory, get data on promotions, get more knowledge about what's going on at the consumer level to enable suppliers to forecast more accurately." This is a shift from practices in the past where "customers told us what they wanted, we tried to fill that, and we really weren't involved with what happened after that." Now "our customers are expecting us to be more involved with how it sells to the final consumer." Suppliers are expected to react "faster to changes whether its color, or model, or size." "Rather than waiting for the customer to tell us, they are actually asking us to anticipate and advise them on those changes." In the future, Mr. Tully expects that "some customers will want to forecast jointly in the true sense of the word, other customers will want to keep forecasting in their venue and share their forecast backwards, and other customers will put the responsibility of forecasting somewhere else in the supply chain."
>
> Source: Phone interview with Mr. Brian Tully, June 11, 1999.

particular situation can be confusing. To begin to pierce that confusion, managers can view these techniques as falling into three broad categories (Mentzer & Bienstock, 1998):

(handwritten: ① Quantitative)

- **Time-Series Forecasting**

A common forecasting task is to predict sales for the next 12 months based on sales of the past 36 months. **Time-series techniques** are **quantitative**—that is, they use values recorded at regular time intervals (sales history) to predicts future values.

- **Correlation or Regression Techniques**

Another common forecasting task is to predict the increase in sales given some marketing action such as a sales promotion or advertising campaign. In this case, correlation or regression techniques are used to compare how a change in one variable (e.g., advertising effort) causes a change in another variable (e.g., sales volume).

- **Qualitative Techniques**

Changes in sales volume may result from the actions of the company or from other factors such as actions by competitors and economic conditions. Time-series techniques cannot foresee and regression techniques cannot account for changes in demand patterns and other relationships that affect sales volume. Instead **qualitative techniques** (also called subjective and judgmental techniques) call on the expertise of people inside and outside the company to adjust the forecast to account for these factors.

The three categories include many different sales forecasting techniques—there are about 60 different time-series techniques alone. However, managers need to understand only a few basic techniques—all the others are variations on the basic group. Sets of quantitative management tools are now available as software packages so that managers can manipulate data in spreadsheets and databases on their desktops instead of having to request an analysis from the management information staff. Because the software performs the calculations, managers can shift their focus to understanding the reasoning behind the mathematics.

Time-Series Forecasting

Time-series forecasting looks only at patterns in sales history and projects those patterns to make a forecast. Time-series techniques look at one or more of the following patterns (Figure 8.1):

- **Level,** the horizontal sales history as if demand was stable with no trend, seasonality, or noise in the sales data.
- **Trend,** the continuing pattern of increasing or decreasing sales represented as a line or curve.
- **Seasonality,** a yearly pattern of increasing or decreasing sales that corresponds to the season.
- **Noise,** the part of sales fluctuations that appears random and cannot be explained because the pattern has not occurred consistently in the past.

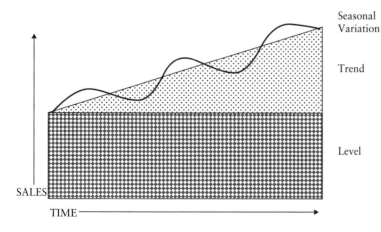

Seasonal Variation

Trend

Level

FIGURE 8.1

Sales data can be decomposed into the components of level, trend, seasonality, and noise.

SALES

TIME

All time-series techniques can be classified as either **open-model time-series (OMTS)** or **fixed-model time-series (FMTS)** techniques.

Open-model time-series techniques, such as, Box Jenkins (the most common statistical analysis in the classification of OMTS), first analyze the time-series to determine the components, then build unique models, and forecast the time-series into the future. Using OMTS forecasting techniques has a number of drawbacks: the method requires training, considerable analysis time, and many periods of sales history, and results vary in accuracy with the skill of the user. Thus, the OMTS techniques have limited use in sales forecasting (Bolt, 1994).

FMTS techniques are simpler and less expensive because they require less data storage. Because they adjust quickly to changing sales conditions, these techniques are appropriate for short-term forecasting. FMTS begins with the idea that the forecast for next month's sales is the average of all past sales. The average "dampens" out fluctuations caused by noise (which cannot be forecast by time-series analysis anyway), trend, and seasonality. So, the average does a good job of identifying the level but ignores two important patterns—trend and seasonality.

Improvements in calculating the average can improve the forecasting power of FMTS techniques (Mentzer & Bienstock, 1998):

- **Moving Average**

The forecaster can improve the forecast by using only the most recent data to calculate the average rather that using all previous data. To do that, the forecaster must decide how many periods of sales data to use in making the forecast. If the forecaster chooses too many, the moving average and the ordinary average for all time periods are practically the same. If the forecaster chooses too few, the moving average projects sales for the next period equal to sales for the last period.

- **Exponential Smoothing**

Exponential smoothing can provide a way to improve on the moving average by weighting the most recent sales period more heavily in the forecast while decreasing weights for the older periods at an exponential rate. A number of additional techniques have been developed to fine-tune the exponential smoothing technique and increase sensitivity to trend and seasonality.

FMTS techniques are useful if changes in the overall level of demand, trend, and seasonality are fairly regular. FMTS techniques do not take into consideration the impact of outside factors such as price changes, sales promotions, or economic activity.

Correlation or Regression Techniques

Correlation or regression techniques look at the relationships between sales and outside factors. Outside factors include marketing mix changes such as price changes, advertising, and promotion. The analysis seeks to answer questions such as the following: Did sales drop off after a price increase? Did sales increase in the time period just after the launching of an advertising campaign?

Correlation or regression techniques are also used to investigate the relationship between sales volume and economic or demographic shifts. In that case, the analysis seeks to answer questions such as these: Did decreasing consumer confidence in the economy lead to decreasing sales? As consumers age, do their purchasing patterns change?

To answer either set of questions, the forecaster needs data sets that include past history on each factor and sales volume. By comparing outside factors and sales volume, the forecaster seeks to discover whether a relationship exists and, if so, its strength. That relationship can then be used to forecast sales under similar situations in the future.

So, unlike time-series techniques, correlation or regression techniques provide a "broad environmental perspective for forecasting sales" (Mentzer & Bienstock, 1998, p. 12). The drawback to these techniques is that they require large amounts of data and are most useful when the time horizon is more than six months.

Government Sources for Data. Some of the data needed for correlation and regression techniques come from the government. Government data provide a comprehensive statistical picture of life in the United States. The government specializes in socioeconomic characteristics of the U.S. population, including age, race, gender, educational attainment, labor-force status, occupation, income, and much more. Other countries do the same. Sales forecasters use this information to put past, current, and expected sales into the larger context of economic life. For forecasting purposes, the following government information is particularly important:

- **The Census Bureau**

The U.S. Census is conducted every ten years and is the basis for the yearly updates by private data companies. The Census Bureau publishes the *Current Population Reports* series, which contains long-range projections of the population by age, sex, and race.

- **The Consumer Expenditure Survey**

This survey provides data on the full range of household expenditures by age group, income, and household type.

- **The Bureau of Labor Statistics (BLS)**

Every other year, the BLS projects the size and characteristics of the labor force and growth projections for various industries and occupations.

Additional Sources for Data. Nonprofit organizations such as trade associations and consumer groups are good sources of information. Consider not only associations in the apparel industry but also others with relevant information about consumer spending trends. For example, the National Association of Realtors publishes studies on home buying activity.

With the coming of the Information Age, more companies began specializing in collecting and selling data from **syndicated surveys**—surveys conducted by a group of sponsors who are interested in the same topic and who share costs and results. Such surveys focus on media use, market studies, and other research efforts. Companies that run such surveys publish directories describing the studies that are available and their cost.

The cliché "timing is everything" holds true for forecasting data. Government surveys are valuable because they track trends over time and are conducted in a consistent way year after year. However, the most up-to-date numbers come from private sources. The forecaster must decide whether to use the no-frills, relatively inexpensive government sources or the quick but sometimes costly private sources.

Activity 8.2 *Statistical* *Treasure Hunt*	The U.S. Government collects an amazing array of statistics related to the economic condition of the country. However, finding useful statistics is not always easy because each government agency publishes its own reports and maintains its own Web site. Avoid tediously picking through sites of individual agencies by using the sites listed in the Resource Pointers section at the end of this chapter. Select one or more statistics that might help explain fluctuations in apparel sales. Making decisions such as this is the first step in using correlation or regression to provide a broad environmental perspective on sales volume.

Qualitative Techniques

Quantitative techniques are predicated on the idea that patterns in sales figures from previous time periods will repeat. If a forecaster doubts that assumption, qualitative techniques provide another forecasting tool. They tap into the expertise of people in the organization. Qualitative techniques are especially useful when:

- Fine-tuning forecasts derived from quantitative techniques.
- Forecasting for new products when historical data are not available.
- Forecasting long range or at the corporate level (see Chapter 9).

Forecasts derived from quantitative techniques are useful beginning points, but they are usually "adjusted" using some subjective or judgmental approach.

In-House Expert. Sometime adjusting a quantitative forecast comes down to a key employee with the knowledge, information resources, and skill to see beyond the numbers and into the dynamics of the marketplace. Such an "expert" has a deep understanding of the market, the consumer, product quality, and other environmental factors that have an impact on sales. The in-house expert uses this expertise to fine-tune the forecast, sometimes on a product-by-product basis. The value of such an employee cannot be overestimated. However, there are drawbacks. The loss of such an employee can be catastrophic to a company's forecasting efforts because the expertise of this person is difficult to transmit to a replacement. And, using one in-house expert introduces the bias inherent in a single viewpoint.

Executive Committee. An alternative to the single in-house expert is to involve groups of executives, salespeople, or outside experts. One approach is to convene a sales forecasting meeting with executives from each functional area in the company, from finance, marketing, and sales to production and distribution. These executives use the sales forecasts generated with quantitative techniques as a take-off point. Then, the group works to arrive at a consensus on needed adjustments to the sales forecast.

Instead of executives, another approach taps into the front-line experience of salespeople to produce or adjust sales forecasts. These are the people closest to the customer and who have the responsibility to generate sales volume. Again, the process begins with sales forecasts generated with quantitative methods. The task for the group is to fine-tune those initial forecasts.

Polling Experts. Meeting to adjust the sales forecast is not always practical. For forecasts with a longer time horizon, a polling process replaces the meeting format. This is also a good approach when forecasting involves new products for which no sales data exist. More time allows for the involvement of experts either within or outside the company in adjusting the quantitative forecasts. Frequently these experts are polled in a process called the **Delphi method,** a "wisdom distillation tool" ("Just the FAQs," 1995).

The goal of Delphi is to generate "best guess" scenarios that represent the consensus of the experts. Usually participants do not know who the other respondents are—a procedure that removes the bias of group dynamics. Participants provide written responses to some question or issue. These responses are summarized and shared with the other participants. In subsequent "rounds," the participants refine and clarify the issues in a series of responses. (See Chapter 9 for an explanation of this technique in the context of long-term forecasting of cultural indicators.)

Handling Bias in Qualitative Techniques. The main problem with qualitative forecasting is the potential to introduce bias into the process. Some typical situations where bias may present problems are:

- When executives, salespeople, and experts use information they already have rather than seeking out additional information that may enhance their decision-making ability.

- When participants bring their corporate political agendas to the table along with their expertise.
- When participants do not have the skills or abilities to process very complex issues.

The first situation can be corrected by supplying market research and other information to the people involved. For the others, if forecasters are aware of these drawbacks and take steps to alleviate the problems as much as possible, qualitative techniques can increase the accuracy of sales forecasting.

Figuring Out Sales Forecasting

A skiwear company is an extreme example of what most apparel companies face (Fisher et al., 1994). Demand for fashion skiwear is dependent on factors that are hard to predict—weather, fashion trends, and the economy (Figure 8.2). The marketplace for skiwear is volatile and seasonal—the peak retailing

FIGURE 8.2

The market for skiwear is volatile and seasonal. Forecasting for skiwear is an extreme example of what most apparel companies face because demand depends on factors that are hard to predict—weather, fashion trends, and the economy.

season lasts only two months. Because the company's products are nearly all new each year, sales forecasting is a challenge. The skiwear company has to speculate on potential sales, not just produce to meet orders. The company has the added complications of having to book production capacity and deal with a more complex supply chain.

After several internal attempts to work on the sales forecasting problem, one company hired a group of consultants to figure out how to improve forecasting (Fisher et al., 1994). Even though the company had shortened its product development process, it still needed an edge.

The company persuaded 25 of its best retail customers to place orders early. This early information helped pinpoint which individual styles in the line were likely to be the most popular. However, there were still two problems: The company was having problems with stockouts and markdowns and about half of its production was still based on risky, speculative demand forecasts.

The skiwear manufacturer was already using a "buying committee" to adjust quantitative forecasts. This group of company managers met to make consensus forecasts for each item in the line. The results were not impressive, as some parka styles outsold the original forecast by 200% and others sold less than 15% of the original forecast. The consultants revised the "buying committee" process. Instead of a single consensus forecast, each member made an independent forecast for each style and color. This shift made each executive responsible individually for the forecasts. Although disturbing to members at first, time showed some interesting implications for forecasting. In the group setting, some people tended to dominate the meeting and the "consensus" forecast was heavily influenced by their views. With each individual forecasting for each style and color, some styles produced obvious high levels of agreement; on others, there was little or no agreement. As sales data came in under the new forecasting system, it became clear that when buying committee members' individual forecasts were in close agreement, they were also accurate forecasts. This finding gave the company a way to sort those styles likely to be forecast accurately from those with high levels of uncertainty. Even forecasting for items with high levels of uncertainty could be improved dramatically by adjusting the forecast using the early order data from retailers.

Within several seasons, the consultants and company executives had evolved a workable combination of forecasting and production planning that practically eliminated markdowns and stockouts. The company replaced highly speculative forecasts of demand with forecasting in carefully thought out stages. When individual forecasts by company executives were in agreement on particular styles, those styles were scheduled for production far ahead of demand. The company used fast and flexible manufacturing for the more unpredictable styles, because it could use market signals such as early season sales to synchronize supply and demand. By blending expert in-house judgement, expertise from its retail customers, and sales data, the skiwear company solved a difficult sales forecasting problem.

Call or write industry contacts and alumni of the university working in the apparel industry to ask about the ways their companies "adjust" the sales forecast. Does an individual employee or a committee of executives perform this task? If a committee performs the task, is the forecast adjusted by consensus in the group or as individual forecasts of each member? How satisfied are they with the way their company accomplishes this task? Summarize the survey results in class.

Blending Quantitative and Qualitative Techniques

The factors that influence a sales forecast can be classified as controllable and uncontrollable (Bolt, 1994). Controllable factors include marketing actions and operating practices. The uncontrollable factors are either direct—those that have an obvious and immediate effect on sales—or indirect. Uncontrollable factors with a direct effect on sales include actions of competitors, access (or loss of access) to channels of distribution, and government regulations. Indirect factors either exert an influence on sales in the mid-range forecast or indicate long-term shifts. Uncontrollable factors with an indirect effect on sales are stages in a product life cycle or shifts in the preference characteristics of the target market for the mid-range forecast. The uncontrollable factors with the longest time horizon are changes in the country's economic situation (cost of living, rate of inflation, currency exchange rates) or in social, political, and cultural aspects (Figure 8.3). A sales forecast rests on a given set of environmental factors—the uncontrollable factors. Although uncertainty is always present in any forecast, accuracy improves if environmental factors are researched and weighed as part of the forecasting process.

Each forecasting method—time-series, correlation or regression, and qualitative techniques—has its purpose and brings advantages and disadvantages. The techniques are complementary. Time-series techniques generate a forecast based on sales history and are used to identify and forecast trends and seasonal patterns. The main advantage of time-series techniques is that they pick up quickly on changes. Correlation and regression analyses take external fac-

FIGURE 8.3

The factors that influence a sales forecast can be classified as controllable and uncontrollable and can be visualized in a tree diagram

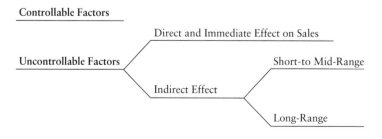

Controllable Factors

Uncontrollable Factors

Direct and Immediate Effect on Sales

Indirect Effect

Short-to Mid-Range

Long-Range

tors into consideration but they do not identify trends or seasonality. Because correlation and regression require more data, they are not useful for picking up quickly on shifts. Qualitative techniques do what time-series, correlation, and regression cannot—they deal with changes in the business environment for which there is no historical data. Best practices for sales forecasting indicate the use of time-series forecasts for an initial forecast, and correlation or regression analysis to provide a broader perspective on environmental factors. Then, qualitative methods can be used to "adjust" or fine-tune the quantitative forecast.

SALES FORECASTING IN CONTEXT

Whether in marketing, sales, finance, production, or distribution, an executive working with short-term sales forecasts needs perspective and context to guide decision making. The quarterly sales figures are small slices of larger cycles (Figure 8.4). Understanding those cycles helps the executive modulate decisions with some recognition of the bigger picture and what is likely to happen next.

The Product Life Cycle

A product progresses through a series of predictable stages called a life cycle from the time when it is merely a concept to the end of its time in the marketplace (Figure 8.5). For marketing executives, this concept has

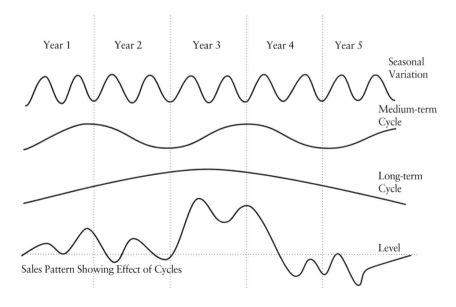

FIGURE 8.4

Medium- and long-term cycles have a cumulative effect on sales figures.

The stages of the product life cycle are a context tool for sales forecasting because they provide a way to gauge the past, present, and future development of a product in the marketplace.

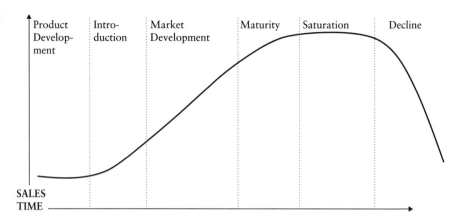

Product Development | Intro-duction | Market Development | Maturity | Saturation | Decline

SALES
TIME

strategic and tactical implications (Bolt, 1994; Levitt, 1986). For new products, the **product life cycle** provides a preview of the stages and duration that can be expected. For existing products, the recognizable stages in the product life cycle indicate what could happen next. The stages of the product life cycle are:

- **Development Stage**

This stage begins when a company identifies a market opportunity; product ideas are researched, screened, and developed to satisfy the needs of a target market; and decisions on pricing are made. During this stage, investments are made but no revenue is generated.

- **Introduction Stage**

Successful introduction depends on whether the product has been tested and is acceptable to the target market, marketing activities have been correctly integrated, and the launch is timed properly. The goal is to entice the consumer to try the product. During this stage, sales will begin and increase in volume or the product will fail.

- **Market Development Stage**

A product may survive introduction because it is novel or unique but to continue to sell it must provide a bundle of tangible and intangible attributes that satisfy consumers enough to generate repeat sales or recommendations to others. The company must convince the consumer to prefer this product and this brand. Sales gain momentum as information spreads through advertising, promotion, and word-of-mouth.

- **Exploitation Stage**

During this stage, a market-oriented company will seek to extend sales beyond the initial target market to other segments and open new distribution channels as a way to extend the market and promote sales volume.

- **Maturity Stage**

Variations and versions of the product become widely available. Competition between brands increases and prices decline. At this point, supply catches up with demand. **Demand** can be characterized as expansion—new customers buying for the first time—and replacement or repeat demand—users replacing the product with the same or similar product.

- **Saturation Stage**

Expansion demand disappears as competitors attempt to take market share from each other using sales promotion activities. Because so much product is available, a "sameness" becomes apparent and brand preference weakens. New substitute products appear and lure customers away. Most companies realign their marketing mix to extend this stage as long as possible.

- **Decline Stage**

All products eventually decline because consumers' needs, wants, or habits have changed, substitute products have appeared, and the product attributes have degenerated. Some companies withdraw the product at this stage and introduce a replacement product. If not, the decline stage sees a strong downward trend in sales volume, with most sales of the repeat type.

Time spent attempting to predict the shape and duration of a new product's life allows a more measured approach to production and merchandising and creates lead time for planning competitive moves. Looking at a product's place in the product life cycle provides lead time to develop ways to extend stages and indicates when a product should be phased out. Attention to the stages of the product's life cycle provides a background of expectations against which sales volume can be viewed and projections for the future made (Shearer, 1994).

Fashion is always evolving and changing. Create a snapshot of this moment in fashion time by creating a presentation board picturing apparel and accessory products in each stage of the product life cycle.

Activity 8.4 Product Life Cycle Detectives

The Business Cycle

When evaluating sales figures, the forecaster uses a process known as **decomposition** to take into account underlying factors that may be influencing the pattern (Shearer, 1994). The sales figures may reflect an underlying trend toward increasing or decreasing sales, seasonal variation, and the existence of medium- and long-term cycles such as the business cycle. Trend and seasonal factors have been discussed earlier in this chapter. The **business cycle** refers to the cyclical nature of the economy as it passes through the rising and falling phases of prosperity and stagnation. The decomposition process attempts to disentangle trend, seasonal, and cyclical effects to gain a clearer picture of the current situation and a glimpse of future directions.

The cyclical nature of the national economy was first recognized in the 19th century and economists have debated the existence and causes of this cycle ever since. A business cycle that rises and falls every four to five years is common in most of the developed nations of the world. A shock to the system such as an oil embargo and higher oil prices can deepen a recession while lower prices can soften a downturn. Even though these shocks increase or decrease the amplitude of the business cycle, the cycles are still present. Government policy attempts to counteract cyclical movement in the economy, but as long as the underlying causes remain and these causes are not fully understood, the business cycle will continue to be a factor that should be considered in sales forecasting.

Although there is general agreement that the sales of durable goods are cyclical, there is less agreement on the existence of an apparel cycle. Some experts agree that there is an apparel cycle but disagree about the length of the cycle. An economist for a marketing research firm (Moin, Edelson, & Tosh, 1996) sees 18- to 24-month expansions periods followed by 6- to 12-month contraction periods. In his view, only two apparel cycles since 1948 have been fashion driven and both occurred during the 1960s. Demographics, pricing, or the general business cycle accounts for the others (Steidtmann, 1996). A CEO of an apparel firm sees the cycles of hot apparel sales followed by a cooling off period in three- to five-year intervals. Others argue that swings in apparel sales are tied to the overall health of the economy and job security. Still others see sales driven not by apparel cycles but by life cycle stages—as the median age of the population rises, priorities shift away from fashion-driven purchasing (see Chapter 3 for a discussion of median age as a factor in fashion dynamics). Some observers suggest that business and apparel cycles are flattening out with fewer peaks and valleys (Moin et al., 1996). When an issue is this controversial, the best approach for forecasters is to monitor the business and apparel cycles, develop ways to predict the timing and amplitude of the cycles, and plan a corporate response. The first step is to understand why cycles happen.

One reason cycles exist is because of the lag between changes in demand and response to that change. Consider the executive watching sales figures for an indication of change in demand level (Shearer, 1994). The figures are naturally variable and it may be some time before the executive recognizes an increase in demand and responds to it (Figure 8.6). Meanwhile, the increased demand will begin to pull down inventory levels. At some point, the executive will see the disparity between demand and inventory and increase production. In time, production will build back inventory to the level of demand. If there

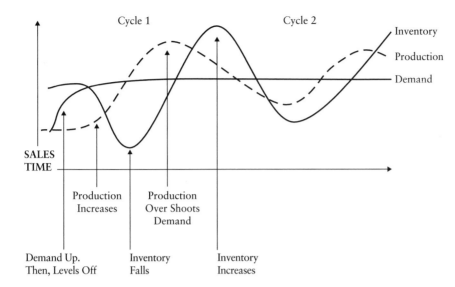

Cycle 1 Cycle 2

Inventory
Production
Demand

SALES
TIME

Production Increases

Production Over Shoots Demand

Demand Up. Then, Levels Off

Inventory Falls

Inventory Increases

FIGURE 8.6

The natural and expected ups and downs of sales can mask a change in demand. The time it takes an executive to recognize the change and respond contributes to the start of another cycle.

were no random variation to obscure this point from the executive's view and if actions could be enacted immediately, cycles would disappear because the executive would be able to synchronize demand, inventory, and production. However, when the executive decides to cut back production, another lag between change and response is likely. During that time production continues to build inventory and inventory levels rise above demand. Once again production is cut back, inventory falls below demand, and another cycle commences. And so the cycle continues. In the worst case scenario, the cycle would be applied not to a single company, but to the industry, and the effect would ripple down the supply chain to industries providing materials and components. Industries close to the consumer are more prone to this kind of cycle.

Consumer Confidence As an Indicator. Inventory levels in key industries within the economy signal phases of the business cycle. Commentators and analysts also look at other factors as indicators of turning points in the business cycle. Levels of retail sales and consumer expenditures are often mentioned as factors. Analysts watch two indexes of consumer sentiment—one by the University of Michigan, one by the Conference Board—which forecast future consumer expenditures and the future of the economy as a whole.

Available since 1969, the Conference Board's **consumer confidence** index reflects Americans' optimism or pessimism about economic conditions in the present and future. The index is based on a 1985 baseline of 100 and is derived from a monthly poll of 5,000 households. The index reports on consumer confidence overall and by region of the country. The index has two parts: consumer reaction to current business conditions, and expectations for the next six months.

The idea behind consumer confidence as an indicator is that consumers react the same way to economic stimuli at different points in time. That is, there is a relationship between economic conditions and consumer behavior. Specifically, consumers are more willing to buy when they expect economic conditions in the future to be favorable to their own well-being (Figure 8.7). If consumer confidence is down, manufacturers anticipate that consumers will spend less overall, shift spending to other categories, postpone purchases, or become more sensitive to price. When anticipating a downturn in consumer confidence, companies are more likely to turn to price promotion.

Like many economic issues, predictability based on consumer confidence is controversial. Some people question whether consumers respond to actual economic conditions or to news about economic conditions. These people argue that consumer confidence is overly influenced by the media's reaction to political, social, and economic issues and to stock market fluctuations. A study by Cotton Incorporated ("Confidence," 1998) shows only a weak correlation between consumer confidence levels and spending for apparel.

Leading Indicators. Forecasting techniques tend to be stronger in predicting trends than in recognizing and anticipating cycles (Shearer, 1994). The **leading indicator** approach attempts to overcome this problem. Forecasters begin with a set of economic factors likely to signal a turning point in the business cycle—factors such as interest rates and housing starts. The factors are chosen

FIGURE 8.7

Measures of consumer confidence reflect Americans' optimism or pessimism about their economic well-being in the present and future. Retailers and manufacturers watching these indexes assume that consumers are more willing to buy when they expect economic conditions in the future to be favorable.

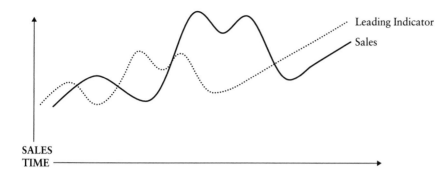

FIGURE 8.8

If well constructed, leading indicators predict what sales will be like 6 to 12 months in the future.

because of their importance to overall economic health, their history of being in sync with the business cycle, and the quick release of the figures for use in analysis. Forecasters construct a set of time-series representing the factors and then take a weighted average to produce a final leading indicator that can be charted. If well constructed, the peaks and troughs of the leading indicator will anticipate those seen in sales by 6 to 12 months (Figure 8.8).

This kind of analysis is more useful in anticipating the turning points in the business cycle and less useful in predicting the amplitude of the upswing or downswing. Because all industries are tied together in the national economy, leading indicators constructed by the government can be helpful in putting sales forecasting in a larger context. The government's leading indicators are frequently discussed on national and business news broadcasts and reported in business and trade publications.

Locate a business news broadcast and monitor it for a month. What breaking news on the health of the economy would be helpful to apparel executives in putting sales figures into a larger context of economic activity? What reports on government statistics would be helpful in understanding and interpreting sales history?

Activity 8.5
News on the Economy

DATA MINING—A STEP TOWARD "REAL-TIME MARKETING"

When data migrated from paper to digital storage on computer, a new era in data analysis and forecasting began. Improved computer technology made it possible to collect and store more and more data. The use of scanners to collect sales data moved analysis away from a retrospective viewpoint to more dynamic, real-time analysis. Companies began to accumulate vast storehouses of historical data about customer transactions. Corresponding improvements were made in software to organize, summarize, and analyze the information. Today, improvements are extending database technology into a process called **data mining.**

The term calls to mind the prospectors of the mid-1800s searching through tons of earth to discover nuggets of pure gold. The data miners search through vast stores of data to ("An introduction," 1997):

- Answer business questions too time consuming to answer using traditional methods.
- Discover patterns hidden in gigabytes of data.
- Find predictive information experts miss because it lies outside of their expectations.

There are several definitions of data mining (Elliott, 1998). In the first, software allows executives to "drill down" through multidimensional databases to discover trends in information, visualize that data graphically, and use those discoveries to support business decisions. In this case, the executive has an idea about a possible relationship, uses analysis to discover why these things are related, and uses available data to verify the hypothesis. This kind of data mining uses software that costs from $500 to $15,000. The second, more sophisticated approach uses software to discover patterns in large databases—patterns not visible to human analysts. In this case, the goal is to generate a hypothesis, not to verify one. The software for this approach costs up to $100,000 and requires a **data warehouse**—a system for storing and delivering massive quantities of data.

A data warehouse organizes information from many databases into a single system. The databases may include consumer shopping behavior, demographics, and attitudes; sales history, promotion and pricing data; competitor actions; and any other information categories that are deemed relevant to decision making.

The data warehouse is useless unless an executive can efficiently call up data to use in decision support. A data warehouse is extensively indexed and specifically designed to answer business questions with a fast access time. High-powered software for data manipulation sits on top of the data warehouse and allows the user to "slice and dice" the data in almost any imaginable way (Figure 8.9). Together, the data warehouse and data manipulation software provide a flexible executive information system (EIS) (Dhar & Stein, 1997).

FIGURE 8.9

A data warehouse combines many databases from multiple sources. High-powered software attached to the data warehouse makes it possible for an executive to gather and analyze data to answer business questions.

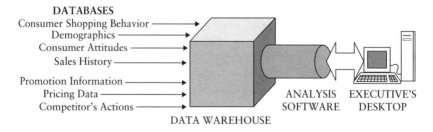

Catalog retailers are making use of data mining to better focus their marketing ("Data miners," 1997). These businesses typically have a huge volume of information generated by transactions. By combining years of transaction data with demographic information from the U.S. Census Bureau and private companies, a cataloger can segment millions of consumers into groups that exhibit similar purchasing characteristics. With that information, they can generate specific marketing plans for certain consumer groups—special catalogs, telemarketing, and special offers such as coupons. Catalog retailers use the same technology to maximize return on investment by fine-tuning mailing lists based on past response. Retailers in both catalogs and stores use data mining to discover patterns such as the purchase of seemingly unrelated products that consumers often buy at the same time. These patterns can lead to cross-marketing the products or to reconfiguring displays.

Marketing on the Web is opening up opportunities to use data mining (Elliott, 1998). Tracking which customers look up which products and their order history means that the Web-based "storefront" can be customized to the customer's preference. In this way, the site looks a little different to each customer and the customer's choice is expedited. Data mining can also be used to identify problems with the Web site that require redesign and a more user-friendly approach.

Data mining works by building a model in a situation where the outcome is known and applying it to situations where the outcome is unknown ("An introduction," 1997). The idea of **model building** in not new—it is a common approach to forecasting. The differences come in the amount of information and the speed of the process. With the extra computing power of today, lots of information about a variety of situations can be stored in a data warehouse. The data mining software runs through that data distilling the characteristics that should be in the model. The software will probably use techniques such as artificial neural networks, genetic algorithms, decision trees, and rule induction.

Artificial neural networks are trained to recognize patterns by repeatedly being presented with examples in a trial-and-error fashion until the network reaches a level of accuracy. **Genetic algorithms** treat rules as if those rules were DNA in biological evolution. Rules evolve by genetic combination, mutation, and natural selection until workable rules sets emerge. **Decision trees** classify a data set in a series of two-way splits that can be expressed as a set of rules. Then, the rules can be applied to a new, unclassified data set. The goal with decision trees is to predict which members of that new data set will have a certain outcome (such as the purchase of a certain product). **Rule induction** extracts useful if-then rules from data using statistical significance as the criteria. While all these techniques sound complicated, they are really extensions of analytical methods such as regression (Small, 1997).

Like regression, these methods model relationships between a set of profile variables and a given outcome. A "good" model can then be used to make some calculated guesses about the outcomes in a new data set. These are still guesses because the models only indicate correlation between variables (Schrage, 1997). One of the oft-repeated mantras of statistical analysis is that correlation is not causation. The relationship can exist without revealing the operation and direction of cause and effect. As long as cause and effect are unknown, the finding is tentative.

As an example of data mining in practice, take the case of a marketing director for a retail catalog hoping to entice the customers of similar catalogs to switch their purchases to her catalog. She knows all about her customers— age, gender, credit history, and buying patterns. She wants to target customers who buy often and spend over $100 on each order. Naturally, the competition is unlikely to share their proprietary information on customer transactions. The answer is to create a model using known information about current customers. Suppose that data mining reveals that 98% of the customers who order from every catalog and spend at least $100 make over $60,000 per year. This model gives the marketing director a way to selectively target new customers.

As another example, consider the mass-market apparel company that test markets styles before making a production commitment. The company knows the demographic information on their customers, transaction information on sales made in the past and currently, and their own marketing plans. Collecting sales information at each test site provides enough data for modeling. Using data mining an executive can take the test market information, identify the characteristics of consumers who respond to the styles, compare that model to the overall market, and predict the potential for those styles to succeed.

Successful data mining depends on the quality of the data warehouse ("An introduction," 1997). The data warehouse should contain an internal data tracking system for all customer contacts along with external market data, information from consumer panels, and competitor activity. The data must be "clean"—free from errors. Databases can be so big that they become cumbersome. The design of the database needs to be based on quality, flexibility, and access rather than sheer size. Some companies find that around 100,000 customer data records is better for analysis than the 27 million in some data warehouses (Miglautsch, 1995). Manipulating huge databases means investing in high-performance computer hardware and a staff of professionals skilled in statistics to manage it. The costs involved mean that data mining is not for every company or every project. Until the techniques are mature, the risks may outweigh the benefits.

If executives see data mining as a magic business booster, they are likely to be disappointed. Building a model is helpful only if it identifies actions that are possible and reasonable. Suppose that data mining models the customer for custom-made suits as between 40 and 50 years old and the owner of a sports car or a luxury car. Unless the company can reach that segment with the right message, the model is useless (Elliott, 1998). Data mining is best viewed as a move toward steady improvement and, occasionally, toward providing an extra competitive edge on a project, with a customer, or for a particular time period. Data mining is just a more sophisticated analysis technique. It cannot replace experience with the business and knowledge about the market. Users still must decide how to interpret the models and how to implement decisions that increase sales revenues (Small, 1997).

One of the drawbacks of data mining may be the insatiable appetite of marketing people for more information and more new analysis tools. Some see this as a vicious circle where "discovering" a correlation unleashes another round of data gathering and investigation. As data mining software reaches the desktops of more and more executives, one spin-off will be a requirement for greater statistical literacy among executives (Schrage, 1997).

Begin a clipping file on data mining and the associated techniques of artificial neural networks, genetic algorithms, decision trees, and rule induction. Run keyword searches on the Internet and on business and industry databases. Although you may not understand everything in the articles, pay special attention to examples related to the textile and apparel industries. Beginning a clipping file is the first step toward self-education about this emerging technology.

Activity 8.6
Clip and File

STRATEGIC DATA PARTNERSHIPS AND REAL-TIME MARKETING

In the past, each segment of the apparel industry from fabrics to apparel manufacturers to retailers developed its own forecasting and planning. Manufacturers overproduced to provide a "safety" stock to meet unpredictable demand, and both manufacturers and retailers shared the costs of keeping these products in inventory. As the season progressed, shortages of hot-selling items could not be restocked and excess items were marked down. Levels of safety stock were necessary to cover delivery dates and to reduce uncertainty about demand.

Now, instead of acting like separate segments, the apparel industry is moving toward becoming a **retail supply chain** with integrated forecasting and planning. Retailers are turning responsibility for forecasting and planning over to their vendors. Manufacturers are sharing forecasts with suppliers of components such as fabric, findings, and trim. Technology makes this shift in strategy toward more collaborative forecasting possible (Power, 1998). The necessity of keeping safety stock is reduced when manufacturing becomes more agile and efficient because products are produced closer to delivery dates. Better forecasting practices reduce uncertainty about demand and that further reduces the need to carry inventory. By reducing the two reasons for carrying inventory—as safety stock, because of uncertainty about demand—the apparel supply chain saves on inventory costs and gains dollars for technology investment.

As forecast in the late 1980s, the vision of real-time marketing in the 21st century is emerging with the following characteristics:

- Active, continuous processing of up-to-the-minute information about consumers, competitor's actions, and the dynamics of the marketplace.

- Quick reaction to opportunities by adjusting the flow of goods or changing prices and promotion strategy.

- The marketer's desktop that is wired into secure global communications networks.

The first step toward the realization of that vision was the introduction of point-of-sales (POS) scanners to capture sales data as it happened. The sales information could be tabulated weekly (or more frequently during peak periods) and shared with vendors through electronic data interchange (EDI). The vision for EDI was as a conduit for forecasting data between vendors and retailers. Instead, it became an excellent way for retailers to transmit electronic versions of standard business documents such as purchase orders and invoices. The standard formats did not allow for the capture of other information relevant to forecasting.

Today, traditional EDI is augmented by **extranets**—private networks that enable users outside a company to access information using Internet-based technology. Extranets allow retailers and manufacturers to share information, create joint forecasts, and monitor results.

Automated Replenishment Systems

Wal-Mart, the Arkansas-based retailer, and Sara Lee's Branded Apparel Group collaborated on a system to share critical sales forecasting information in an **automated replenishment system** (Hye, 1998). This pilot program had implications for the way business will be conducted in the future. The goal is more precise forecasting and improved in-stock positions in stores. In this kind of collaboration, manufacturers gain access to retailers' information about promotion plans, store openings, local events, and other factors that have an impact on forecasts. Retailers gain access to order status and are alerted to any problems in production or distribution as it effects delivery times. Additionally, partners can share more subtle information such as insights about how sales in one department may spur increased sales in a related department—information with significant impact on forecasts.

Canadian-based Nygard International, a manufacturer of women's moderate and bridge apparel, is an example of a company taking Quick Response (QR) to a higher level by developing automated replenishment systems (Zimmermann, 1998c). The Nygard approach is based on the idea that retailers do 80 percent of their business on 20 percent of their products. Nygard combines highly automated production with an extranet for EDI transactions with suppliers and customers such as Dillard's. The company's response to orders is so quick that retailers need no inventory except what is on the sales floor and out-of-stock situations on fast-selling items are virtually eliminated. In some cases, orders received at Nygard in the morning are shipped within 24 hours. The manufacturer accomplishes this feat by having a constant accurate picture of its inventory position with retailers and suppliers. Using POS data, the system identifies slower selling items and generates an alert to reduce production on those items. The system is further augmented with a customer database system to provide more accurate information about the women who purchase Nygard apparel. This information is used to make decisions about new products.

Some companies are even converting lost sales into customer service opportunities. In its automated replenishment system, Duck Head Apparel allows retailers to enter an item missing from the sales floor into the POS system as a sale. A ticket is generated and the item is shipped from Duck Head's distribution center directly to the customer in 48 hours (Zimmermann, 1998a).

Category Management

Category management is another collaborative strategy between manufacturers and retailers. In category management, the manufacturer provides expertise in a category including trends, fit, silhouettes, and finishes and makes recommendations on merchandising assortment, display, and inventory controls in that product category on a store-by-store basis. While the store retains control and often modifies the suggestions, the manufacturer acts as a specialist in forecasting to keep the right flow of merchandise going to the selling floor. The exchange of sales data allows the vendor to pinpoint emerging trends and restock accordingly.

More manufacturers have the potential to participate in category management because more companies own multiple brands in a product category through mergers and acquisitions. For example, VF Corporation owns several jeanswear brands. They range from Marithè & Francois Girbaud at the high end, to moderately priced Lee and Wrangler for department stores, to Rustler and Rider priced for mass-market channels. With several denim brands the company can position each for a different target consumer and different retail channels. VF Corporation differentiates the brands in image, pricing, packaging, placement, and presentation (Ozzard, 1996). The **brand tiers** or a multiple-brand strategy enables the company to cover more of the market. Because VF Corporation has a multiple-brand strategy in the denim business, a corporate infrastructure of EDI, and automatic replenishment programs, the company is in position to partner with top retail accounts in category management.

Category management radically alters traditional relationships between manufacturers and retailers, bringing changes in organizational structure and corporate culture. Such sweeping change takes time to implement and to prove its viability (Reda, 1995).

As these collaborative efforts to create a retail supply chain strategy become more common, so do advances in forecasting software. New software packages can produce forecasts for each SKU, categorized by type of product, location, and channel of distribution. The software determines which methods produce the best forecast by analyzing demand data (historical sales data), testing multiple methodologies, and comparing forecasts to actual results. The system is designed to adjust forecasts to consider the impact of holidays and sales. Picking the best forecast for product, consumer type, region, and channel of distribution is possible because of advanced mathematical modeling, artificial intelligence, and advanced computing technologies.

Key Terms and Concepts

Aggregated
Artificial Neural
   Networks
Automated Replenishment
   System
Brand Tiers
Business Cycle
Category Management
Consumer Confidence
Correlation or Regression
   Techniques
Data Mining
Data Warehouse
Decision Trees
Decomposition
Delphi Method

Demand
Extranets
Fixed-Model Time-Series
   (FMTS)
Genetic Algorithms
Just in Time
Leading Indicators
Level (in Time-Series
   Forecasting)
Markdowns
Model Building
Noise (in Time-Series
   Forecasting)
Open-Model Time-Series
   (OMTS)
Product Life Cycle

Qualitative Techniques
Quantitative Techniques
Quick Response
Retail Supply Chain
Rule Induction
Sales Channel
Sales Forecast
Sales History
Sales Plan
Seasonality (in Time-Series
   Forecasting)
Stockouts
Syndicated Surveys
Time-Series Forecasting
Trend (in Time-Series
   Forecasting)

Case Revisited: Data on Demand

Patricia has noticed a possible new trend in the sales data from stores in the Northeast. The sales figures are up for the most colorful items and holding steady or declining for basic colors. As the Northeast is traditionally a region where people prefer basic colors, Patricia wonders what is driving sales. Use the following discussion questions to summarize this chapter and review the possibilities open to Patricia.

Data needed to answer the question: *Does Patricia need sales volume reports by SKU, individual products, or product families (apparel groups or lines)? Or, would it be more helpful to look at sales by salesperson or distribution channel? Or, is the answer really one of location, in which the revenues should be broken down by city within the region? The need of a sales manager for data is interactive—as Patricia examines the situation, should she "drill down" to layers with more detailed information on a particular salesperson, a particular store, or a particular product?*

Analysis needed to answer the question: *Can this question be answered with quantitative methods? What will time-series analysis disclose? Will Patricia learn anything helpful from correlation or regression analysis? Are there any qualitative methods that could be used to answer the question?*

Technology: *How can technology assist Patricia in her quest for an answer? What technology assistance should Patricia's company invest in so that they can capitalize on the sales forecasting process?*

Modeling: *If Patricia discovers a model—a pattern of spending, a profile of a consumer—that relates to the popularity of color in sportswear, what then?*

Additional Forecasting Activities

Tapping into Executive Expertise. Use the Delphi method to inquire about the concepts of real-time marketing in the textile and apparel industries. Let marketing executives at various companies be the experts. In Round One, contact each executive by e-mail, present the real-time marketing scenario from the beginning of this chapter, ask for an evaluation of the concept and a prediction of when real-time marketing will happen. For Round Two, summarize the answers from the group, removing all possible identifiers, and send the summary to each participant. Ask each person to comment, revise, or evaluate the group response. Because these executives are busy, do not take the exercise beyond the two rounds. Summarize Round Two responses and present your findings to the class.

Data Mining and Apparel. Interview experts on the potential of data mining and its applications to the apparel business. One expert might be a professor of management information systems. Another could be an expert in consumer behavior research. Gather the views of several industry executives through telephone interviews. Write up the results of your interviews as a news article for a trade paper.

What Catalog Executives Know about You. Collect all the catalogs that come to your household over the course of one month. Categorize the catalogs by type of merchandise, style, and price point. Think about your purchases from each catalog over the past two years. Were your purchases spread over the year or did you tend to buy seasonally? How much did you spend on average in each transaction? Did you return merchandise and provide the reason why? Can you identify a purchase in a product category that may have led to your receiving catalogs from other companies offering the same kind of merchandise? What can the catalog merchandisers deduce from your purchase behavior? How would they categorize you as a customer? Pool your findings with the other members of the class. Can you discover a pattern that relates to the demographics of the class members? Discuss the positive and negative aspects of data mining from the point of view of the consumer. Discuss the positive and negative aspects of data mining from the point of view of the catalog company.

Resource Pointers

Find government statistics that provide a picture of the the changing economic picture on the following sites:

- Fedstats—www.fedstats.gov
- Economic Statistics Briefing Room—www.whitehouse.gov/fsbr/income. html
- The Dismal Scientist—www.dismal.com

Chapter 9

CULTURAL INDICATORS

"The trick to anticipating the future is not to determine what is likely to happen, but what has already happened that will create the future."
—Peter Drucker

Objectives

- Understand the characteristics of long-term forecasting.

- Explain the place for long-term forecasting in supporting the decision making of executives in the textile and apparel industries.

- Cultivate skills in the methodology of long-term forecasting.

- Understand the criteria for evaluating long-term forecasts.

CASE: THE FUTURE OF INFORMATION

Tywanda has held several merchandising positions with an apparel company manufacturing branded and private label lines for men and women. Recently she has been asked to head the e-commerce division of her company. She and her staff will be responsible for developing the Web site to market the branded lines to consumers. One of the first decisions facing the group is whether to sell to consumers on the Web or merely show the company's product and direct consumers to a list of stores that carry the line in their region. If they sell directly to customers, retailers who carry the brand may see this as competition for consumer sales. If the company does not sell on the Web site, consumers may be irritated and feel they are wasting their time because they cannot complete the transaction online. Other issues relate to the look of the site and the degree of interactivity necessary to interest savvy online shoppers.

Tywanda and her staff need to develop a long-range vision for the way that this division should relate to customers. They want to discover what forecasters and futurists are saying about the evolution of the marketplace over the next five, ten, or more years. Tywanda begins the search with Michael Detouzos, head of the MIT Laboratory for Computer Science, home of the World Wide Web and place of origin for may high-tech products and processes. Detouzos describes the Information Marketplace as "a twenty-first century village marketplace where people and computers buy, sell, and freely exchange information and information services" (1997). Tywanda is also interested in the concept of consumer tribes—groups with an affinity based on similar interests and lifestyles.

This chapter will introduce the research strategies and techniques that Tywanda and her staff can use to explore the challenges of e-commerce. The staff will need to design their own environmental scanning system to detect consumer tribes, identify trends, and monitor the technology of the 21st-century village marketplace.

NAVIGATING CHANGE

Imagine yourself in a canoe on a wild river. A canoe is an unstable craft for such a dangerous situation. However, skilled paddlers can deftly maneuver the canoe with different strokes—strokes to propel the craft forward, back-paddling to slow forward progress, side strokes to direct the canoe away from obstacles, or techniques for keeping the canoe in place while the paddler rests and reads the river. The torrent of change in social, cultural, economic, and technological domains is like the river. Just as the canoeist cannot alter the flow of the river so individuals, companies, and industries are powerless to alter the flow of change. The business executive, like the paddler in the canoe, reads the river watching for clear passages and for hidden obstacles. An accurate reading of change allows the executive to select the maneuver best suited to the situation. Reading the current of change means identifying trends that have long-term impact on the way people live—trends that change not only products but also entire industries. Long-term forecasting is valuable when it enables the executive to look far ahead, begin early to position the product, company, and industry advantageously in the flow, and avoid some of the obvious obstacles. The trip downstream will still be bumpy and exciting, but long-term forecasting can make the passage safer and, ultimately, more rewarding.

The signals for sweeping change are present long before the results begin to be evident to most people. Most people worry that they will not recognize a trend early enough to capitalize on it. Why spend the effort on forecasting the future without the expectation of a payoff? Faith Popcorn (1991), one of the most frequently quoted trend forecasters, says that a trend takes about ten years to work through the culture and reach all market levels. Here, she is not talking about style trends because those move very quickly through culture aided by media and the Internet. She is talking about lifestyle trends that reorganize consumer priorities and influence decisions in every aspect of life. As these long-term trends play out over time, people in many industries participate in translating the new priorities and preferences into many short-term style trends.

In the apparel field, companies need an early warning system so that specific product categories can be fine-tuned to trends within a market segment. While timing is important, an agile, responsive company will be able to capitalize on trends whenever they are spotted—sometimes just as a glimmer far in the future, sometimes as a phenomenon in the building stage. Waning trends are another signal. When some avocation, interest, or lifestyle loses cultural power, that is a good time to survey the information landscape for the next big thing.

Just as there are guides to wild rivers, so are there guides to the river of change. These guides are forecasters and futurists who make it their business to chart the currents and map the obstacles. Working on a long timeline—five years, ten years, or even longer—forecasters and futurists anticipate the future by linking breakthroughs in science, technology, and medicine to the likely course of demographic trends. Then they examine the likely result of those changes on the economy, political system, and environment. Most large businesses utilize long-term forecasters as consultants or subscribe to trend reports published by their companies.

THE PROCESS OF LONG-TERM FORECASTING

The best way to understand the process of long-term forecasting is to look at the approach and predictions of professionals in the field. Each forecaster and futurist can be characterized by the approach used to arrive at a long-term forecast. The approach has four characteristics:

- The time frame for predictions—five years ahead, a decade, or more.
- The techniques used for capturing signals.
- The methods used to interpret the signals and make the forecasts.
- The range of the forecasts, whether general or restricted to certain countries or economic systems, particular cohorts, or specific industries.

Following are three profiles of forecasters working on long time lines beginning with the book that first introduced trendspotting to the public. These three profiles were chosen because they represent the spectrum of techniques generally used by professionals in the field and because these particular forecasters have received substantial coverage in the media for their views including both praise and criticism.

Naisbitt: Megatrends. In 1968, John Naisbitt was reading a history of the Civil War when he realized that the author was using newspapers of that period as primary sources. Thinking of newspapers as a "first draft of history," Naisbitt began methodically sifting newspapers for the fleeting hints of developing trends. He founded a business consulting firm and began publishing a newsletter based on this idea (Dougherty & Hoover, 1990). When Naisbitt's book *Megatrends* was published in 1982, a new word entered the vocabulary—a "megatrend" is a critical restructuring that defines a new direction for society.

Megatrends was a bestseller and continues to be one of the best-known trend books. In the book Naisbitt identified ten megatrends including:

- The move toward an information-based economy.
- The dual compensations of "high tech" and "high-touch" products—high-touch products have soft contours and cozy, handmade, or artsy attributes (Figure 9.1).
- The shift to a global economy.
- The shift away from hierarchical structures in favor of informal networks.
- The shift from an either/or to a multiple-option society.

In the years since the book was published, these general trends have been demonstrated in the growth of the Internet and other computer-based changes

FIGURE 9.1

A fur coat by Karl Lagerfeld features the attributes of "high-touch" apparel because it looks soft, cozy, and warm.

in business and in a more flexible approach to career development and lifestyle choices. However, long-term general forecasts are never completely accurate because intervening events deflect or even reverse trends. Such was the case in Naisbitt's megatrend predicting a shift in population and investment capital from the North to the Sunbelt, a shift that did not occur to the extent predicted and did not have an appreciable negative impact on the Northeast.

Careful readers of trend books and subscribers to trend reports need to pay special attention to the methodology used to make predictions. In *Megatrends,* the methodology is clearly spelled out in the introduction. Data were gathered by continually monitoring 6,000 local newspapers each month to "pinpoint, trace, and evaluate the important issues and trends" (Naisbitt, 1982). The idea was that trends and ideas began in cities and local communities rather than in urban centers like New York and Washington, D.C. Content analysis of local papers revealed those issues and trends that were competing for the scarce resource of space in the newspaper. Over time, these issues and trends could be observed emerging, gaining importance, and then losing space as interest declined.

Although Naisbitt and his wife Patricia Aburdene have written other trend books—*Megatrends 2000* (Naisbitt & Aburdene, 1990), *Megatrends for Women* (Aburdene & Naisbitt, 1992), and *Megatrends Asia* (Naisbitt, & Brealey, 1996)—those books were less clear about the underlying methodology. Because all Naisbitt's books are relentlessly upbeat about the future, critics have called the forecasts "megababble" (Kanfer, 1990). However, in that first book, Naisbitt did identify key transitions in the culture and economy using content analysis of media sources.

Look at Naisbitt's predictions about high-tech/high-touch products or the shift from hierarchical structures to networks—trends that were introduced nearly two decades ago. How do they play out in today's culture? List examples of products, processes, careers, organizations, or businesses that exemplify these trends. For balance, list any examples that run counter to the trend or that contradict Naisbitt's predictions. Will these trends continue or disappear over the next five or ten years?

Activity 9.1 Megatrends Ahead

Faith Popcorn: Clicking. Cultural trends arise from three sources: **high culture** (fine and performance arts), **low culture** (activities pursued locally by special interest groups outside of mainstream awareness), and **pop culture** (movies, television, music and celebrity). All three interest forecaster Faith Popcorn, who co-founded the company BrainReserve in 1974 (Figure 9.2). BrainReserve is a marketing consultancy working with a wide array of clients

Faith Popcorn, co-founder of the marketing consultancy BrainReserve, is credited as the trendspotter who recognized the trend for "cocooning" as early as 1981—a trend with variations that are still visible in culture today.

in many product categories. As she puts it in her first book, *The Popcorn Report* (1991), "It's our business to study how consumers are feeling today and how they'll be feeling tomorrow" and to make those predictions based on "a sound methodology developed and refined over the years."

Popcorn is credited as the trendspotter who saw a stay-at-home syndrome building in 1981 and called it "cocooning." Popcorn made the connection between people's stressful work lives and hectic social lives and their wish for a tranquil haven at home. Her company tracked the trend as it reached full bloom in the late 1980s. That single trend had repercussions in multiple industries. For the home building and renovation industry it meant that consumers demanded master bedroom suites, larger baths with all the amenities of a spa, and media rooms. For the apparel industry, it meant consumers were staying home and demanding casual, no-frills, basic fashion.

The trend was still in play in the mid-1990s when sales of bed linens, towels, and housewares continued the trend upward (Reda, 1994). Even among teens and young adults, half the women and one-third of the men list home as their favorite place to be. Instead of ending, Popcorn sees the trend continuing for 20 to 25 years but in a transformed state that reflects the times (Pfaff, 1998). One example is the expansion of cocooning beyond the home to the car with portable phone and fax and elaborate sound systems. Another is the shift from cozy nesting to protecting the cocoon in the mid-1990s with increased interest in unlisted numbers, caller ID, and home security systems (Vargo, 1996). The trend continues to play out in the new demographic trend for Gen Xers to become GenNesters (Edwards, 1997)—that is, the shift of twenty-somethings away from the club and bar scene and into serious relationships, intimate dinner parties, and self-definition through homemaking.

The power of trends for the business executive is clearly illustrated by the life cycle of the cocooning trend. People's desire for home as a retreat from the stress of everyday life had the energy, stability, longevity, and viability to power purchases for two decades and influence multiple industries. But it was up to the executives in each of those industries to shape their product and their business plan to take advantage of the opportunity.

The BrainReserve methodology begins with people in the company building collective knowledge on potential change by:

- Scanning a continuous stream of about 350 magazines, trade journals, newspapers, and newsletters in categories such as business news, women's and men's fashion magazines, health, home decor, travel, health, food, entertainment and gossip, science, economics, environmental issues, and politics.

- Monitoring the top television shows, first-run movies, Broadway plays, best-selling books, and hit music.

- Shopping stores in America and abroad for new products.

- Interviewing about 4,000 consumers each year about 20 different product categories.

The methodology results in what Popcorn calls a "brailling of the culture," and that leads to the identification of trends—the forces shaping the future (Popcorn, 1991).

In her book *Clicking* (1997), Popcorn identifies cocooning and 16 other specific trends including:

- Clanning—the tendency for people to group together around a shared common interest.

- Fantasy Adventure—consumers' need for excitement and stimulation but without sacrificing safety and security.

- Egonomics—products that are customized to an individual consumer to offset the impersonal feeling of modern culture.

- FemaleThink—the idea that women are more comfortable in an environment that is compatible with the way they think and behave, and that such an environment is less hierarchical and more relational.

Spining out the methodology further, BrainReserve develops concepts by spending time interviewing experts. People in their "TalentBank"—more than 5,000 people with interesting jobs or points of view—may be asked to assist in reviewing creative concepts.

The final component of the BrainReserve methodology is **brainstorming** sessions. The idea is to gather a diverse group of individuals and ask them to concentrate on a particular subject. A neutral moderator stands at an easel pad and jots down everything that is suggested. The moderator keeps the session on track by reminding the people in the group to avoid rambling and negativity and by pushing and probing for answers and solutions. This technique may be used at several points in the process of generating new concepts or applying trends to future business plans.

Popcorn's word for the clear, definite connection between a trend and a business concept is "click." To be "on-trend" (compatible with the prevailing trends), a business concept should click with at least 4 of her 17 identified trends. If it does, the concept is more likely to succeed because it will have the energy, stability, and longevity to work through the market over a period of years and because it will appeal to a large enough audience to be viable commercially (Popcorn, 1997).

Popcorn readily recognizes the contradictory nature of working with trends. Some concepts can click with one or more trends and be contradicted by others. After all, people and the societies they create are not completely consistent. For every trend, there are **counter-trends** or "flip-sides"(Popcorn, 1991). This contradictory aspect of working with trends mirrors the sometimes contradictory aspects of human behavior: The same person may watch his diet, exercise strenuously, and reward himself with a pint of premium ice cream! According to Popcorn, money can be made on a trend and on its flip side if business executives are canny enough to see the "click" (Figure 9.3).

Popcorn, like Naisbitt, comes in for criticism as well as praise. In one highly critical article, Popcorn's methodology is attacked because results are not reported as "quantified trend data," trends tend to get renamed and repackaged over time, and the names of trends sound like media sound bites (Shalit, 1994). Popcorn (1994), in a response to the article, pointed out that her approach is to interview, observe, and then make a creative leap to identify trends shaping the future—a qualitative approach rather than a quantitative one (for more on quantitative and qualitative approaches to consumer research, see Chapters 2, 7 and 8). As for repackaging, Popcorn claims that her business is tracking the evolution of trends—a process that includes redefining trends. Popcorn's early job experience was in advertising where she honed the ability to use words (including self-invented jargon) to inform, convince, and persuade. This ability has made her one of the most quoted futurists in the media, a situation that irritates her competitors in the field (Shalit, 1994). Even in an article critical of Popcorn's approach, clients of BrainReserve are quoted expressing satisfaction with the services provided. These

FIGURE 9.3

The flip side of the trend toward modern, sleek, minimalist styles is a more embellished look. Both trends, while seeming contradictory, exist side-by-side, and offer business opportunities.

clients point out that thinking about long-term trends promotes fresh thinking and focuses executive's attention on consumer lifestyle.

Is apparel "clicking" with Popcorn's trends of cocooning, clanning, fantasy adventure, egonomics, and female-think? Select an apparel product or brand and profile its status as "on-trend" or "off-trend." Do the same for a store, mall, or a visual merchandising approach. If the profiles show an "off-trend" status, how can the situation be altered to bring it "on-trend"?

Activity 9.2 The Apparel Click

Taylor and Wacker: The 500-Year Delta. The turn of the century and the millennium offer a unique vantage point to observe social trends. A child born in the early 1900s saw many firsts in technology—the first animated cartoons, television, computers, trips into space—and in medicine—the first vaccines, successful organ transplants, and births where the child was conceived outside the mother's body. All these advances and many more had social implications. Civil rights and liberation movements for African Americans, women, and gays had profound effects on social institutions and lifestyles. Hints of changes to come in the next century are present as instabilities within the social fabric of today. One futurist looking at those instabilities on a long timeline is Watts Wacker who wrote the book *The 500-Year Delta* (1997) with public relations and marketing executive Jim Taylor.

Who are Taylor and Wacker and what gives them the ability to see such large-scale shifts? They call themselves "number crunchers and content analysts" because of their backgrounds in consumer survey research and as consultants with leading companies. Taylor directs global marketing for the computer company Gateway 2000; Wacker had been resident futurist at several well-known market research firms before starting his own firm.

Wacker researches change by becoming a **participant observer** in selected situations. A participant observer enters a situation and interacts with the people and activities found there as a way of exploring and understanding the meaning of people's behavior. He claims that studying people and social situations at the "edge" of culture informs his understanding of change at the "center" of society. Each summer Wacker assumes the persona of Mitch, a Montana cowhand, and takes guests on day-hikes. He has also worked in a fast-food restaurant, been a baggage handler at an international airport, and begged on the streets of Harlem (Doyle, 1998).

Together Taylor and Wacker have written a book with a controversial premise: every half-millenium the world experiences a radical shift. Wacker and Taylor contend that the world is at the end of a 500-year experiment with reason and the scientific method that began with the Renaissance and the invention of the printing press. During this experiment, natural and social sciences sought to explain events based on causality—the goal was to discover a logical link between cause and effect. These causal chains became more intricate as scientists linked multiple causes for every effect and multiple effects for every cause (Figure 9.4). According to Wacker and Taylor, the current pervasive sense of anxiety comes from the loss of certainty that the modern condition can be sufficiently explained in terms of reason. Instead, they see chaos theory as offering insights into the way that the world will work in the future.

The concepts of chaos theory were introduced to a wide audience in a bestselling book (Gleick, 1987). People in a number of fields began to be dissatisfied with the **linear** explanations of the scientific method with its attempts to link cause and effect. Instead they saw potential in the **nonlinear** concepts in the new science of chaos. In nonlinear systems—and the marketplace certainly qualifies as nonlinear—simple, seemingly inconsequential events give rise to astonishingly complicated dynamics (see Chapter 10 for a more extended discussion of chaos theory as it applies to forecasting).

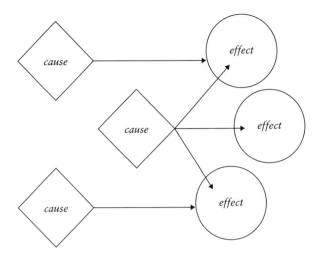

FIGURE 9.4

Traditional science is based on understanding cause and effect. The problem is the complexity—for every cause there are multiple effects and for every effect there are multiple causes. Unraveling the cause-and-effect chains has proven very difficult.

As an example of a nonlinear approach to marketing, Taylor and Wacker (1997) cite the case of the Tommy Hilfiger brand. Hilfiger executives noticed what seemed to be a relatively inconsequential event—as soon as new products would hit the stores, a small but significant number of garments would be pilfered from stores in urban areas. Reason would dictate that the company act to eliminate shoplifting by installing new security systems or withdrawing from stores where the shoplifting was most prevalent. Instead, the Hilfiger executives did what Taylor and Wacker see as the right thing—nothing. Taylor and Wacker explain that the executives understood that the Hilfiger brand was popular among young, urban trendsetters who, by wearing the styles on the streets, became billboards for the brand. Further, they understood the dynamics of the system: these trendsetting early adopters influenced others so that the looks diffused through the teenage clothing market. Thus, a seemingly inconsequential event—lost sales at certain stores due to pilfering—plays out in a complex dynamic that drives brand awareness and sales volume.

Using a combination of social science techniques, industry experience, and observation, Taylor and Wacker predict a flood tide of changes and transitions occurring during the next 500-year experiment including:

- The creation of demand-based markets rather than those driven by production efficiencies.
- The rise of tribalism and the need for marketing to the new tribal organization of society (see the discussion of "style tribes" in Chapter 6).
- The movement away from conspicuous consumption to "stealth wealth," where it is more important to have a few good things.
- The rising value of personal energy as time pressure intersects with stress.

Profile

Iconoculture®

In 1992 **Mary Meehan, Larry Samuel,** and **Vickie Abrahamson** started a trend forecasting firm called Iconoculture®. Based in Minneapolis, Minnesota, the trio ventures far afield to research trends and present findings to clients at companies such as Dayton Hudson Corporation, The Limited, Inc., Target Stores, Rockport shoes, *Details* magazine, and advertising agencies. Ms. Meehan spent 10 years at Dayton Hudson, rising to manager of new product development and then moved into an agency specializing in marketing and licensing (Gale, 1995). She functions as the firm's resident media maven. Mr. Samuel, a futurist who has a Ph.D. in American Studies, uses the Internet to sleuth the edges of cultural change and visits clubs to check out the fashions in clothes, drinks, and music. Ms. Abrahamson travels throughout the country talking to people in small towns, shopping in local stores, and reading local newspapers. When they get together, they try to "make sense out of the cultural chaos, make key connections, and discuss the implication" for their clients (Abrahamson, Meehan, & Samuel, 1997, p. xiv). They think of their firm as "a cultural weathercaster, reading the prevailing trendwinds to forecast marketing dewpoints" (p. xiii).

Every business needs to differentiate itself from others in the field. The partners in Iconoculture® see themselves as different from other trend-spotters or research firms that report on street trends for two reasons: their "vision is broader than just looking at what's 'in' right now" (Tillotson, 1998, p. 01E), they go beyond identifying trends to "draw out the implications of trends on business" (Moore, 1999, p. 01D). The role of the firm is to help retailers and other businesses to recognize shifts in society that will make the difference in thriving for the future. Mr. Samuel says, "So many companies are so caught up in the next year, they're not really attuned to the larger picture" (Moore, 1999, p. 01D).

As consultants, Iconoculture® offers a menu of options designed to "lead to actionable marketing and advertising opportunities" for clients ("Iconoculture," 1999, p. 1). The firm's Web site lists the following types of presentations and proprietary techniques ("Iconoculture," 1999):

- The Trend Commandment™ outlines the firm's methodological approach and illustrates the presentation with visual evidence of trends they have identified and translated into business ideas.
- Signs of Times™ is a multi-sensory presentation on current and emerging cultural trends likely to impact businesses and designed to be the starting point for long-range business planning and concept development.
- Iconoclock™ shows the historical development of a product, industry, or market decade-by-decade through the 20th Century and projects "a future scenario based on its cultural arc" (p. 2).

- Cool Monitor™ is a biannual or quarterly report on the people, places, and products that are on the leading edge of cultural change.

- Global Monitor™ reports on findings from an international network of informants who "track, interpret, and translate a society's values" so that business can develop global marketing strategies (p. 2).

- Culturama™ is the firm's term for custom projects which could include scenario planning based on different cultural paradigms, workshops on how advertising works and why or what makes some brands dynamic, or collections "trend-smart cultural artifacts."

Ms. Meehan points out that the firm is "less obsessed with what's driven by cool than what's driven by other things, like environmentalism or spirituality" (Moore, 1999, p. 01D). The partners' book on trends uses people's "passion points"—for Americans these include mind, body, spirit, experience, identity, society, nature, relationships, fear, and technology—to cluster trends. According to the partners, these passion points have lifestyle and marketing implications, offer compelling ways to sell, and are as stable as people's values. Each passion point is covered in a chapter of the book with three or more "signs of the times"—cultural trends with a distinctive label that captures its personality. The book includes forty trends including "biomorphing" (shaping the anatomy using science and the imagination), "zentrepreneurism" (fusing personal vision, social philosophy, and one's profession), "beehiving" (communities based on tight-knit affinity groups), and "technomorphing" (the evolutionary effects of technology on people's lives). Each trend is explained using people, places, and products as examples and concludes with suggestions on how the core trend can be used as a marketing opportunity (Abrahamson, Meehan, Samuel, 1997). Because these trends relate to different "cohort characteristics," they may seem overlapping or even contradictory. Yet, the partners see the trends as a first step in linking attitudes and behavior to brand positioning ("Iconoculture", 1999).

The book was written knowing the specifics would be out-of-date, perhaps within months. But, the trends will continue evolving just as aromatherapy evolved into "sensatherapy" (using the senses in diagnosing and treating ailments). As Samuel sees it, "The narrow trends will be gone, but the way we cluster them will still be here" (Tillotson, 1998, p. 01E). Mr. Samuel compares the firm's work to being an outfielder: "You don't move to where the ball is, you move to where the ball is going" (Furchgott, 1998, p. 12). To accomplish that feat, the partners look for a trend and then take it apart into mini-trends. The trend might be for a cultural emphasis on well-being but that might be played out in concerns for mental and physical health, desire for balance in one's life, focus on home life, or a new interest in spirituality. Businesses in many industries could be impacted by the trend and its associated mini-trends (Furchgott, 1998).

Sources

Abrahamson, V., Meehan, M., Samuel, L. (1997). *The future ain't what it used to be: The 40 cultural trends transforming your job, your life, your world.* New York: Riverhead Books.

Furchgott, R. (1998, March 2). Trend-spotting: Anyone can play. *Business Week,* 12ENT.

Gale, E. (1995, October 23). Trend-watch maven takes of Jeune Lune board. *Minneapolis Star Tribune,* p. 08D.

Iconoculture [Web]. Available: *http://www.iconoculture.com* [1999, July 19].

Moore, J. (1999, January 17). On the trail of the next big thing. *Minneapolis Star Tribune,* p. 01D.

Tillotson, K. (1998, January 31). Selling futures. *Minneapolis Star Tribune,* p. 01E.

The future, especially on the time scale attempted by Taylor and Wacker, is unknowable. Any attempt to do so depends on sweeping generalizations. The authors' vision depends on a continuation of today's consumer society projected into a future of challenges and opportunities. Critics point out that futurists with a more pessimistic view—usually academicians and journalists—are less likely to appeal to CEOs and other business people (Goldman, 1998).

Unlike other forecasters, Wacker and Taylor's synthesis of the future goes beyond identifying general trend directions. They suggest a different way of thinking about issues—a nonlinear approach in which the emphasis is less on linking cause and effect and more on the dynamics of a system. It is this fusion between forecasting and the new sciences of chaos and complexity that distinguishes their synthesis from that of other forecasters.

Activity 9.3
Stealth Wealth
Style

Taylor and Wacker see a trend toward owning a few good things, things that symbolize a person's style. Conduct consumer research to determine what product categories and specific products are coveted as "stealth wealth." Ask people to make a collage of pictures showing the things they aspire to own. Good sources for making the collages are magazine ads and catalogs. Ask them to avoid big-ticket items such as houses and cars and focus on personal belongings they would use every day. Then, ask them to list three items they would save and sacrifice to own. Collate the responses to create a map of aspirational products likely to receive consumer attention now and in the future.

IMPLICATIONS FOR THE TEXTILE AND APPAREL INDUSTRIES

Companies such as the Italian firm Mandarina Duck use cultural indicators in shaping their company identity and for product development (Ilari, 1998). Not interested in presenting a total look, the company instead offers an eclectic group of accessories and apparel that can be mixed and matched. Their goal is to research the market, study products that transcend fashion trends, and create a futuristic line with an urban feel. Export manager Elena Moretti explains, "We analyze social trends and filter them into our collections."

When analyzing trends, it is easy to see links between the forecasts made by different people at different times and using various methods. Compare Naisbitt's view in 1982 of the shift away from hierarchical structures in favor of informal networks and Popcorn's 1997 trend called FemaleThink, which contends that women are more comfortable in nonhierarchical, more relational settings. Popcorn calls the tendency for people to form groups around a shared interest "clanning," while Taylor and Wacker call it "tribalism." Popcorn's "egonomics"—customizing products for the individual consumer to offset the impersonal feeling of modern culture—echoes Naisbitt's view that "high tech" must be offset by "high touch" products and Taylor and Wacker's views on demand-based markets. All these forecasters see the continuing centrality of information to the economy and to the lifestyles of individuals.

The implications of some of these trends have already been introduced in previous chapters. Demand-based markets necessitate close attention to consumer research (Chapter 7) and focus attention on the process of mass customization, the complete connection between consumer preferences and product. Consumer tribes create a look as a badge of identification and that behavior influences the way clothing is marketed (Chapter 6). Taylor and Wacker's observations about "stealth wealth" are another facet of conspicuous consumption and reverse conspicuous consumption introduced in the discussion of fashion dynamics (Chapter 3). The way people invest personal energy relates to the way clothing is marketed and sold, particularly the growing potential of selling online. Each of these trends affects the way consumers buy and use clothing today and each has the potential to be useful in shaping business strategies.

Long-term forecasting looks for **cultural drift,** directional pointers for the way society is moving (Popcorn, 1997). While major events such as war, political turmoil, and economic downturns can interrupt or even reverse such drifts, a company cannot plan for such unexpected disruptions. What it can plan for is continuation of the drift at the same rate, acceleration of the drift, or tapering off of the drift—three scenarios of alternative, but possible futures. Long-term forecasts provide:

- Insights that are valuable in evaluating current business practices.
- Indications that a business needs to reposition the product or the way of relating to customers.
- Input for a company's strategic planning.
- A backdrop for understanding and evaluating short-term forecasting.

THE LONG-TERM FORECASTER'S TOOLBOX

Forecasters charge customers thousands of dollars for a seminar at a national sales meeting, a one-year subscription to a trend report, or a concept development project. Companies find the price reasonable when the trends reported point to a new business or an investment opportunity. Learning about trends can be useful in other ways such as expanding an executive's time horizon, encouraging creative thinking, or explaining behaviors that previously seemed insignificant. For companies that overemphasize number crunching and linear analysis, trendspotters can provide balance by showing other measures of consumer reality. Obscure events signal change at the fringes, and these changes can move toward the mainstream. Most executives are blind to such signals because, as specialists in their fields, their expectations limit their vision—they see what they expect to see. Trendspotters interpret soft data, are more receptive to change, and make connections using imaginative thinking.

The raw material of forecasting is information. Most trendspotters look for trends by scanning media and through observation. Critics of trendspotters wonder why companies would pay for a service that anyone can do. Although the techniques of media content analysis, interviewing, and observation seem simple, they must be carried out continuously and systematically to be effective. Trendspotting depends on being able to filter the trends from the stream of information. The forecaster is looking for:

- Shifts in demographics that can restructure society.
- Changes in industry and market structure.
- Differences in consumer interests, values, and motivation.
- Breakthroughs in technology and science.
- Changes in the economic picture.
- Alteration in political, cultural, and economic alliances between countries.

A plan for systematic **environmental scanning** enables the forecaster to find signals of change and signposts to the future in today's media. Every executive already casually samples media and tracks trends by clipping attention-grabbing items or discussing news stories with colleagues. Expanding those efforts and using a more systematic approach to collecting and analyzing observations is the first step in creating an environmental scan for cultural indicators. The skill comes in recognizing the link between seemingly unrelated bits of information and the talent in recognizing the implications. The following summary of research strategies and analysis techniques provides a toolbox for those who want to emulate the techniques used by long-term forecasters.

Research Strategy 1: Media Scan

A magazine writer who writes on emerging trends says she lives by the maxim "three's a trend"—if she sees, hears, or reads about something three times, that signals a trend (Greco, 1994). Scanning media for clues to change is a method many trendspotters share. Forecasters are media mavens with vast appetites for information. No individual can match the effort of a company like BrainReserve. So, how can an individual be successful at spotting cultural indicators? By building on personal observations of friends and family and media habits (magazines, movies, television, music, books), any individual already has a start on forecasting.

While an executive (or even a company) cannot devote the time and energy to scanning that the professional forecaster does, it is wise to include some provision for this kind of broad-based scanning in the workday. See Chapter 11 for the details on how any executive can bring environmental scanning to the desktop using print, broadcast, and online sources.

Research Strategy 2: Interviewing

Ask People. Faith Popcorn once said she got some of her best signals about lifestyle trends by talking to people in airports. By simply asking them what was making them happy or unhappy, she opened up a discussion about lifestyle changes they were contemplating. Forecasting executives have been known to recognize social change in the conversation at a dinner party. People engage in conversation everyday but fail to discern underlying trend indicators. Merely becoming aware that ordinary conversations hold deeper meaning is a first step to tapping into this rich source of cultural information.

Focus groups take the dynamic of the dinner party conversation into a more formal interview setting. The moderator uses a predesigned set of questions to guide the discussion to topics of interest to the research sponsor. Still, it is not unusual for focus group interviews to yield unexpected richness in terms of directional information (see Chapter 7 for a more detailed discussion of focus group interviewing).

In contrast to group interview situations, the **in-depth interview** is conducted one-on-one in an attempt to gain a deep understanding of a consumer's relationship to a product or product category. The interviews can last several hours and many involve more than one session. A researcher conducting a number of in-depth interviews can use the insights gained in earlier interviews as questions and probes in subsequent interviews. Often the person interviewed reveals something interesting and unexpected. The researcher is free to pursue this new topic if it seems to hold promise. This flexibility is the chief advantage of one-on-one interviews.

When trying to understand a shift in social rules or a change in lifestyle among a cohort group, a forecaster may decide to conduct a number of interviews—sometimes 100 or more. When the findings show a cultural drift that has gone unnoticed or the significance of the change has not been fully appreciated, the studies may be published in a book or article. Disseminated to a larger public, the trends can be discussed and evaluated for their impact on a particular product category or industry.

Activity 9.4 Asking Around

List issues related to price, quality, style, or sizing of fashion products. From the list, select one issue to research. Watch for opportunities to bring up the topic in conversation during one day. Report on these conversations and the implications of what you discover for the textile and apparel industries.

Ask Experts. One way to scan for hints about the future is to listen to experts in the field when they appear on panels and participate in the question and answer period. An alternative is to conduct a method of research called the Delphi method. The Delphi method was devised in a "think tank" environment in California in the early 1960s (Gordon, 1994). The reasoning was that experts, when they agree, are more likely than others to be correct on questions related to their field of expertise. The goal of the Delphi method is to encourage debate by making the interaction independent of personality. The following list shows the stages in using the Delphi method:

- **Identify the Experts**

Experts are often quoted in articles or cited in the literature of the field. Once a few such people have been identified and recruited, other experts are added in a "daisy chain" fashion through recommendations of those already on the panel. Expert participants are assured of anonymity—that is, comments made in the debate are not identified with the individual expert.

- **Introduce an Issue for Debate**

The rearchers conducting the Delphi pose a question to the experts. The question may involve the size of a future market, what policy will bring about a particular business goal, or the likely outcomes of a particular action.

- **Round One—Obtain Initial Response from Experts**

Participants state their positions, the reasoning behind those positions, and provide supporting materials if they exist. The responses can be communicated back to the researchers in a letter, fax, or e-mail.

- **Summarize the Responses**

The researchers summarize the responses, identifying the range of opinions. Usually there are a few extreme opinions on either side of the issue. Most responses are likely to fall in the moderate range. All comments are given equal weight and are not identified by the expert's name or title.

- **Report on Round One; Initiate Round Two**

The researchers present the summary to the group. They ask people holding extreme opinions to reassess their views given the group's more moderate response. Often those with extreme opinions will be asked to provide additional reasons for their positions. Once again responses are returned to the researchers.

- **Report on Round Two; Initiate Round Three**

The researchers report on the group judgment and the reasons for the extreme opinions. Each expert is asked to reassess his or her opinion. They may also be asked to refute the reasons given for the extreme opinions using information known to them as insiders. The experts return their responses to the researchers.

- **Report on Round Three; Initiate Round Four**

Researchers summarize the arguments and the evolving group consensus. In this final round, the experts are once again asked to reassess their opinions if the arguments of others on the panel are compelling.

Because personalities are removed from the situation, the Delphi method is like a debate but without the anger, spin, bias, or rancor that a face-to-face debate can engender. Often experts reach consensus. When they do not, at least the reasons for different opinions become clearer. The researchers and planners now have insights to use in making decisions on the issue. The value of the Delphi method is in the ideas it generates and the clarification that comes from experts debating a complex issue.

Research Strategy 3: Observation

In the late 1980s, a group of consumer behavior researchers set out to illustrate the power of observation (Wallendorf, Belk, & Heisley, 1988). Two dozen researchers participated in the Consumer Behavior Odyssey—a trip from coast to coast in a recreational vehicle observing consumers in naturalistic settings while conducting qualitative research. The researchers stopped at fairs, swap meets, flea markets, and festivals—anywhere consumers congregated to shop. They used photography and interviewing along with participating and observing the interactions. What they discovered was a rich and virtually untapped reservoir of relationships between people and their possessions.

New products in the grocery store, new services offered by the phone companies, an art show at a new gallery in a quaint part of town—all offer the chance to become a participant observer in change. The essence of the participant observer method is the way it provides access to the "insider's viewpoint" (Jorgensen, 1989). Being an insider provides the opportunity to understand the meaning of everyday happenings and the reality of situations as defined by the participants (Figure 9.5).

The methodology of participant observer invites involvement in concrete activities in natural settings as a way to understand people's behaviors, attitudes, and belief structure. The actual methodology has a long history and practitioners follow careful protocols in collecting and reporting on their experiences. However, to a lesser extent, any person interested in forecasting can become a participant observer when he or she explores a new offering in the marketplace. A forecaster is constantly aware of the potential for discovery in any and all daily activities.

Activity 9.5 On the Spot

Go to a mall, collection of small shops, downtown intersection, or other observation post. What can you learn from just observing? Spend at least one hour observing the activities of consumers and report on the interesting, unusual, or unexpected things that you see. Do any of these observations suggest a cultural drift that needs further research and explanation?

Reviewing, Organizing, and Editing Trend Folders

Collecting bits and pieces from a broad spectrum of sources, seeing hints and glimpses of possible futures, hearing about new directions is only a first step. These signals must be linked, shaped into a vision of what the future may be, and logically supported before being dubbed a trend. Even a minimum level of environmental scanning will produce a wealth of information for analysis. How do forecasters decide what things to pay attention to and what things to ignore? They pay careful attention to the following signals of the future:

- New and unusual businesses.
- Innovative and novel products.
- Unusual travel destinations.
- New, rediscovered, or redesigned leisure-related activities.
- Shifts in the workplace and the way people do their jobs.

FIGURE 9.5

Every shopping trip offers the forecaster a chance to observe consumer behavior and recognize emerging trends, whether the trip is to an upscale specialty retailer, a discount store, or a trendy boutique that taps into New Age philosophies.

- New shopping locations, store designs, and services for customers.
- Stories about people and their unique adjustments to life's challenges.
- Stories about neighborhoods with an interesting mix of people, shopping, or ethnic cultures.

Most trendspotters begin with lists of themes or issues that capture their attention. Trends require labels. At first, the label may be general and descriptive—for example, new music, financial issues, cult movies, and unusual jobs. Trendspotters often move from lists into a set of file folders representing major categories of interest. Remember the maxim "three's a trend"? When something interesting and attention grabbing comes along, forecasters capture it and add it a "trends" folder—either an actual folder or on a computer disk. By reviewing the folders occasionally, the forecaster begins to see links. If three or more items seem related, the forecaster may start a separate folder with a label that captures the trend—for example, "Cyberstyle" or "Asian Influence" or "GenNesters." Once the trend begins to emerge, the next step is to think about how the trend relates to a specific product category or target market.

Reviewing, editing, and organizing the trend folders is part of the process of making connections. To keep the job manageable, Merriam and Makower (1988) suggest the following guidelines:

- Restrict the process to about ten major topics with possible subsets for each. Discard folders from time to time—a trendspotter can only manage about 50 major and minor categories and still be able see the subtle relationships between the categories.
- Include both objective and subjective views of an issue (e.g., downsizing of a corporation from the financial viewpoint of the company and the personal stories of workers who are losing their jobs).
- Include intuitive categories—those where the forecaster sees a glimmer of meaning or a subtle connection but is unsure whether the matter will evolve into a trend.

Activity 9.6 Forecaster's Motto— Be Aware	Buy a set of colored folders and some labels. Begin clipping directional items from newspapers and magazines. Make notes of interesting items on television. Add one or more items to your set of folders every day for the next 21 days. About halfway into the process, stop and organize your clippings into folders, giving each folder a label that stands for a topic or trend name. At the end of the 21 days you will have become more aware of the signals of change in the cultural environment and established the habits of a trendspotter.

Looking into the Future

A baby born in January 2000 has a better chance than any previous generation to live to see 2100. What kind of world will that person live in? Forecasts for the cohort born into the new century include (Adler, 1998; Garber, 1998; Stein, 1999):

- An increasing population in the United States, particularly in California, Texas, and Florida, where crowding means smaller median lot sizes for single family homes.
- Technology-driven prosperity, creating a "long-boom" economic cycle, increased worker mobility, and demand for technical savvy.
- Retirement of the baby boom generation, bringing great deals on family homes and good job prospects to the younger generations.
- A widening gap between haves and have-nots in terms of economic and technology factors.
- Increasing population among minority groups with the American population one-quarter black, Asian, or Native American and one-quarter Hispanic by 2050 according to the Census Bureau.
- Genetically tailored plants and animals producing more food to support a doubling of the world population.
- Continuing penetration of personal computers—in 38 percent of homes in 1995, 70 percent in 2005—along with cheaper rates and faster transmission for voice-data-video over the same line.
- Loss of trust in things people used to count on, like safe food and water.
- Customized clothes, home furnishings, and other consumer products.
- Leisure time becoming so rare that it will be elevated to a status symbol.

Long-term forecasts contain optimistic predictions about amazing advances and pessimistic warnings about eroding quality of life caused by population pressures on the environment. Often predictions from different futurists seem contradictory because each predicts large-scale change and effects on large population groups and many industries.

Analysis and Implication Assessment. Just as an executive may have multiple color forecasts to work with, so the executive will have multiple long-term forecasts—some internal from strategic planners and consultants and other external from newsletters, books, industry groups, government reports. The executive needs a framework that will highlight the niche each forecast fills, conflict or agreement between forecasts, and voids in the forecasts. In 1928, Nystrom proposed a list of the elements that compose the "spirit of the times"—a list updated and expanded on in Chapter 2. Nystrom's framework provides a way to evaluate and organize cultural indicators.

In addition to applying a framework, it is important to use research strategies such as environmental scanning, interviewing, and observation to customize predictions to the textile and apparel industries and to specific target audiences. Customized long-term forecasts can provide meaningful guides to decision making if they focus on the effect of change on **consumer cohorts** (groups of consumers who share similar demographic and psychographic characteristics). The goal of long-term forecasting is to translate broad directional tendencies into an understanding of how they will affect consumer preferences and behaviors. The process begins with environmental scanning, interviewing, and observation, but only becomes meaningful when the information is analyzed and implications assessed.

Scenario Writing. Looking into the future helps inform decisions in the present. Futurists do not predict the future (Tanaka, 1998). They look at data, identify trends, and extrapolate the trends into the future. To do this they consider alternative futures and lay out paths of probability as to which is more likely. Looking at alternative futures can encourage executives to think more creatively about long-range planning.

The term **scenario** was borrowed from the theatrical arts, where it refers to the plot of a story or a summary of the action in a movie. In the business world, a scenario describes the evolution from the present situation to one or more possible futures (Fahey & Randall, 1998). There are many variations on how to write scenarios. One approach is to start with a vision of the future and work backward to discover the path to that future. Another is to project present forces into the future, plotting their likely evolution.

The process usually begins when executives identify an issue or decision that will influence future business decisions. The next step is to identify forces and trends in the environment that influence the issue. Then, rank these influences in terms of their importance and the degree of uncertainty associated with each. With this outline in hand, locate any quantitative data that can be used to support scenario writing (e.g., demographic data, consumer statistics, and economic indicators).

A single scenario is useless because it fails to consider alternative futures. Instead, futurists recommend a minimum of three scenarios (Kania, 1998):

* The "surprise-free" scenario—a scenario projecting the continuation of current conditions.
* The "best-case" scenario—a scenario that takes an optimistic view toward technological breakthroughs and economic conditions.
* The "worst-case" scenario—a scenario built using more negative possibilities and a pessimistic view.

To be effective, the scenarios must be vivid and plausible.

Together these three alternative futures provide executives with the basis for discussion of long-term plans. Scenarios lead to actionable decisions if they are tracked and monitored as the future unfolds. The final step in scenario writing is to decide on some key indicators and signposts to watch. Writing and discussing scenarios helps executives make decisions that lead to a particular and preferable path into the future.

Some products are classics created in the 20th century and emblematic of the times—Barbie Dolls, VW Beetles, and Rollerblades. Forecasting classic products of the future begins with looking at the classics of the past. Examine fashion history in the 20th century for classic examples such as jeans, khaki pants, the little black dress, and T-shirts. Select one classic and research the current situation by locating quantitative and qualitative data. Then write two scenarios—one optimistic about the future of this item in the 21st century, one pessimistic. Discuss the plausibility of each scenario in class.

Activity 9.7
Classic Products of the Twenty-first Century

Key Terms and Concepts

Brainstorming	High Culture	Participant Observer
Consumer Cohorts	In-Depth Interview	Pop Culture
Counter-Trends	Linear	Scenario
Cultural Drift	Low Culture	
Environmental Scanning	Nonlinear	

Case Revisited: The Future of Information

Tywanda and her staff are in the planning stage for their company's entrance into e-commerce. They began with the concept of style tribes and the idea that the Web is like a 21st century village marketplace. From there the staff will use long-term forecasting techniques to devise an entrance strategy and a strategic plan so that the company can become a prominent player in e-commerce. Use the following discussion question to review and summarize the strategies and techniques presented in this chapter.

The four characteristics of long-term forecasting: *What time frame should Tywanda's team use? What techniques should they use for capturing signals? What methods should they use to interpret the signals and make the forecasts? How general or restricted will the forecasts be?*

Scenarios for cultural drifts: What cultural drifts moving though society now provide a beginning point for the forecasts Tywanda's team want to make? What scenarios are more likely for each drift—continuation at the same rate of change, acceleration, or tapering off?

Tools for long-term forecasting: How will media scanning help the team? Should the team conduct interviews? What part should observation play in the team's task? How will the team review, organize, and edit their findings?

Additional Forecasting Activities

Checking Out the Forecasters. Make a special folder for collecting long-term predictions. When you have several sets of predictions, identify the items where there is general agreement and items where there is disagreement between forecasters. If possible, check into the background and credentials of those making the predictions. Which predictions seem overly optimistic or pessimistic? Which predictions are likely to impact the textile and apparel industries? Synthesize your own customized set of predictions related to your career in the industry.

Experts on the Future. Use the list of issues developed in Activity 9.6. Choose one issue as the seed for the Delphi technique. Identify a "dream team" of experts you would like to participate. Using online databases, locate speeches and interviews with your experts. Use these sources to construct a set of likely Round One responses from these experts on the issue you have chosen.

E-Commerce and the Future of Stores. Using online databases, locate articles about the future of e-commerce, including those that project future participation by companies and consumers and potential revenues. Also locate articles about the future of store retailing, including department stores, specialty stores, discount stores, malls, outlet malls, and independent stores. Organize the projections stated in these articles for a side-by-side comparison of these forms of retailing. Analyze the sources for each prediction and the level of uncertainty each represents. Evaluate which predictions seem to project current conditions into the future and which take an optimistic or a pessimistic view. This type of content analysis helps an executive clarify a seemingly confused and contradictory set of predictions about future directions.

Part Four

FORECASTING
AT WORK

Chapter 10

THE FUTURE OF FORECASTING

"Technology allows a company to 'come up with ideas faster than they can be stolen'."
—Pat Danahy, former Cone Mills CEO

Objectives

• Become aware of the new sciences of chaos and complexity and the implications for fashion forecasting in the 21st century.

• Understand the shift from forecasting as input for planning to forecasting as decision support under conditions of anticipation, improvisation, and continuously evolving strategy.

• Become better consumers of forecasts by understanding why forecasts fail.

• Recognize forecasting as a collaborative process based on enterprise-wide teamwork.

BALANCING ACT: THE EDGE OF CHAOS

At the beginning of the 1990s, news about the new sciences of chaos and complexity began reaching the general public (Gleick, 1987; Waldrop, 1992). People in fields from biology to business discovered links between the new sciences and difficult to understand questions in their own fields. The new sciences offered an alternative way of viewing the world. The traditional view, a method of knowing that had roots in 17th-century physics, holds that the way to understand how things work is to separate the process, phenomenon, or article into parts; study the parts to discover cause-and-effect relationships; and then learn how to apply controls. This approach made possible many breakthroughs and innovations in the modern world. But by the 20th century, people were identifying problems where understanding the parts did not explain the whole and where applying controls did not work. The new sciences of chaos and complexity offered a different way to think—a way that looks at how systems evolve and suggests that order and disorder are complementary.

Almost immediately people in business recognized that insights from the new sciences provided a new view of organizations (Anderla, Dunning, & Forge, 1997; Brown & Eisenhardt, 1998; Wheatley, 1992). More fluid, agile, and entrepreneurial companies were besting mechanistic, control-oriented, bureaucracies. This new kind of business initiated new kinds of competition, especially time-based competition. Traditional explanations could not explain these new "learning organizations," which functioned without boundaries and seemed to be self-renewing.

The world itself had changed. The 20th century experienced more change than occurred in all centuries that proceeded it. The Industrial Age that replaced the Agricultural Age had itself been replaced by the Information Age (Figure 10.1). By the 1990s, the emphasis had switched from information to intelligence (Tyson, 1997). The most forward-thinking companies sought competitive intelligence as a part of continuously evolving strategies. The traditional view of forecasting as input for planning works only under the tradi-

FIGURE 10.1

The 20th century experienced more change than occurred in all centuries that proceeded. Instead of disappearing, the characteristics of each age persisted even as a new age emerged.

ERA	PRODUCTION	SOCIETY	TIME	CULTURAL	FORECASTING
Agricultural 1000 BC to 1450 AD	Land-based	Ruling Class Peasants	Slow	Aristocratic	Seasonal
Industrial 1450 AD to 1960 AD	Mass Production	Owners & Workers	Linear	Mass-Culture Urbanization	Planning
Information 1960 AD to present	Networks	Knowledge Workers	Fast Cyclical	Global Postmodern	Anticipation Improvisation

tional, bureaucratic scheme. What do the new sciences of chaos and complexity offer that is useful to today's forecaster? Where does forecasting fit into the accelerated time-based competition? How do the most forward-thinking companies think of forecasting?

Insights from Chaos Theory

Chaos in scientific terms does not mean confusion, turmoil, and agitation as it does in everyday language. Instead, scientists use chaos to refer to orderly disorder—recognizable but complex patterns that form, dissolve, and reform in infinite diversity. Some of the pioneering work in **chaos theory** was done in the field of weather forecasting by a scientist named Lorenz (Gleick, 1987). Lorenz's intuition told him that weather repeated familiar patterns over time. By reducing weather to a bare bones algorithm on a primitive computer set-up, Lorenz began amassing printouts. What he saw was a kind of orderly disorder—a system containing periodic components that were predictable and nonperiodical parts that created unpredictability. In other words, a weather system is much like the fashion system.

Visualization makes this easier to grasp. Whereas linear relationships can be captured with straight lines on graph paper, Lorenz was looking at nonlinear relationships. Nonlinear relationships are usually displayed on two planes that share an axis. The changing relationship is thus represented in dimensional space (Figure 10.2). By plotting data in dimensional space, Lorenz re-

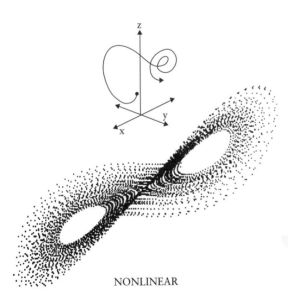

NONLINEAR

FIGURE 10.2

Unlike linear relationships, which can be captured on a single plane, nonlinear relationships require dimensional space for a pattern to emerge. In this example, the system never exactly repeats itself and the trajectory never intersects—an orderly but unpredictable pattern with an underlying "strange attractor" that keeps the system within boundaries.

vealed order in a stream of data that appeared to be disorderly. He discovered a system that never exactly repeats itself, with a trajectory that never intersects itself—an orderly but unpredictable, **nonlinear pattern.** Underlying the pattern is a **strange attractor**—a pull that keeps the system within boundaries.

The most important insight that came out of Lorenz's work is known as the **butterfly effect**—nonlinear systems have points of instability where a small push can have large consequences. The idea is that in a dynamic system such as weather, a butterfly flapping its wings in Brazil sets off a series of connecting events that results in a tornado in Texas a month later. Put another way, tiny differences in the initial conditions of an event swell into overwhelming differences later on.

Weather forecasting is like fashion forecasting—a field with the technical sophistication to collect data and store it in huge data warehouses, but a field where forecasting still depends on intuitive ability and guesswork. The same insights found in Lorenz's work apply to fashion systems. Fashion systems exhibit an orderly but nonlinear pattern, a strange attractor underlies the pattern, and points of instability in the system mean that a small push can lead to large consequences.

These insights offer fashion executives new ways to think about their business. The unpredictability of fashion is just a case of a nonlinear system in which order exists but is not apparent when the system is viewed in two dimensions. If the system could be viewed from a multidimensional viewpoint, the viewer would see an orderly pattern associated with a strange attractor. In such a system, a simple action can give rise to astonishingly complicated dynamics. A royal wedding, a hit movie, or the emergence of a rock band can have complicated outcomes that play out over an extended timeline within the fashion system. In nonlinear systems—and the marketplace certainly qualifies as nonlinear—chaos theory suggests that the slightest uncertainty in a forecaster's knowledge of the initial conditions will inevitably turn predictions into nonsense. Does that mean efforts at forecasting are also nonsense?

Insight about Self-Organizing Systems

People behaving within a marketplace are not completely rational agents with easy predictability. They think and act on the basis of expectations and strategies. To understand such behavior, consider a new paradigm of the marketplace as a complex, spontaneous, adaptive, dynamic, self-organizing system (Waldrop, 1992). A system is complex when a great many independent agents (consumers, fashion firms, media) interact with each other in a great many ways. The richness of these interactions allows the system to undergo spontaneous self-organization. The system itself is adaptive to events, actively trying to turn them to some advantage. The system is dynamic in the ways suggested by chaos theory. Still, chaos theory with its explanation that simple rules can give rise to intricate behavior only partly explains the structure, coherence, and cohesiveness of complex, spontaneous, adaptive, dynamic, self-organizing systems.

Here is how a complex adaptive system works (Holland, 1995):

- **The Agents**

A system is a network of many agents. Each agent finds itself in an environment produced by the interaction among agents in the system. It constantly acts and reacts to what the other agents are doing. Therefore, nothing in its environment is fixed.

- **The System**

Control of the system is highly dispersed since each agent acts automonously. Coherent behavior arises from competition and cooperation among the agents themselves.

- **Building Blocks**

A system has levels of organization, with the agents of one level serving as the building blocks of agents at a higher level. For example, individual workers compose a department, a group of departments compose a division, and on through companies, economic sectors, national economies, and finally the world economy.

- **Learning**

Complex adaptive systems constantly revise and rearrange their building blocks based on experience. This adaptive response means that agents and systems learn.

- **Internal Models**

Complex adaptive systems anticipate the future by making predictions based on internal models. Like subroutines in a computer program, these routines come to life in a given situation and execute to produce behavior. For example, consumer confidence is a measure of expectations about how the economy will effect an individual's well-being. If a consumer feels he or she will be worse off within the next few months as the economy enters a recessionary period, that individual will hold back on buying. If many consumers do the same, that will guarantee that the recession will be extended. Internal models are constantly tested, refined, and rearranged as the system gains experience.

- **Niches**

Complex adaptive systems have many niches to be exploited by an agent. That is, there are many ways for an agent to prosper or fail to prosper within the system. The success of an agent depends on the mix of other agents in the system.

- **Lack of Static Equilibrium**

Complex adaptive systems are essentially open—they never reach equilibrium, agents never optimize their fitness or utility. Therefore, complex adaptive systems are characterized by perpetual novelty.

Complex systems bring order and chaos together at a balance point poetically called the **edge of chaos**. At this point the components of a system never lock into place yet never dissolve into turbulence. Here, there is stability, unity, and structure but also change, creativity, and lack of structure—all in a sort of rolling equilibrium.

The heart of the new science of complexity is the recognition that a system is composed of agents—they might be consumers or corporations or economies. These agents constantly reorganize themselves into larger structures through mutual accommodation and mutual rivalry. These larger structures acquire collective properties beyond those of the individual agents involved. Consider, for example, the collective properties of style tribes where individuals form a group based on shared viewpoint, lifestyle, and way of dressing. Or, consider the collective properties of partnerships between retailers and manufacturers in licensing agreements to produce private-label merchandise. Co-evolution on each level inevitably leads to the emergence of new structures that engage in new behaviors. The trend is always to more and more complex behaviors. It is this worldview that helps executives in the fashion world manage high-velocity change in the next millennium.

The Balancing Act: Anticipation and Improvisation

Think of the marketplace as a kaleidoscope where the handful of beads lock into one pattern, hold it briefly, and then cascade into a new configuration with the slightest touch or turn of the barrel (Waldrop, 1992). In the marketplace, those shifts may correlate with changes in tastes, lifestyles, immigration, or technological developments, shifts in the prices of raw materials, and other such factors. If, as chaos theory suggests, things are not repeating, not in equilibrium, how can anyone predict anything?

Now think of the marketplace as a pile of sand on a tabletop with a steady drizzle of new sand grains raining down from above (Figure 10.3). The grains

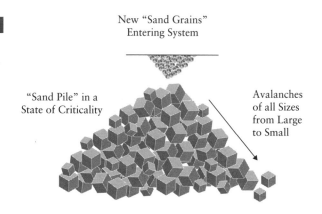

FIGURE 10.3

The sand grains represent new styles, colors, or fashion directions being introduced to the marketplace. The sand grains are barely stable. When a new falling grain hits, there is no telling what will happen—perhaps nothing, perhaps the shift a few grains, or perhaps a chain reaction with a catastrophic landslide—a new style or look becomes fashionable.

New "Sand Grains" Entering System

"Sand Pile" in a State of Criticality

Avalanches of all Sizes from Large to Small

represent new styles, colors, or fashion directions being introduced to the marketplace. The pile of sand represents the styles already in the system, those adopted by the fashion-forward few and the more numerous fashion followers. The pile grows until it cannot grow any higher and old sand cascades down the sides and off the table at the same rate as new sand dribbles down. The resulting sand pile is self-organized in that it reaches a steady state by itself. It is in a state of criticality because the sand grains are barely stable—the microscopic surfaces and edges are interlocked in every possible combination, but they are ready to give way. When a new falling grain hits, there is no telling what will happen—perhaps nothing, perhaps the shift of a few grains, perhaps a chain reaction with a catastrophic landslide.

This exact experiment that has been done in computer simulation and with real sand (Bak, 1996). Scientists discovered that big avalanches are rare and small ones frequent—a relationship so common in nature that mathematicians call it a power law distribution. A system such as this is an example of **self-organized criticality** because the changes form a dynamic that can be understood only from a holistic viewpoint, one that considers the entire system, not just the individual elements.

The Fashion System on the Edge. Fashion, like many systems, can be characterized as a mass of intricately interlocking subsystems, just barely on the edge of criticality, with avalanches of all sizes rippling through and rearranging things. Such a system is always poised on the edge—just as the fashion system is always poised on the edge of change. Self-organized criticality, like the phase transitions at the edge of chaos, offers an intriguing visualization that allows executives to explore fashion as a nonlinear system and question the role of fashion forecasting in the future.

Imagine that the sand on the table is like apparel in the pipeline. There is a lot of sand on the table (apparel in the pipeline) when an innovation in fabrication, color, or styling is dropped on the pile. Will it have no effect, create a small avalanche of interest, or set off a huge chain reaction that changes the entire system?

Imagine that the sand on the table is like consumer preferences. Consumers begin to experiment with a new lifestyle component or consumer confidence shifts and the change ripples through the system. A new movie or music video introduces street fashion to a larger audience and a kind of "information contagion" passes the look from one individual to another, from one social group to another.

Buyers and sellers behave like agents in a complex system because they interact with each other, sharing information in a social transaction called word-of-mouth (Figure 10.4). Through self-selection some buyers cluster around certain products or styles, forming patterns of preference. When an innovation enters the system, it may disappear almost immediately or some agents may adopt it and spread news of the innovation to others. On occasion

FIGURE 10.4

The marketplace is viewed as a complex system because the agents (buyers and sellers) network with each other, share information, form groups and alliances—all without an outside force coordinating the activity.

these activities reach a critical mass and set off a chain reaction of decisions resulting in a "hit" (Farrell, 1998). What appears to be many people simultaneously coming to the same decision, really started with a single innovation that built in popularity as networks formed and patterns of interaction emerged. None of this happened because some outside force was coordinating the action. A hit moves through a social system creating new preference structures and networks. Some hits are so powerful that they fundamentally change the relationships between agents, dissolving some connections and forging others.

Decision Making on the Edge. What do these ideas have to do with executives making the everyday decisions in the fashion industry? Essentially, any decision maker lives within a system that is very difficult to analyze. The traditional theories and models do not provide the kind of information needed to make real-time decisions given risk and uncertainty because they leave out the most important variables—social, psychological, and political factors. The insights from chaos and **complexity theory** are threatening to traditional organizations following the 20th century industrial model of planning and control, but they are empowering to companies dealing with high-velocity change (Tetenbaum 1997). In those companies, creativity and experimentation are valued as much as control and efficiency.

For the most innovative companies, managing chaos means seeking order in a disorderly way until something workable emerges (Wheatley, 1992). Competing on the edge of chaos means creating a relentless flow of innovations. Together, these innovations create a stream of competitive advantages that merge into a "semicoherent strategic direction"—semicoherent because of uncertainty and uncontrollable factors, strategic because a company can assume a proactive stance toward change (Brown & Eisenhardt, 1998). The goal is not a single "correct" path into the future but instead acceptance of constant change, where strategies emerge through anticipation and improvisation.

Managers play a critical role in balancing on the edge of chaos (Figure 10.5). Their decisions maintain competitiveness by encouraging innovation but promote stability enough for survival. Perhaps the best approach involves two focal points (Tetenbaum, 1997): (1) the present with order and stability to daily business, and (2) the future where disorder and instability must be tolerated, and if possible, embraced.

In this view, short-term forecasting helps managers recognize and build on order as it emerges close to the present. Long-term forecasting helps managers anticipate alternate futures and recognize possible points of instability, where a push could result in enormous consequences.

The new sciences of chaos and complexity offer the promise of recognizing order in seemingly disorderly data—not order that leads to long-range planning schemes, but order that leads to improvisation. Instead of looking for a single linear solution that can be locked into place and executed through time, the decision maker uses forecasting to anticipate the implications of various options, the way situations may develop, and how the most

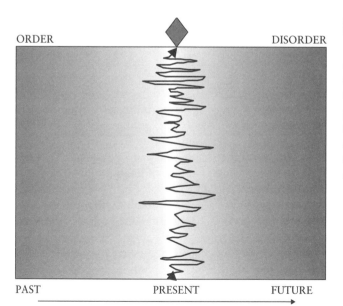

ORDER   DISORDER

PAST   PRESENT   FUTURE

FIGURE 10.5

Order and chaos are complementary in a system balanced on the edge of chaos—a point where stability and structure, change and disorder balance in a sort of rolling equilibrium.

important variables interact. Such analysis will not help predict what new fashion will emerge next week, but it will provide measures of the process and guidance in answering business questions such as, When do you introduce a new product? How big an impact will it cause? How many other goods and services does the innovation bring to market with it and how many old ones go out? How do you recognize when a good has become central to a system as opposed to a fad? This way of thinking enhances an executive's understanding of the underlying order in the gyrations of seemingly random phenomena.

Fashion as a Balancing Act. It is easy to find exemplars of the new style manager in the computer industry, one only has to look at the way Bill Gates runs Microsoft (Pitta, 1998). He does not conform to traditional styles of business management. Instead, Gates goes into businesses, finds that they are unworkable, and drops them. Or, he buys into a company that has a potentially interesting product before the product has been fully developed and tested. He puts out "feelers" as a way to anticipate change. He hires top professionals to work on "blue-sky projects"—innovations that may or may not generate big business in the future. Sometimes Microsoft looks like a company running in contradictory directions. Instead, it is a company that anticipates the future by hedging its bets about the direction of that future.

Fashion companies do the same thing. They acquire or create brand tiers so that a drop-off in one business is offset by an increase in another division. They share the risk by licensing some lines to companies with expertise in manufacturing that product category at a certain price point. Fashion companies pick up early signs of change using point-of-sale data and improvise on the theme to build sales. They buy out small entrepreneurial firms with a fashion-forward product line and test the market for expansion opportunities. They put out "feelers" for consumer preference by showing design innovations as trial balloons that can be developed in later seasons into design trends. They conduct consumer research to gauge changes in lifestyles and preferences that will effect purchasing.

Competition in the 21st century will require more anticipation and improvisation than ever before. To do that, companies will need to build competitive knowledge about their customers, competitors, suppliers, partners, future opportunities, and future threats (Tyson, 1997). The way to build competitive knowledge is to gather bits and pieces of information, collaborate as a team to put the puzzle pieces together, and continuously improvise strategy. As the future unfolds, forecasting will focus on providing perspective rather than on precision. The process begins with gathering the bits and pieces—the puzzle parts that come from continuous monitoring of the external environment.

Scan profiles in trade and business publications to identify technology and apparel companies that already behave like 21st-century competitors using anticipation, improvisation, and continuously evolving strategies. Compare the decision-making process in these companies with that in more traditional, bureaucratic companies.

Activity 10.1
Twenty-First-Century Competitors

The Balancing Act: Multiple Time Horizons

If flexibility is the key characteristic of executives of the future, that flexibility must be demonstrated by thinking in multiple time horizons (Brown & Eisenhardt, 1998). Here is another balancing act—decisions poised in the present but with an awareness of the past and future. That awareness must not tip over into attachment. An executive captivated by the past will make decisions that are dated because they are tied to old strategies. An executive enthralled with the future can get too far ahead of the action. At the same time, the executive cannot fail to capitalize on past experiences or ignore the future. In addition to balancing on the edge of chaos between order and disorder, an executive must balance in time by managing multiple time horizons simultaneously.

Even in an information-rich environment, only human intelligence can turn information into knowledge on which to base decisions. This process includes recognizing patterns, interpreting meanings, and determining the speed and direction of fashion change. The forecasting frameworks, theories about how trends move through social systems, help the executive see and understand multiple time horizons.

Diffusion Curves   The idea that fashion diffuses across consumer segments in a predictable way provides the forecaster with a powerful tool to use in analyzing emerging trends. The links between the stages of diffusion and retailing and promotion are well established. The decisions of fashion executives can be traced back to the power of this paradigm including the goal of identifying and communicating with innovative early adopters and opinion leaders (discussed in detail in Chapter 2). Diffusion curves aid forecasters in identifying the probable adoption pattern within a consumer segment; visualizing the sales volume that can be expected from adoption across the segment, and the likelihood of transferring the trend to additional consumer segments; and estimating the timing involved at each stage.

The Spirit of the Times   Difficult to spot in the present, in retrospect each period has an identifiable style or personality. The theory of collective selection taps into this concept because it suggests that certain fashions gain quick and general acceptance because they embody the spirit of the times, a quality consumers recognize but often cannot articulate. Characterizing this spirit of the times, also called the *Zeitgeist*, is part of a forecaster's job (a detailed framework is provided in Chapter 2). Incorporating consideration of the *Zeitgeist* and cultural indicators (Chapter 9) places the forecaster in the present with a window on the future.

The Direction of Fashion Movement   The theories of fashion change provide a set of filters that forecasters can use in trend analysis. The theories of fashion leadership, popularly know as trickle down, trickle up, and trickle across, indicate the origination point for fashion ideas, the directions of adoption across consumer segments, the speed of diffusion, and the gatekeepers for the process. Using these theories (discussed in detail in Chapter 3) becomes intuitive for the experienced forecaster.

Fashion Cycles   Although the dream of discovering some numerical cycle that determines the return of a fashion to popularity has been dashed, the concepts underlying the idea of fashion cycles still provide a framework for trend analysis. Fashions that once were considered hideous are revived and travel once more through the marketplace. Here, the issue of time lag is critical. The ideas of oscillation between extremes, shifting erogenous zones, time-linked changes in appropriateness and acceptability, and generational effects (discussed in detail in Chapter 3) provide the forecaster with tools useful in trend analysis.

FORECASTING TRAPS FOR THE UNWARY

The entire history of American sportswear cautions the forecaster to separate trends from hype. The couture houses of Paris were in charge of fashion innovation until the early 1950s, when the American designer Claire McCardell offered an alternative—more casual, functional style that suited the woman with an active lifestyle (Figure 10.6). This sportswear look of separates made more sense to American women than the dressed up, constricting fashions of the same period. After all, it was Americans, not Europeans, who most fervently embraced Coco Chanel's 1950s cardigan suit for its easy stylish practicality. This dynamic continues to play out in American fashion today (Figure 10.7)

Now as then, fashion journalists often push trends better suited to socialites, celebrities, or urban youths than the everyday lifestyle of most Americans. Although these trends are interesting from a strictly aesthetic viewpoint and certainly novel, they do not always match the needs of the majority of the market. The barrage of stylistic trends, one piled on another, can confuse consumers, causing them to withdraw from purchasing or shift discretionary income to other categories.

In the early 1950s, designer Claire McCardell offered an alternative to dressed up and restrictive fashion—a more casual, functional style that suited American women with an active lifestyle.

The look popularized by Claire McCardell continues to play out in the collections of American designers.

This book proposes an integrated approach to forecasting (Figure 10.8); that is, a balanced view that seeks out the newest styles breaking on the cultural edge and the reality of changing demographics, identifies the fad and the long wave of change, and uses consumer preference research and fashion analysis. The forecaster, acting as an advance guard, must be sure to make the connection between innovations proposed and potential markets, never forgetting the consumer's role as final arbiter between what is in and what is not.

Forecasting has become a growth industry, perhaps spurred on by the turning of a decade and a millennium, perhaps encouraged by the increasing complexity of business. In the rush to capture the attention of clients and the public, forecasters sometimes identify trends that fail to materialize. When these trends are picked up by journalists and broadcast widely, the unwary business executive may be caught up in these nonexistent trends.

Executives today and in the future will be bombarded with forecasts in the business books they read, in the news, and at conferences and seminars. Companies will subscribe to multiple forecasting services and increase forecasting efforts in-house. With so many forecasts, an executive may have a difficult time deciding which are applicable to specific business problems. To avoid forecasting traps, executives must become good consumers of forecasting information—that is, they must be able to evaluate which forecasts are sound

FIGURE 10.8

Fashion forecasting requires a balanced view that seeks out the newest styles breaking on the cultural edge and the reality of changing demographics, identifies the fad and the long wave of change, and uses consumer preference research and fashion analysis.

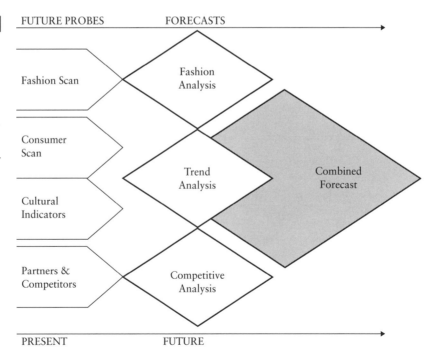

and plausible, which are poorly researched and reasoned. The forecasting traps to avoid are oversimplification, exaggeration, and distortion.

There is no science of forecasting that can guarantee predictions. However, the forecasting frameworks (Chapters 2 and 3), the multiple viewpoints generated by the various forecasting disciplines (Chapters 4 through 9), the blending of quantitative and qualitative approaches, and the collaboration of teams help avoid forecasting traps. Following are some guidelines for evaluating the quality of forecasts.

Avoiding Traps in Forecasting Methods

Time Horizons, Limitations, and Assumptions. Strategic business decisions rely on forecasts. To use forecasts appropriately it is necessary to understand the purpose and limitations of each forecasting method. Because economic conditions fluctuate widely over time, economic forecasts are short-range projections based on assumptions about the future. Demographic forecasts have a longer horizon because the underlying trends in mortality, fertility, and migration rates rarely change quickly or dramatically. Assumptions in economic forecasts are often derived from demographic forecasts. Focus groups only show the range of response to an issue with hints about the whys. Focus groups are not projections of who or how many people will feel the same way. As these brief examples illustrate, all forecasting methods have time horizons, built-in assumptions, and limitations. Using the methods incorrectly or interpreting them without consideration of the limitations results in faulty forecasting.

Connecting the Dots. The forecaster's job is to see connections between dissimilar phenomena—to connect the dots (Mahaffie, 1995; Russell, 1989). The danger is in making a broad jump to the wrong conclusion using faulty assumptions. Examine the social or technological developments that are associated with the forecast. How likely is it that these developments will happen in the same timeline as the forecast? Step back and consider the "real world" constraints of human nature and economic realities. Be sure the linkages between intermediate steps make sense and are supported by evidence.

Statistics As Truth. It is really very easy to lie with statistics (Huff, 1954). People put faith in statistics because numbers carry the promise of precision and accuracy. But using statistics to size up a situation requires a deep understanding of statistical methods and care in interpreting findings. The careful forecaster does not manipulate statistics to make a point or leave out data that tend to disconfirm a hypothesis. Instead, the forecaster looks for all possible explanations and facts with bearing on the interpretation. Anyone relying on a statistical forecast should understand the methods in at least a general way and be willing to ask questions until he or she is comfortable with the analysis and the findings.

Avoiding Traps in the Forecast

Lack of Imagination and Insight. Forecasts can be too conservative, missing some interesting possibilities. Consider the implications of the forecast on other related fields and estimate the effects on other products and market segments (Mahaffie, 1995). Extend the forecast to include potential spin-offs from the change. Early closure or narrow thinking can doom a forecast to limited usefulness. Of course, some possibilities (e.g., the end of the organization, the phasing out of a product line) can be so daunting that they are difficult to consider.

Excessive Optimism. Over optimistic forecasts fail to consider the "downside risk" associated with the shift, change, or innovation (Mahaffie, 1995). These upbeat views are easy to listen to and pleasant to contemplate. However, failure to consider limiting factors—those conditions likely to inhibit or deflect the forecast—can lead to overestimating the impact of the change.

Hidden Agendas. Caught in an enthusiasm for a particular pet idea, technology, product, or social change, forecasters and their clients can overlook information that fails to conform with their desires (Spindler, 1995). Forecasters are often pressured to find evidence supporting the client's preconceived ideas. **Normative forecasting** is done on purpose to motivate people to take actions toward some desirable result. If it is recognized and labeled appropriately, there is no problem (Mahaffie, 1995). But "normative forecasting" is not identical to nor a substitute for detached, objective forecasting about the future.

Estimating Speed and Time. Some forecasts overestimate the speed at which an innovation will spread through society. Diffusion of innovation occurs in two steps, with early adopters increasing the visibility of the new style and opinion leaders endorsing the style within their social groups. It takes time for the first stage of impersonal, media- and marketer-based influence and the second stage word-of-mouth to build so that a new style becomes a mass fashion. Evaluate the plausibility of the timing based on clues in consumer research and cultural indicators.

Avoiding Traps in Trend Analysis

Tall Tales versus Statistical Analysis. The passion for trends in media coverage leads to stories based entirely on anecdotes. These stories make interesting points but are only directional if backed up by well-designed research studies or population data (Russell, 1989). The existence of the story alerts the forecaster to an emerging issue, but prediction requires more. Trend analysis comes down to evaluating the evidence—both qualitative and quantitative—

supporting that trend. If stories abound but there is little other valid backing for the trend, use caution when acting on the predictions.

Wish Fulfillment versus Reality Check. Consumer research often reports on the unmet longings of people and translates these into trends. However, these "wishes" must be submitted to a reality check to fine-tune predictions (Russell, 1989). Sometimes consumer wishes are mere nostalgia for a simpler life or some other projection that may be impossible to satisfy. Still, such clues may provide the basis for an effective ad campaign, promotional effort, or a revised list of store services.

Two Sides of the Coin. Every trend has two sides—the trend and the counter-trend (Popcorn, 1991). Trend analysis includes investigating both since the two sides of the trend can be interpreted for different market segments. The clever forecaster takes these trend dynamics into consideration and the clever marketer makes profit on both the trend and the counter-trend.

The Generational Lens. Every forecaster would be wise to use a generational lens to examine trends and make predictions (Russell, 1989). Cohorts of consumers move through predictable life stages that influence purchasing priorities. The preferences of consumers often reflect those formed at a particular age, and these preferences persist throughout the life cycle. Generational cohorts develop a personality and a style that marks their consumption behavior. For all these reasons, the age structure of the American population and the changes in that structure are fundamental building blocks for accurate predictions.

Influential Segments. If key market segments such as working women and the older baby boomers fail to accept a trend, it has virtually no chance of becoming a major trend. Even so, acceptance by these two groups does not guarantee a trend's success because the absolute population numbers are too small and because these groups have specific preferences that may not be reflected in the overall population. Acceptance by key consumer segments is necessary but not sufficient for a trend to succeed.

Trends in Collision. Consumer trends are not easy to sort out. Rarely are there clear-cut moments when one trend ends and another begins (Letscher, 1994).

- Overlapping Trends

Changes in one area have carryover or overlap to others. The classic example of overlap came with the adoption of the miniskirt in the mid-1960s and the subsequent increase in pantyhose sales, from 10 percent of the market to 80 percent of the market in less than two years.

- **Offsetting Trends**

With offsetting trends, one set of lifestyle changes may be congruent, another incongruent with an innovation. For example, smaller families and the desire for a convenient shopping experience would appear to work against warehouse-club outlets, but the desire for low prices and wide selection made them destinations that offset these negatives.

- **Discontinuity**

Some events cause discontinuity in a trend so that it changes course, merges with another trend, or terminates. The event may be the introduction of a new style, a change in consumer priorities, or an economic upturn or downturn. Recognizing the event is the first step. The canny forecaster works out these potential interactions as part of the forecast or recalibrates the forecast as events unfold.

Fads versus Trends. Companies make money on short-term fads and on long-term trends. The trick is to be able to distinguish between them early on to determine entrance and exit strategies (Letscher, 1994). A trend is supported by multiple lifestyle changes, presents clear long-term benefits to the consumer, and parallels changes in other areas. The more adaptable an innovation is, the more likely it will be a trend because it can be modified for broader audiences. A trend is a basic theme in society (e.g., the value of exercise and healthy eating). It can be expressed in many ways (e.g., jogging, aerobics, and in-line skating, or increased selection of fish and poultry over beef). As one apparel executive put it: "It's not going to be so much about trends anymore" because people are more interested in their lifestyles—they will ask instead, "Is this trend fitting in with my lifestyle?" (Hammond, 1999). If the innovation is more unidimensional, it is more likely a fad.

"Fringe" versus "Mainstream." Forecasters and journalists often spotlight fringe products, services, and looks that tend to be exaggerated, extreme, or impractical—the kind of things avoided by mainstream American consumers. These innovations have the potential to become mainstream trends only if they have a desirable set of tangible and intangible benefits and can be modified and expressed in different ways to appeal to a broader public (Letscher, 1994).

Specificity versus Direction. Especially in fashion but also in other forecasting fields, it is impossible to have control over or access to all variables that impact on change. Recognizing this situation, a careful forecast will be as objective and comprehensive as possible while pointing out missing details. Such forecasts only show direction and the probable characteristics of change, not the specifics of how those variables will actually interact (Mahaffie, 1995).

Avoiding Traps As a Forecaster

Don't Oversell Accuracy. Forecasts are based on assumptions. If those assumptions are within historical trends and inside normal limits, the forecast is said to be "reasonable ." Careful forecasters present alternative futures—a set of scenarios showing low, medium, and high impact from the projection. If the forecaster stamps one of the scenarios as "likely," then that is the forecaster's interpretation based on expertise and experience. Reasonable forecasts may be inaccurate if other factors not initially considered turn out to be important. Likely forecasts may not happen because unexpected outcomes sometimes do occur. The only real gauge of forecasting accuracy is when a prediction actually comes to pass. One way to improve accuracy is to include "milestones" in the forecasts—points where the forecast can be evaluated and adjustments made (Mahaffie, 1995; "What is a forecast," 1995).

Don't Oversell Expertise. Forecasting is too multifaceted for any one person to master. Encourage the use of integrated forecasting so that factors associated with fashion change, consumer behavior, cultural shifts, and competitive position can be correlated for decision support. No single forecasting discipline has the answer, but each serves a complementary function.

Locate several articles in a newsmagazine or newspaper forecasting future developments. The articles do not have to relate to fashion. The purpose of this activity is to practice a quick and graphic way to analyze forecasting information using highlighter pens. Analyze the content by highlighting anecdotes with one color, statistics and research findings with another, and quotes from experts with a third. Are the forecasts tall tales or are they backed up by statistics and research? What would be the next step in verifying the forecast?

Activity 10.2 Tall Tales?

FORECASTING AS A TEAM SPORT

The most potent competitive weapon is new ideas (Amabile, 1998). Business creativity has similarities and differences with creativity in the arts. Both kinds of creativity are practiced by people who see potential in new combinations of existing ideas, products, and processes and by people who persevere during slow, dry periods. But new business ideas must be appropriate and actionable—that is, they must somehow enhance the way business gets done. Creativity in business is based on expertise. Expertise consists of everything a person knows about his or her work domain. The larger the intellectual space that comprises this expertise, the more chance to discover new possibilities, new connections, new combinations that solve problems. Working in homogeneous teams does little to enhance creativity because everyone has the same mindset. Working in supportive but diverse teams builds expertise by introducing different perspectives into the dialogue.

Forming teams is like breaking a larger institution into a series of small groups, each with an assignment. These teams build an allegiance to the team, participate in decision making, and are rewarded for meeting team objectives. Unless these teams are linked into the larger institution, the teams may become isolated with barriers that prevent between-group communication, learning, and collaboration. Of course, the best outcome would be empowered, high-performing small teams (decentralization of decision making) and collaboration among teams enterprise-wide (Haskins, Leidtka, & Rosenblum, 1997). Forecasting with its many disciplines, multiple time horizons, and focus on business creativity is an ideal shared activity that encourages collaboration within and between teams in pursuit of enterprise-wide goals.

Forecasting professionals hired by the company for their expertise are also team members, but with a very special function. Some bring the ability to bridge the gap between the corporation and a particular market segment, such as the under-30 consumer. These forecasters help sort out the difference between a fad and a trend. As one of the partners of Sputnik, a research firm that uses young correspondents to track their peers, explains: "A trend is a shift in the prevailing thought process that eventually manifests itself in a range of popular tastes and, ultimately, consumer goods" (McMurdy, 1998). These professional "trend trekkers" work in fashion and in related industries such as cosmetics and fragrance. Lori Smith, a trend forecaster for one of the world's largest makers of perfume puts it this way: "What I do is bring the outside world in" (Green, 1998). Reports from forecasting professionals—whether working inside the company or as consultants—may affect the way a product is designed, the way it is sold, or where it is sold.

Problems Inside and Outside the Box

Solving problems is the essential element in business: Which new products to introduce? How to put products and likely consumers together in a space conducive to buying? How much to spend on new tools or processes? How to prosper given changing technology and a dynamic marketplace? The first step is to realize the difference between "tame" and "wicked" problems (Pacanowsky, 1995). Tame problems are those that are manageable, easy to define, and lend themselves to a solution that can be applied consistently across time. Wicked problems (a name derived not from the first dictionary meaning of the word, morally bad, but from another meaning, harmful and damaging) are so complex that they are very difficult to solve (Figure 10.9).

Because tame problems are manageable, it is relatively easy to gather relevant information and apply traditional methods to discover the solution. The

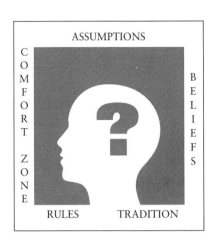

Thinking Inside The Box

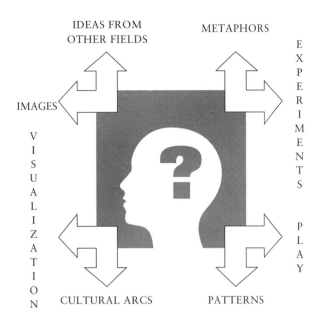

Thinking Outside The Box

solution to tame problems requires **thinking inside the box** of normal practices. Solving tame problems involves the following steps:

Step 1: Define the problem.

Step 2: Generate alternative solutions.

Step 3: Specify criteria to use in evaluating the solutions.

Step 4: Apply the criteria to choose a solution from among the alternatives.

Step 5: Implement the solution.

Step 6: Collect feedback on the effectiveness of the solution.

Wicked problems are so difficult that they require **thinking outside the box.** The preceding linear problem-solving method fails at the first stage because wicked problems defy easy definition. Forecasting, planning, and strategy development involve wicked problems. Solving wicked problems involves a process:

Step 1: Generate the greatest possible understanding of the problem from diverse viewpoints. The trick is to avoid seeking closure too quickly or bogging down into a polarizing argument between positions. Instead, generate a large number of questions that start out:

FIGURE 10.9

Solving tame problems requires thinking inside the box. Solving wicked problems mean thinking outside the box.

- "What if . . ." (questions about possibilities)
- "What is . . ." (questions about fact)
- "What should . . ." (questions requiring judgment and opinions)

Step 2: Sort through the questions for those that need to be pushed farther.

Step 3: Look for relationships and patterns.

One way to prospect for relationships and patterns is to create a **mind map**—a kind of outline but without the rigid structure of the traditional form. Draw a box in the center of a piece of paper and pose a question inside that box. Surround the square with words that identify key variables or factors involved in the question. Add layers of terms building a tree-like structure that grows from the central question (Figure 10.10). When all the factors are listed, use circles or lines to show relationships between them.

Because wicked problems are so complex, a team approach is especially helpful. The questions in step 1 can be generated in a brainstorming session. The mind maps can be produced in a group session or by individuals. At some point the work of individuals and the group is merged in a "shared display" (either flip chart pages displayed around a room, a transcript of notes, or photocopies of the maps) to allow the team to capture thinking as it happens. In this way team members work as individuals on different elements and the insights are integrated into an overall team-designed solution.

FIGURE 10.10

A mind map of the disciplines of forecasting illustrates how complex the field is and how connections and relationships can be captured.

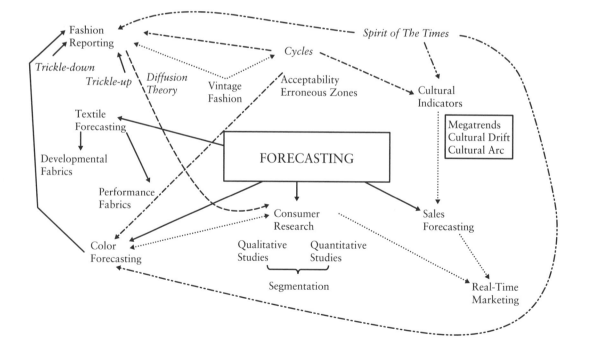

W.L. Gore & Associates, makers of Gore-Tex™, use teams to deal with wicked problems. One team responsible for a major market segment had a problem that had eluded resolution for 18 months. Using the mind mapping approach, each team member drew all the characteristics and features of the problem. When the maps were pooled, team members first glimpsed the true complexity of their problem. Using the question generating task, the team came up with hundreds of questions and then identified the most important to answer. Individual team members committed themselves to getting answers within one month. At the meeting one month later, team members were able to reach consensus on a solution they were willing to implement.

Eighteen months wrestling with a wicked problem using traditional methods probably is not that unusual. It is just one example of how frustrating it can be to use the approach that works on tame problems on wicked problems. Wicked problems must instead be engaged through a dialogue where the definition of the problem, relevant information, the solution, and the outcomes all evolve together. Solving problems this way dovetails with the concepts that come from chaos and complexity theory because the process recognizes the nonlinearity and multidimensionality of wicked problems.

Discuss in class some difficult and complex issues in the domain of fashion. To jog the discussion, use the editor's letters from fashion magazines or articles that expose problems related to the industry. Select one issue as a "wicked problem" and brainstorm as many questions as possible. Create a mind map of the issue showing connections and relationships. Select one or two questions for further exploration. Let each student research possible solutions to one of the questions. Share the possible solutions with the class and try to arrive at a consensus solution that is appropriate and actionable.

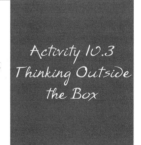

Activity 10.3
Thinking Outside the Box

Shared Information, Shared Forecasting

Forecasting is an ideal forum for information sharing and collaboration. The information environment is so rich, no one person can possibly locate and interpret all the signs and signals across multiple time horizons. Information is only the raw material. It must be processed, spun, and woven into a forecast. A team approach to forecasting means continuous information sharing between functional groups with the goal of increasing the quality of the forecast.

Technology can facilitate shared information and interpretation. Software packages allow executives to capture an article or report, use an electronic highlighter to emphasize key points, attach notes like electronic Post-It Notes™, and send it to team members. The team members then add their own interpretations. In this way information is turned into knowledge and knowledge is leveraged along the decision chain.

Apparel companies continue upgrading their network communications to add applications and make access faster (Zimmermann, 1998d). Companies are pushing more timely and critical information through these corporate networks, called **Intranets**. An Intranet uses similar technology to the Internet, but Intranets are proprietary—restricted to the internal use of a corporation. Corporate networks usually include both Intranet and Internet access.

The next phase of network development is **enterprise portals** (Wilder, Davis & Dalton, 1999)—the use of Web-type browsers in corporate situations to enable managers and knowledge workers to access real-time and historical information. The idea of the portals is to pool the three kinds of networks currently in use: the Internet, Intranets, and extranets (business-to-business networks for transactions and collaborative forecasting between suppliers and customers). What differentiates this newest approach is the ability to gather data from multiple sources and in multiple formats and make it accessible from a single, easy-to-use menu. Portals may incorporate triggers to alert users to new information, signal the start-up of enterprise-wide events, and let users conduct business transactions. The goal with all network systems is to share information seamlessly within an organization to enhance business performance.

Forecasting and Multimedia Reporting. Graphic images of store layouts, proposed products, and advertising campaigns require large files that can slow network traffic. However, the trend is toward more graphics on company networks. Computer-aided design (CAD) is moving out of design departments to become enterprise-wide technology ("CAD," 1998). Manufacturers plan to use CAD to communicate new lines to retailers for early reaction, even before samples are made (Figure 10.11). CAD is being used in computer-generated presentations and on business-to-business Web sites. The availability of graphic images enhances the opportunity to share information and presentations related to fashion forecasting among functional teams from design and production to marketing and sales.

Forecasting is entering an era of multimedia reporting. Information from online and video sources and images scanned into the computer or gathered with the digital camera provide a rich visual resource for multimedia reporting on trends and forecasts. CAD, drawing programs, and presentation software further expand the options for visual communication. Photostyling software and image presentation software allow forecasters to sequence digital images, add titles and text, and create polished computer-based slide shows. Spreadsheet packages offer charting capabilities that turn numbers into graphics. Desktop publishing and advanced color printers facilitate the creation of hard-copy versions of trend analysis and forecasts. Powerful lap-

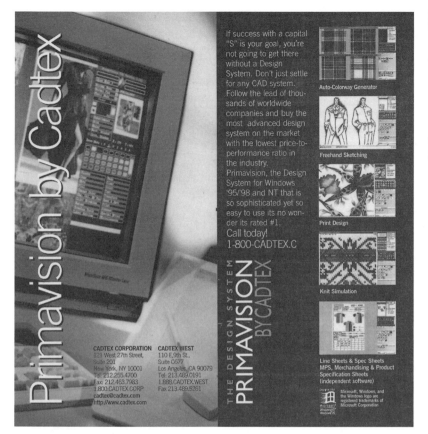

FIGURE 10.11

CAD (computer-aided design) is being used in new ways, including communicating new lines to retailers for early reaction, in forecasting presentation, and on business-to-business Web sites.

top computers and conferencing equipment such as data projectors make multimedia reporting portable. Together, these techniques equip the forecaster to communicate trends, styles, and forecasts more quickly, accurately, and imaginatively than traditional methods.

Develop an inventory of the skills useful in multimedia reporting. Which skills do you already possess? What software packages do you already have experience using? Which skills can you develop as part of working on assignments? Which skills can you develop on your own using software tutorials? Which do you need to see demonstrated? Which will require instruction in a classroom or workshop setting? Develop a plan to explore multimedia reporting and develop the necessary professional-level skills.

*Activity 10.4
Skill Assessment
and Inventory*

Implementing the Forecast. Developing forecasts is one challenge. Even more important is implementing the forecast enterprise-wide. Cultural indicators and competitive analysis provide the context for forecasting and have the longest time horizon. Seasonal product development depends on forecasts for textiles, color, and styling with a time horizon of fewer than two years. The same trends and themes that guide product development spin out through merchandising, marketing, advertising, promotion, retailing, and visual merchandising. Diagnosing the quality of a trend, its trajectory, and its timeline has a tremendous impact on the success of a company in attracting consumer interest, generating sales, and making profits. Like other business ventures, the key to implementing the forecast lies in teamwork and partnerships between experts at every stage of the supply chain.

Key Terms and Concepts

Butterfly Effect	Intranets	Strange Attractor
Chaos Theory	Mind Map	Thinking Inside the Box
Complexity Theory	Nonlinear Patterns	Thinking Outside the Box
Edge of Chaos	Normative Forecasting	
Enterprise Portals	Self-Organized Criticality	

Discussion Questions

The future of forecasting involves rethinking traditional approaches and incorporating insights from chaos and complexity theory. Forecasting has become more collaborative between manufacturers and retailers. Computer networks such as the Internet, Intranets, and extranets bring information to the desktops of apparel executives. Now and in the future, forecasting will be less about prediction and more about anticipation and improvisation. Fashion forecasting has become an enterprise-wide activity involving specialists in the various disciplines from textile development to sales forecasting, from color to fashion trends, from consumer research to cultural indicators. Use the following questions to summarize and review this chapter on new directions in fashion forecasting.

Teams: How do enterprise-wide forecasting and collaborative forecasting hinge on teamwork? How can communication between teams be encouraged?

Company networks: How can a company's computer network be used as a linking device between the functional groups to facilitate the forecasting process? Of what use would an enterprise portal be in encouraging executives to anticipate change? Why is graphics capability an important aspect of the company's network?

Forecasting traps: When an apparel executive reads a forecast, what are some of the points that should be questioned before incorporating the recommendations into decision making? When the executive is also the forecaster, what pitfalls must be avoided?

Forecasting and the future: What do the new sciences of chaos and complexity contribute to forecasting practice? What are the implications of these sciences for the way business will be conducted in the 21st century?

Additional Forecasting Activities

Reading into the Future. Read either *Competing on the Edge* by Brown and Eisenhardt or *Leadership and the New Science* by Wheatley (see the References at the back of this book for a complete citation). Each book makes the connection between the new sciences of chaos and complexity and business issues. Each book also discusses other emerging scientific fields. Explore what these other new sciences may contribute to forecasting practice.

Teamwork Solutions. Locate an apparel company that uses teams in either production or management. Arrange to interview members of one team. Ask for their assessment of the teamwork concept. How does working in teams improve job satisfaction and productivity? Are there any drawbacks to working in teams? How can the work of teams be enhanced?

Multimedia Workstation. Collect brochures, ads, printouts from Web sites, and articles on software and hardware (digital cameras, scanners, and data projectors) related to multimedia reporting. Design a computer workstation equipped to facilitate multimedia reporting on fashion change.

Chapter 11

WINDOWS ON THE FUTURE: MEDIA SCANS AND COMPETITIVE ANALYSIS

"Today competitive advantage goes to the company with the 'er' component—faster, smoother, smarter."
—Paul R. Charron, Chairman and CEO, Liz Claiborne, Inc. (1998)

Objectives

- Appreciate the potential of customized media scanning as low-cost probes of the future.

- Understand the connection between acquiring and analyzing forecasting information and applying the insights to competitive situations.

- Recognize the steps in competitive analysis from question forming and information gathering to analysis and reporting.

- Identify the multiple sources of information useful in forecasting and competitive analysis.

- Become aware of the ethical and legal issues involved in information gathering.

INFORMATION AS AN ASSET

By education and training, executives develop a specialty, one that restricts their view to a relatively small information domain. These executives tend to restrict themselves to only a narrow scan of information generated within a specialty or within an industry segment. In doing so, they risk developing tunnel vision by focusing on information internal to the company and industry to the exclusion of the broader cultural perspective. Tunnel vision reduces the flexibility that is so essential for decision making under conditions of high-velocity change.

Even though apparel experts must become experts in an information domain bounded by their placement on the supply chain, product category, or job description, all apparel executives share the same problem space—how to make the right product, introduce it at the right time, distribute it in the right channels, and capture the attention of the right consumers. When specialists talk only to each other or talk to others in technical jargon, then the chance to collaborate on solutions is squandered. Collaborative forecasting within a company and between companies in partnership encourages communication across domain boundaries.

Forecasting for the long-term (five years or more) is a way to explore possible futures and to build a shared vision of an organization's direction and development. A compelling vision draws people toward a preferred future. Short-term forecasting (more than one year ahead) involves periodic monitoring of the long-term vision and revision as circumstances dictate. Short-term forecasting also acts to coordinate the operations of a company within the context of the industry and the marketplace. Forecasting keeps the momentum going because it forces a perspective of the future on the day-to-day business decisions.

The focus of this book is on managing information as a corporate asset, an asset that can be managed like any other. Executives balance on a point in the present. Their decisions are supported by past experience—fashion history,

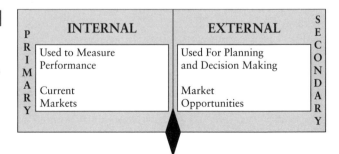

sales history, and traditional ways of doing business. To keep their balance, executives need a window on the future—new innovations, cultural change, and alternative ways to do business. Scanning today's media opens that window on the future. In this way, an executive has on his or her desktop the important external information that blends with internal information to support decision making (Figure 11.1).

PROBING THE FUTURE WITH MEDIA SCANS

In an atmosphere of change, flexibility is the key characteristic of successful executives. Environmental scanning is a method of tracking and analyzing trends using media sources. These low-cost probes improve flexibility by providing insights into the future—insights that help executives to anticipate changes and react quickly to shifts in the marketplace (Brown & Eisenhardt, 1998). The sources include print (newspapers, magazines, newsletters, trade periodicals), broadcast (television and radio), and online sources. In an interview, June Roche of Milliken suggested watching talk shows because when people air their problems, it provides insights on cultural change; looking at "zines" on the Web to locate small groups with special needs and wants; and watching junk mail because it follows the pulse of change (Trentham, 1994).

Developing a systematic environmental scanning plan means considering the payoffs of a broad, cross-sectional scan versus a specialized, narrow scan. Executives and consultants who depend exclusively on quantitative measures and demographic data may miss the "X-factor for fashion"—the unknown element that makes an item seem "hot" to a consumer (Spindler, 1995). The first mention of Prada bags was in tiny news items in fashion magazines reporting that the bags were prized by fashion journalists and models coming back to the United States from the European runway shows. Those first small items were precursors for the growing interest in the accessories and clothing from that company. When the designer Miuccia Prada was featured in the fashion issue of *The New Yorker* (Sischy, 1994), interest in the Prada approach to fashion—the plain, undesigned, uniform-like look—was just beginning. Prada became a directional influence for a larger market, but this influence was first detected among the young, slightly rebellious, slightly disenfranchised women. Executives handicapped by an insufficient flow of information or by outmoded information management techniques risk missing opportunities.

The Basic Scan: National News Media

A publicist with over 20 years of experience pointed out the cross-pollination between media (Skenazy, 1989). A relatively few influential media sources serve as feeder lines to all the rest. So, it is not necessary to read everything—just the media outlets that feed all the rest. The media sources that everyone watches provide the background for trendspotting (Celente, 1990; Merriam & Makower, 1988). Spotting a future trend begins with being fully aware of the present situation. Following the news is the essential first step in recognizing shifts in social and economic spheres. Select some sources from the following list:

- Televised news on the major networks (NBC, CBS, ABC) and on the cable news networks (CNN and MSNBC).
- Newsweeklies (*Newsweek, Time,* and *U.S. News & World Report*).
- National newspapers (*The New York Times, The Washington Post, USA Today*).

The Basic Scan with a Slant

Business News   To add a more specific business news slant, include one or more of the following sources:

- Televised business news (CNN, CNBC, PBS).
- A business news publication (*Business Week, The Wall Street Journal*).
- One or more periodicals focusing on business (*Fortune, Forbes*).

Cultural News   To add a more cultural slant to the scan, include one or more sources—either trade publications or those written for the sophisticated consumer—covering high or pop culture. Specialize further by adding media covering particular interests of professionals and consumer in the field:

- The fine arts—painting, sculpture, and photography.
- The performing arts—dance, theater, music.
- The popular culture scene—music, movies, and television (e.g., *Billboard, Rolling Stone, Premiere,* and *Variety*).

Technology News   To add a technology slant, select one or more of the computer magazines targeted at users. Or, subscribe to a magazine such as *Yahoo Internet Life* or *Wired* to discover how the early adopters of technology are making it part of their lifestyle. Watch technology news programs such as *Computer Chronicles* on PBS.

International Views   People in other countries frequently see international issues in ways not usually covered by U.S. media. To gain insight with a more international slant, include *The International Herald Tribune* and *The Economist*.

Choose one of the possible ways to individualize scans. Research other publications, broadcasts, and Web sites that could enhance the scan. Build the ultimate list of possible sources. Because no executive will have the time to scan all the possible sources on a continuous basis, develop a strategy for choosing a few to scan often, a few to scan regularly but less frequently, a few to scan occasionally, and a few sites to keep an eye on as potentially important at some future time. Be sure to think about the reasons for your choices.

Activity 11.1
Slant of Choice

Extensions to Basic Scan

Precursor Media   Precursor sources offer the opportunity to spot a trend at the earliest possible time (Merrian & Makower, 1988). Journalists and other influential people who hope to recognize and promote emerging trends read these publications. Reading such sources means going outside the confines of business and fashion to read about science, medicine, and social science. The *Utne Reader*, a compendium of items from the alternative liberal press, functions as one of these precursor sources for social and economic trends. *American Demographics* is a magazine that specifically attempts to identify and analyze emerging trends.

   Precursor sources in fashion include those publications covering avant-garde, alternative, "downtown," and New Age lifestyles and looks.

Trade Media   Do not confine trade sources only to those in the fashion field (see Chapters 4, 5, and 6 for suggestions). Advertising is a field that is particularly sensitive to developing trends. Monitoring *Advertising Age*, the trade paper of the advertising industry, keeps executives current with trends across many product categories. Trade publications are rich sources for trend information before it is picked up by mass media.

Regional Media (United States)   Geographic diversity still exists in this country and the dedicated trendspotter will want to sample media from areas recognized as breeding grounds for trends. The newspaper or city magazine of the largest city in a region provides a convenient way to monitor developing trends. Specific suggestions include: *The New York Times* and *New York Magazine*, *The Los Angeles Times*, and *The Miami Herald*. Look at the articles and lifestyle sections, but also check out the letters to the editor and the smaller ads. The ads are an ideal hunting ground for new products and services and novel retail concepts. Some regional newspapers have Web sites and monitoring these sites can give the trendspotter the flavor of lifestyles and preferences in different part of the United States.

Explore newspaper sites on the Web. Look for national papers, papers in regional centers in each geographic region in the United States (Northeast, Southeast, Southwest, Middle West, West, Northwest), and papers in small cities and towns. Devise a scanning system to discover the similarities and differences between different parts of the country. Discuss how these findings could help product developers, merchandisers, and retailers fine-tune their operations.

Media Scan Shortcuts. Just because every executive needs access to a continuous flow of forecasting information, it does not mean they have time to become media mavens and information junkies. By using a few shortcuts, executives can increase the flow of relevant information across their desktops without a large outlay of time and effort.

The first shortcut does take time and effort initially, but that investment will pay off in increased access to key information. Take time to learn how to use the information management tools described in the next section. Building those skills will make all the other shortcuts much more useful.

Shortcut 1: One for Many   One media source can serve as a proxy for many others. Trend watching experts Merriam and Makeower (1988) recommend selecting a few sources as proxies for the others. For example, reading just the front page of *The Wall Street Journal* daily serves as a proxy for a more detailed scan of business news.

Shortcut 2: A Minimalist Scan   A minimalist scan uses only a few sources but, because these few sources are well chosen, the scan will pull in most of the trends important to know. An example of a minimalist scan with a business focus would include reading *The Wall Street Journal* daily, adding a trade journal, and finding one source that tends toward the avant-garde to monitor the leading edge of change. Print or online subscriptions to carefully chosen sources may be sufficient environmental scanning for some executives.

Shortcut 3: The Keywords Scan   For a broader scan within a small time investment, executives can use keyword searches of computer databases that provide abstracts of articles. Select a database that indexes nearly all the journals in the business field, provides a short summary of the article, and identifies all the keywords associated with the article. By searching with the same set of keywords on a daily or weekly basis, this shortcut approach can save time and effort although delivering the benefits of the broader scan. Any articles of particular interest can be located for a more complete reading.

Shortcut 4: Forecasting Bookmarks   Nowadays most print and broadcast media have Web sites. Some sites are free; others are by subscription. Even with subscription sites there is usually a free section of the site as an inducement to visit. Web sites offer a useful shortcut for environmental scanning because the Web browsers allow users to bookmark sites they want to return to often. The bookmarks can be grouped and each category of sites given a name. This convenient organizational technique allows even busy people to check useful sites on a daily, weekly, or monthly basis as part of environmental scanning. To make it even more efficient, software is available to alert the user to changes at sites of interest.

Tricks of the Trade: Technology Tools for Scanning

Relatively few jobs focus exclusively on forecasting with the travel budgets to attend trade shows, see runway presentations, and shop exotic locations. Instead most jobs involve attending a few trade shows related to a specific product category and reading the trade news. But because all executives make decisions in an environment of uncertainty, all executives have a need for forecasting information. With the dawning of the Information Age, the sources of forecasting information became available to a wide range of executives right on their desktops. The networked computer promises instant access to almost all human knowledge. One writer compared the result to trying to drink from a firehose because the gush of information can overwhelm attempts to organize and analyze it. Environmental scanning, as a low-cost probe of the future, is only low-cost if the executive's time is not taxed with information management duties. Locating, retrieving, and filtering information can still be frustrating and time consuming, but help is on the way. Software is being designed to make information management tasks more efficient. As the online toolbox expands, forecasters who are knowledgeable about how to use these tools will be able to scan the information environment more easily and efficiently.

Executives who master information management tools gain access to forecasting and competitive information on their desktops instead of waiting for it to be delivered by consultants outside the company or specialized units inside the company. Forecasting information suggests alternative futures—possible directions for current trends in fashion and the marketplace. Competitive analysis indicates the possible moves competitors will make to capitalize on trends. Together, forecasting information and competitive analysis provide support for the decisions executives make everyday.

Search Strategy.   Although many people "surf" the Net, browsing until they become lost in a web of hyperlinks, few search using any kind of strategy (Pfaffenberger, 1996). The forecaster needs a more systematic approach with tools that are designed to find and capture the right information for decision support.

Pinpoint Searches   If the executive needs to locate specific information on a topic, then a pinpoint search using a **search engine** is the answer. Search engines allow users to type in keywords to initiate a search, locate documents that match, and see the retrieved list of documents ranked by relevancy (relevancy is computed according to the frequency of key words in the document). The low precision of such searches can be improved by using advanced search techniques that allow the user to more fully specify keywords, restrict the search to a particular information domain, or confine the search to a certain time span.

Sampling Sources   If the executive wants to explore a topic by collecting a few high-quality sources, the best place to begin is with the **subject tree** of a search engine such as Yahoo. Locate Web sites developed by subject matter specialists and experts that feature an extensive list of links to all the key sources on a specialized topic. Sampling sources in this way indicates which topics are worth pursuing, which to keep a periodic check on, and which are irrelevant to the executive's current interests.

Collecting Everything   Occasionally the executive wants to discover and collect all possible documents on a given topic. To perform these kinds of searches, the executive uses the same tools as a professional research librarian:

- **Boolean operators,** the words AND, OR, and NOT attached to a keyword search to indicate the relationships (Figure 11.2).
- **Proximity operators,** which allow users to specify how close the keywords are to each other in the text.

The most frequently used proximity operator is "phrase searching" in which the document retrieved must contain the keywords in the exact order specified. Search engines that allow users to apply proximity operators offer the options in a drop-down menu or explain their system under advanced search options.

Intelligent Text Retrieval.   Much of the content of newsstands and libraries is now available electronically. Searchers have the option of reading headlines, abstracts, or full text. With so much information only a keystroke away, the busy executive needs a way to search and capture that small but important fragment of the information environment that is relevant to decision making. Intelligent text retrieval means using software tools to locate information and sift it for the most significant sources—a saving to the searcher in time and effort.

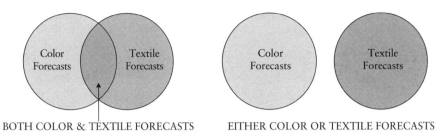

BOTH COLOR & TEXTILE FORECASTS   EITHER COLOR OR TEXTILE FORECASTS

The AND Operators   **The OR Operators**

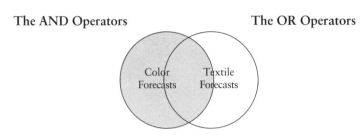

COLOR FORECASTS AND NOT TEXTILE FORECASTS

The NOT Operators

FIGURE 11.2

Boolean operators allow users to fine-tune their keyword searches to locate relevant information while screening out less useful sources.

Information retrieval is becoming more automated as **Internet agents** become widely available. Internet agents are software programs that traverse the World Wide Web, moving from one document to another through the hyperlinks at the sites (Cheong, 1996). A user launches these "infobots" to search for new resources, index Web space for keyword searches, and update Web addresses. Some agents help users build keyword profiles by suggesting related topics. Some go beyond keywords to suggest sources other users have found relevant. Some can be customized to create a "daily news digest" based on specific categories of news. These software assistants are a boon to the busy trend watcher.

Finding information is only the first step. Software developments promise to help with the next step, interpretation. Imagine a software helper that digests documents, analyzes them for similarities and relationships between concepts, and produces a visualization of the "information landscape." Relationships between the concepts translate into colors and shapes to make the connections visual. Looking at the information landscape points to ways to extend or refine the search.

While Internet agents help locate information and sift through it for relationships, they are only tools. The user's deep understanding of the information domain—the specialized knowledge of the field—turns the information into knowledge useful in everyday decision making.

Activity 11.3
Keys to the
information
Kingdom

Keywords unlock information in databases making it available to users. Begin a list of keywords associated with fashion forecasting using the Key Terms and Concepts lists in this book. Select a few words that particularly interest you and relate to your career goals. Search databases available online or in the library using your keywords list. When the search locates a list of articles, scan the titles and mark those that seem the most relevant to your interests. Next, read the abstracts for the selected articles. For each article that still sounds relevant, look at the keyword list attached to the abstract. Add new keywords to your list and use them in your next search. By linking a set of keywords with your own interests, you are working like an Internet agent, identifying similarities and relationships. The keyword list becomes a valuable resource for intelligent text retrieval.

News Reader with Intelligent Agent Filter   An information-rich environment is not automatically helpful unless the executive has the capacity to ignore selectively—that is, to screen out unimportant or useless articles while never missing an article with interesting or important information. Software designers are creating applications that will automatically connect to a site, request articles on a particular topic, download them to the computer, and filter out unwanted articles (Bigus & Bigus, 1998). The filter consists of three parts:

- A keyword filter that matches a keyword profile entered by the user with keywords attached to the articles.
- A cluster filter that maps the similarity between articles (similar to the information landscapes idea).
- A feedback filter that allows the user to "train" the software about which articles are the most useful by providing positive or negative feedback on each article.

Because the user grades the usefulness of each article in the first few searches, over time the software "learns" which articles are wanted and which are not. When fully trained, this kind of software can reduce the flow of information while improving the likelihood that important information will not be missed.

Push versus Pull Approaches   The World Wide Web began as a "pull" concept—users hunted for information they could pull into their own computers. In the mid-1990s a new "push" concept was introduced—users specified the information wanted, a service provider gathered it and pushed it onto the desktop, ready whenever the user signed on to the Internet (Shannon, 1998). Push technology was designed to save the user's time and provide professional search expertise because the information universe was growing so fast. The push approach shows up in several versions:

- Customizing the news displayed from the Web sites of national print and broadcast organizations so that topics of interest from stock prices to fast-breaking news are updated continuously.

- Subscription to a service in which the user selects the information channels of interest and these are automatically updated on a continuous basis.

- Connection to an in-company system that provides the user with news updates via e-mail from a service provider.

- Connection to an in-company system for internal updates on information to improve customer service, keep the sales force ahead of the competition, deliver software revisions, or report on manufacturing status.

Permutations of push are likely to continue to develop as a way to deliver targeted information to users in the most timely way possible. Push technology is a business tool that brings external information to the executive's desktop and updates the executive about time-sensitive company information.

Use the customizing features of news organizations on the Web to design your own customized news gathering service. See the Resource Pointers at the end of the chapter for suggested sites with this capability.

Activity 11.4
Customized
News

Individualized, Customized Scans

Executives gather useful external information when they scan a daily newspaper, watch TV news, listen to the radio while commuting to work, and chat with people at a dinner party. The difference between information gathered in this informal way and environmental scanning is a more systematic approach and use of information management tools. The building blocks of such a system are presented as chapters in this book (Figure 11.3). Using this template,

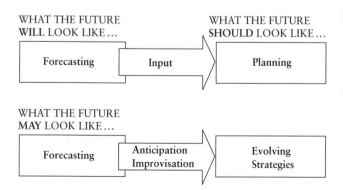

WHAT THE FUTURE WILL LOOK LIKE...

Forecasting → Input → WHAT THE FUTURE SHOULD LOOK LIKE... Planning

WHAT THE FUTURE MAY LOOK LIKE...

Forecasting → Anticipation Improvisation → Evolving Strategies

FIGURE 11.3

Past, present, future—forecasting harmonizes time perspectives to produce a picture of what the future may look like. Thus, forecasting provides input for tactical decisions in the present and long-term strategic planning. In times of high-velocity change, forecasting enables the executive to anticipate the future and improvise continuously evolving strategies.

individual executives can design a continuous, computer-based, environmental scanning system to augment their usual sources of information.

The purpose of a media scan is to provide the information an executive needs to create a customized set of trends (see Figure 10.8). Although the scan is customized to an executive's interests and needs, it should not omit broad scans. It is these broad scans that provide context and early warnings about changes that will eventually hit closer to home.

Cultural Indicators Scan for Context. Trends start as experiments, trial balloons, and self-expression. Many die at this level but some begin to gain momentum as they are adopted, first by other trendsetters, then by the gatekeepers of our culture—designers, fashion scouts, creative directors, and journalists. It is at this stage that trends start to appear in media coverage. Monitoring emerging trends over time provides a context for understanding the other scans on fashion and lifestyles. Monitoring cultural indicators also provides a context for the qualitative adjustment of internal company sales forecasts.

The best overview of what is happening and what might happen in society comes from media sources received across the population as a whole. Continuous monitoring of cultural indicators (see Chapter 9) enables the executive to recognize genuine buzz, manufactured hype, and spin and figure them into the analysis. The cultural indicators scan can be customized by slant (business, cultural, international) to focus on breeding grounds for trend formation. Shortcuts allow the executive to gather important pieces of the puzzle more efficiently.

Fashion Scan for Innovation. Fashion professionals are always eager to keep up with the latest fashion news. Print, broadcast, and online sources are available for this phase of trendspotting. The apparel industry is part of a larger complex of industries—architecture, interior design, cosmetics, autos, and entertainment—primarily in the business of stylistic innovation to service consumers' desire for continual revision of the status quo (Robinson, 1958). Color trends often cut across these fields. Take the color purple—called "aubergine" for its resemblance to the skin of an eggplant—which appeared in the late 1980s as a store-wide apparel promotion at Bloomingdale's, a popular accent color in decorating, the "hot" color in automobiles, and, eventually, the newest look in nail polish. Because these fields are so interrelated, an apparel executive needs access to coverage of all these fields.

Fashion professionals in all fields need an overview of innovations in color forecasting (Chapter 4), textile development (Chapter 5), and design concepts (Chapter 6). Along with the overview, fashion professionals within the different segments of the fashion industry can customize the scan to reflect their special interests:

• Textile specialization—individualize the scans with more science-oriented sources and focus on business-to-business marketing.

- Fabric and print development—customize the scan for color forecasting and focus on precursor sources, because this phase of the apparel supply chain involves longer lead times.

- Apparel product developer—customize for spotting fashion trends developing around the globe.

- Apparel retailers—focus on new retail concepts and fashion-forward neighborhoods where entrepreneurs experiment with new merchandise and visual merchandising.

Consumer Scan for Shifts in Preferences and Lifestyles. Recognizing a trend is only the first step for a fashion professional. Shaping the trend for a particular market segment is just as essential. Consulting firms, market research organizations, advertising agencies, the government, and companies are constantly conducting consumer research. Research conducted by companies is usually proprietary—that is, it belongs to the organization that funded it and is used internally for decision support. Short summaries of this kind of research are often available in trade publications and from print and broadcast news sources. Keyword searching is an excellent way to locate this useful trend information (Chapter 7).

Product development and marketing executives use information about consumer segments to identify emerging target markets. Retailers and merchandisers use the information as an early warning system of long-term social trends because changes within consumer segments eventually have an impact on store design, merchandise assortments, and staffing. By keeping up to date on findings from consumer research, an executive increases the likelihood of making the connection between an emerging trend and the market segment most likely to be interested in related products.

Scan Template for Collaborative Forecasting. Executives on the fashion and business side of apparel need a shared information base to enhance collaboration. A basic information template would include:

- *The Wall Street Journal* as a substitute for a more extensive scan of business news.

- A national newspaper such as *The New York Times* or another daily from an urban center as a substitute for a more expansive news scan.

- *Women's Wear Daily* (*WWD*), for women's wear, or *Daily News Record* (*DNR*), for men's wear, the key trade papers for coverage of fashion and apparel industry news.

- *Advertising Age* for coverage of marketing trends.

- Fashion and lifestyle magazines for coverage of popular culture and opinion leaders that influence fashion trends.

From this base, executives on the fashion side and the business side can individualize the plan by adding one or more specialized scans. In this way, environmental scanning becomes a platform for company forecasting with executives in functional areas sharing a common information domain.

COMPETITIVE ADVANTAGE: MEDIA SCANS FOR MARKET INFORMATION

Digital communication brings with it a shift in the factors that contribute to competitiveness (DuMont, 1997). Instead of low value-added activities, the industry is moving to strategies based on agility, faster response times, and demand-activated production (Figure 11.4).

In today's competitive marketplace, it is important to track news about the industry and about a company's current and potential partners and competitors. Forecasting information is only useful when it can be applied to decision making about the future. The success of a company's decisions rests not only on what action it takes but also on the actions of its competitors. An executive must have information about fashion change and competitors in order to decide on short-range tactics and long-term strategies. Combining forecasts with competitor information makes it possible to formulate actionable decisions.

Competitive intelligence or **competitive analysis** means using public sources to develop a detailed and accurate view of the market environment, both trends in the industry and what the competition is likely to do. The goal of the competitive analysis is to take the pulse of companies whose actions may have an impact on an executive's decision making. A climate of fast-paced

FIGURE 11.4	FUNCTIONS	OLD	NEW
The transformation of the textile and apparel industries means shifting from low value-added activities to strategies based on agility, faster response times, and demand-activated production.	**DESIGN**	Runaway Shows Status Appeals	Demand-Activated Product Development Mass Customization
	DEVELOP	Low Cost Labor Mass Production Long Production Runs	Partnerships Networks
	DISTRIBUTION	Efficiency with Volume	Speed Dynamic Management
	RETAIL	Real Estate Location Superior Service Reputation	Convenience Entertainment Online Access

technological development and an international marketplace increase the importance of competitive analysis.

Like environmental scanning in general, competitive analysis is a continuous process of collecting information from published sources, public government documents, and interviews ("Frequently," 1998). It does not mean gathering proprietary information in illegal or unethical ways. Competitive analysis scans can be customized to capture news about companies considered to be industry leaders as a way to measure operations against the best practices. Or, the scan can be customized to focus specifically on companies that are allies or direct competitors. As it is impossible to gather all the information needed, any gaps are identified and, where possible, filled in by reasoning during the analysis stage. The analysis makes the information useful to executives as support for planning and decision making.

Competitive analysis shares commonalities with other forecasting activities because it also involves data gathering, analysis, and interpretation. Competitive analysis takes into account past and current situations as part of a proactive stance toward business challenges and opportunities. It can be applied to planning **tactics**—scoping out seasonal direction and planning short-range strategy. Or, it can be used to forecast the competitor's **mid-range strategies** two to five years ahead. Or, it can be applied to more long-range **strategic planning** to gain competitive advantage and ensure business survival and long-term growth. The tactical approach means focusing attention on a particular project or the implementation of a current business strategy. A strategic approach means having a longer time horizon and a more comprehensive view. Tactical, mid-range, and strategic planning require an ongoing flow of information about the industry, business climate, and competitive situation (Prescott & Smith, 1989).

Competitive analysis offers two benefits: it confirms what the company thinks it knows and it warns of change in cases where having the right information is crucial. The potential benefits of using competitive analysis are not restricted to large corporations. Companies of every size benefit from competitive analysis (McGonagle & Vella, 1990):

- **Large Apparel Companies**

Corporations with brand tiers—several brands for similar products but at different price levels—or brand extension—multiple product lines from eyeglasses to apparel to towels based on lifestyle concepts—use competitive analysis to monitor and control their own activities. For these large companies, it is vital that senior management have the best information about the different brands within their own company in comparison to rival companies. Competitive analysis is important in making far-reaching decisions about business strategy.

- **Mid-Sized Apparel Companies**

To survive, mid-sized companies must sustain and strengthen current markets and look for new opportunities. In a climate of acquisition, mid-sized companies may seek to acquire other companies as part of their growth plans or they may be the targets of an acquisition. Competitive analysis benefits these mid-sized companies by identifying market threats and opportunities.

- **New Businesses**

Entrepreneurs, whether designers, manufacturers, or retailers, need to identify potential backers with deep pockets to finance the first critical years of establishing the company's name and market niche. Business start-ups require competitive information for solid business planning and to justify investment to venture capitalists.

Large corporations frequently have a staff dedicated to gathering and analyzing information about competitors. Companies also hire consultants for specific projects. Membership in the Society of Competitive Intelligence Professionals (SCIP), a professional association for consultants and corporate employees, grew from 1,800 in 1994 to over 4,000 in 1998, indicating that demand for expertise in information gathering and analysis is increasing ("Frequently," 1998; Heath, 1996b).

An executive's company may hire professionals who specialize in competitive analysis either on staff or as consultants. But any executive can benefit from having a personal competitive analysis system in place as a support for business decisions, as an early warning system for shifts in the business landscape, and as a part of career planning. There are four parts to a competitive analysis system: question forming, information gathering, data analysis, and communication of results ("Curriculum," 1998).

The first steps in competitive analysis are things an executive already does—attending trade shows, reading the trade and business press, and networking with others in the industry. The next step is making gathering and analyzing competitor information more systematic and continuous ("Curriculum," 1998).

The goal of competitive analysis is to provide a company or an individual with **competitive advantage**. Competitive advantage occurs when for a period of time there is an asymmetry in the marketplace that favors one company over another. To sustain competitive advantage in its favor, a company must anticipate the responses of rivals (Amit, Domowitz, & Fershtman, 1988). Analyzing a rival company's position opens up several opportunities for executives (Gelb, Saxton, Zinkhan, & Albers, 1991):

- The opportunity to try to outsmart the competition by exploiting their weaknesses.
- The opportunity to avoid surprises that may upset a company's strategic plan.
- The opportunity to imitate the competition in a search for a better way to do the task or a better way to make decisions.

- The opportunity to recognize as early as possible when a company is on the wrong path and cannot compete in a particular market.
- The opportunity to identify a new niche where the company can be competitive.

Analysts categorize these as informational, offensive, and defensive opportunities (Prescott & Smith, 1989): informational, because a company's executives need an overall understanding of their industry and their competitors; offensive, because competitive analysis attempts to discover where competitors are vulnerable and what actions can be taken to capitalize on that temporary advantage; defensive, because competitive analysis involves thinking ahead about competitor moves that could threaten the firm's position in the market.

Use databases to identify technologies that will influence competitive strategies in apparel retailing or apparel production over the next five years. For example, technologies such as smart cards, in-store kiosks, and e-commerce will affect the future of retailing; technologies such as three-dimensional body scanning and digital printing will affect apparel production. Find three articles on one of the new technologies and analyze them to discover how these technologies will provide a competitive advantage to some companies and not to others.

Activity 11.5
The Technology
Advantage

Question Forming and Information Gathering

The first step in competitive analysis is to identify the decisions or issues that will become the focus of the process. Issues might involve changes in the regulatory, technological, or competitive environment. Decisions might involve fashion direction, marketing, and promotional strategy. By listing the kind of information they need for decisions, executives set priorities and structure information gathering in categories—what is critical, relatively important, or merely nice to know. As there will not be time or resources to gather all the information, the search will concentrate on the critical and important categories (Heath, 1996b).

The quest for information uses four sources (Heath, 1996b):

- Published sources, including information in newspapers and magazines, trade publications, government documents, company reports, investment and financial publications, and presentations by company executives at conferences.

- **Fieldwork**—direct observation and interviews with employees, suppliers, customers, and experts quoted in published articles.
- **"Soft information"** from the popular press, TV shows that mention the company or product, and industry rumors.
- In-house sources such as the sales force, customer service, technical support, and other front-line workers who know before managers about the competitor's newest products and plans (Heath, 1996a).

Companies leave paper trails whenever they take actions such as hiring or firing people, buying supplies, opening new plants, or expanding their distribution channels. Companies must deal with local, state, and federal governments in undertaking actions, and that makes government sources a good place for basic information on financials, plant size, and regulatory issues.

Competitive analysis can be undertaken for a specific project and have a specific ending date. But companies that use competitive analysis most successfully monitor information by category and frequency (Prescott & Smith, 1989):

- Continuous monitoring of general industry trends and technological development.
- Continuous monitoring of marketing, sales, and financial information on key partners and competitors.
- Periodic monitoring on a weekly, monthly, or seasonal basis of partners' and competitors' organizational goals, customer profiles, services, and channels of distribution.
- Occasional monitoring of public and international affairs, human resources, general administrative structure, and other business practices as changing situations require.

Continuous, periodic, and occasional monitoring can be focused on a specific goal—to keep tabs on the competitive environment, changes in the marketplace, the actions of a direct competitor, or the management style of a company as it influences decisions.

It may seem strange to monitor not only the competition but also **business-to-business partners**—firms closely allied with the company as suppliers or customers. However, competitive analysis can be a way to pick up on signals that promote better understanding between firms that do business with each other. Missing signals from business partners can be costly when it leads to a disruption in either the supply or the demand side of a business. Partner firms are probably also doing business with others, and part of achieving total quality management is finding out if a competitor is doing a better job in terms of products or services (Fuld, 1992). Monitoring business partners provides an early warning of changes or shifts in alliances that can have long-term effects on the business.

Fieldwork is one way to gather information about a competitor's business—shop their stores and wear their product. Pick a specialty store chain as a "client" for competitive analysis. Then, take on the role of a **"secret shopper"**—a person who appears to be just a customer but who is actually noting the operational details of a business. Compare the product, visual merchandising, pricing, and service at two or more of your client's competitors. Prepare a chart comparing the stores. Conclude with ways your "client" can meet or surpass the competition.

Activity 11.6 Be a "Secret Shopper"

Competitive Environment Scan. An executive makes decisions contingent on the decisions of counterparts at competing firms. That is, an executive must anticipate the effect a decision will have on his or her own company and the likely response from competitors (Zajac & Bazerman, 1991). A competitive environment scan provides the background for those decisions. Depending on the executive's needs, the scan can be updated on either a continuous or periodic basis. The purpose of this scan is to locate general information on an industry and the relative position of the companies in that industry. This type of scan will include information on industry size, market share by company, and trends in the industry.

Trade magazines usually publish one issue a year as an overview of an industry. These issues provide good background data and suggest ways to organize information on the industry—perhaps by size of companies, product categories, or geographic location. Tracking back a few years using these special issues provides directional information on the industry and highlights issues and trends that are of perennial interest and those just emerging. Other sources for industry overview information include:

- U.S. Department of Commerce and other government sources.
- Reports prepared for investors.
- Databases of magazine and newspaper articles on the industry and the companies in the industry.
- Trade associations that conduct surveys of industry practices.

Investor reports may be free through databases compiling company profiles and from brokerage firms seeking new investors. The newspaper and magazine articles contain data on companies in the industry but also the names of experts who can be contacted for interviews for more detailed information.

Some companies compile a company history on each of their key partners and competitors (Fuld, 1985). The company history includes a chronology of the company's activities, including acquisitions of other firms, name changes, and major changes after a new chief executive officer (CEO) or management team was installed. Trade magazines often profile one company per issue and these profiles are a good first step in compiling a company history. By adding articles on the company gleaned from other newspapers and magazines and a recent annual report from the company, the executive has the sources needed to compile a timeline for the company and a company history.

Activity 11.7 Competitive Analysis Start-Up	Start a competitive analysis filing system on the apparel industry. Begin with a file for material on the total industry. Add files for two or three major companies. Develop a one-page company history on the major companies in timeline form showing the development of the company, its brands by product category and price, and quotes taken from recent articles about the company's direction in the future.

Market Scan. Executives have a good idea who their direct competitors are but often fail to consider indirect or hidden competitors. **Direct competitors** sell the same general product to the same customers in the same distribution channels. **Indirect competitors** are those that offer alternatives that may deflect a customer away from a purchasing situation. Using competitive analysis techniques to develop a market overview promotes a more comprehensive answer to questions about who the firm's competitors are now and in the future.

All companies going after the same target customer with products that can be substituted for each other or competing for that customer's discretionary spending are competitors. Customers are notoriously fickle and can decide to change brands, trade up or down in terms of quality and price, substitute a different product, or shift spending to another category of goods at any time. The purpose of a market scan is to identify trends, shifts in consumer preferences, and changes in competitor strategies that may have an impact on the firm in the short and long term.

The scan begins with an overview of the size of the market and expected growth rates for key customer segments—age range, income levels, geographic concentration, and lifestyle. Government documents from the Census Bureau are a good starting point. Business and industry databases provide articles projecting growth or contraction of market segments and reports on lifestyle surveys covering the market segments. Important directional information includes consumer preferences for styling, fabrications, and brands. Suggestions that consumer preferences vary by regions of the country or by ethnicity indicate that different strategies must be formulated for each region or group.

The scan continues with the identification of key brands and estimates of their market share. How do they vary in terms of pricing, styling, fashion, and fabrication? Do these key brands use different distribution channels? Do the companies vary in their marketing and promotional strategy? What is the strength of brand identity for each company? Breaking down the key brands into subsegments by product line produces a better, more fine-grained picture of the market.

Executives looking ahead will analyze the threats that exist to this market. Possible threats include emerging companies with a novel approach to attracting customers, shifts in consumer preferences or lifestyle, and reallocation of consumers' discretionary spending away from apparel products and toward another category such as home décor, entertainment, or travel. If there are threats, there are also untapped opportunities in this market.

Market reports containing this kind of information are available from market research firms, publishing companies specializing in marketing, and consultants. Market reports can cost thousands of dollars and may go out of date quickly. Executives who conduct their own market scan and update it periodically will be in a better position to evaluate competitive moves by rival firms and to position their own products and company to gain competitive advantage now and in the future.

Search the Internet for sites offering market reports. Write to market research firms to obtain promotional literature about commercially available market reports. Pay close attention to the way these reports are packaged, the listed contents, and the date they were published. Examining the commercial reports may suggest ways in which to organize market information in your own filing system and expand the topics you will look for.

Activity 11.8 Who's Got the Report?

Competitor Profile. Executives need a detailed profile of their direct competitors, including a breakdown of each product line by design, quality, distribution, packaging, marketing, and promotion. Supplementing the breakdown with figures about costs associated with each aspect is helpful but such information is among the most difficult to obtain. Sometimes historical data can be used to trace developments up to the current time. These historical data can be used to hypothesize about future directions (Schlossberg, 1990). Important insights can result from an understanding of the **corporate culture** in the competing firm. Even details such as how offices are allocated and the frequency of meetings suggest how the company functions internally, how executives relate to each other, and how decisions are made.

To provide decision support, a competitor profile should include the following (Gelb et al., 1991):

- Overview and history of the company.
- A breakdown of product lines including sales figures and pricing.
- An overview of the company's marketing strategies, including defining and developing new target customers.
- An overview of corporate strategy on issues such as technology and research and development.

- A financial analysis of the company, including costs, profits, and overhead.
- Information on international strategies in terms of marketing and production.

In addition to a company history (see earlier suggestions under "Competitive Environment Scan"), an executive collects announcements about new products, price changes, new promotional initiatives, personnel changes, plant openings or closings, and openings of new distribution centers. Even ads for the company's products indicate the competitor's positioning strategy in different markets. Information about the company in the trade press and business and industry databases fills out the profile (Martin, 1992).

Governmental data, public documents, and investor reports help executives assess the financial health and market share of a competitor. Some computer databases require only entering the company name to locate this information. Many companies overlook internal sources of competitor information such as the sales staff and suppliers who can discuss sales levels, floor space, or other details about how the competitor is doing business.

An excellent way to organize information in a competitor profile is to use three categories: (1) what competitors say about themselves, (2) what other competitors say about them, and (3) what third parties such as reporters, suppliers, and customers say about them. Evaluating each of these categories separately gives a much clearer picture and raises more interesting questions than combining them (McGonagle & Vella, 1990).

Gathering information for competitive analysis is a creative process. One professional suggests using the "small pond theory"—that is, look for information close to where the company or the corporate division has its headquarters (Schlossberg, 1990). Many apparel companies have showrooms or sales offices in fashion centers such as New York but others are headquartered where the company was founded, often in small and mid-sized cities. Over the past decade, some apparel firms have moved their headquarters out of New York. When a large company is headquartered in a smaller city, that company is big news and will be covered extensively in the local press. For information on those firms, instead of going to national sources, check local sources first. For example, use the local paper in the city where the corporate headquarters are located or tap into the clipping files and expertise of the research librarian at the library nearest the company headquarters.

Another creative and frequently overlooked source of information on competitors is help wanted ads in trade publications and newspapers. In describing themselves to potential employees, companies frequently provide insights about new initiatives in the company. Perhaps the company is changing computer-aided design (CAD) systems or expanding the number of designers. In either case, the ad may signal that more emphasis is being placed on product development than in the past. Similarly, help wanted ads that mention expansion plans, new equipment, or other changes are helpful in developing a profile that anticipates the competitor's moves (Fuld, 1988).

The more detailed the profile of the competitor, the more helpful it is to an executive in supporting tactical and strategic decision making. The profile on a key competitor should be continuously updated to provide the most up-to-the-minute picture of the competitive situation. Only with such detailed and current information can an executive recognize a competitive advantage and act on the opportunity.

Collect help wanted ads for positions in the apparel industry in product development and design, production, quality control, sales, visual merchandising, advertising and promotion, buying, and retail management. Use trade publications and company Internet sites to locate the ads. When you have a collection of ads, examine what they reveal about companies. Compare ads across companies: How do the ads reflect the corporate culture of each firm? What specific information do the ads reveal about the company structure? Are there any hints about changes in the way that the company is doing business?

Activity 11.9 Help Wanted Ads

Management Profile. The corporate culture of a rival firm may give it some sort of competitive edge. A new CEO comes to a company with the experience of what worked and what did not at other firms and a mandate to increase profits. A firm changes from a chain-of-command system to a functional team approach to product development. A competitor based in another part of the country seeks to acquire a retail chain. Today's rising young executive is tomorrow's president of a rival firm. In all these cases and many more, the management style and background of the executives in the rival firm are essential to understanding the situation and predicting what comes next. Competitive analysis includes profiling key decision makers as a way to anticipate and explain their strategic moves.

Occasionally a trade publication, business magazine, or newspaper will profile an executive focusing on his or her successes, management style, and financial acumen. Television cable channels that focus on business sometimes offer interview programs with executives who have become prominent in an industry. Other sources for assembling management profiles include articles in trade publications and newspapers about an executive's promotion, who's who directories for business and industry, and brief biographies in annual reports and convention materials when the executive is on the program.

In the case of a firm's president or CEO, the chances are that the person has been prominent in business news about the industry prior to assuming the position. A search of databases using the executive's name or that of his or her former company may provide articles in which the executive was interviewed over a range of issues. Another source of information comes from interviews with colleagues and co-workers who discuss how this executive approaches business decisions.

Attending trade shows and conventions that feature executives from rival firms on the program offers the chance to gain insight on the direction the firm will be taking in the future. There is usually a question-and-answer session and the executives' responses during this period can be more revealing than the prepared remarks.

Assembling a profile of the executive's education, work history, philanthropic interests, and management philosophy requires time, patience, and creativity. But such a profile opens a window into the behavior and customary approach of a key executive in business situations—a critical piece of information in a competitive environment.

Activity 11.10
CEO Profile

Select a company in which you are particularly interested. Find out the name of the president or CEO of the firm. Use database searching to locate profiles of the company and the CEO. Some databases contain not only the text of print articles but also transcripts of media interviews. The interviews are particularly helpful in developing a CEO profile. Using several articles or interviews, compile a profile that includes:

- Background information on the executive's early life, education, and career path.
- The situation when the CEO stepped into this position, the challenges faced, actions taken, and the outcome.
- Information about the executive's style of management and philosophy of business.

Complete the profile by selecting several recent quotes by the executive that suggest the probable direction the firm will take over the next year.

Ethical and Legal Issues. In the mid-1990s, Johnson Industries hosted an eager graduate student working on his master's degree and an investment banker claiming to represent Swiss investors. The visitors were given access to company executives and to plant tours. These visitors left knowing things that no one outside the company did. According to a lawsuit filed in 1998, these visitors were corporate spies allegedly working for a rival (the rival company denied the allegations). In the suit, Johnson Industries claimed that the information gleaned by the corporate spies cost the company as much as $30 million in business losses ("Grad student," 1998).

Industrial espionage occurs when someone breaks the law to collect data. Examples of industrial espionage include "hacking" into a company's computer to steal files, stealing samples from a trade show display, or entering a firm's plant or distribution center surreptitiously to spy on operations.

Some information gathering activities are not illegal but are considered **unethical practices**. Examples of these kinds of activities include misrepresenting a person's identity to extract information from a firm's employees, and giving a competitor's employee an employment interview solely to debrief them about the other company's operations. Other activities fall in a gray area—not illegal put perhaps questionable. An example is going through a competitor's trash when it has been put on the curb for pick up. The competitor does have the option to guard against this form of intelligence gathering by shredding all documents before discarding.

Although there are no government regulations on competitive intelligence gathering and there is no licensing system for practitioners, most people in the field voluntarily abide by a code of ethics such as that published to members by the Society of Competitor Intelligence Professionals (SCIP). Common sense and a sense of fair play will guide the actions of most executives, but there are some activities to avoid (Murphy & Laczniak, 1992; Paine, 1991):

- Purposeful searches for confidential business information or classified government information.

- Covert surveillance.

- Obtaining information under false pretenses, deceit, or misrepresentation.

- Encouraging other professionals such as bankers and lawyers to leak confidential information.

- Seeking information in ways that interfere with a person's privacy.

Illegal or unethical practices are unnecessary to successful competitive analysis because there are so many public sources of information and computer databases that make obtaining information so much easier than in the past.

Methods of Data Analysis

Competitive analysis is different from market research. One professional explained it this way: In market research, the analyst has 997 pieces of the puzzle and has to figure out the last three; in competitive analysis, the analyst has three pieces and has to figure out what the whole picture looks like (Heath, 1996b). Strictly factual information such as the organizational structure of a company or the location of distribution centers requires very little analysis. The information on general industry trends, potential competitors, and technological developments require more extensive analysis to determine the short- and long-term implications for a company (Prescott & Smith, 1989). If looking at competitive analysis is like a puzzle, some pieces may not belong in the picture and must be discarded because of unreliability or inaccuracy.

Having gathered the information is only the first step. Next, the analyst must evaluate the information for **reliability** and **accuracy**—the first clue to consider is the original source and the creditability of that source. "**Disinformation**" results from inaccuracies in published articles, from people misrepresenting their knowledge or expertise, and from countering moves by competitors seeking to protect their secrets. The only protection from inaccurate information is to check and cross check information using multiple sources.

Another source of inaccuracy is related to the timeliness of information. Facts in a magazine story are already months old and in a book years old. Evaluating the accuracy of data involves evaluation of its timeliness—the best sources contain information that is less than a year old (Heath, 1996b).

The next step is organizing the information using an outline of key topics (see the earlier discussion of scans and profiles for organizational structures) and make inferences about what it means. There are many forms of analysis, and they may be performed by a team or by an individual analyst. The most frequently used methods include:

- **Content Analysis**

Content analysis involves extracting significant data from the sources and classifying it by topic and reliability. Content analysis condenses the information into meaningful clusters that can be evaluated to determine their implications.

- **Pattern Recognition**

Look for patterns in the information—an apparel company hiring more designers may be changing strategies, a division that was barely mentioned in last year's annual report but is prominent in this year's probably means that the division's status has changed within the company. Having background and historical information makes it more likely that the analyst will spot an emerging pattern in the data.

- **Anomalies, Outliers, and Omissions**

Anomalies are data that do not fit expectations. **Outliers** are cases or facts that are unexpectedly high or low in value. **Omissions** are missing reasons for an action or a business decision. These unanticipated gaps in the information gathered during a competitive analysis may be mistakes or misunderstandings or they may be important clues. It is important to recognize anomalies, outliers, and omissions and diligently search for an explanation. Ignoring these gaps may lead the analyst to incorrect conclusions.

It is important during the analysis phase to keep the information separate from conclusions. Experienced analysts organize the information first, then draw conclusions, and, finally, check to see that they have enough data to support each conclusion. If a conclusion lacks support, it is dropped until additional information confirms it (McGonagle & Vella, 1990).

From Scanning to Implementation

Competitive analysis assists executives in corporate-level planning by identifying the nature and intensity of competition in the industry, the characteristics of the dominant firms, and projections for the future size of the market. Competitive analysis assists executives at the business planning level in developing a competitive strategy and in making the frequent tactical decisions required to compete effectively in a marketplace (McGonagle & Vella, 1990). Competitive analysis contributes to the overall planning and forecasting functions by justifying projects, priorities, and actions and by generating new ideas about how to solve problems or take advantage of opportunities.

In addition to these basic uses of competitive analysis, there are other more sophisticated applications.

- **Shadow Market Planning**

The goal in **shadow market planning** is to have one or more people in a company be so familiar with a competitor that they can answer "what if" questions about that competitor's strategy on a current and continuous basis. They accomplish this task by regularly monitoring the elements of a competitor's marketing efforts to such an extent that they can put themselves in the competitor's place (McGonagle & Vella, 1990).

- **"Best Practices" Benchmarking**

Benchmarking means comparing a company with other firms considered best in terms of efficient operations. In "best practices" benchmarking, the firms chosen for comparison may not even be in the same industry. For example, an apparel firm beginning a mail-order operation may choose to study the practices of a successful catalog of gourmet cooking items because that firm is tops in fulfillment and customer satisfaction with catalog buyers.

- **Competitive Benchmarking**

In **competitive benchmarking,** the firms chosen for comparison are the company's direct competitors. A set of specific measures such as capital investment, productivity, and product quality is used to create a side-by-side comparison of how the company fits into the competition with other firms (Ghoshal & Westney, 1991).

- **Sensitization**

The goal of **sensitization** is to shake up a company's assumptions about its place in relationship to competitors. Sensitization uses information about competitors to build a sense of urgency in a company by alerting executives to gains by competitors or an emerging challenge from a new company (Ghoshal & Westney, 1991).

- **Reverse Engineering for Products**

Reverse engineering means purchasing and dismantling a product to determine how it was designed and constructed. The purpose of this process is to estimate the costs and evaluate the quality of the product to determine how to produce a more competitive product. Beyond the product itself, reverse engineering may involve the way the product is packed or shipped or the way it is manufactured. For certain types of products, such as computer software, reverse engineering is mostly illegal.

- **Reverse Engineering for Services**

Customer satisfaction is essential to business success in today's market. If a rival firm has a reputation for better service from sales associates, fulfillment of phone orders, or some other service component, that service can become the target for competitive analysis. The process involves profiling the steps and attributes of the service and comparing it to current practices in the industry.

Any corporate program of competitive analysis involves both quantitative and qualitative data. Few executives have the full range of skills to accomplish competitive analysis. A much better approach is to see competitive analysis as a shared responsibility among executives. Today's computer networks makes this easier to accomplish. One approach involves having each executive list and prioritize issues and topics of interest. A computerized search of databases overnight allows the newest information to be delivered to the executive's computer desktop the next morning (Roush, 1991). Another approach based on networked executives involves collaborative information processing: any executive in the group puts information on a competitor on the network and the information is annotated with electronic Post-It Notes™ from other executives in the group. In this way the work group builds corporate knowledge bases on key competitors and partners. Whatever the approach, competitive analysis is an important part of forecasting and planning—a process that involves executives at all levels and in all job categories. To be effective, competitive information must be communicated widely throughout the company using formal reporting methods such as memos and newsletters and less formal methods such as e-mail and bulletin boards (Fuld, 1988).

Key Terms and Concepts

Anomalies	Corporate Culture	Reliability of Information
Benchmarking	Direct Competitors	Reverse Engineering
Boolean Operators	Disinformation	Search Engines
Business-to-Business Partners	Fieldwork	Secret Shopper
Competitive Advantage	Indirect Competitors	Sensitization
Competitive Analysis	Industrial Espionage	Shadow Market Planning
Competitive Benchmarking	Internet Agents	Soft Information
Competitive Intelligence	Mid-Range Strategies	Strategic Planning
Content Analysis	Omissions	Subject Tree
	Outliers	Tactics
	Proximity Operators	Unethical Practices

Discussion Questions

This chapter looks at ways an apparel executive can probe the future using the techniques of media scanning and competitive analysis. These two approaches can provide support for decision making and improve a company's planning and forecasting.

Environmental scanning: How can an individual executive use media scans to gain the information he or she needs for decision making? How can teams collaborate on finding the relevant bits and pieces of information to support forecasting? How can an executive or team build customized sets of trends based on media scans? What are some shortcuts and technology tools that can reduce the time executives spend on media scanning?

Questions forming: What decisions or issues are the focus of competitive analysis? Do they involve regulatory, technological, or competitive environment changes on the horizon? Fashion direction, marketing, and promotional strategy?

Competitors: The direct competitors are obvious. Are there any indirect competitors who should be considered?

Probable uses of the analysis: Is the analysis likely to be used as informational, offensive, or defensive? What kinds of decisions will depend on the analysis—tactical or strategic or both?

Priorities for information gathering: List the kind of information needed, then set priorities about which kinds of information to gather. What methods will be employed in gathering this information?

Analysis model: Which analysis model—competitive environment, market scan, competitor profile, or management profile—will be most helpful to decision makers?

Additional Forecasting Activities

Ethics on Trial. Consider the role of ethics in information gathering. Gather some actual cases involving intelligence gathering where companies have filed cases or complained of competitors' unfair practices. Invite a panel of executives to discuss these cases and the financial implications for both the companies paying for the information and the companies being monitored.

Touring for Information. Plan a plant tour to a textile or apparel manufacturer or to a retail distribution center. In addition to observing the facilities, consider what a competitor could gain on such a tour. What would they look for? What questions would they ask? Discuss with your hosts the security aspects of plant tours.

Career Building. Competitive analysis is helpful to individual executives in career building because it alerts them to changes within the industry, their own company, partner companies, and competitors. Go through the steps of competitive analysis with career planning in mind. What questions are important from this point of view? What information gathering methods will be used? How frequently should information be updated? What scans and profiles will be helpful? Are there any ethical issues that apply when the competitive analysis focuses on career building?

Resource Pointers

A Web site has been created to aid in developing an individualized, customized environmental scanning system. It offers access to the online souces suggested in this chapter organized in a menu form that makes navigation easier and quicker. Find this site at: http://www.humsc.auburn.edu/ca/brannon/elbhome.html

The *New York Times* provides a homepage used by their newsroom personnel as an entrance portal to the Web. It offers excellent links on business, economics, entertainment, and other environmental scanning topics. Find the home page at: http://www.nytimes.com/learning/general/navigator/index.html

Chapter 12

PRESENTING THE FORECAST

"People rarely distinguish among data, information, knowledge, and wisdom. Yet they are as different from one another—and as interlocking—as starch molecules, flour, bread, and the flavorful memory of a superb morning croissant."
—Lewis Branscomb, IBM

Objectives

• Explain the differences between data, information, knowledge, and wisdom.

• Define the steps of presentation design as information design, interaction design, and sensory design.

• Introduce the guidelines for performance, effective visuals, and use of audiovisual equipment.

• Clarify the purpose and characteristics of trend reporting.

• Explore traditional and leading edge presentation techniques and the role of technology.

PRESENTATION DESIGN AS A CREATIVE PROCESS

An eager audience has gathered for a presentation on the latest fashion trends. The room buzzes with conversation. People maneuver for a good seat, trying to find a spot near friends but with a view of both the screen and the presenter. The mood is expectant. Today they will see a multimedia presentation tying together ideas, images, and themes to show the direction of fashion change (Figure 12.1).

The fashion forecaster prepared for the occasion by aggressively collecting ideas, hints, innovations, signals, signs, and indications. The process involved traveling to the fashion capitals, visiting showrooms and boutiques, watching trendsetters, scanning media, and reading everything possible that might relate to fashion change. Some discoveries were made because of her deliberate efforts, some through serendipity. The forecaster saturated her senses and her environment with all the possibilities. Identifying trends was a necessary first step, but that alone is not sufficient to prepare a presentation. At some point she began to sort, organize, and edit the material searching for relationships and patterns. This process creates meaning, which she will convey in her presentation. Just as creative is the process of choosing the style of the presentation and collecting or devising the visuals to illustrate key points.

The audience awaits an experience. Their goal is to depart with knowledge that will guide and support decisions for their companies. The success of this

FIGURE 12.1

The audience for a presentation on the latest fashion trends expects the forecaster to tie together ideas, images, and themes to show the direction of fashion change.

venture for both presenter and audience depends on transforming data into information and knowledge. The presentation allows each audience member the opportunity to understand, consider, evaluate, and interpret the content—a personal process that leads to wisdom.

Data Gathering and Pattern Recognition

The metaphor of a kaleidoscope versus a teleidoscope explains the forecasting process. The kaleidoscope creates new patterns and combinations as light passes through the translucent cover and hits the chips and bits that are inside the barrel. Moving the kaleidoscope causes patterns to form and reform. The teleidoscope is similar in construction except that the cover is transparent and the new patterns and combinations are formed from the changing environment wherever the scope in pointed. So it is with a creative person who uses what is stored inside but also seeks a continuous flow of new viewpoints. Creative behavior is a function of knowing, imagining, and evaluating. The more data a person has to work with, the more ideas, patterns, and combinations can be generated (Parnes, 1984).

The fashion forecaster scopes out the patterns forming and reforming in the worlds of fashion. Looking inside the textile and apparel industries, the forecaster sees how the elements inside the structure shift, move, and reshape themselves (the kaleidoscope approach). Looking at the social, cultural, and economic world, the forecaster examines the fusion and fragmentation of tastes, styles, and ideas (the teleidoscope approach).

Pulling together all these images and impressions involves creative problem solving. The human brain "knows" in two different but collaborative ways: by using logical, linear, **analytical thinking** based on facts and reason and by using **intuition**, feelings about how things fit together, pattern recognition, and leaps of insight. Everyone uses logic and intuition, reason and insight, but the fashion forecaster must be especially adept at using both approaches.

During the creative process leading up to the presentation, the forecaster's mind oscillates between **divergent thinking**—generating many alternatives, many possible meanings—and **convergent thinking**—seeking one conclusion, the best alternative, one meaning (Parnes, 1984). The brain rapidly generates hypotheses to explain data, makes new connections, and evaluates alternative explanations imaginatively (without externally testing each and every one).

Given all the possibilities and sources available, the forecaster runs the risk of flooding the audience with images. The presentation fails if audience members are left on their own to sort and make sense of what they have seen. Instead it is the presenter's job to create meaning by reporting on trends and suggesting applications for specific situations in product development, merchandising, promotion, retailing, and visual merchandising.

Transforming Data into Information and Knowledge

Forecasters begin by defining the goals of the presentation and the experience to be shared by the presenter and the audience—the needs and wants of the audience, their probable level of interest, and their level of **knowledge.** Every decision, from what the presenter wears to the kind of visuals, relates back to this definition. The goal of the presentation becomes the standard for selecting appropriate graphics, techniques, and technology.

Effective communication depends on clarity. Clarity is not the same as simplicity. Fashion forecasting involves complex relationships that can only be explained by presenting many examples (data). Over-simplification or "dumbing down" the information can make it meaningless. Instead, effective presentations focus on a particular message and make it clear through organization and the careful selection of presentation techniques. Making a few important points is better than clouding the communication by attempting too much in a limited time frame.

Suppose the presenter's task was to describe a canoe instead of a fashion trend. Perhaps the presenter would begin to describe the shape, dimensions, materials, and method of construction. That works if audience members need to recognize a canoe when they see it or if they need to build one. If they need to use a canoe, then it would be better to describe the functions of a canoe. If they need to understand the experience of paddling a canoe, it would be better not to speak directly about the canoe but instead about what can be seen of lakes, creeks, and forests from the canoe. These three forms of defining a canoe also apply to defining other activities, experiences, and observations (Volk, 1995). Designing a fashion presentation means:

- Describing the trend so well that the audience can recognize it.
- Analyzing the trend so that the audience understands how it functions.
- Showing the trend in its natural habitat so that the audience participates vicariously in its discovery.

To accomplish this task, the presenter must consider three modes of design: information design, interaction design, and sensory design (Shedroff, 1997).

Information Design. Data are researched, created, gathered, and discovered. **Data** are the raw material of communication—not meant to be seen by the audience, only by the producers of the presentation. Data are incomplete and boring as the basis for a presentation. Information is the first level of design suitable for communication to the audience. **Information design** transforms data into valuable, meaningful information by identifying and explaining the relationships and patterns between data (Shedroff, 1997).

Organizational Schemes for Data   Data can be left as random bits, but organization adds value by showing order, connections, and relationships. All data can be organized in basic ways (Flacks & Rasberry, 1982; Wurman, 1989):

- **By Location in Space**

Maps and diagrams organize relationships geographically. This same approach works when visualizing mental space because the forecaster is showing the relative location of data points and the ways they are connected. Physical or mental space can be organized right to left, top to bottom, and outside to inside. The explanation can define the relationship of parts to parts or how the parts relate to the whole. This system of interacting, interrelated parts has more power than the simple sum of those individual parts.

- **By Time**

A schedule where time is organized by minutes and hours and historical timelines where time is organized by decades or centuries clarifies relationships. How-to instructions for all kinds of activities from gardening to sewing are organized in chronological order. The organization may be as simple as listing events over time, the logical sequence in a process, or arraying trends from the past, present, and future.

- **On a Continuum**

Grades (from A to F) or rating systems for movies (from four stars to one star) imply a **continuum**—an underlying value scale. Organizing in numerical or alphabetical order is another form of continuum.

- **By Category**

Grouping similar things together and giving the group a name form a **category**. One form of categorizing involves recognizing the similarities between the items—the aspect that shows that they belong together. Another form of categorizing involves recognizing differences between items or groups of items—the aspects that make each distinctive. If there are several groups and they can be ranked in importance, then the organizational scheme has an underlying order.

- **By Metaphor**

One other way to organize data so that people can quickly understand relationships is by using metaphors. Using a **metaphor** means perceiving resemblance between two separate areas and linking them together. When using metaphors, the presenter compares some concept or mechanism that is difficult to understand to one that is familiar and well understood. The dynamics of street fashion can be compared to atoms joining to make molecules, bumper cars at the fair, and a layer cake—each becomes a metaphor for the way people interact in the fashion system.

Organizational Structures for Presentations. If the purpose of the presentation is to influence actions, consider organizing the content in one of the following patterns (Flacks & Rasberry, 1982):

- **Pro and Con**

This organizational structure is useful when there are several alternatives and strong arguments can be made for each viewpoint. The presenter begins with a short background summary of the issue, then presents the alternatives and the arguments on both sides.

• **Cause and Effect**

The world is much too complex to allow easy, simple identification of cause-and-effect relationships. For any effect, there are multiple causes. Every cause has multiple effects. The presenter attempts to show the web of connections, the meaning of those connections, and possible actions to be taken.

• **Problem and Solution**

This organizational structure begins with an explanation of the problem and proceeds to discuss possible ways to resolve that problem. The resolution should include consideration of the costs in terms of time and money.

The best presenters do not settle immediately for a traditional or stereotypical organizational pattern. New ways to organize and present data capture attention and delight the audience. Professionals brainstorm ways to use the same set of ideas in different organizations as a way to discover unexpected patterns, relationships, and connections.

All organizational forms can be nested into multiple layer organizations (Figure 12.2). Information design provides the structure for a presentation, a structure enhanced by interaction design and sensory design.

Interaction Design. **Interaction design** involves creating compelling experiences for the audience (Shedroff, 1997). Considering the audience in this way acknowledges the interactive nature of presentations. Experiences range between passive situations such as watching television to full interactivity. The interaction may be with other people or with tools such as simulations or animated sequences or video clips. The presenter determines the level of interactivity that is most appropriate for the goals of the presentation. Because building knowledge requires participation, designing interactivity into the presentation helps the audience integrate and understand the content.

FIGURE 12.2

For more complex presentations, organize by nesting the basic organizational forms.

TOPIC

S T R U C T U R E

FASHION FOR A SPECIFIC TARGET AUDIENCE

PRO & CON
• Size of Market
• Communication channel
• Barriers to positioning
  ↳ CAUSE & EFFECT
    • Cynical about advertising
    • Anti-mass media
    • Difficult to target
      ↳ PROBLEM & SOLUTION
        • Hard-to-reach audience
        • Viral marketing
          ↳ PRO & CON
            • New, fresh approach
            • Expense
            • Expertise

THE NEXT NEW THING

CAUSE & EFFECT
• Description
• Initial source
• Appeal
• Potential
  ↳ PRO & CON
    • Possible adaptation
    • Possible markets
    • Difficulties in product development
    • Difficulties in marketing
      ↳ PROBLEM & SOLUTION
        • Barriers to acceptance
        • Positioning
        • Timing

CROSSOVER FROM PERFORMANCE FABRIC TO CONSUMER APPAREL

PROBLEM & SOLUTION
• Dyeing & finishing
• Comfort
• Adaptations
  ↳ PRO & CON
    • Consumer Demand
    • Sport Connection
    • Costs
      ↳ CAUSE & EFFECT
        • Raw materials
        • Alternate finishes
        • Aesthetics

The best conversations involve listening as well as talking, thinking as well as acting. To enrich the experience for audience members, the activities should engage them as participants in a shared experience. The best patterns for interaction design come from the performing arts—dance, theatre, songs, improvisational acting—and from fields such as scriptwriting and storytelling. Storytelling is an especially powerful way to present a forecast—stories about how the information was gathered, innovators, and trendsetters. One common thread in the design of the performing arts is an intriguing beginning, a careful buildup, and a strong conclusion.

Sensory Design. **Sensory design** means employing techniques that communicate to others through their senses (Shedroff, 1997). Visual design includes graphics, video, typography, illustration, and photography—the most commonly used to appeal to the senses in a presentation. However, appealing to the other senses can enrich the experience. Using sound design—music, sound effects, vocal talents—is an appropriate way to communicate about fashion. Fabrics and yarns appeal to the sense of touch. The use of fragrance appeals to the olfactory senses.

Engaging the senses may involve experts from different disciplines collaborating on a presentation. When the presenter chooses to engage a number of senses with the presentation, coordination becomes an issue. Even a seemingly minor detail such as design of the type on visuals changes the audience's perception of the message. Decisions involving font style, size, and how the text is aligned (flush left, flush right, centered, justified, or unjustified) make a difference in communicating effectively.

It is important for the presentation coordinator (usually the fashion forecaster) to understand the potential in sensory design and coordinate its use to reinforce the content of the presentation. What is appropriate depends on the goals for the presentation but carefully integrated sensory design leads to a more compelling, engaging experience for the audience.

Think back to the best lecture, speech, or presentation you sat through. List the characteristics that made it memorable. Think back to the worst lecture, speech, or presentation you ever sat through. List the characteristics that made it so bad. Analyze the positive and negative characteristics from the audience's point of view using the framework of information design, interaction design, and sensory design.

Activity 12.1 Sitting in the Audience

TREND REPORTING

The role of a fashion forecaster is to identify, develop, and present fashion directions in fabrics, color, and style and put them into the context of the culture and lifestyles of consumer. The forecaster explains what is happening, why the trend in developing, and who is leading the trend. Fashion forecasting is a resource for product development, merchandising, marketing, and retailing executives (Figure 12.3). Trend reporting helps these executives interpret fashion change by relating new directions to brand or store strategy.

Trend reporting begins by describing the appeal of a trend via labeling. The label may refer to:

- A look—retro, minimalist, Japanese influence.
- The mood or spirit—youthful, sophisticated, playful.
- A lifestyle message.
- A tie-in with a celebrity.
- A target market—urban youth, working women, early retirees.
- A brand image or designer's name.
- A concept—career casual, investment dressing, mix-and-match.
- The source of inspiration, whether historical or ethnic—*la Belle Époque,* Moroccan.
- A pop culture influence such as a hit movie or TV series.

FIGURE 12.3

Trend forecasting is a resource for product development, merchandising, marketing, and retailing executives because it alerts them to new directions that relate to brand or store strategy.

Trend reporting continues the labeling process by describing the basic elements of the trend:

- Fabric—fiber content, functional attributes, texture, pattern.
- Color—hue, value, intensity, color schemes.
- Silhouette—shape of the garment, hemline, coordinating elements of the total ensemble.
- Details and design features.
- Subtleties of fit, proportion, and coordination.

The description may also include attributes such as the size category (juniors, misses, plus size, petites), price category (designer, bridge, better, moderate), and the season (Fall/Winter, Spring/Summer, Cruise).

Describing the trend is only the first step in trend reporting. The forecaster must also provide a trend map detailing the stage in development and probable scope of each trend.

Trend Map

The **trend map** identifies which trends are just emerging, continuing to build, or declining. The theories about fashion dynamics (see Chapters 2 and 3) and the product life cycle (see Chapter 8) provide frameworks for these observations. To the apparel executive, the mainstream, continuing trends are the core business. Exit strategies must be devised for clearing merchandise associated with declining trends. Emerging trends represent the opportunity to test the potential and get in on the ground floor of "the next big thing."

Quality of the Trend. The trend map draws distinctions between **major trends**—those that will appeal to large groups of consumers—and **minor trends**—those with niche appeal to small groups of consumers (Perna, 1987). Major trends are fabrics, colors, styles, and looks that are likely to move into the mainstream. These trends have already been tested in the market and continue to receive support in terms of sales and media coverage. They represent volume sales potential. Minor trends have more limited sales potential because they are too avant-garde, too distinctive, or too complex to appeal to a broad audience. However, these trends have potential for regional sales or in retail settings congenial to the look. Minor trends often appear at the top of the price range or at the bottom. Fads often play out as interesting and fun minor trends.

The trend map must indicate the quality of each trend. Some items, styles, or looks are **trial balloons**—designer experiments to gauge the effect and potential of a new idea (Perna, 1987). These trial balloons are likely to be commented on by fashion insiders and the media but will not receive support from most retailers. Occasionally, a trial balloon has strong, instantaneous appeal because it is the perfect statement mirroring the spirit of the times (see Chapter 2 for a discussion of the *Zeitgeist*). In those rare occasions, the item or look becomes suddenly "hot" and sells out quickly. The initial restricted availability and strong reaction (sometimes fueled by media coverage) combine to drive the popularity of that item.

Some items, styles, or looks represent **embryonic trends**—that is, trends in the very first stages of development (Perna, 1987). Perhaps a trial balloon in one season is further developed and given more prominence in the next season. The trend has not yet developed, but the look is poised to take off; fashion insiders are tracking its development (Figure 12.4); but the public is largely unaware of its existence.

If fashion innovators and fashion-forward retailers adopted a specific look, it is termed a **directional trend** (Perna, 1987). For more mainstream companies, directional trends offer the opportunity to introduce the thrill of the avant-garde by featuring the trend in a promotion, through visual merchandising, or in fashion shows. While most customers will end up buying only merchandise associated with major trends, the directional trends bring excitement and a feeling of forward motion to fashion.

Interactions with Other Product Categories. It is important for the trend map to establish relationships between classifications:

- Skirt length and pants styles influences shoe design and height of heels.
- Style and design of ready-to-wear influences hosiery.

FIGURE 12.4

Fashion displays at international trade shows help participants track evolving trends.

- Outerwear coordinates with the style and fit of dressy and casual looks.
- The structure and fit of apparel relates to the styling of innerwear and vice versa.
- Accessory stories closely parallel the fashion story, tapping into the same design inspiration.
- Makeup and hairstyles coordinate with apparel styles.

Estimating the Relative Strength of Trends. Finally, the forecaster must make recommendations. Based on an understanding of the marketplace and fashion dynamics, the forecaster estimates the **timing of a trend**—how soon the trend will "hit," how long will it continue. In addition to timing, the forecaster must estimate the **scope of a trend**—how big will it be, how broad an impact will it have on markets. Recommendations indicate the relative strength of various trends and the kind of investment in product development and merchandising that they merit (Perna, 1987).

Use Web sites First View (firstview.com) and Vogue (vogue.com) to look at the designer collections for last season. These Web sites give you a chance to come to your own conclusions without commentary or analysis from others. Select two designers with very different approaches to fashion. Comb through their collections looking for trial balloons and embryonic, major, and minor trends. Develop a brief presentation explaining fashion change as experimentation and illustrate the talk using these two designers' work.

*Activity 12.2
Basic Training*

Trend Boards

Concept boards are used in the product development stage to coordinate the efforts of the design team (Chase, 1997; Tain, 1997). Having a visual "concept" of the fashion direction helps in the editing process—the decision making when the design team selects from the many ideas proposed those that have the strongest potential to succeed in the marketplace. The strength of that potential rests on reading fashion rightly and projecting a consistent image within each coordinated group and across the groups that make up the line.

Concept boards are used in selling apparel internally to the manufacturer's sales force and externally to retail buyers. Sometimes a single concept board is used to convey the source of inspiration, the color and fabric story, the styling, pricing, and key specifications in a visual way. Other companies opt to use one board for the color story, one for the trend story, and another to suggest visual merchandising options. The boards facilitate communication between the buyer and seller. As one accessories executive put it: "When [buyers] see the boards, it all clicks" (Feitelberg, 1998b).

Information on concept boards can often be traced back to **trend boards** for the fashion forecast. Trend boards identify the mood or spirit of each trend and its thematic focus. The best themes fuse visual and verbal elements into a vivid image (Figure 12.5). Here are two examples where the combination of an evocative theme, the visual development of the theme in fashion, and the verbal flourish engages the viewer's psyche.

- **Classical Jazz**

The forecaster may recognize a pattern among suits on fashion runways around the world—classical styling but with just a touch of the unconventional in fabrics, design details, and colors. The forecaster creates a presentation board to convey this trend by creating a collage of examples by many designers and adding the phrase "Classical Jazz." The phrase captures perfectly the idea that designers are improvising on a classic silhouette in the same way that jazz musicians improvise on a classic tune.

- **Desert Drama**

Perhaps the biggest movie coming out next year features a love story set in the 1930s where the lovers make a long trek through the desert. The costumes inspire an interest in the clothes worn by liberated women of the thirties who were explorers, pilots, photographers, and foreign correspondents. The fashion fore-

FIGURE 12.5

Trend boards use visuals, graphics, and text to identify the mood or spirit of each trend.

caster reports this direction on a trend board juxtaposing stills from the movie, ravishing photographs of the sculptural shapes of sand dunes, and new fashions. He ties together the inspiration and the look in the phrase "Desert Drama."

When designers, manufacturers, and retailers pick up on the trend, each is likely to recast the theme slightly to reflect their own customers' interests and sophistication. For example, a mainstream department store may pick up on the adventurer theme and the neutral color scheme from "Desert Drama," pair it with a promotion of rugged, functional casual clothes, and call it "Entering Neutral Territory." The underlying trend information is present but the theme has been translated in a way that gives the user an opportunity to craft an image.

Coming up with the concept is a high form of communication, one that involves many levels of meaning. Fashion forecasters must be masters of this form of communication. Finding themes that capture the essence of a trend is a creative challenge for the forecaster. The themes may be inspired by something occurring in the culture—in science, current events, fine arts, performance arts, sports, or popular culture. Or, the inspiration may come from travel destinations and ethnic influences. Trends often resonate with past fashion periods, and the words and images of those times are used to convey the connection.

The theme, once identified, becomes the unifying force. The typeface, graphics, borders, and background color are selected to further the theme. Computer-generated type avoids the amateurish effect of hand lettering. Experimenting with the typeface—upper and lower case, effects such as bold letters, and other techniques—connects the message of the text with the theme (Figure 12.6). Photographs, sketches, fabric swatches, and color palette are all coordinated to the theme. If color names are used, the names

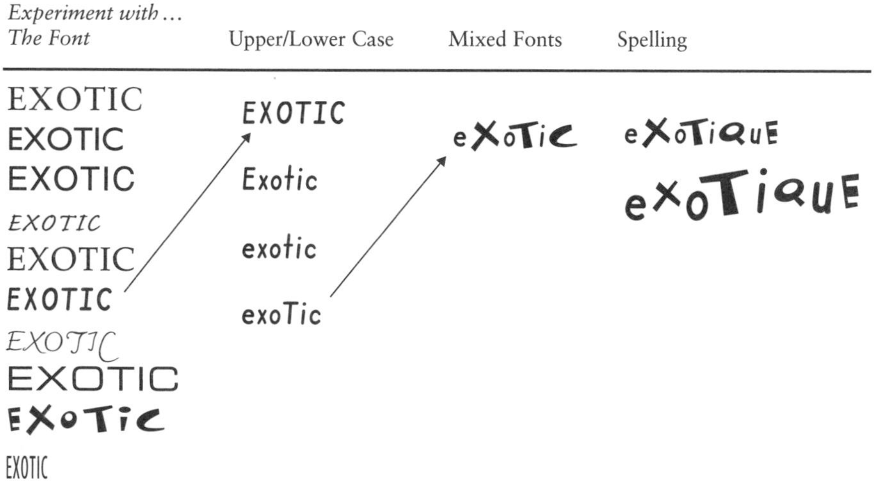

Experiment with ... The Font	Upper/Lower Case	Mixed Fonts	Spelling
EXOTIC EXOTIC EXOTIC EXOTIC EXOTIC EXOTIC EXOTIC EXOTIC EXOTIC EXOTIC	EXOTIC Exotic exotic exoTic	eXoTic	eXoTiQuE eXoTiQuE

FIGURE 12.6

The font selected for titles and labels conveys the theme of the trend board.

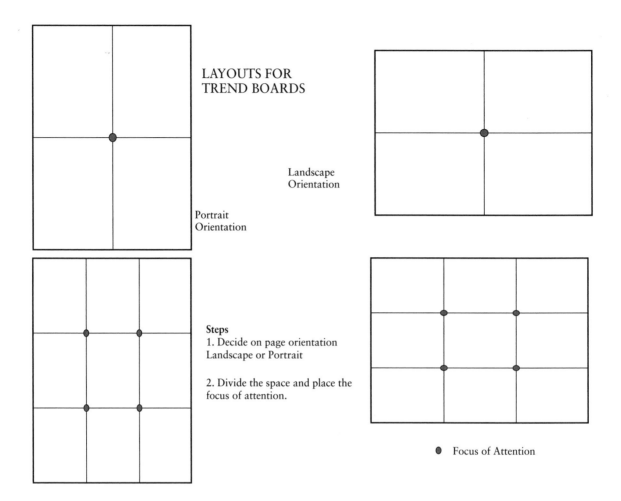

LAYOUTS FOR
TREND BOARDS

Landscape
Orientation

Portrait
Orientation

Steps
1. Decide on page orientation
Landscape or Portrait

2. Divide the space and place the
focus of attention.

● Focus of Attention

FIGURE 12.7

*The layout of the
trend board directs
the way the viewer's
eye takes in the
content. (Continued
on page 389.)*

relate to the theme. For example, colors associated with the jazz theme
might be red hot, blue note, and brass while colors in a trend story about
the influence of China on fashion might have names such as lacquer red,
jade, and ming blue.

The layout of the trend board controls how the viewer sees and compre-
hends the content (Figure 12.7). Forecasters use every design device to keep
the eye of the viewer moving within the borders of the trend board. The best
trend boards have a focal point with all the items arranged to move the
viewer's eye on a path around the board. Weak trend boards direct the
viewer's eye away from the images. "White space" (unfilled portions of

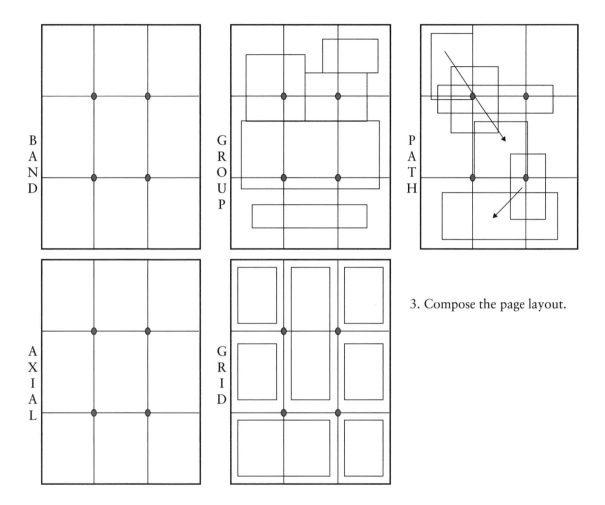

B
A
N
D

G
R
O
U
P

P
A
T
H

A
X
I
A
L

G
R
I
D

3. Compose the page layout.

the board) allow the viewer's eye to rest, but too much space can detract from interest in the images. The best effects are achieved when the space on the board is divided into interesting, arresting, uneven units rather than the more ordinary half-and-half.

Forecasters use trend boards at every stage in the forecasting process. Trend reporting begins with new developments in fibers, yarns, blends, and fabrics (Figure 12.8). Color forecasters use trend boards to communicate the seasonal color forecast. Fashion directors working for manufacturers and buying offices working for retailers use trend boards to report on fashion trends from the runways and the streets.

FIGURE 12.8

Forecasters scout for new developments in fibers, yarns, blends, and fabrics at international trade shows and then report their findings in trend presentations.

Activity 12.3 *Turn of Phrase*	Clip clever headlines from fashion stories and ads in magazines and trade journals. Analyze the inspiration and connections captured in these turns of phrase. Hear the rhythms as you read the headlines. Try revising them using your own concepts and ideas. Writing such headlines is a skill that can be cultivated. The first stage in developing the skill is awareness and the rest is practice.

Activity 12.4 *Colorful* *Language*	Select a trend identified in a fashion broadcast, magazine, or trade journal. Devise a set of five or more color names in harmony with that trend.

Activity 12.5 *Trend Board* *Evolution*	Begin trend board development by pinning up images on a bulletin board. Add and subtract images, add text, move things around. Let the trend board develop over several days. Consider making a formal trend board from the materials collected on the bulletin board only when the trend is clearly communicated in text and images.

PRESENTATION TECHNIQUES

The traditional way to communicate trend information is in a meeting. The forecaster speaks to the group using many types of visuals—trend boards, slides or videotapes of runway shows, sample garments, fabric swatches or short yardage, and color chips—to illustrate the trends and drive home points. To be effective, the forecaster needs public speaking ability. Performance issues such as tone of voice and gestures can make or break a presentation. The technical mastery of all possible visual techniques is beyond one person, but the fashion forecaster coordinates artists, graphic designers, and video production staff in developing the elements of the presentation.

Speaking about Fashion

Narrative Drive: Beginning, Middle, and End. Aggressive research and brilliant analysis of fashion trends can come to nothing if the presentation is lackluster. Research and analysis transform data into information, but the fashion forecaster must also be a performer interacting with the audience. Ideas are exciting only if they are communicated with power and assurance (Flacks & Rasberry, 1982).

The audience is on the side of the speaker. They come to the meeting with high hopes of spending an entertaining interlude learning new things. They also come with the distractions of their business and personal lives and the fear that they may be wasting time attending this meeting. It is up to the speaker to engage the audience immediately in a shared experience with a strong introduction.

Many speakers focus so much energy on the body of the speech—the main points, the actions that must occur, the recommendations—that they fail to prepare a compelling beginning. Yet, it is this beginning that introduces the audience to the style of the speaker and sets the tone of the presentation.

It is a myth that a good presentation begins with a joke. It is also a mistake to begin a speech with an apology: "I'm sorry I'm late," "I hope you will bear with me because I have a cold," "I haven't had time to prepare for this occasion because I was rushing to complete the trend boards." These openings turn audiences off. Such openings also cause the audience to focus on mistakes and on the presenter's nervousness (Flacks & Rasberry, 1982).

Instead, a good opening acknowledges the purpose of the meeting, sets the stage for the body of the speech, and captures the audience's attention. For example, surprise the audience with several examples of fashion behavior that seem unrelated and show a connection. Or, bring the audience into the data gathering experience by showing a street scene with a variety of people wearing looks that relate to the trends in the presentation. Or, enlighten the audience by showing the parallel between fashion behavior and something else happening in the culture such as a new dance craze or direction for interior design. Brief clips of interviews with consumers who are very pleased or very displeased with the state of fashion set the tone for a lively session. It is not difficult to find a creative and colorful way to begin a trend report. All it takes is brainstorming and a commitment to getting off on the right foot with the audience.

Speakers are frequently advised to "tell them what you're going to tell them, tell them, and then tell them what you told them." This is good advice. Hearing information presented is not as effective as reading for the transfer of knowledge. By repeating the main points three times in different ways, the presenter allows the audience to take in and process the meaning. Presenters often introduce the topic and provide a brief overview—a kind of teaser that will keep the audience looking forward to the unfolding of the ideas and information in the talk. Then, they proceed in an organized way to the core presentation using variety and change of pace to maintain interest. The final repetition comes in the conclusion of the presentation.

The ending is just as important as the beginning of a speech. The goal of the conclusion is to drive home the key points, motivate action, and leave the audience inspired and energized. The conclusion is not tacked on but flows smoothly from the core presentation. Perhaps the speaker returns to the images used in the beginning of the speech and elaborates on the content and meanings. Or, the conclusion could be a flash summary of the key trends. Whatever the content of the conclusion, there are several pitfalls to avoid. Some presenters attempt to present new information in the conclusion—a problem for the audience because there is not time for processing the ideas. Other presenters tell the audience that they are going to stop and then proceed on for several more points and several more minutes—a technique that irritates the audience. The audience needs a clear signal that the speech is over. The most poised presenters stop talking, smile, pause while maintaining eye contact with the audience, and either ask for questions or leave the podium if no question-and-answer session is scheduled.

Visuals with Impact. Trend boards are only one form of visuals used by forecasters. Actual trend boards can be used in a presentation or the trend board can be photographed either by conventional or digital camera and reproduced in sizes ranging from postcard to poster. The trend boards can be shown as slides, scanned into computer programs to become part of computer-generated slide shows, or printed as transparencies to be shown on an overhead projector.

In a short presentation of 10 to 30 minutes, it is difficult to find the time to show a video. But if the tape is edited and cued up properly, a short video segment can add realism to a presentation. Videos of runway shows and street fashion give the audience the feeling of seeing trends firsthand. When trends tie into larger cultural issues, video clips help the audience see the bigger picture. Videos of interviews either with consumers or with designers enliven a presentation.

The backbone of many presentations is computer-generated images using presentation software. With this technology everyone gets to be a graphic artist but the results are often amateurish. Visual impact improves when presenters follow a few guidelines by:

- Keeping the color choices simple, limiting the number of colors to three or four for the whole presentation, and avoiding complex screen patterns and shading.

- Creating a "master slide" with the color scheme, page design, and design elements such as bullets, and using that template consistently throughout the presentation.

- Improving the readability of the text by using a large, easy to read font and making the contrast between background and text strong—dark on a light background or light on a dark background.

- Following the K.I.S.S. principle in designing each slide: Keep It Simple and Short.

- Using appropriate clip art and importing graphics (photographs and sketches in digital form) to enhance the presentation.

Whatever the production method, visuals should not overpower the speaker or the content. The first task is finding the best, most representative visuals; the next, writing clear and compelling titles that are easy to read. Whether on a trend board or a computer-generated slide, a visually pleasing layout helps convey the message. When visuals are integrated carefully into the organization of a presentation, they add appeal and make the content more accessible to the audience.

Speaking with Confidence. Most people, even experienced speakers, have stage fright. After all, the speaker has lots to think about:

- The content of the speech.

- The comfort of the audience. (Can the audience hear? Is it too warm or too cool in the room? Are there distractions such as sounds coming from other rooms?)

- The attention level of the audience.

- Whether the speech is running too long or too short.

Still, there are ways to make the speaker more comfortable and more confident. The best tips come from actors for whom stage fright is just another challenge that comes along with their career choice (Flack & Rasberry, 1982).

The best remedy for stage fright is good preparation so that the speaker is completely fluent with the content, visuals, and order of presentation. Actors swear by rehearsal and so should speakers. Too often, the last minute rush to complete preparations deprives the speaker of time for practice. If a speaker is convinced that he or she has something worth listening to, then that confidence has a magnetic effect on the attention of the audience.

Stage fright just before getting up to speak is normal. A slight case of nerves gets the mind and body sharply awake and ready for a challenge. Excessive nervousness may come from worries about whether the audience will like the speaker. Skilled presenters shift the focus away from the personal by asking instead whether the audience will understand the trends. If the speech is well researched and thought out, the answer will be yes. With this realization comes confidence.

Nervousness sometimes results in shallow breathing. Taking slow deep breaths before arising to speak means that the body has stored enough oxygen to provide the energy to begin talking. After that, the momentum of the narrative and the importance of the points will carry the talk forward.

The audience is most comfortable when the presenter talks in a relaxed but energetic way. The style should be conversational. By speaking to different parts of the room during the talk and maintaining eye contact with the audience whenever possible the presenter draws more people into the content. Making points with gestures can be overdone, but gestures are appropriate to emphasize points. If the speaker enjoys the presentation and gets involved with the content, the audience will, too.

A professional forecaster is also a professional communicator. Polishing these skills is just as important as any other aspect of the job. There are excellent books on the topic for those who prefer to learn on their own. There are also classes and seminars for those who like group learning situations. There are organizations for people who want to continuously improve their speaking abilities through practice with helpful feedback from fellow members. Finally, there are vocal coaches who work with people one-on-one to overcome problems and improve their comfort level with public speaking.

Activity 12.6 Breathing Lessons	Invite an acting teacher, vocal coach, or speech teacher to class to discuss breathing techniques and performance. Ask them to teach several breathing exercises that are helpful to public speakers in preparing and delivering a talk.

Equipment Management. Ask any teacher, salesperson, or lecturer about what can go wrong during a presentation and he or she will talk about equipment problems—a slide projector that jams, an overhead projector that blows a bulb, a VCR that keeps stopping abruptly and ejecting the tape, a data projector that will not focus. Even an easel that is the wrong size or too light to hold a trend board can cause problems. Anything can happen and frequently does!

The only cure for these disasters is a sense of humor and some technical expertise. Sometimes the sponsoring group or the meeting facility provides equipment managers who troubleshoot problems. If none of these helpers are available, then the presenter must come up with a solution.

A trend report has some built-in problems and solutions in terms of equipment. The forecaster may use actual trend boards in the presentation. Even if there is no easel, trend boards can be propped up against a chair or even against the wall and the talk can proceed. Trend boards that have been reproduced as slides or transparencies carry the risk of equipment failure, but slide and transparency projectors are generally reliable and replacement equipment and bulbs are usually available. If trend boards have been scanned or digitally photographed as part of a computer-generated slide show, then both a computer and a data projector are required. The most common problem in this situation is failing to have the proper cables to join the equipment together. Whatever the equipment, here are some tips for the fashion forecaster who is also a road warrior (a person who travels and must perform in unfamiliar surrounding):

- **Call Ahead**

Check with the presentation sponsor well ahead of the date of the talk. Discuss the equipment available, size of the room, and technical assistance.

- **Come Equipped**

If there are any doubts about equipment at the location, bring equipment along. Portable overhead projectors, laptop computers, and data projectors are all made to travel. Equipment can often be rented if the presentation is in a metropolitan location. All equipment should include backup bulbs, cables, power cords, and extension cords.

- **Carry Backup**

If the presentation is on the hard drive of a laptop computer, carry a duplicate on a floppy disk. If a computer-generated presentation has been transferred to slides, carry a set of the identical presentation as transparencies. If the presentation consists of slides picturing fashions, street scenes, and trend boards, carry an extra copy of key slides just in case slides are lost or destroyed by an equipment malfunction. If possible, carry two copies of any videotape that will be used in the presentation.

- **Leave a Paper Trail**

Regardless of the equipment, plan to distribute printed copies of the key points to the audience. It is a courtesy to provide paper for notes and a reminder of the key points. Computer-generated slide shows offer a convenient way to accomplish this task because they allow the presentation to be printed out six slides to the page. Some speakers have the handout on the chairs prior to the arrival of the audience. Others pass them out before the beginning of the talk. With notes in hand, even if all the equipment fails, the speaker and audience have a joint reference point and the talk can proceed.

Whenever possible, an experienced speaker will scout the room ahead of time, rearranging the equipment in a way that suits the presentation content and the audience. Sometimes a room is not set up for a meeting until a few minutes before time to begin, but if there is time, a little practice in the space where the presentation will take place helps build confidence. Finally, visuals are an important part of a trend report but they are not the most important part. The most important part is the speaker and the insights and information he or she is there to share. An experienced speaker does not let equipment (or equipment problems) stand between the messenger, the message, and the audience.

Activity 12.7 *Familiarity* *Banishes Fear*	Gather up every different type of slide and overhead transparency projector available. Learn how to turn them on, how to focus the images, and how to operate all the features such as remote controls. Check through the manuals (if they still exist) for directions about changing bulbs. If a "wired classroom" is available (one equipped with several projection devises, a VCR and monitor, and perhaps a computer), schedule a demonstration and practice using the equipment.

New Presentation Tools

Today, trend boards and other presentations can be completely computer generated. Graphics can be captured into the computer from Web sites, scanned in, copied from disks, and transferred from digital cameras. Images can be manipulated with software packages that crop, resize, shift colors, alter focus, and create many other special effects. Text can be added in different fonts, sizes, and colors. Original graphics can be created with drawing and painting programs. Styles, colorways, and textile designs can be illustrated with computer-aided design (CAD) programs. CAD makes sharing images between design teams, manufacturers, and retailers routine.

Although this sounds like a great advance, not all problems have been eliminated. Computer hardware and software for such graphic-intensive uses are expensive. Graphics take up a lot of storage space on computer hard drives and floppies. Decisions must be made about the resolution (the number of pixels horizontally and vertically that make up the graphic) depending on the image, the scanner, and the computer. The higher the resolution, the more memory required to store the graphic. Without sophisticated color calibration software and color matching between the original color of the images, how they appear on the computer screen and how they look printed out require compromise or careful trial-and-error experimentation. Because all the problems are not worked out, most forecasters use a combination of traditional and computer-based techniques.

Nowadays multimedia presentations of forecasting information arrive as interactive CD-ROMs or on Web sites. Many of the design principles for creating presentations can be transferred to the design of a Web site. Software packages and books are available to guide users in designing Web sites. Web sites can incorporate short video clips and sound bites along with text, graphics, and photographs. Additionally, Web sites offer the opportunity for interactive participation by visitors in chat rooms and feedback via e-mail. Taking full advantage of these possibilities awaits a new wave of fashion forecasting professionals.

Key Terms and Concepts

Analytical Thinking	Embryonic Trends	Minor Trends
Category	Information Design	Scope of a Trend
Concept Boards	Interaction Design	Sensory Design
Continuum	Intuition	Timing of a Trend
Convergent Thinking	Knowledge	Trend Boards
Data	Major Trends	Trend Map
Directional Trend	Metaphor	Trial Balloons
Divergent Thinking		

Discussion Questions

A forecaster is preparing for a presentation on seasonal fashion change. In the audience will be design, merchandising, and marketing executives. Use the following questions to summarize the chapter and review the steps a forecaster would use in preparing and presenting trend information.

Data gathering and pattern recognition: What are data for a trend presentation and how are they gathered? What two ways of thinking about the data aid in pattern recognition?

Transforming the data into knowledge: What is information design? How can data be organized in a way that creates knowledge? What is interaction design? Why is it important? What is sensory design? What does sensory design have to do with the fashion forecaster's job of presenting fashion trends?

Trend reporting: Why is labeling a trend important to communicating a trend? What is the difference between major and minor trends? How is the quality of a trend assessed? What are the attributes of a good trend or concept board? What stages are involved in the development of the theme for a concept board?

Presentation techniques: How can a fashion forecaster improve the performance aspects of the presentation? What are the attributes of a good visual presentation?

Technology issues: How can a presenter handle equipment and technology as they relate to information design and interaction design? How effective will the Web-based and CAD-based presentations be compared to traditional trend board presentations?

Additional Forecasting Activities

Trends on Board. Develop trend boards in class. Collect a large number of clippings from catalogs and magazines. Brainstorm possible themes that unite the elements. Choose a phrase that captures the theme. Develop a text style that works with the theme. Use care and craftsmanship to complete the board. Display the trend boards in class and discuss the content and the techniques of actually making a trend board.

Forum of Experts. Invite a representative from the local art supply store, a local artist, and a product developer or merchandiser from an apparel or accessory firm in your area to critique the trend boards. Ask the art supply representative to make suggestions about the selection of the board itself (usually mat board, illustration board, or foamcore board) and the choice of adhesives. Ask the artist to discuss design composition of paintings and how the concepts transfer to trend boards. Ask the company representative to evaluate the quality of the themes, the connection between the theme and the illustrations, and the level of professionalism. The company representatives may also be able to share techniques used in the industry.

Critiquing the Pros. Regional apparel marts usually include trend seminars for attendees. Fashion students are often invited to attend these presentations. As an audience member, students have the dual opportunity to learn about new fashion directions and to evaluate the skills of the presenter. Observe which visuals are particularly helpful and vivid, what qualities of voice and manner are especially engaging, and how the presenter relates to the audience. Incorporate the best techniques into your next presentation.

APPENDIX

Bill Glazer & Associates
7955 West Third Street
Los Angeles, CA 90048
213 937-7956
Forecasting and retail reporting on Los Angeles and Europe for men's, women's, and children's markets.

Color Association of the United States
589 Eighth Avenue, 12th Floor
New York, NY 10018
212 582-6884
http://www.colorassociation.com
Color forecasting.

The Color Box
29 West 38th Street, 9th Floor
New York, NY 10018
212 921-1399
Color forecasting.

Color Marketing Group
5904 Richmond Highway, Suite 408
Alexandria, VA 22303-1864
703 329-8500
http://www.colormarketing.org

Color Portfolio
201 East 17th Street
New York, NY 10003

Color Prospective by Marie-Pierre
488 Seventh Avenue, Suite #9H
New York, NY 10018
212 563-4604
Color and trend forecasting.

Concepts in Colour
2 West 32nd Street, Suite #301
New York, NY 10001
212 967-5688
Color forecasting.

THE COTTONWORKS Fabric Library
Cotton Incorporated
488 Madison Avenue
New York, NY 10022
212 413-8300
http://www.cottoninc.com
Color and textile forecasting for cotton and cotton-rich fabrics.

D-3/Doneger Design Direction
463 Seventh Avenue, 3rd Floor
New York, NY 10018
212 560-3720
http://www.doneger.com
Color and trend forecasts for women's, men's, and children's wear.

Design Options
112 West Ninth Street, Suite #1026
Los Angeles, CA 90015
213 622-9094
Color forecasting, fabric research, and
retail shopping.

Eiseman Center for Color Information
and Training
Leatrice Eiseman, Director
8555 Ferncliff Avenue
Bainbridge Island, WA 98110
206 842-4456
Color forecasting.

Eleanor Douglas Analyst
48 Churchill Drive
Clifton, NJ 07013
201 471-3484
Trend reports on ready-to-wear, accessories, and children's markets.

Fashion Dossier
1359 Broadway, 22nd Floor
New York, NY 10018
212 967-1919
Forecasting for knits and wovens.

The Fashion Service
1412 Broadway, Suite #1410
New York, NY 10018
212 704-0035
Color and trend reporting and forecasting.

Here & There
104 West 40th Street, 11th Floor
New York, NY 10018-3617
212 354-9014
Fashion forecasting and reporting.

Huepoint
39 West 37th Street, 18th Floor
New York, NY 10018-6217
Phone: 212 921-2025
Color forecasting services.

Lucey Harley Associates
135 East 83rd Street
New York, NY 10018
212 768-4111
Forecasts future megatrends, color,
silhouettes, and fabric.

Norma Morris Design Products
110 West 40th Street, Suite #306
New York, NY 10018
212 730-0758
Seasonal colors for men's, women's, and
children's markets. Also forecasting style
and theme inspiration.

Pantone Inc.
590 Commerce Blvd.
Carlstadt, NJ 07072
201 935-5500
http://www.pantone.com
Color forecasting and color specification
system.

Pat Tunsky, Inc.
1040 Avenue of the Americas, 23rd Floor
New York, NY 10018
Color and fashion forecasting.

Promostyl USA
80 West 40th Street
New York, NY 10018
212 921-7930
http://www.promostyl.com
Color and fashion forecasting.

Trend Union
90 Riverside Drive, Suite, #9D
New York, NY 10024
212 724-3825
Color and fashion forecasting.

Fashion Reporting

Bureau de Style
Hayson Hahn, Director
989 Avenue of the Americas
New York, NY 10015-5410
212 947-4600

The Photo Report
11 Fourth Avenue, Suite #9K
New York, NY 10003
212 477-3075
Photo reporting on retail in Europe and
Rio de Janiero.

Money in the Bank
121 Madison Avenue
New York, NY 10016
212 683-7418
Photo retail report with print, color, textile, and apparel direction from European
boutiques.

Design Resources/Trends West
315 West Ninth Street, Suite #701
Los Angeles, CA 90015
213 623-9400
Reports on Los Angeles retail scene.

Style Masters International
110 West 40th Street, Suite #508
New York, NY 10018
212 764-2411
Fashion forecasting photo service.

Fabric Councils & Commissions

Acrylic Council Inc.
1285 Avenue of the Americas, 35th Floor
New York, NY 10019
212 554-4040

American Wool Council
50 Rockefeller Plaza, Suite #830
New York, NY 10020
212 245-6710

Cotton Incorporated
488 Madison Avenue
New York, NY 10022
212 413-8300
http://www.cottoninc.com

International Linen Promotion
Commission
200 Lexington Avenue, Suite 225
New York, NY 10016

Mohair Council of America
499 Seventh Avenue, 12th Floor
New York, NY 10018
212 736-1898

Natural Cotton Colours, Inc.
67 North Tegner Street
P.O. Box #66
Wickenburg, AZ 85390
520 684-7199

Polyester Council of America
1675 Broadway
New York, NY 10018

The Woolmark Co. (formerly The Wool Bureau)
330 Madison Avenue, 19th Floor
New York, NY 10017
212 986-6222

Consumer Research

About Women, Inc.
33 Broad Street
Boston, MA 02109
617 723-7107
Specializes in marketing to women.

Age Wave, Inc.
2000 Powell St. #1555
Emeryville, CA 94608-1804
510 652-9099
www.agewave.com
Tracking lifestyle factors among consumers over 50.

Claritas
1525 Wilson Blvd, Suite 1000
Arlington, VA 22209
703 812-2700
PRIZM®, a lifestyle cluster system for consumer segmentation by neighborhoods.

Cooper Marketing Group Inc.
1043 Forest Ave.
Oak Park, IL 60302-1311
708 386-1233

Emerging Adult Research, Inc. (EAR)
73 Spring Street, Suite 205
New York, NY 10012
212 925-3800
http://www.earinc.net
Tracks youth culture.

Iconoculture
2105 Irving Avenue South
Minneapolis, MN 55405
612 377-0087
http://www.iconoculture.com
Trends forecasting as a marketing tool.

Kidfacts Research
34405 West Twelve Mile Road, Suite 121
Farmington Hills, MI 48331
810 489-7056
Tracks youth culture.

Lambesis
100 Via De La Valle
Solana Beach, CA 92075-1913
619 794-6444
Tracks youth culture.

Langer Associates, Inc.
Judith Langer, President
19 West 44th Street, Suite 1601
New York, NY 10036
212 391-0350
http://www.qualitative.com
Specialists in qualitative studies—focus groups, interviewing.

Strategic Mapping
70 Seaview Avenue
P.O. Box 10250
Stamford, CT 06904
ClusterPLUS®, consumer segmentation based on clustering by U.S. neighborhoods.

Teenage Research Unlimited/Kids
Research Unlimited
601 Skokie Blvd.
Northbrook, IL 60062
708 564-3440
Tracks youth culture.

Yankelovich Partners, Inc.
101 Merritt 7 Corporate Park
Norwalk, CN 06851
203 846-0100
Marketing research and consulting including syndicated research programs
like the Yankelovich MONITOR®.

Youth Market Intelligence
149 Fifth Ave.
New York, NY 10010-6801
212 777-2063
Tracks youth culture.

Zandl Group (formerly Xtreme, Inc.)
270 Lafayette Street #612
New York, NY 10012-3327
212 274-1222
Tracks youth culture.

Business Consulting / Marketing

Inferential Focus
200 Madison Ave #1904
New York, NY 10016-4001
212 683-2060

Faith Popcorn's BrainReserve
59 East 64th Street
New York, NY 10021
http://wwwfaithpopcorn.com

Carol Farmer Associates, Inc.
2250 Bethel Blvd.
Boca Raton, FL
561 243-2800
www.carolfarmer.com
Consumer trend analyst and futurist.

Futurists

Paul Saffo
Institute for the Future
2744 Sand Hill Rd.
Menlo Park, CA 94025-7020
650 854-6322

Marvin Cetron
Forecasting International Ltd.
3612 Boat Dock Dr.
Falls Church, VA 22041-1413
703 379-5600

Lester Brown
Worldwatch Institute
1776 Massachusetts Ave NW, 8th Floor
Washington, DC 20036-1904
202 452-1999
Environmental & economic issues.

Roger Selbert
Growth Strategies (formerly FutureScan)
1930 Century Park West, 2nd Floor
Los Angeles, CA 90067
310 552-3757
Trend-based business, strategic, communications consulting.

Media Analysis

Weiner, Edrich, Brown, Inc.
200 E. 33rd St.
Suite 9I
New York, NY 10016-4827
212 889-7007
Detect emerging trends in media.

The Trends Research Institute Inc.
Gerald Celente, Director
P.O. Box 660
Rhineback, NY 12572-0660
914-876-6700
www.trendsresearch.com

GLOSSARY

Abstracting The process of identifying underlying similarities or differences in individual elements and interrelationships across products and design collections.

Achromatic Pure neutrals such as black, white, and gray.

Aggregated The term for point-of-sale data when figures on individual products or stock-keeping units (SKUs) are summarized and combined by categories.

Analogous Color combinations made from closely related colors adjacent on the color wheel.

Analysis The phase in forecasting when a trend or phenomenon is dissected to achieve a more complete understanding of its components.

Analytical Thinking Thinking that is logical, linear, and based on facts.

Androgyny Appearance styles that combine traits associated with masculinity and femininity.

Anomalies In information analysis, data that do not fit expectations.

Artificial Neural Networks Computer software that can be trained to recognize patterns by repeatedly being presented with examples in a trial-and-error fashion until the network reaches a level of accuracy.

Automated Replenishment System A collaborative effort between a retailer and a manufacturer involving vendor-designed assortment plans and automatic shipping to keep stock at optimum levels.

Backcast A method of tracing the development of fashion ideas or trends backward to their origin points.

Benchmarking In competitive analysis, comparing a company with other firms considered best in terms of efficient operations.

Blend A combination of two or more natural, man-made, or manufactured fibers in a single yarn or fabric to provide desirable attributes.

Boolean Operators The words AND, OR, and NOT attached to a keyword search to indicate relationships.

Boom and Bust Cycles Periodic swings in popularity between times when an item is "in" and "out" of fashion.

Brainstorming Group creativity session in which a diverse group of individuals meets to discuss some issue or topic with a neutral moderator keeping the session on track.

Brand Image A distinct set of tangible and intangible characteristics that identify a brand to a target customer.

Brand Loyalty The degree to which a consumer purchases and repurchases a brand again and again.

Brand Name The trademarked and proprietary name a company uses to promote its products through advertising, labeling, and other marketing initiatives.

Brand Recognition The degree to which consumers are aware of a brand name and brand image.

Brand Tiers A strategy in which a company owns multiple brands in a product category and positions each for a different target consumer and different retail channels, differentiating between the brands in image, pricing, packaging, placement, and presentation.

Branding A competitive strategy that targets customers with products, advertising, and promotion organized around a coherent message as a way to encourage purchase and repurchase of products from the same company.

Bubble Up (also known as the **Trickle-Up Theory**) A chain of events beginning with streetstyle innovation, picked up and popularized through media, disseminated to street kids in other locales, and finally finding its way into a designer's collection.

Business Cycle The cyclical nature of the economy as it passes through the rising and falling phases of prosperity and stagnation.

Business-to-Business Partners Firms closely allied as suppliers, manufacturers, or customers.

Butterfly Effect An insight derived from chaos theory—points of instability in the system mean that a small push in a nonlinear system can have large consequences and that tiny differences in the initial conditions of an event swell into overwhelming differences later on.

Buzz The way trends spread through the media; the excitement about something new, and a feeling of being in the know because of insider information.

Category A form of organization based on the similarities or differences between elements.

Category Management A collaborative strategy between a retailer and a manufacturer in which the manufacturer acts as a specialist in forecasting, keeping the right flow of merchandise going to the selling floor; provides expertise in a category, including trends, fit, silhouettes, and finishes; and makes recommendations on merchandising assortment, display, and inventory controls in that product category on a store-by-store basis.

Change Agents The small group of innovators who begin the diffusion process by spreading trends visually and verbally to others in their group.

Chaos Theory A scientific theory based on the concept of orderly disorder—recognizable but complex patterns that form, dissolve, and reform in infinite diversity.

Chase and Flight (also known as the **Trickle-Down Theory**) The idea that fashion change is triggered by imitators who chase the status markers of the elite in a drive toward upward social mobility; flight because the elite responded by flying away toward new forms of differentiation.

Chroma (see **Saturation**)

Classic An item or style that is introduced, gains visibility, generates multiple purchases or replacement purchases, and reaches a plateau level of widespread acceptance that persists over a long time period; an item or style that delivers at least the core attributes desirable to the consumer while avoiding extremes in styling.

Coattail Effect The phase in the life cycle of a trend when it catches the attention of people in the industry who recognize the potential of the trend and rush to produce it in their own lines.

Cohort A group of consumers who share preferences and demographic characteristics—the basic unit of consumer research.

Collective Selection The idea that individuals in large numbers choose among competing styles those that "click" or "connect" with the spirit of the times, thereby forming a feedback loop between the fashion industry and the consumer —a feedback loop moderated by aesthetic trends and social-psychological processes.

Color Association of the United States (CAUS) Based in Manhattan, a not-for-profit trade association formed in 1915 to provide color forecasting to members, including corporations and designers concerned with apparel, interiors and furnishings, paint, and automobiles.

Color Cycles Periodic shifts in color preferences and the patterns of repetition in the popularity of colors.

Color Key Program A system developed to assist in coordinating paint colors and apparel based on whether a color has cool or warm overtones.

Color Marketing Group (CMG) An international nonprofit association formed in 1962 to provide advanced color information for industries from apparel to automobiles, from health care to corporate identity, and based in the Washington, D.C., area.

Color Palette The eight to ten colors selected during the initial design phase that signal the personality of the collection.

Color Story (see **Color Palette**)

Color Wheel The simplest version of organizing color into a graphic form that helps designers form harmonious color groupings and specify colors.

Colorways Color groups and combinations used for an item, ensemble, or group within a line.

Compatibility An estimate of harmony between the innovation and the values and norms of potential adopters.

Competitive Advantage A situation in which, for a period of time, there is an asymmetry in the marketplace that favors one company over another.

Competitive Analysis The process of using public sources to develop a detailed and accurate view of the market environment—both trends in the industry and what the competition is likely to do.

Competitive Benchmarking In competitive analysis, comparing a company with its direct competitors on a set of measures such as capital investment, productivity, and product quality.

Competitive Intelligence (see **Competitive Analysis**)

Complementary A color scheme formed from colors directly across from each other on the color wheel.

Complexity A gauge of the difficulty faced by a consumer in understanding and using the innovation.

Complexity Theory A scientific theory that looks at complex systems composed of many independent agents (consumers, fashion firms, media) that interact with each other in a great many ways, interactions that allow the system to undergo spontaneous self-organization.

Computer-Aided Design (CAD) Computer hardware and software designed to assist the designer in creating and presenting design concepts.

Concept Boards Collections of clipping, objects, fabrics, color chips, and other items arrayed on a stiff cardboard foundation and used in the product development stage to coordinate the efforts of the design team or to present visual concepts to the manufacturer's sales force and retail buyers.

Concept Garments Sample garments made to show the potential of developmental, performance, or other innovative fabrics in apparel.

Conspicuous Consumption The behavior of the upper strata of the social system who display wealth by participating in an extravagant lifestyle, including the acquisition of homes and furnishings and the wearing of apparel made by expensive modes of production and using costly materials; originally used to refer to the lifestyle of the wealthy around the turn of the 20th century.

Conspicuous Counterconsumption The practice of status denial, as when people with wealth and status choose to dress down.

Conspicuous Leisure An attribute of the upper strata of the social system that does not have to work for a living and can participate in an extravagant lifestyle of travel, entertainment, and the pursuit of pleasure.

Consumer Adoption Process The mental process used by individual consumers in deciding between adopting or failing to adopt an innovation.

Consumer Cohorts Groups of consumers who share similar demographic and psychographic characteristics.

Consumer Confidence An index of consumer feelings of economic well-being, used to predict future consumer expenditures and turning points in the business cycle.

Consumer Segment A portion of the population identified by demographic characteristics such as age, gender, ethnicity, and income.

Consumer Segmentation The practice of dividing the total population into homogeneous groups that can be targeted with products and product promotion.

Consumer Stylists Innovative individuals who combine apparel, accessories, and other appearance characteristics to create variations on fashionable styles or to create new styles.

Content Analysis A method of analyzing information involving extracting significant data from source material, classifying it, and noting patterns and regularities in the data.

Continuum A form of organization that arrays items in terms of an underlying value scale.

Convergent Thinking A style of thinking that seeks one conclusion, the best alternative, one meaning.

Converters Companies that specialize in sourcing base fabrics and using contractors to dye, print, and finish them for apparel manufacturers unable to meet large minimum orders or who require short lead times.

Corporate Culture The personality of a company, including the way it does business, its relationship to consumers, its style of communication, and the way the company operates internally.

Correlation or Regression Techniques Statistical techniques for comparing how a change in one variable (e.g., advertising effort or some outside factor) causes a change in another variable (e.g., sales volume).

Counterfeit The term for a product that is a close copy of a designer's product and is passed off as authentic.

Counter-Trends Trends that contrast with another prevailing set of trends, both of which offer opportunities for businesses because of the contradictory aspects of human behavior.

Couture Extravagant, high-priced clothing that shows off the ultimate level of dressmaking design and skill, and which is made-to-order for specific clients; also known as haute couture.

Cross Dyeing A piece dyeing process that produces multiple colors in a blended fabric when dyes that are reactive with each fiber are used in a single dye bath.

Cross-Shoppers Consumers who shop up and down the spectrum from discount stores to luxury lines at department stores

Cultural Drift Directional pointers for the way society is moving.

Cycles Reoccurring rhythmic patterns in styles or prices with a fixed, regular alternation between highs and lows.

Data The raw material of forecasting, including the observations, research findings, and discoveries uncovered during the exploratory stages of the process.

Data Mining The ability to search through vast stores of data to answer complex business questions, discover patterns in databases, and find predictive information that lies outside experts' expectations.

Data Warehouse A system for storing and delivering massive quantities of data.

Decision Trees Analysis software that classifies a data set in a series of two-way splits that can be expressed as a set of rules that can be applied to a new, unclassified data set.

Decomposition The process of breaking down a pattern to analyze the underlying factors influencing it.

Delphi Method A method of polling used to elicit expert input using a method that combines brainstorming and debate to generate ideas, clarify complex issues, and reach consensus.

Demand An expansion of orders resulting from an influx of new customers buying for the first time or replacement or repeat purchases by users.

Demi-Couture Various experiments by designers seeking to expand the client base for couture by mixing designer ready-to-wear for simple pieces with more elaborate made-to-order pieces.

Demographics Consumer characteristics such as age, gender, marital status, and occupation.

Depth Interview A research technique in which a researcher interviews a single consumer at a time in a lengthy dialogue aimed at discovering the meaning products or brands have for that consumer.

Designer Name Brands Brands based on the aesthetic taste and reputation of a known designer; these products are developed by the designer's firm or through licenses, sold to retailers through the wholesale market, and carried by retailers who often compete in the same market area.

Designer Ready-to-Wear Expensive, luxurious, and beautifully executed clothes manufactured using mass production techniques and, therefore, not as costly as couture.

Developmental Fabrics Newly developed innovations in fiber, yarn, or finishing that provide special characteristics or properties and that are presented for consideration to designers and manufacturers.

Differentiation The attempt to present a product in a way that highlights how it is different and better than other products of its type.

Diffusion Curve A visualization of diffusion of innovation as a bell curve showing the progressive participation of consumers, beginning with innovators and early adopters, proceeding to majority adoption, and concluding with laggards.

Diffusion Process The process by which innovations spread within a social system, including the kind of consumers participating in each stage.

Direct Competitors Companies that sell the same general product to the same customers in the same distribution channels.

Directional Trend The stage of trend development when fashion innovators and fashion forward retailers adopted the look, style, detail, accessory, or other fashion idea and public awareness of the idea begins to build.

Disinformation In competitive analysis, inaccuracies in published articles, from people misrepresenting their knowledge or expertise, and from countering moves by competitors seeking to protect their secrets.

Dissonance A stage in the consumer adoption process that occurs after purchase when the consumer questions the adoption decision and seeks reassurance.

Distant Opinion Leader The idea that celebrities and popular culture serve as a source of new meanings and as a conduit to transmit those meanings to consumers.

Divergent Thinking A style of thinking in which the goal is to generate many alternatives, many possible meanings.

Double Complement Color combinations consisting of two sets of complementary colors.

Drape The way the finished fabric hangs on the body—whether it stands away from the body or clings to the curves.

Economic Risk The risk of performance problems after the purchase, the risk that the purchase price may reduce the ability to buy other products, or the risk that the price will fall after purchase.

Edge of Chaos The balance point in complex systems where order and chaos come together in a sort of rolling equilibrium.

Embryonic Trends The first stages of trend development when a look, style, detail, accessory, or other fashion idea is poised to take off, fashion insiders are tracking its development, but the public is largely unaware of its existence.

Enjoyment Risk The risk of becoming bored by the purchase or not liking it as much as expected.

Enterprise Portals The use of Web-type browsers in corporate situations to enable managers and knowledge workers to access real-time and historical information.

Environmental Scanning A method of systematically tracking and analyzing trends using media sources.

Erogenous Zone The idea that any part of the female body may become the focus of erotic attention and that fashion change is partly powered by the shifting of this zone.

Evolution of a Trend Developmental stages for a trend including introduction, awareness, participation by early adopters, increasing visibility until mainstream consumers join in—each stage offering the opportunity for corporations, brands, and entrepreneurs to take note of the trend and capitalize on it.

Extranets Business-to-business private networks for transactions and collaborative forecasting between suppliers and customers.

Fabric Finishing Processes used to manipulate the appearance characteristics, performance, or hand of a fabric, including mechanical or chemical techniques and the application of films to the fabric surface.

Fabric Libraries A collection of seasonal fabric samples where designers and product developers come to research fabrications and source fabrics from many manufacturers.

Fad A trend of short duration that is introduced, gains rapid visibility and acceptance among a relatively small contingent of consumers, and fades quickly because it is not supported by corresponding lifestyle changes.

Fashion A style that is popular in the present or a set of trends that have been accepted by a wide audience.

Fashion Counts A method for researching fashion change that consists of finding a suitable source for fashion images, sampling the images in a systematic way, applying a standardized set of measurements or observations to each image, and analyzing the data to reveal patterns of fashion change.

Fashion Cycles The idea that there exist discernible cyclical patterns in fashion that recur over time.

Fashion Leaders People to whom others look for advice about clothes or other aesthetic products; also known as opinion leaders.

Fashion Weeks Periods of time when seasonal fashion shows are held in each of the four fashion capitals—New York, London, Milan, and Paris—along with associated trade shows and showroom events.

Fieldwork A method of data gathering involving observation and interviews.

Filament A continuous strand of man-made or manufactured fiber as it comes from the spinneret or a continuous strand from the unwound cocoon of a silk moth.

Findings Functional items on apparel such as elastic, interfacing, thread, and zippers.

Fixed-Model Time-Series (FMTS) A set of statistical techniques that begins with the idea that the forecast for next month's sales is the average of all past sales.

Flow The process that occurs when a trend passes from a relatively small group of fashion-forward consumers to other groups across social boundaries of age, income, and lifestyle.

Focus Group(s) A qualitative method of research based on informal, uncensored talk about products in a group interview setting.

Focus Group Moderator The research professional who leads the focus group discussion using a schedule of questions previously agreed to by the client.

Forecasting The process of anticipating future developments by watching for signals of change in current situations and events and applying the forecasting frameworks to predict possible outcomes.

Garment Dyeing The process of applying color after the fabric has been made into garments.

Gatekeepers People or groups that filter the innovative ideas proposed by designers and street fashion and determine which will be disseminated widely and which will be discarded—a role played today by journalists, manufacturers, and retailers.

Gender Bending (see **Androgyny**) Slang for styles that combine masculine and feminine characteristics, including those that border on caricature.

Gender Blending Slang for combining masculine and feminine characteristics in a way that merges the two sensibilities.

Generational Cohorts Group of consumers who share the same "age location" in history and a collective mindset.

Generic Name The common name given to a new fiber when it is developed by the U.S. Federal Trade Commission (e.g., nylon, polyester, spandex, and lyocell).

Genetic Algorithms Computer software that treats rules as if those rules were DNA in biological evolution and allows those rules to evolve by genetic combination, mutation, and natural selection until workable rules sets emerge.

Geodemographics A research approach that links geography and demographics to show the clustering of similar people in a neighborhood and associate the cluster with purchase behavior.

Hand The way finished fabric feels when handled, including properties such as its ability to recover when stretched or compressed.

High Culture Events, activities, directions, and trends derived from the fine and performance arts.

Historic Continuity The concept that fashion is a steady evolution of styles, including the continual recurring of symbolism and elements of decoration.

Hue The color itself in a color system.

Hype Awareness and excitement about an innovation created through the purposeful efforts of public relations executives.

Idea Chain A set of linked events that move a phenomenon from a subculture to the mainstream or a graphic representation of that movement.

In-Depth Interview (see **Depth Interview**)

Indirect Competitors Companies that do not sell the same or similar products but offer alternatives that may deflect a customer away from a purchasing situation.

Industrial Espionage Information-gathering activities that involve breaking the law to collect competitive data.

Influentials Change agents who are recognized by others for their abilities to adopt and display innovations and who tend to establish the standards of dress for others in the social group.

Information Cascades The process that occurs when a fashion leader acts to adopt or reject the innovation; frequently others imitate the action, beginning a cascade of decisions either positive (all individuals in the group adopt the innovation) or negative (all reject the innovation).

Information Design A process in presentation planning that transforms data, the raw material of presentations, into valuable, meaningful information by identifying and explaining the relationships and patterns between data.

Innovation Something new submitted to the public's attention for approval and adoption.

Innovators People who adopt new product innovations relatively earlier than others in their social group.

Intensity (see **Saturation**)

Interaction Design A process in presentation planning in which consideration is given to creating compelling experiences for the audience.

Internet Agents Software programs that traverse the World Wide Web, moving from one document to another through the hyperlinks at the sites, and retrieving relevant information.

Intranets Corporate information networks that use similar technology to the Internet but are restricted to the internal use of a corporation.

Intuition Perceptive feelings about how things fit together, including pattern recognition and leaps of insight.

Just in Time An approach to inventory control whereby components are not stockpiled but are instead made available close to the time when they are needed in the production process.

Knitting The process of forming fabric by looping together yarns in successive rows.

Knockoff The practice of copying designs from higher priced lines into lower priced lines either as line-for-line copies or as close facsimiles, but without labeling the result with originator's label.

Knowledge The goal of presentation design, achieved when the audience understands the information and can use it in decision making.

Labeling A name, label, or slogan that acts as an identifier for a trend and serves to connect the trend to spirit of the times in an original and catchy way.

Leading Indicators A statistically weighted set of economic factors likely to signal a turning point in the business cycle—peaks and troughs of the leading indicator anticipate those seen in sales by 6 to 12 months.

Legitimation An optional stage in a consumer's adoption process during which the consumer seeks additional information about the innovation.

Level (in Time-Series Forecasting) The horizontal line showing sales history as if demand was stable with no trend, seasonality, or noise in the sales data.

Linear Explanations such as the scientific method which attempt to link cause and effect and establish relationships that can be graphed in two dimensions.

Long Wave Phenomenon A reoccurring pattern in prices or styles in which the movement rises and falls with differences in duration and magnitude, velocity and momentum across time periods.

Long-Term Forecasting A forecasting timeline sufficient for decisions related to repositioning or extending product lines, initiating new businesses, reviving brand images, or planning new retail concepts.

Low Culture Events, activities, directions, and trends derived from local special interest groups outside of mainstream awareness.

Mainstream Trends or styles that are acceptable to the majority of consumers.

Major Trends A distinction applied by a forecaster when a trend is expected to have broad public appeal.

Mall Intercept Research Market research conducted for a client using consumers recruited from shoppers in a mall who satisfy the requirements of the client.

Man-Made Fibers Fibers manufactured from chemicals (acrylic, spandex, nylon, polyester, and polyolefin) and formed into fiber by extrusion through a spinneret.

Manufactured Fibers Fibers chemically engineered from biological raw materials such as wood pulp (rayon, lyocell, and acetate) and formed into fiber by extrusion through a spinneret.

Manufacturing Cycle In apparel planning and scheduling, a rolling forecast where long term is usually 12 months but can be as short as 6 months to as long as 18 months.

Markdowns Unwanted goods remaining at the end of a selling period that must be reduced in price in order to sell.

Market Intelligence Information and analysis combined to provide an understanding of customers' needs and preferences, and challenges and opportunities in the marketplace.

Market Orientation An approach to business in which the core themes are customer focus, profitability, and coordinated marketing; responsibility for marketing is shared across functional units; and attention is given to generating intelligence about future directions in the marketplace.

Mass Customization The process of delivering a unique, personalized, or customized product using mass production techniques and at a cost competitive with mass production.

Mass Market Theory (see **Trickle-Across Theory**)

Mega Niche Brand/Mega Nichers A powerful brand name with a generic image that taps into the consciousness of a broad consumer population and then extends out to fill more and more product niches with its branded merchandise.

Megatrend A trend so fundamental that it indicates a critical restructuring of culture.

Memes Self-replicating ideas—advertising slogans, catchy bits of dialogue from television or a movie, a product, look, or brand—that move through time and space without continuing support from their original source.

Metaphor A form of comparison in which a term that ordinarily designates an object or idea is used to designate a dissimilar object or idea to form an analogy.

Microfibers Fibers produced when man-made or manufactured fibers are extruded through very small holes in the spinneret to produce fabrics that are softer, with more drape.

Mid-Range Strategies Business approaches focused on actions two to five years ahead.

Mind Map A kind of outline, but without the rigid structure of the traditional form, that organizes a topic by building out from the center in a tree-like structure.

Minor Trends Distinction applied by a forecaster when a trend is expected to be limited to a small, specialized group of consumers.

Model Building Forecasting method that uses a situation in which the outcome is known and applies the same pattern to situations in which the outcome is unknown.

Modernity A stage in the evolution of culture and an associated aesthetic that emerged with technological innovations such as the automobile, telephone, plastics, synthetic dyes, and man-made fibers and with mass media and entertainment such as the movies.

Munsell Color System A color specification system that includes a color atlas, the *Munsell Book of Color,* with about 1,600 chips arranged in equal steps of hue, value, and chroma (intensity or saturation) and a notation for each.

Muse A woman—often a client or employee of the design house or a celebrity—who embodies the ideal look for a designer.

National Brands Brands developed and promoted by manufacturers who sell to retailers through wholesale channels.

Natural Fibers Fibers that originate from animals (alpaca, angora, camel's hair, cashmere, mohair, silk, vicuna, wool) or plants (cotton, linen, and hemp).

Noise (in Time-Series Forecasting) The part of sales fluctuations that appears random and cannot be explained because the pattern has not occurred consistently in the past.

Nonlinear Systems that cannot be solved by simple means because seemingly inconsequential events give rise to complicated dynamics.

Nonlinear Patterns Unlike linear relationships which can be captured with straight lines on graph paper, relationships that emerge only when graphed in three-dimensional space because the orderly but unpredictable patterns never repeat exactly.

Normative Forecasting Forecasting done on purpose to motivate people to take actions toward some desirable result, rather than as detached, objective forecasting about the future.

Novelty Fabrics Fabrics formed through processes other than weaving or knitting, including bonding, crocheting, felting, knotting, or laminating.

Observability In the consumer adoption process, the degree of visibility afforded an innovation.

Omissions In information analysis, missing facts or reasons for an action or business decision.

Open-Model Time-Series (OMTS) Techniques (e.g., Box Jenkins) that first analyze the time-series to determine the components, then build unique models and forecast the time series into the future.

Outliers In information analysis, cases or facts that are unexpectedly high or low in value.

Panel Studies Studies that ask questions of a group of people over time in order to track changes in consumer attitudes and opinions.

Pantone ® Professional Color System A color specification system that includes a color atlas, *The Pantone Book of Color* (1990), with 1,225 colors identified by name and color code.

Participant Observer A qualitative strategy in which a researcher enters a situation and interacts with the people and activities found there as a way of exploring and understanding the meaning of people's behavior.

Perceived Risk The imagined potential consequences of purchasing something new and novel.

Performance Fabrics High-tech fabrics originally developed for industrial, active sports, or rugged outdoor usage which are adapted to use in high fashion and streetwear.

Piece Dyeing Fabric dyed after weaving but before other apparel manufacturing processes.

Point-of-Sale (POS) Data Information captured at the time of sale—the starting point for sophisticated sales forecasting techniques.

Pop Culture/Popular Culture Events, activities, directions, and trends—derived from advertising, magazines, movies, television, music, and other media and popularized by celebrities—that serve as a source of inspiration for consumer purchasing.

Positioning A unique marketing approach that appeals directly to a specific consumer segment in a way that differentiates the product from all others in the category.

Postmodern(ism) A stage in the evolution of culture and an aesthetic associated with an emerging global economy, fragmentation in society, extreme eclecticism in the use of signs and symbols, unease with the consequences of modernity, and fluidity in social identities.

Première Vision An important trade show for color and textile forecasters held in Paris.

Primary Colors The fundamental colors in a color system from which all other colors are mixed.

Primary Sources Original sources written at the time the change or action or event was taking place.

Private-Label Brands Brands owned by retailers and merchandised solely through the retailers' stores.

Product Life Cycle A series of predictable stages from the development of a product until it disappears from the marketplace.

Product Segmentation A segmentation strategy that focuses on differences between brands on product-specific criteria, including brand image, brand associations, and consumer perceptions of brand similarities at critical points in the purchase decision—before purchase, at the point of purchase, and in use.

Proximity Operators Specifications used in keyword searches to allow users to indicate how close the keywords should be to each other in the text to be meaningful.

Psychographics Aspects of lifestyles, consumer preferences, and consumer psychology that are used to identify a consumer segment by shared values, attitudes, preferences, and behaviors.

Qualitative Research An approach to research based on ethnography, case studies, and phenomenological studies in which human experiences are observed in a natural setting and described or explained using the natural language, categories, and frameworks of the subjects.

Qualitative Techniques (in Sales Forecasting) A set of techniques that are used to tap into the expertise of people inside and outside the company to adjust the quantitative forecast to account for environmental factors; also called subjective and judgmental techniques.

Quantitative Research An approach to research that uses experimental methods or surveys to collect data on a sample in order to generalize finding to a population.

Quantitative Techniques (in Sales Forecasting) A set of statistical techniques used to analyze sales history data.

Quick Response A strategy that seeks to shorten product development cycles and make other adjustments to make apparel manufacturing agile and responsive to market demand.

Regional Markets Centers that lease space to manufacturers and sales representatives who carry multiple lines in permanent showrooms and for seasonal shows.

Relational Marketing A marketing strategy based on building a "learning relationship" with customers—an ongoing, interactive connection that encourages collaboration between a company and its customers on how to meet consumers' needs.

Relative Advantage The perception that an innovation is more satisfactory than items that already exist in the same class of products.

Reliability of Information The trustworthiness of information as measured by the credibility of the source.

Retail Supply Chain The linked segments of the apparel industry, especially when those segments share integrated forecasting and planning.

Retro Fashion The revival of a look or style from a former period but not exactly in the same form or with the same companion elements or for the same use or occasion.

Reverse Engineering A way of gaining competitive information by purchasing and dismantling a product to determine how it was designed and constructed.

Reverse Ostentation (see **Conspicuous Counterconsumption**)

Rule Induction Analysis software that extracts useful if-then rules from data using statistical significance as the criteria.

Runway Shows Designers and apparel manufacturers promote new seasonal lines to the press and merchants during fashion weeks in productions that involve models, music, lighting, and staging. Term also used generically for fashion shows of similar type presented at regional markets to promote lines to retail buyers and those by retailers and other sponsors that promote seasonal fashions to consumers.

Sales Channel A particular form of retailing or category of retail distribution.

Sales Forecast A projection of expected demand given a set of environmental conditions, which is developed using quantitative and qualitative methods.

Sales History Data on products in terms of which sold and in what quantities.

Sales Plan A plan that defines goals and provides motivation for sales levels that meet or exceed the sales forecast.

Sampling In product development, ordering a minimum amount of fabric as a trial order.

Saturation (also called **Intensity** or **Chroma**) The strength or purity of a color.

Scenario A technique used by futurists consisting of a series of stories or summaries that describe the evolution from the present situation to one or more possible futures.

Scope of a Trend The forecaster's estimate of how important a trend will be and how broad an impact it will have on markets.

S-Curve The cumulative form of the diffusion curve; interlocking sets of S-curves can be used to represent the spread of an innovation from one consumer segment to another or from one company to another.

Search Engines Web utilities that allow users to type in keywords to initiate a search, locate documents that match, and see the retrieved list of documents.

Seasonal Color Analysis An idea promoted in the 1980s to help consumers select the "right" colors to enhance their personal coloring and avoid the "wrong" colors, in which color groupings were named for the four seasons and varied in undertone (warm or cool) and saturation (clear, bright, and vivid versus subdued and less intense).

Seasonality (in Time-Series Forecasting) A yearly pattern of increasing or decreasing sales that corresponds to the season.

Secondary Colors A set of colors mixed from two primary colors.

Secret Shopper A person who appears to be just a customer but who is actually noting the operational details of a business for the purpose of competitive research.

Self-Organized Criticality The state of a system in which change is constant, the components of the systems are barely stable, and the next change in the system may have no effect or set off a catastrophic chain reaction.

Semiotics The science of analyzing culture as a system of signs.

Sensitization A strategy that intends to shake up a company's assumptions about its place in relationship to competitors by using information to build a sense of urgency about competitive challenges.

Sensory Design The process in presentation design that considers enhancing communication by involving the audience's senses.

Shade A color mixed with black.

Shadow Market Planning A technique in competitive analysis in which one or more people in a company are so familiar with a competitor that they can answer "what if" questions about that competitor's strategy on a current and continuous basis.

Short-Term Forecasting In the fashion industry, the process that begins two to three years before the arrival of merchandise in the retail store, a process that is allows the segments of the textile/apparel pipeline to coordinate seasonal goods around looks that can be communicated to the customer through the press and stores.

Showcase or Laboratory Stores Stores where mega niche and 3-D brands can present their entire line as a billboard for the brand, an educational environment for retailers on the latest in visual merchandising, and a research site for gathering intelligence about what consumers want, which products in the line are heating up and which cooling down, and which packaging and promotional initiatives are most effective.

Showrooms The part of a designer's or manufacturer's facility where buyers and the press come to see the seasonal line.

Simultaneous Adoption Theory (see **Trickle-Across Theory**)

Social Risk The risk that the consumer's social group will not approve of an innovative purchase.

Soft Information Information from the popular press, TV shows that mention the company or product, and industry rumors.

Solution Dyeing A process specific to man-made and manufactured fibers whereby the color is added to the liquefied fiber before it is extruded as a filament.

Split Complements Based on a simple complement; a color combination that includes a color and the two colors on either side of its complement.

Staple Length The relatively short lengths of a fiber either from natural sources or cut from the filament form of man-made or manufactured fibers.

Status Float Phenomenon (also called the **Trickle-Up Theory**) The view that higher status segments with more power imitate those with lower status and that status markers float up (rather than down) the status pyramid.

Status Markers Styles, fashion details, accessories, or any appearance factors that denote high rank, wealth, or achievement.

Stockouts Situations when merchandise is not available at the time when consumers request it, resulting in lost sales.

Store Brands Brands developed and merchandised through a company's own stores.

Strange Attractor A pull within a nonlinear pattern that keeps the system within boundaries.

Strategic Planning A business approach that focuses on gaining competitive advantage and ensuring business survival and long-term growth—planning with a long time horizon and a more comprehensive view.

Strategic Windows A strategy that involves timing the firm's product offerings to the customers' readiness and willingness to accept and adopt those products.

Style Testing Pretesting styles with consumers to identify "winners" and "losers" early enough in the product development cycle to enable styles with low consumer interest to be eliminated from further development.

Style Tribes A group that has adopted a distinctive style of dress as a marker of membership, providing satisfaction of the dual drives to fit in and stand out.

Subcultures Groups that invent or adopt specific aesthetic codes that differentiate them from other subcultures and from the mainstream.

Subject Tree A method of locating information at a Web site in which the user "drills down" through category listings that become progressively more specific.

Supply Chain The linked functions that begin with a fiber that is processed into yarn, then into fabric, and ends with fabric finishing, including dyeing and printing.

Survey Research A method of data gathering in which consumers are asked to answer a set of carefully designed questions about themselves, attitudes toward shopping, opinions of products and services, and other issues of interest to the researcher.

Syndicated Surveys Surveys conducted by a group of sponsors who are interested in the same topic and who share costs and results.

Synthesis The phase in forecasting when the forecaster achieves a creative reintegration of the parts of a trend or phenomenon and projects future directions.

Tactics Business approach that focuses on seasonal direction, planning short-range strategy, and current business matters.

Target Audience A slice of the population more likely than others to adopt an innovation at a particular time in the diffusion process or be attracted to the tangible and intangible attributes of a product, company image, or service.

Target Market An approach that focuses on attracting a specific potential purchaser, one whose lifestyle, preferences, and aspirations predispose them to see a match with the offer.

Technical Fabrics (see **Performance Fabrics**)

Tertiary Colors Colors mixed from one primary color and one secondary color.

Texture The surface variations of fabric from hard and slick to soft and fuzzy, including effects produced by interaction of light and the surface (dull or shiny).

Thinking Inside the Box An approach to problem solving used when it is relatively easy to gather relevant information and apply traditional methods to discover the solution.

Thinking Outside the Box An approach to problems solving used when problems are so difficult that traditional methods do not work; a holistic approach that looks at the problem from multiple viewpoints and seeks to recognize patterns and relationships.

3-D Brand A brand that focuses on a lifestyle concept, produces products in many categories, and creates a three-dimensional world defined by the brand image.

Time-Series Forecasting Quantitative techniques that use values recorded at regular time intervals (sales history) to predicts future values.

Timing of a Trend The forecaster's estimate of how soon the trend will "hit" and how long it will continue.

Tint A color to which white is added.

Tone A grayed color—a color plus gray.

Trade Dress A form of trademark infringement that allows owners to protect ownership of the way a product looks or is presented and to prevent others from trading on their reputation, image, and customers' goodwill.

Trade Organizations Groups formed by producers of both natural and man-made fibers to promote use of their fiber by providing forecasting information, public relations support, and fabric sourcing for apparel manufacturers.

Trade Shows Expositions open only to people in the industry that are centered on selling fashion but also showcase new design talent and identify trends for specific product categories, price points, and target audiences.

Trend (in Time-Series Forecasting) The continuing pattern of increasing or decreasing sales represented as a line or curve.

Trend Identifiable similarities across information sources related to styles, details, or other aspects of appearance characterized by a building awareness of this new look and an accelerating demand among consumers.

Trend Boards Collections of clipping, objects, fabrics, color chips, and other items arrayed on a stiff cardboard foundation and used to identify the mood or spirit of each trend and its thematic focus.

Trend Map Part of the forecaster's task, a framework that identifies which trends are just emerging, continuing to build, or declining.

Triads Color combinations with three colors equally spaced on the color wheel—the primary triad is red, blue, and yellow; the secondary triad is orange, green, and violet.

Trial Balloons Designer experiments presented to merchants, the press, and the public to gauge the effect and potential of a new idea.

Trialability In the consumer adoption process, an evaluation of the ease of testing out the innovation before making a decision.

Trickle-Across Theory (also known as **Mass Market** or **Simultaneous Adoption Theory**) A theory that holds that fashion information trickles across horizontally *within* social strata rather than vertically *across* strata because mass media and advances in manufacturing allow access to fashion ideas by consumers in all socioeconomic groups simultaneously.

Trickle-Down Theory (see also **Chase and Flight**) A theory that holds that fashion spreads downward through the class structure from the fashionable elite—the rich and socially prominent—to the lower classes.

Trickle-Up Theory (see **Status Float Phenomenon** and **Bubble Up**)

Trims All the items used to embellish and finish a garment, whether functional—buttons, buckles, belts—or decorative—appliqué, beading, binding, and lace.

Two-Step Flow The visualization of diffusion in which the initial flow of information is through mass media channels and marketer-based information to the innovators, then from the innovators to the opinion leaders and others through personal influence.

Unethical Practices Information-gathering activities that are not illegal but involve misrepresentation.

Value The lightness or darkness of the color.

Vintage Fashion Recycled clothing sold to fashion-forward consumers interested in the quality and aesthetics of earlier fashion eras.

Viral Marketing A type of Internet marketing designed to encourage customers to try a software product, share it with the people they know, and thereby propagate the product on behalf of the company that created it—a digital form of word-of-mouth advertising.

Virtual Dressing Rooms Software that lets users try fabrics, patterns, and colors together while making mix-and-match decisions, sometimes on a computerized model that resembles the user in terms of shape and hair color.

Visualization An approach to understanding a process by illustrating it in graphs, pictures, or other visual or graphic ways.

Weaving The process of forming fabric by interlacing yarns at right angles in patterns called weaves; each weave has its own characteristics and properties.

Word-of-Mouth The way trends spread among personal networks when one person visually or verbally recommends a new fashion to friends and acquaintances.

Zeitgeist Generally translated as the "spirit of the times."

BIBLIOGRAPHY

Abel, D. F. (1978). Strategic windows. *Journal of Marketing, 42,* 21–28.

Aburdene, P. and Naisbitt, J. (1992). *Megatrends for women.* New York: Villard.

Adler, J. (1995, February 20). Have we become a nation of slobs? *Newsweek,* 56–62.

Adler, J. (1998, November 2). Tomorrow's child. *Newsweek,* 54–64.

Agins, T. (1994a, December 20). As leather gets cheaper, it loses its cool. *Wall Street Journal,* pp. B1, B8.

Agins, T. (1994b, August 8). Copy shops: Fashion knockoffs hit stores before originals as designers seethe. *Wall Street Journal,* pp. A1, A4.

Agins, T. (1995, February 28). Out of fashion: Many women lose interest in clothes, to retailers' dismay. *Wall Street Journal,* p. A1.

Aikman, B. (1997, October 26). Reel stories: Hollywood looks to journalists for fresh ideas. *Newsday,* p. F08.

Allen, J. (1985). *Showing your colors.* San Francisco: Chronicle.

Allen, J. P., and Turner, E. (1990, August). Where diversity? *American Demographics,* 34–38.

Allenby, G. M., Jen, L., and Leone, R. P. (1996). Economic trends and being trendy: The influence of consumer confidence on retail fashion sales. *Journal of Business & Economic Statistics, 14,* 103–112.

Alter, J. (1992, October 5). The cultural elite. *Newsweek,* 30–34.

Amabile, T. M. (1998, September/July). How to kill creativity. *Harvard Business Review, 76* (5), 76–77.

Amit, R., Domowitz, I., and Fershtman, C. (1988). Thinking one step ahead: The use of conjectures in competitor analysis. *Strategic Management Journal, 9,* 431–442.

Anderla, G., Dunning, A., and Forge, S. (1997). *Chaotics.* Westport, CT: Praeger.

Anderson, L. J., Brannon, E. L., Ulrich, P. V., & Marshall, T. (1998). Toward a consumer-driven model for mass customization in the apparel market. Unpublished working paper of the National Textile Center, Auburn University, Auburn, Alabama.

Back to the 50s. (1972, October, 16). *Newsweek,* 78–79, 81.

Bak, P. (1996). *How nature works.* New York: Springer-Verlag.

Banner, L. W. (1983). *American beauty.* Chicago: University of Chicago Press.

Barry, E. (1999, February/March). The color guard. *Metropolis,* 60–65, 99, 101.

Bass, F. M. (1969). A new product growth model for consumer durables. *Management Science, 15* (January), 215–227.

Bathory-Kitsz, D. (1996, January/February). "Tea. Earl Grey. Hot.": Mass customization presents major opportunities and major threats. *Consumer Goods,* 13–14, 16, 18.

Behling, D. (1985/1986). Fashion change and demographics: A model. *Clothing and Textiles Research Journal, 4,* (1), 18–23.

Behling, D. (1992). Three and a half decades of fashion adoption research: What have we learned? *Clothing and Textiles Research Journal, 10* (2), 34–41.

Belleau, B. (1987). Cyclical fashion movement: Women's day dresses: 1860–1980. *Clothing and Textiles Research Journal, 5* (2), 15–20.

Betts, K. (1992, May). La mode destroy. *Vogue,* 106–107, 116.

Betts, K. (1994, September). Up front: Copy rites. *Vogue,* 148, 154.

Betts, K. (1998a, June). Generation vexed. *Vogue,* 98, 100.

Betts, K. (1998b, September). Some nerve. *Vogue,* 614–621.

Beyond blue denim/Lifestyle Monitor. (1998, May 12). *Women's Wear Daily* [Web], 3 pp. Available: www.cottoninc.com [1998, June 17].

Bigus, J. P., and Bigus, J. (1998). *Constructing intelligent agents with Java.* New York: Wiley.

Bikhchandani, S., Hirshleifer, D., and Welch, I. (1992). A theory of fads, fashion, custom, and cultural change as informational cascades. *Journal of Political Economy, 100* (5), 992–1026.

Bird, L. (1995, September 6). Tired of T-shirts and no-name watches, shoppers return to Tiffany and Chanel. *Wall Street Journal,* p. B1.

Birren, F. (1987). *Creative color.* West Chester, PA: Schiffer.

Blumberg, P. (1975). The decline and fall of the status symbol: Some thoughts on status in a post-industrial society. *Social Problems, 21* (4), 480–497.

Blumer, H. (1969, Summer). Fashion: From class differentiation to collective selection. *Sociological Quarterly, 10* (3), 275–291.

Bolt, G. J. (1994). *Market and sales forecasting: A total approach.* London: Kogan Page.

Bowles, H. (1998, November). Trend trekker. *Vogue,* 190.

Bragg, R. (1994, July 15). Nowadays, workers enjoy dressing down for the job. *New York Times,* pp. A1, A8.

Brampton, S. (1993, July). The new direction: A handful of forward thinkers are defying all the conventions, stripping fashion down to its most basic elements in order to build its future. *Bazaar,* 67–68, 134.

Brannon, E. L. (1993). Affect and cognition in appearance management: A review. In S. J. Lennon and L. D. Burns (Eds.), *Social science aspects of dress: New directions* (pp. 82–92). Monument, CO: International Textile and Apparel Association.

Brantley, B. (1992, March). Zoran *Zeitgeist. Elle,* 201–208, 218.

Braun, H. D. (1993, March). The catalog shopper of the '90s. *Direct Marketing,* 15–18.

Brenninkmeyer, I. (1963). The diffusion of fashion. In G. Wills and D. Midgley (Eds.) (1973). *Fashion marketing: An anthology of viewpoints and perspectives* (pp. 259–302). London: Allen and Unwin.

Bridging the gender gap. (1996, June). *Children's Business, 11* (6), 58.

Brimming with trimmings. (1998, May). *Body Fashions Intimate Apparel, 28* (5), 18.

Brown, E. (1994). Designer of distinction. In H. Linton (Ed.), *Color forecasting* (pp. 136–145). New York: Van Nostand Reinhold.

Brown, R. (1992). Managing the "S" curves of innovation. *Journal of Consumer Marketing, 9* (4), 61–72.

Brown, S. L., and Eisenhardt, K. M. (1998). *Competing on the edge: Strategy as structured chaos.* Boston: Harvard Business School Press.

Browne, A. (1994, September). Revival of the fittest. *Bazaar,* 130, 136.

Brubach, H. (1994, February 20). Style: Cut above. *New York Times,* p. 67.

Brubach, H. (1998, May 3). Style; Spectator sportswear. *New York Times* [Web], 2 pp. Available: www.archives.nytimes.com [1998, May 5].

Business: The changing fabric of Italian fashion. (1998, April 11). *The Economist, 347* (8063), 47–48.

CAD branching out. (1998, August 26). *Women's Wear Daily,* p. 18.

Calvert, D. (1994). Textile design and apparel. In H. Linton (Ed.), *Color forecasting* (pp. 190–192). New York: Van Nostrand Reinhold.

Calvin, Helmut reignite show date debate. (1998, July 9). *Women's Wear Daily*, pp. 8–9.

Cardin, M. M. (Producer), and Charney, N. (Director). (1992). *Christian Dior: The legend* [Video]. New York: VideoFashion, Inc.

Carman, J. M. (1966) The fate of fashion cycles in our modern society. In R. M. Hass (Ed.), *Science, technology and marketing* (pp. 722–737). Chicago: American Marketing Association.

Carpenter, D. L. (1998, May). Return on innovation—The power of being different. *Retailing Issues Letter*, 1–5.

Caughey, J. L. (1978). Artificial social relationships in modern America. *American Quarterly, 30,* 70–89.

Celente, G. (1990). *Trend tracking.* New York: Warner.

Chambers, V., and Davis, A. (1998, April 13). Direct from Paris . . . to the mall. *Newsweek,* 64–65.

Chase, R. (1997). *CAD for fashion design.* Upper Saddle River, NJ: Prentice Hall.

Cheong, F. (1996). *Internet agents.* Indianapolis, IN: New Riders.

Chirls, S. (1996a, November 12). Prints make fast break for spring. *Women's Wear Daily,* p. 12.

Chirls, S. (1996b, June 11). Sales on rise, but profits stall. *Women's Wear Daily,* p. 12.

Chirls, S. (1997, June 24). Pantone out to keep colors real as they connect with the Internet. *Women's Wear Daily,* [Web], pp. 1–2. Available: www.pantone.com [1998, May 12].

Chirls, S. (1998a, July 7). Novelties may lift market. *Women's Wear Daily,* pp. 12, 14–15.

Chirls, S. (1998b, June 23). TDA told: Price squeeze goes on. *Women's Wear Daily,* pp. 9, 11.

Chirls, S. (1998c). Telling the high tech story. *Merchandising Activewear/Women's Wear Daily,* pp. 16–17.

Chute, E. (1988, October 5). Panelists criticize SA on responsiveness. *Women's Wear Daily,* p. 18.

City slickers. (1998, January). *Sportstyle,* 20 (1), 43.

Cleland, K. (1995, July 24). Arbitron analysis probes lifestyles. *Advertising Age,* 66 (30), 18.

Collins, K. (1974). Fashion cycles. In J. A. Jarnow and B. Judelle (Eds.), *Inside the fashion business* (2nd ed., p. 24). New York: Wiley.

Colman, D. (1998, January 4). Abandon ship: Fashion follies of the year. *New York Times* (Section 9), p. 1.

Confidence in consumer confidence? Tread carefully, look closely. (1998, March). *Textile Consumer* [Web], 2 pp. Available: www.cottonin.com/Textile Consumer [1998, June 17].

The cool ones. (1996, May 31). *Women's Wear Daily,* p. 10.

Cooper, N. (1998, September). Maximum security. *Vogue,* 256.

Cotton Incorporated unveils 18 groups of developmental apparel fabrics. (1998) [Web], 3 pp. Available: www.cottoninc.com/FabricDevelopme [1998, June 17].

Courting and keeping the catalog customer. (1997). *Women's Wear Daily* [Web], 3 pp. Available: www.cottoninc.com [1998, June 17].

Craik, J. (1994). *The face of fashion: Cultural studies in fashion.* London: Routledge.

Creative woman's world. (1971, June). *Family Circle,* 8.

Crispell, D. (1997, December). Pre-millennial purples. *American Demographics* [Web], 1 p. Available: www.demographics.com [1998, May 5].

Crockett, B. (1998, November 25). Online shopping like never before. *CNBC and The Wall Street Journal* [Web], 5 pp. Available: www.msnbc.com/news [1998, November 28].

Cuneo, A. Z. (1994, September 12). Prying the truth out of consumers. *Advertising Age,* 65 (37), p. S-4.

Curriculum modules for educational programs. (1998). [Web], 1 p. Available: Society of Competitive Intelligence Professionals: www.scip.org/miller3.html [1998, September 17].

D'Innocenzio, A. (1993, December 28). Study explains shopping shift. *Women's Wear Daily,* p. 8.

D'Innocenzio, A. (1995, June 7). The casual glut. *Women's Wear Daily,* p. 8.

D'Innocenzio, A. (1996, July 3). Dealing with downsizing. *Women's Wear Daily,* pp. 4–5.

D'Innocenzio, A. (1998a, April 15). It's a longish story as the industry faces a new hemline dilemma. *Women's Wear Daily,* pp. 1, 4.

D'Innocenzio, A. (1998b, June 24). Retro brands battle back. *Women's Wear Daily,* p. 9.

D'Innocenzio, A. (1998c, August 26). Spiegel redefines its niche. *Women's Wear Daily,* p. 10.

Danger, E. P. (1968). *Using colour to sell.* New York: Gower.

Danielson, D. R. (1989). The changing figure ideal in fashion illustration. *Clothing and Textiles Research Journal, 8* (1), 35–48.

Darmstadt, C. (1982). *Farbige Rassungen für Bügerhauser des Historismus und des Jugendstils unter hertigen Aspekten.* Dissertation, Dortmund University.

Darmstadt, C. (1985, June 6). Farbe in der Architektur ab 1800. *DBZ,* 743–748.

Darnton, N. (1992, April 6). Night of the living dead. *Newsweek,* 50–51.

Data miners dig for consumer information to predict buying trends. (1997, September 7). *Minneapolis-St. Paul Star Tribune* [Web], 3 pp. Available: www.elibrary.com [1999, January 9].

Davis, F. (1991). Herbert Blumer and the study of fashion: A reminiscence and a critique. *Symbolic Interaction, 14* (1), 1–21.

Davis, M. L. (1996). *Visual design in dress* (3rd Ed.). Upper Saddle River, NJ: Prentice Hall.

Dean, B. (1998, January). Measuring catalog effectiveness. *WWD/DNR Specialty Stores,* pp. 4, 6.

DeCaro, F. (1997). Style over substance; Junk today, on runways tomorrow. *New York Times* [Web], 3 pp. Available: www.archives.nytimes.com [1998, May 5].

Defining a new market. (1996, October 31). *Women's Wear Daily,* (Section II), p. 2.

The descent of the "Wally" dress. (1931, August 19). *Life, 13* (6), 57.

Designer's customers 'shop like a celebrity' on Internet. (1998, November 26). *The Gadsden Times,* p. D3.

Designer's guide to color 2. (1984). San Francisco: Chronicle.

Designers: Endangered or extinct? (1992, April 7). *Women's Wear Daily,* pp. 1, 10–12.

Detouzos, M. (1997). *What will be: How the new world of information will change our lives.* New York: Harper Collins.

Dhar, V., and Stein, R. (1997*). Seven methods for transforming corporate data into business intelligence.* Upper Saddle River, NJ: Prentice Hall.

Dougherty, S., and Hoover, E. (1990, July 30). Pages: John Naisbitt and Pat Aburdene reap profits as mega-prophets. *People,* 57.

Doyle, M. (1998, October 3). The man with a 500-year plan. *The Daily Telegraph* (UK), p. 33.

Dransfield, A. (1994, Spring). Forecasting color demand at Ciba-Geigy. *Journal of Business Forecasting* [Web], 4 pp. Available: www.proquest.umi.com [1998, May 6].

Drier, M. (1998, August 17). CPD: A fashion turnaround. *Women's Wear Daily,* p. 21.

Duff, C. (1994, February 11). Six reasons women aren't buying as many clothes. *The Wall Street Journal,* pp. B1, B3.

DuMont, S. R. (1997, February 1). The global textile/apparel industry meets the digital revolution. Paper presented at the World Economic Forum, Governors for Textile and Apparel, Davos, Switzerland.

Eckman, M., Damhorst, M. L., and Kadolph, S. J. (1990). Toward a model of the in-store purchase decision process: Consumer use of criteria for evaluating women's apparel. *Clothing and Textiles Research Journal, 8* (2), 13–22.

Edelson, S. (1991, July 19). Painting the town with MAC. *Women's Wear Daily,* p. 16.

Edelson, S. (1994, August 16). MTV rocks shopping format. *Women's Wear Daily,* p. 14.

Edelson, S. (1995, November 8). Fashion reevaluated flickering fortunes of TV home shopping. *Women's Wear Daily,* pp. 1, 8–9.

Edwards, T. M. (1997, November 10). The young and the nested. *Time,* 88–89.

Eiseman, L. (1994). Color forecasting: Crystal ball or educated choice? In H. Linton (Ed.), *Color forecasting* (pp. 148–158). New York: Van Nostrand Reinhold.

Eiseman, L. (1997). All about color. Pantone [Web] 3 pp. Available: www.pantone.com [1998, May 12].

Eiseman, L., and Hebert, L. (1990). *The Pantone book of color.* New York: Abrams.

Elliott, C. (1998, June 1). Trends: Give your data a workout. *Internet Week,* p. 32.

Ellis, K. (1999, June 3), Viral marketing 'creeps in.' *Women's Wear Daily*, p. 14.

Erlichman, J. (1998, April). Click here to get to the past. *Washington Post* [Web], 2 pp. Available: www.washingtonpost.com [1998, May 29].

Eysenck, H. J. (1941). A critical and experimental study of colour preferences. *American Journal of Psychology, 34*, 385–394.

Fahey, L., and Randall, R. M. (1998). What is scenario learning? In L. Fahey and R. M. Randall (Eds.), *Learning from the future* (pp. 3–21). New York: Wiley.

Fallon, J. (1998, November 25). Shop spawns Shopgirl tops. *Women's Wear Daily*, p. 6.

Farrell, W. (1998). *How hits happen*. New York: Harper Business.

Fashion depression. (1995, April 3). *Women's Wear Daily*, pp. 1, 6–9.

Fashion noir/Lifestyle Monitor. (1998, April 9). *Women's Wear Daily*, p.2.

Fashion on the internet. (1997, March). *Women's Wear Daily* [Web], 2 pp. Available: www.cottoninc.com [1998, June 17].

Feitelberg, R. (1995, November 17). The teen mystique: How to relate. *Women's Wear Daily*, p. 10.

Feitelberg, R. (1996, February 22). Girls will be boys: Unisex looks. *Women's Wear Daily*, pp. 22–23.

Feitelberg, R. (1998a, June 25). Designers told: Vary the vision. *Women's Wear Daily*, p. 10.

Feitelberg, R. (1998b, August 17). Trend boards make everything click. *Women's Wear Daily*, p. 10.

Fennell, G. (1991). The role of qualitative research in making what the consumer wants to buy. In R. H. Holman and M. R. Solomon (Eds.), *Advances in Consumer Research,* Vol. 18 (pp. 271–279). Provo, UT: Association of Consumer Research.

Fibers: The foundation of fashion. (1998, June 23). *Women's Wear Daily*, pp. 1–31.

Field, G. A. (1970). The status float phenomenon—The upward diffusion of innovation. *Business Horizons, 8*, 45–52.

Fiore, A. M., and Kimle, P. A. (1997). *Understanding aesthetics for the merchandising and design professional*. New York: Fairchild.

Fischer, D. H. (1996). *The great wave*. New York: Oxford University Press.

Fisher, C. (1991, May 13). To buy, or not to buy: Retailers focus on computerized sessions. *Advertising Age, 62* (20), 27.

Fisher, M. L., Hammond, J. H., Obermeyer, W. R., and Raman, A. (1994, May/June). Making supply meet demand in an uncertain world. *Harvard Business Review, 72* (3), 83–89.

Fitzgerald, K. (1992, January 27). Marketers learn to 'just do it.' *Advertising Age, 63* (4), S-7.

Fitzgerald, K. (1994, March 21). Home shopping comes up short. *Advertising Age, 65* (12), IM-14.

Flacks, N., and Rasberry, R. W. (1982). *Power talk*. New York: Free Press.

Flugel, J. C. (1930). *The psychology of fashion*. London: Hogarth.

Foley, B. (1998, July 8). The dating game: Calvin joining Helmut with a September show. *Women's Wear Daily*, pp. 1, 14.

Fox, S. (1984). *The mirror makers: A history of American advertising and its creators*. New York: Vintage.

Freed, J. C. (1994, August 14). Spreadsheets beware, demographic mapping is here. *New York Times,* p. 8.

Frequently asked questions. (1998). Society of Competitive Intelligence Professionals [Web], 3 pp. Available: www.scip.org/faq.html [1998, June 8].

Friedman, A. (1990, August 28). Loose looks scoring well in tough fall. *Women's Wear Daily*, pp. 1, 6–7.

Friedman, A. (1996a, December 6). A blueprint for brand licensing. *Women's Wear Daily*, p. 14.

Friedman, A. (1996b, July 24). Panel: Real women want real fashion. *Women's Wear Daily*, p. 18.

Friedman, A. (1997, July 7). RTW's personality problem. *Women's Wear Daily* [Web], 5 pp. Available: www.Women's Wear Daily.com [1998, July 8].

Friedman, A., and Pogoda, D. M. (1990, August 7). SA debates the loose and the sexy. *Women's Wear Daily*, p. 10.

From stupidity to greed, why business is bad. (1988, October 18). *Women's Wear Daily*, pp. 1, 4–6.

Fuld, L. M. (1985). *Competitor intelligence: How to get it; how to use it*. New York: Wiley.

Fuld, L. M. (1988). *Monitoring the competition.* New York: Wiley.

Fuld, L. M. (1992). Achieving total quality through intelligence. *Long Range Planning, 25* (1), 109–115.

Furchgott, R. (1998, June 28). For cool hunters, tomorrow's trend is the trophy. *New York Times,* p. 10.

Gandee, C. (1993, September). The dressing down of America. *Vogue,* 524–529.

Garber, J. R. (1998). Tea leaves. *Forbes, 76.*

Gardner, M. (1995, July 27). Trend-spotting—Chasing the future with a butterfly net. *Christian Science Monitor,* p. 12.

Gelb, B. D. (1997). Creating "memes" while creating advertising. *Journal of Advertising Research, 37* (6), 57–59.

Gelb, B. D., Saxton, M. J., Zinkhan, G. M., and Albers, N. D. (1991, January/February). Competitive intelligence: Insights from executives. *Business Horizons, 34,* 43–47.

Ghoshal, S., and Westney, D. E. (1991). Organizing competitor analysis systems. *Strategic Management Journal, 12,* 17–31.

Giannovario, B. (1998, March 4). Implementation of 3-dimensional body scanning for apparel mass customization. Paper presented at the International Apparel Research Conference, American Apparel Manufacturers Association, Atlanta, Georgia.

Gladwell, M. (1996, November). The science of shopping. *The New Yorker,* 66–75.

Gleick, J. (1987). *Chaos: Making a new science.* New York: Penquin.

Glusac, E., Brown, B., Emert, C., and Edelson, S. (1995, September 20). 'What are you wearing to work today?' *Women's Wear Daily,* p. 13.

Goldman, D. (1998, September 7). Future imperfect. *Adweek, 39* (36), 54.

Goldsmith, R. E., Flynn, L. R., and Moore, M. A. (1996). The self-concept of fashion leaders. *Clothing and Textiles Research Journal, 14* (4), 242–248.

Gopnik, A. (1994, November 7). What it all means. *The New Yorker,* 15–16.

Gordon, I. J. (1994). The Delphi method. A publication of the United Nations University Millennium Project Feasibility Study (Phase II).

Gordon, M. (1990, August 31). Levi's to open stores to test merchandise. *Women's Wear Daily,* p. 13.

Gordon, M., Hartlein, R., Pogoda, D. M., and White, C. (1990, September 26). SA offers stores a helping hand in tough times. *Women's Wear Daily,* pp. 1, 6–7.

Grad student and banker accused of being spies. (1998, October 13). *Opelika-Auburn News,* p. A7.

Greco, J. (1994, February). Name that trend . . . and sell! *Writer's Digest,* 40–41.

Green, P. (1998, August 24). Perfume futurist is a "trend trekker" with a nose for what's new. *Star Tribune,* pp. 03E.

Gross, M. (1988, April 11). Paris when it dithers. *New York Magazine,* 35–37.

Hammond, T. (1999). A new twist. *WWD/WWD-Magic,* p. 26.

Haskins, M. E., Leidtka, J., and Rosenblum, J. (1997). Beyond teams: Toward an ethic of collaboration. *Organizational Dynamics* [Web], *26,* 14 pp. Available: www.elibrary.com [1999, February 22].

Hastreiter, K. (1997, December). The world war of fashion. *Paper,* 64.

Heath, R. P. (1996a, September). The competitive edge. *Marketing Tools* [Web], 6 pp. Available: www.demographics.com [1998, September 17].

Heath, R. P. (1996b, July/August). Competitive intelligence. *Marketing Tools* [Web], 6 pp. Available: www.demographics.com [1998, September 20].

Heath, R. P. (1996c, July 1). The frontiers of psychographics. *American Demographics, 18,* 38–44.

Heath, R. P. (1997a, October). Blue, blue, my world is blue. *Marketing Tools* [Web], 1 p. Available: www.demographics.com [1998, May 5].

Heath, R. P. (1997b, October). The wonderful world of color. *Marketing Tools* [Web], 5 pp. Available: www.demographics.com [1998, May 5].

Hirschman, E. C. (1980). Innovativeness, novelty seeking, and consumer creativity. *Journal of Consumer Research, 7,* 288–295.

Hirschman, E. C., and Stampfl, R. W. (1980). Roles of retailing in the diffusion of popular culture: Microperspectives. *Journal of Retailing, 56* (1), 16–36.

Holch, A. (1996a, July 23). Getting lacy. *Women's Wear Daily*, pp. 6–7.

Holch, A. (1996b, November 26). Tencel's variety show. *Women's Wear Daily*, p. 11.

Holch, A. (1997, February 4). Wool blends bloom for Spring '98. *Women's Wear Daily*, p. 9.

Holch, A. (1998a, July 14). A luxury buying. *Women's Wear Daily*, pp. 16–17, 19.

Holch, A. (1998b, April 1). New York: A touching moment. *Women's Wear Daily*, p. 12.

Holch, A., and Chirls, S. (1998, August 25). Yarn fair: New colors look to kick knitwear's blues. *Women's Wear Daily*, pp. 10–12.

Holch, A., and McNamara, M. (1995, May 5). Polyester: Back with a bang. *Women's Wear Daily*, p. 8.

Holland, J. J. (1995). *Hidden order*. Reading, MA: Addison-Wesley.

Hollander, A. (1994). *Sex and suits: The evolution of modern dress*. New York: Knopf.

Hope, A., and Walch, M. (1990). *The color compendium*. New York: Van Nostrand Reinhold.

Hope, P. (1990). Fashion: Geography of color. In A. Hope and M. Walch (Eds.), *The color compendium* (p. 127). New York: Van Nostrand Reinhold.

Horn, M. J. (1965). The second skin. Boston: Houghton-Mifflin.

Horton, D., and Wohl, R. (1956). Mass communication and para-social interaction. In G. Gumpert and R. Cathcart (Eds.), *Inter/Media* (pp. 32–55). New York: Oxford

Horton, R. L. (1979). Some relationships between personality and consumer decision making. *Journal of Marketing Research, 16,* 233–246.

Horyn, C. (1997, September). Courtney Love and the coming of age of American style. *Bazaar*, 426–431, 481.

Huff, D. (1954). *How to lie with statistics*. New York: Norton.

Hye, J. (1998, April 8). Wal-Mart and Sara Lee: Collaborating on the Internet. *Women's Wear Daily*, p. 16.

Ilari, A. (1998, August). Ducking the future. *Women's Wear Daily/Italy '98,* pp. 38–39.

Ingrassia, M. (1994, June 6). A not-so-little black dress. *Newsweek*, 72.

An introduction to data mining. (1997). Pilot Software [Web], 11 pp. Available: www.santafe.edu [1997, September 16].

Isbecque, D. (1990). Personal color analysis. In A. Hope and M. Walch (Eds.), *The color compendium* (p. 242). New York: Van Nostrand Reinhold.

Jack, N. K., and Schiffer, B. (1948). The limits of fashion control. *American Sociological Review, 13,* 731–738.

Jackson, J. (1998, October). Crazy for Colette. *Bazaar*, 128.

Jacobs, D. L. (1994, May 29). The titans of tint make their picks. *New York Times*, p. 7.

Jorgensen, D. L. (1989). *Participant observation: A methodology for human studies*. Newbury Park, CA: Sage.

Just the FAQs, Ma'am. (1995, May). *Marketing Tools*, 61–62.

Kaiser, S. (1990). *The social psychology of clothing*. New York: Macmillan.

Kaiser, S. B., Nagasawa, R., and Hutton, S. S. (1995). Construction of an SI theory of fashion: Part 1. Ambivalence and change. *Clothing and Textiles Research Journal, 13* (3), 172–183.

Kanfer, S. (1990, January 8). Millennial megababble. *Time*, 72.

Kania, J. (1998). Customer-driven scenario planning. In L. Fahey and R. M. Randall (Eds.), *Learning from the future* (pp. 264–284). New York: Wiley.

Kanner, B. (1989, April 3). Color schemes. *New York Magazine*, 22–23.

Kantrowitz, B., Witherspoon, D., and King, P. (1988, December 5). The fashion revolt: Who would wear this stuff? *Newsweek*, 60–64.

Katz, E., and Lazarsfeld, P. (1955). *Personal influence*. New York: Macmillan/Free Press.

Kauffman, S. (1995). *At home in the universe*. Oxford, England: Oxford University Press.

Kaufman, L. (1997, August 18). Enough talk. *Newsweek*, 48–49.

Kelly, K. J. (1994, June 20). 'Consumer culture' overrules income. *Advertising Age, 65* (26), 4.

King, C., and Ring, L. (1980). Fashion theory: The dynamics of style and taste, adoption and diffusion. In J. Olson (Ed.), *Advances in consumer research*, Vol. 7 (pp. 13–16). Ann Arbor, MI: Association for Consumer Research.

King, C. W. (1963). A rebuttal to the 'trickle down' theory. In S. A. Greyer (Ed.), *Towards scientific marketing* (pp. 108–125). Chicago: American Marketing Association.

Kinning, D. (1994). Colourcast services. In H. Linton (Ed.), *Color forecasting* (pp. 174–178). New York: Van Nostrand Reinhold.

Klepacki, L. (1998, June). Fall's rich harvest. *Women's Wear Daily*, pp. 42–43.

Kline, B., and Wagner, J. (1994). Information sources and retail buyer decision-making: The effect of product specific buying experience. *Journal of Retailing, 70* (1) 75–88.

Kobayashi, S. (1981, Summer). The aim and method of the color image scale. *Color Research and Applications, 6* (2), 93–107.

Kohli, A. K., and Jaworski, B. J. (1990). Market orientation: The construct, research propositions, and managerial implications. *Journal of Marketing, 54,* 1–18.

Koppelmann, U., and Kuthe, E. (1987). Präferenzwellen beim Gestaltungsmittel Farbe. *Markeint-AFP, 2,* 113–122.

Kroeber, A. L. (1919, July). On the principle of order in civilization as exemplified by changes of fashion. *American Anthropologist, 21* (3), 235–263.

Krueger, R. (1988). *Focus groups: A practical guide for applied research.* Beverly Hills, CA: Sage.

Lacina, J. (1996, March). Auto update. *Better Homes and Gardens, 242.*

Lamb, M. (1997). Trend 101 [Web]. Available: www.trendcurve.com [1998, May 5].

Lannon, L. (1988, March). Swatch watch. *Savvy,* 40–43, 100–101.

Lauerman, C. (1997, October 7). Money talks and its voice is increasingly female, marketers say. *Chicago Tribune,* p. 1.

Laver, J. (1937). *Taste and fashion.* New York: Harrap.

Laver, J. (1973). Taste and fashion since The French Revolution. In G. Wills & D. Midgley (Eds.), *Fashion Marketing* (pp. 379–389). London: George Allen: Irwin.

Lee's lifestyle trends. (1999, January 7). *Women's Wear Daily,* p. 17

Lencek, L. (1996). *Nothing to hide: History of the bathing suit.* [Video: TLC/Australian Film].

Lenclos, J. (1994). Atelier 3D Couleur: Trends, signs, and symbols. In H. Linton (Ed.), *Color forecasting* (pp. 36–59). New York: Van Nostrand Reinhold.

Letscher, M. G. (1994, December). How to tell fads from trends. *American Demographics* [Web], 6 pp. Available: www.demographics.com [July 22, 1998].

Levanas, T. (1998, January 1). You are what you buy—that's the premise of 'clustering.' *Gannett News Service* [Web], 2 pp. Available: www. elibrary.com [1999, February 16].

Levenbach, H., and Cleary, J. P. (1981). *The beginning forecaster: The forecasting process through data analysis.* Belmont, CA: Lifetime Learning.

Levin, G. (1989, June 26). JWT researchers stages, not ages. *Advertising Age, 60* (26), 30.

Levin, G. (1992, February 24). Anthropologists in adland. *Advertising Age, 63* (8), 3, 49.

Levine, J. (1997, April 21). The streets don't lie. *Forbes,* 145.

Levitt, T. (1986). *The marketing imagination.* New York: Free Press.

Lewis, R. (1995, November 8). What's a brand worth? *Women's Wear Daily*, pp. 10–11.

Lewis, R. (1996a, May). Power to the consumer. *Women's Wear Daily/Infotracs,* p. 5.

Lewis, R. (1996b, October 31). Observations: The 3-D brands: Creators of dreams and dollars. *Women's Wear Daily* (Section II), p. 34.

Linton, H. (1994). *Color forecasting.* New York: Van Nostrand Reinhold.

Lipovetsky, G. (1994). *The empire of fashion.* Princeton, NJ: Princeton University Press.

Lockwood, L. (1996, February 9). Mademoiselle hits its target. *Women's Wear Daily*, p. 8.

Lohrer, R. (1998, June 8). Playing the price game. *Women's Wear Daily*, p.12.

Loose vs. tight. (1990, September 19). *Women's Wear Daily*, pp. 1, 6–7, 28.

Lopiano-Misdom, J., and DeLuca, J. (1997). *Street trends*. New York: Harper.

Lowe, E. D., and Lowe, J. W. G. (1985). Quantitative analysis of women's dress. In M. R. Solomon (Ed.), *The psychology of fashion* (pp. 193–206). Lexington: Heath/Lexington.

Lowe, E. D., and Lowe, J. W. G. (1990). Velocity of the fashion process in women's formal evening dress, 1789–1980. *Clothing and Textile Research Journal, 9* (1), 50–58.

Lowe, J. W. G., and Lowe, E. D. (1982). Cultural pattern and process: Stylistic change and fashion in women's dress. *American Anthropologist, 84* (3), 521–544.

Lowe, J. W. G., and Lowe, E. D. (1984). Stylistic change and fashion in women's dress: Regularity or randomness? In T. C. Kinnear (Ed.), *Advances in consumer research*, Vol. 11 (pp. 731–734). Provo, UT: Association of Consumer Research.

Lüscher, M. (1969). *The Lüscher color test*. New York: Random House.

MacLaughlin, P. (1996, May 1). Tracking trends: A keen observer can see into fashion's future. *Star Tribune*, p. 3E.

Mahaffie, J. B. (1995, March). Why forecasts fail. *American Demographics* [Web], 6 pp. Available: www.demographics.com [1998, July 22].

Makridakis, S. G. (1990). *Forecasting, planning, and strategy for the 21st century*. New York: Free Press.

Malarcher, P. (1995, Winter). Coloring the future. *Surface Design Journal*, 20–21.

Malone, S. (1999, January 12). Speed: The upsides and the downsides. *Women's Wear Daily*, pp. 12–13.

Marin, R., and Van Boven, S. (1998, July 27). The buzz machine. *Newsweek*, 22–26.

Martin, J. S. (1992). Building an information resource center for competitive intelligence. *Online Review, 16* (6), 379–389.

Mass sees separates getting women's back on track. (1997, July 21). *Discount Store News, 36* (14), 17.

Masterson, P. (1994, March 14). Brands seek subconscious boost. *Advertising Age, 65* (11), 29.

Maycumber, S. G. (1998, March 16). New fabric development aim to grow cotton market. *Daily News Record*, p. 16.

Mazzaraco, M. (1990, May 15). SA: Trekking to Europe for fabric direction. *Women's Wear Daily*, pp. 16, 18.

McCracken, G. (1988a). Consumer goods, gender construction, and a rehabilitated trickle-down theory. In *Culture and consumption* (pp. 93–103). Bloomington, IN: Indiana University Press.

McCracken, G. (1988b). Meaning manufacture and movement in the world of goods. In *Culture and consumption* (pp. 69–89). Bloomington, IN: Indiana University Press.

McGonagle, J. J., and Vella, C. M. (1990). *Outsmarting the competition: Practical approaches to finding and using competitive information*. Napierville, IL: Sourcebooks.

McMurdy, D. (1998, January 12). Corporate fortune-tellers. *Maclean's*, 33.

McQuarrie, E. F., and McIntyre, S. H. (1988). Conceptual underpinnings for the use of group interviews in consumer research. In M. S. Houston (Ed.), *Advances in consumer research*, Vol. 15 (pp. 580–586). Provo, UT: Association of Consumer Research.

Menkes, S. (1996). Couture: Some like it haute, but others are going demi. *International Herald Tribune* [Web], 2 pp. Available: www.iht.com [1998, September].

Mentzer, J. T., and Bienstock, C. C. (1998). *Sales forecasting management*. Thousand Oaks, CA: Sage.

Merriam, J. E., and Makower, J. (1988). *Trend watching: How the media create trends and how to uncover them first*. New York: AMACOM.

Meyersohn, R., and Katz, E. (1957). Notes on a natural history of fads. *American Journal of Sociology, 62*, 594–601.

Michaud, H. A. (1989). *Integrated forecasting, scheduling, and planning: Generic model*. Wilmington, DE: Dupont Information Systems.

Miglautsch, J. (1995). Drowning in data? *Marketing Tools* [Web], 4 pp. Available: www. demographics.com [1998, July 22].

Modis, T. (1992). *Predictions.* New York: Simon and Schuster.

Moin, D. (1990, September 25). Stores making hard decisions for hard times. *Women's Wear Daily,* pp. 1, 4–5.

Moin, D. (1999, January 19). More retailers on Internet, but future may have blips. *Women's Wear Daily,* pp. 2, 6.

Moin, D., Edelson, S., and Tosh, M. (1996, March 25). Charting the cycles: Predictable patterns meet chaos theory. *Women's Wear Daily,* pp. 1, 14–15.

Moin, D., and Socha, M. (1998). Industry leaders thrash out merits of creativity vs. caution. *Women's Wear Daily,* pp. 1, 6.

Morris, B. (1998). Millennium. New York Style [Web], 2 pp.. Available: www.nystyle.com [1998, July 6].

Mower, S. (1996, February). A question of taste. *Bazaar,* 161–162, 208.

Munsell book of color (1976). Baltimore: Munsell Color Company.

Munsell system of color notation. Munsell [Web], 3 pp. Available: www.munsell.com [1998, July 6].

Murphy, P. E., and Laczniak, G. R. (1992). Emerging ethical issues facing marketing researchers. *Marketing Research, 4* (2), 6–11.

Musselman, F. (1997, August). Suiting up Generation X: Tailored clothing gets a makeover. *Apparel Industry Magazine, 58* (8), 56–64.

Musselman, F. (1998, March). Clear on the concept. *Apparel Industry Magazine, 59* (3), 46–50.

Naisbitt, J. (1982). *Megatrends.* New York: Warner.

Naisbitt, J., and Aburdene, P. (1990). *Megatrends 2000.* New York: Morrow.

Naisbitt, J., and Brealey, N. (1996). *Megatrends Asia.* New York: Simon and Schuster.

Nayak, P. R. (1991, July 15). Secrets of better faster innovation. *Boardroom Reports,* 1–2.

Nelson, E. (1998, December 9). The hunt for hip: A trend scout's trail. *Wall Street Journal,* pp. B1, B3.

Nichols, P. (1996, May). Shades of change. *American Demographics* [Web], 1 p. Available: www.demogaphics.com [1998, May 5].

1988: In retrospect. (1988, December 28). *Women's Wear Daily,* p. 10.

Nippon Color and Design Institute (1994). Color and image forecasting. In H. Linton (Ed.), *Color forecasting* (pp. 25–31). New York: Van Nostrand Reinhold.

Noh, M. (1997). *Fashion forecasting information and timing for product development and merchandise selection.* Unpublished master's thesis, Auburn University, Auburn, AL.

Norris, F. (1994, October 23). A bleak year for apparel makers like Van Heusen. *New York Times,* p. 13.

NPD: Clothes buying down for core females. (1999, February 16). *Women's Wear Daily,* p. 4.

Nystrom, P. (1928). Character and direction of fashion movement. In *Economics of fashion.* New York: Ronald Press.

O'Neill, J. (1989, September). Forecasting—Fact or fiction? *Textile Horizons, 9* (9), 26–28.

Oberascher, L. (1994). Cyclic recurrence of collective color preferences. In H. Linton (Ed.), *Color forecasting* (pp. 66–77). New York: Van Nostrand Reinhold.

One-stop shops/Lifestyle Monitor. (1998, July 2). *Women's Wear Daily,* p.2.

Owens, J. (1998, August 26). Survey says loyalty to brands is fleeting. *Women's Wear Daily,* p. 14.

Ozzard, J. (1993, August 18). Ruff Hewn: Living large. *Women's Wear Daily,* p.11.

Ozzard, J. (1995, February). Levi's takes to the streets. *Women's Wear Daily/Denim Network,* p. 26.

Ozzard, J. (1996, May 8). VF's brands serve a broad market. *Women's Wear Daily,* p. 12.

Ozzard, J., and Seckler, V. (1996, September 19). Fashion revolution: The 3-D mega niche. *Women's Wear Daily,* pp. 1, 6–9.

Pacanowsky, M (1995). Team tools for wicked problems. *Organizational Dynamics* [Web], 23, 13 pp. Available: www.elibrary.com [1999, February 22].

Paine, L. S. (1991). Corporate policy and the ethics of competitor intelligence gathering. *Journal of Business Ethics, 10*, 423–436.

Palmieri, J. E. (1998). Eddie Bauer heading back to classics after orgy of orange. *Women's Wear Daily, 1*, 22–23.

Parnes, S. J. (1984). Learning creative behavior. *The Futurist*, 30–32.

Parr, K. (1996, October 31). The image makers. *Women's Wear Daily*, p. 16.

Parr, K. (1997, January 16). Tickling teens with trends. *Women's Wear Daily*, p. 28.

Parr, K. (1998a, April 9). More BP Style. *Women's Wear Daily*, p. 10.

Parr, K. (1998b, July 16). Sweet on vintage. *Women's Wear Daily*, p. 9.

Pasnak, M. F. D., and Ayres, R. W. (1969). Fashion innovators. *Journal of Home Economics, 61* (9), 698–702.

Patterson, G. A. (1993, September 10). Newer ten fashion trip up hip-hop. *Wall Street Journal*, pp. B1–B2.

Peavy, K. K. (1996). *Investigation of expert evaluations of market turbulence in the apparel industry.* Unpublished master's thesis, Auburn University, Auburn, Alabama.

Perna, R. (1987). *Fashion forecasting.* New York: Fairchild.

Pfaff, K. (1998, June). Divining woman. *High Points, 5* (6), 28–30.

Pfaffenberger, B. (1996). *Web search strategies.* New York: MIS Press.

Piirto, Rebecca (1991). *Beyond mind games: The marketing power of psychographics.* New York: American Demographics.

Pine, B. J., Peppers, D., and Rogers, M. (1995, March-April). Do you want to keep your customers forever? *Harvard Business Review, 73* (2), 103–114.

Pine, J. (1993). *Mass customization: The new frontier in business competition.* Boston: Harvard Business School Press.

Pitta, J. (1998, May 18). Putting out feelers. *Forbes Magazine*, 206.

The polarity of retail. (1998, Summer). *Ideations, 5* (2), 1, 4.

Polegato, R. and Wall, M. (1980). Information seeking by fashion opinion leaders and followers. *Home Economics Research Journal, 8*, 327–338.

Polhemus, T. (1994). *Streetstyle: From sidewalk to catwalk.* London: Thames and Hudson.

Polhemus, T. (1996). *Style surfing.* London: Thames and Hudson.

Poling, J. (1963, September 21). Piracy on 7th Avenue. *Saturday Evening Post*, 28–34.

Popcorn, F. (1991). *The Popcorn report.* New York: Doubleday.

Popcorn, F. (1994, May 16). Pop to the editors. *The New Republic*, 4.

Porpcorn, F. (1997). *Clicking.* New York: Harper Collins.

Porter, T. (1994). Color in the looking glass. In H. Linton (Ed,), *Color forecasting* (pp. 1–9). New York: Van Nostrand Reinhold.

Potts, M. (1990, April 15). Purchasing power. *Washington Post*, p. H1.

Power, D. (1998, March 4). Executives taking new look at role of technology. *Daily News Record*, p. 3.

Prescott, J. E., and Smith, D. C. (1989, May-June). The largest survey of "leading-edge" competitor intelligence managers. *Planning Review, 17*, 6–13.

Pressler, M. W. (1995, February 19). From riches to rags? Grunge's flop, other trends wear on the apparel industry. *Washington Post*, pp. H1, H7.

Radeloff, D. J. (1991). Psychological types, color attributes, and color preferences of clothing, textiles, and design students. *Clothing and Textiles Research Journal, 9* (3), 59–67.

Ramey, J. (1995, September 20). Getting the word out. *Women's Wear Daily*, p. 12.

Raper, S. (1998, July). Changing the ways of the couture. *Women's Wear Daily/Global*, pp. 9, 33.

Raper, S., and Weisman, K. (1998, May 27). Paris: The boutique boom. *Women's Wear Daily*, pp. 40, 44.

Reda, S. (1994, August). Home and hearth motivate shoppers. *Stores*, 46–49.

Reda, S. (1995, April). Category management: Who wins? Who loses? *Stores*, 16–19.

Results of the Roper/Pantone consumer color preference study (1997/1998). [Web], 4 pp. Available: www.issihk.com [1998, July 13].

Revamping mail order. (1998, February 26). *Women's Wear Daily* [Web], 3 pp. Available: www.cottoninc.com [1998, June 17].

Reynold, W. H. (1968, July). Cars and clothing: Understanding fashion trends. *Journal of Marketing, 32*, 44–49.

Rice, F. (1994, June 26). Come of age. *Fortune*, 110–113.

Richardson, J. and Kroeber, A. L. (1940). Three centuries of women's dress fashion: A quantitative analysis. *Anthropological Records, 5* (2), 111–153.

Riche, M. F. (1990, June). New frontiers for geodemographics. *American Demographics*, 20.

Rickard, L. (1993). Goodyear text-drives the Visionary shopper for market research. *Advertising Age, 64* (45), 24.

Rickard, L. (1994, July 11). Helping put data in focus. *Advertising Age, 65* (28), 18.

Ries, A. and Trout, J. (1986). *Positioning: The battle for your mind.* New York: McGraw-Hill.

Robertson, T. S. (1971). *Innovative behavior and communication.* New York: Holt, Rinehart and Winston.

Robertson, T. S., Zielinski, J., and Ward, S. (1984). *Consumer behavior.* Blenview, IL: Scott, Foresman.

Robinson, D. E. (1958, November/December). Fashion theory and product design. *Harvard Business Review, 36* (6), 126–138.

Robinson, D. E. (1975, November/December). Style changes: Cyclical, inexorable, and foreseeable. *Harvard Business Review, 53* (6), 121–131.

Rock, A. (1995, July 31). 'Ad generation' still spending. *Advertising Age, 65* (30), 26.

Rogers, E. M. (1962). *Diffusion of innovations.* New York: Glencoe.

Rogers, E. M. (1983). *Diffusion of innovations* (3rd ed.). New York: Free Press.

Roush, G. B. (1991, January-February). A program for sharing corporate intelligence. *Journal of Business Strategy, 12*, 4–7.

Rueff, R. (1991, February 4). Demographics won't find the bull's eye. *Advertising Age, 62* (6), 20.

Russell, C. (1989). Lifestyles of the ordinary and anonymous: A guided tour of the real American market. Presented at the Consumer Outlook conference, New York City.

Sandburg, J. (1999, April 12). The friendly virus. *Newsweek, 65,* 67.

Sapir, E. (1931). Fashion. In R. A. Seligman (Ed.), *Encyclopedia of the Social Sciences,* Vol. 6 (pp. 139–141). New York: Macmillan.

Schiro, A. (1998, May 5). Sign of Autumn: "Watch for falling hemlines." *New York Times* [Web] 4 pp. Available: www.nytimes.com [1998, May 5].

Schiro, A. (1999, February 2). Denim turned every which way but loose. *New York Times,* p. B10.

Schlossberg, H. (1990, March 5). Competitive intelligence pros seek formal role in marketing. *Marketing News, 24,* 2, 28.

Schrage, M. (1997, June 30). Data mining in a vicious circle. *Computerworld,* 37.

Schrank, H. L. (1973). Correlates of fashion leadership: Implications for fashion process theory. *Sociological Quarterly, 14,* 534–543.

Schroeder, M. (1991). *Fractals, chaos, power laws: Minutes from a infinite paradise.* New York: Freeman.

Schweiss-Hankins, D. (1998, November 20). Retail fashion programs and fashion trends. Presentation at the Annual Meeting of the International Textiles and Apparel Association, Dallas, Texas.

Seckler, V. (1995, July 17). Analysts: Women's retail faces uphill trek to skimpy payoff. *Women's Wear Daily,* pp.1, 14–19.

Seckler, V. (1998a, June 24). On-line reminders: What's in store. *Women's Wear Daily,* p. 13.

Seckler, V. (1998b, November 11). Target's successful formula: Upscale trends with discounts. *Women's Wear Daily,* pp. 2, 16.

Seckler, V. (1999, February 12). 41% of U.S. Online by 2002. *Women's Wear Daily,* p. 11.

Shalit, R. (1994, April 18). The business of faith. *The New Republic,* 23–28.

Shannon, V. (1998, December 10). "Push" didn't get the shove. *International Herald Tribune* [Web], 2 pp. Available: www.elibrary.com [1999, February 25].

Shearer, P. (1994). *Business forecasting and planning.* New York: Prentice Hall.

Shedroff, N. (1997). Information interaction design: A unified field theory of design. In R. Jacobson (Ed.), *Information design.* New York: MIT Press.

Shupe, R. (1993, March 29). Grunge: 1992–1993, R.I.P. *New York Magazine,* 24.

Silverman, D. (1998a, August 6). The clout of baby boomers. *Women's Wear Daily,* p. 39.

Silverman, D. (1998b, May 11). Malls have that teen spirit again. *Daily News Record,* pp. 8–9.

Silverman, D. (1998c, March 16). Minority rules: Ethnic buying on the rise. *Daily News Record,* p. 6.

Simmel, G. (1904). Fashion. *International Quarterly, 10,* 130–155.

Simon-Miller, F. (1985). Commentary: Signs and cycles in the fashion system. In M.R. Solomon (Ed.), *The psychology of fashion* (pp. 71–81). Lexington: Heath/Lexington.

Sischy, I. (1994, February 7). Some clothes of one's own. *The New Yorker,* 44–47.

Skenazy, L. (1989, March 20). Publicist Caruba lists most powerful media. *Advertising Age, 60* (12), 62.

Skinner, R. C. (1993, February). Oxford Shirtings tries fashion forecasting. *Consumer Goods Manufacturer, 2* (1), 104–105.

Sloan, P. (1988, October). Makeup: The hue and dye. *Savvy,* 94–96.

Sloan, P. (1991, December 16). Bozell rewires media strategy. *Advertising Age, 62* (53), 12.

Small, R. D. (1997, January 20). Debunking data-mining myths. *Information Week,* 55.

Smith, J. W. (1989, June). Keeping up with the consumer information revolution. Paper presented at the Consumer Outlook Conference sponsored by American Demographics, New York.

Snyder, R. (1991, January). Interview with John Wittenbraker, Vice-President, ARBOR, a Philadelphia Market Research Company. *The Communicator, 26* (1), 6–7.

Socha, M. (1998a, June 8). Differentiate or die—product. *Women's Wear Daily,* pp. 10, 14.

Socha, M. (1998b, May 8). Runways to aisles, picks stick. *Women's Wear Daily,* p. 12.

Socha, M. (1998c, July 23). Tuning in to the street beat. *Women's Wear Daily,* p. 10.

Socha, M., and Lee, G. (1999, February 25). Gucci: The hole truth. *Women's Wear Daily/Denim Network* [Section II], p. 12.

Spindler, A. (1993, September 5). Piety on parade: Fashion seeks inspiration. *New York Times,* pp. 1, 10.

Spindler, A. (1994, September 27). How fashion gave the waif a makeover. *New York Times,* pp. B1. B4.

Spindler, A. (1995, June 13). Are retail consultants missing fashion's X-factor? *The New York Times,* p. B10.

Spindler, A. (1997, June 3). Taking stereotyping to a new level in fashion. *New York Times* [Web], 4 pp. Available: www.archives.nytimes.com [1998, May 5].

Standing out from the crowd/Lifestyle Monitor. (1998, May 14). *Women's Wear Daily,* p. 2.

Stark, S., and Johnson-Carroll, K. (1994, July). Study finds color choices far from random. *Bobbin,* 16, 18.

Steidtmann, C. (1996, October 31). The future of fashion. *Women's Wear Daily* Section II, p. 35.

Stein, J. (1999, January 8). Will ride to the turn of the century. *Los Angeles Times* (Home Edition: Southern California Living), p.1.

Steinhauer, J. (1997, November 7). The most sincere form of flattery: Mass marketing. *New York Times* [Web], 3 pp. Available: www.archives.nytimes.com [1998, May 5].

Steinhauer, J. (1998a, February 24). The Los Angeles contemporary look. *New York Times* [Web], 4 pp. Available: www.archives.nytimes.com [1998, May 5].

Steinhauer, J. (1998b, March 15). The stores that cross class lines. *New York Times/Money and Business,* pp. 1, 11.

Stores lament designer sales. (1990, June 12). *Women's Wear Daily,* pp. 1, 12–13.

Strauss, W., and Howe, N. (1991*). Generations: The history of America's future, 1585 to 2069.* New York: Morrow.

Strom, S. (1994, February 6). After 12 years, Boogie is back on the Merry-Go-Round. *New York Times,* p. 5.

Sullivan, R. (1998, August). Teen tribes. *Vogue,* 217–224.

Sutton, S. M. (1993, March/April). Honing in on the hottest markets. *Monitor, 23* (2), 34–37.

Sykes, S. A. (1994). Color forecasting and marketing for home furnishings. In H. Linton (Ed.), *Color forecasting* (pp. 1–9). New York: Van Nostrand Reinhold.

Szwarce, D. (1994). A colorful experience. In H. Linton (Ed.), *Color forecasting* (pp. 138–145). New York: Van Nostand Reinhold.

Tahmincioglu, E. (1990, June 14). Penney's to offer satellite service. *Women's Wear Daily,* p. 8.

Tain, L. (1997). *Portfolio presentation for fashion designers.* New York: Fairchild.

Talley, A. L. (1998, July). Style fax. *Vogue,* 26.

Tanaka, J. (1998, March 2). Futurism—the trendiest profession. *Newsweek,* 14.

Tapert, A. (1998, September). The American comfort class. *Bazaar,* 474, 550.

The taste test. (1995, October 19). *Women's Wear Daily,* pp. 1, 4–8.

Taylor, J., and Wacker, W. (1997). *The 500 year delta.* New York: Harper Collins.

Teen cool factor: Most top brands gain, some lose ground. (1997, September). *Youth Markets Alert, IX* (9), p. 1.

Tempting the shopper appetite. (1997, April 28). *Women's Wear Daily,* 2.

Terrazas, B., and Huang, T. (1998, February 12). A word to the Y's: Children of baby boomers are growing into the largest teen population in U.S. history. *Dallas Morning News,* p. 1C.

Tetenbaum, T. J. (1997). Shifting paradigms: From Newton to chaos. *Organizational Dynamics* [Web], *26,* 12 pp. Available: www.elibrary.com [1998, December 14].

Tilberis, L. (1995, October). Editor's note. *Bazaar,* 50.

Tilberis, L. (1998, January). Editor's note. *Bazaar,* 18.

Trentham, G. L. (1994). Interview with June Roche, Milliken. Unpublished working paper, Computer-Integrated Forecasting, National Textile Center, Auburn University.

Tunsky, P. (1994). Pat Tunsky, Inc. In H. Linton (Ed.), *Color forecasting* (pp. 179–180). New York: Van Nostrand Reinhold.

Turk, R. (1989, December 3). Fashion taboos are yielding to 'anything goes.' *Birmingham News,* p. 18E.

A 12-step program to revive fashion. (1995, June 21). *Women's Wear Daily,* pp. 1, 6–9.

Tyson, K. W. M. (1997). *Competition in the 21st century.* Delray Beach, FL: St. Lucie Press.

Valle, C. D. (1994, February 7). They know where you live—and how you buy. *Business Week,* 89.

Vargo, J. (1996, August 9). The armored cocoon: Are houses becoming prisons with all the comforts of home? *Dallas Morning News,* p. 1G.

Vasilopoulos, V. (1998, March 2). Kiton, Brioni Windsor some, lose some at Sotheby's. *Daily News Record,* p. 1.

Veblen, T. (1899). *The theory of the leisure class.* New York: Macmillan.

Venkatraman, M. P. (1991). The impact of inovativeness and innovation type on adoption. *Journal of Retailing, 67* (1), 51–67.

Venkatraman, M. P., and Price, L. (1990). Differentiating between cognitive and sensory innovativeness: Concepts, measurement and their implications. *Journal of Business Research, 20,* 293–315.

Verlodt, P. (1994a). Beyond the crystal ball. In H. Linton (Ed.), *Color forecasting* (pp. 159–164). New York: Van Nostrand Reinhold.

Verlodt, P. (1994b). Color Marketing Group. In H. Linton (Ed.), *Color forecasting* (pp. 32–35). New York: Van Nostrand Reinhold.

Volk, T. (1995). *Metapatterns.* New York: Columbia University Press.

Waldrop, M. M. (1992). *Complexity: The emerging science at the edge of order and chaos.* New York: Simon and Schuster.

Wallendorf, M., Belk, R., and Heisley, D. (1988). Deep meaning in possessions: The paper. In M. S. Houston (Ed.), *Advances in Consumer Research,* Vol. 15 (pp. 528–530). Provo, UT: Association of Consumer Research.

Ward, S. (1992, October 1). Harsh '80s shift to soft '90s. *USA Today,* p. E1.

Wasson, C. R. (1968, July). How predictable are fashion and other product life cycles? *Journal of Marketing, 32,* 36–43.

Webb, A. L. (1994). Timing is everything. In H. Linton (Ed.), *Color forecasting* (pp. 203–206). New York: Van Nostrand Reinhold.

Weeden, P. (1977). Study patterned on Kroeber's investigation of style. *Dress, 3,* 8–19.

Weir, J. (1994, November 7). Casual look 'defining character of the '90s.' *Advertising Age, 65* (45), S-2, S-12.

Weiss, M. J. (1988). *The clustering of America.* New York: Harper and Row.

What is a forecast? (1995, December). *American Demographics* [Web], 3 pp. Available: www.demographics.com [1998, July 22].

Wheatley, M. J. (1992). *Leadership and the new science.* San Francisco: Barrett-Koehler.

White, C. (1992, April 1). SA creates new basics from old hits. *Women's Wear Daily,* pp. 1, 6–7.

White, C. C. R. (1997, November 7). Review/Fashion; Invoking tribal spirits in 90's muses. *New York Times* [Web], pp. 3. Available: archives.nytimes.com [1998, May 5].

Wilder, C., Davis, B., and Dalton, G. (1999, February 8). Top of the week: Data gateway—Businesses are adopting the Web portal model as a way of transforming Intranets into more powerful data-delivery platforms. *Information Week,* 18.

Wilke, M. (1995, October). The reluctant shopper in the pink. *American Demographics* [Web], 2 pp. Available: www.marketingpower.com [1998, May 5].

Will cigars stay hot? How to track the trend. (1997, July 21). *Newsweek, 59.*

Wilner, R. (1995, July 17). Factors: Pressure is mounting. *Women's Wear Daily,* p. 17.

Wilson, E. (1985). *Adorned in dreams.* Berkeley: University of California Press.

Wilson, E., and Friedman, A. (1998, June 23). Evening's myriad muses. *Women's Wear Daily,* pp. 6–7.

Winter, D. (1996, September 1). Uh, oh: Colors and fabrics of the '70s are making a comeback. *Ward's Auto World, 32,* 38–41.

Wintour, A. (1998a, July). Letter from the editor. *Vogue,* 22.

Wintour, A. (1998b, August). Letter from the editor: Clans and cliques. *Vogue,* 50.

Wolcott, J. (1998, August). Tanks for the memories. *Vanity Fair, 68,* 70, 73–74, 76.

Wolfe, D. (1989, January 2). Fashion statements [Letter to the editor]. *Newsweek,* 11.

Wolfe, D. (1997, Winter). The cult of cool. *Couture* [Web], 3 pp. Available: www.fashionmall.com [1998, July 13].

Wolfe, D. (1998, January). The state of fashion 1998. Paper presented at the annual meeting of the National Retail Federation, New York.

Wolfe, D. (1999, January). The state of fashion 1999. Paper presented at the annual meeting of the National Retail Federation, New York.

Wolfe, D. B. (1993). *Marketing to boomers and beyond.* New York: McGraw-Hill.

Wolfe, D. B. (1998, April 1). The psychological center of gravity. *American Demographics, 20,* 16–20.

Wood, D. (1990, August 10). Fashion vs. natural looks: Two ways to pick a palette. *Women's Wear Daily,* pp. 8, 10.

Wrack, K. S. (1994). Shopping is in-depth market research. In H. Linton, (Ed.), *Color forecasting* (pp. 181–188). New York: Van Nostrand Reinhold.

Wurman, R. S. (1989). *Hats (Design Quarterly #145).* New York: MIT Press.

Young, A. B. (1937). *Recurring cycles of fashion 1760–1937.* New York: Harper and Row.

Young, V. M. (1998, September 14). Copycat suits increase with competition. *Women's Wear Daily,* pp. 20–21.

Zajac, E. J., and Bazerman, M. H. (1991). Blind spots in industry and competitor analysis: Implications of interfirm (mis)perceptions for strategic decision. *Academy of Management Review, 16* (1), 37–56.

Zessler, I. (1994). Peclers Paris. In H. Linton (Ed.), *Color forecasting* (pp. 195–202). New York: Van Nostrand Reinhold.

Zimbalist, K. (1998a, April). Fashion conspiracy. *Vogue,* 154, 164

Zimbalist, K. (1998b, September). Story of a store. *Vogue,* 274, 278.

Zimmermann, K. A. (1998a, April 4). Duck head shifting into automatic. *Women's Wear Daily,* p. 20.

Zimmermann, K. A. (1998b, December 9). Mass-produced for individual looks. *Women's Wear Daily,* p. 24.

Zimmermann, K. A. (1998c, March 18). Nygard's Quick Response: Paperless and profitable. *Women's Wear Daily,* p. 20.

Zimmermann, K. A. (1998d, July 15). Upgrades for Hudson's Bay. *Women's Wear Daily,* p. 31.

INDEX

A

Abstracting, 203
Accuracy, 370
Achromatic colors, 130
Acrylic Council, 167
Adoption, 42
Advertising Age, 349, 357
A&F Quarterly, 227
Age
    and fashion change, 78
    and preferences, 249–50
Agents in self-organizing systems, 321
Aggregate data, 259
American Demographics, 349
American sportswear, 189
American Wool Council, 144
Analogous colors, 124
Analysis, 213. *See also* Competitive
    analysis; Content analysis;
    Cost/benefit analysis; Statistic
    analysis
Analytical thinking, 377
Androgyny, 78
Anomalies, 370
Apparel industry
    color planning inside, 148–53
    competitive analysis in, 359–60
    forecasting in, 27–31
    forecasting in planning and
        scheduling in, 29–30
    implications of cultural indicators
        in, 303–4
Apparel product developer, 357
Apparel retailers, 357
Appropriateness, visual core concepts
    referencing, 205

Arizona, 222
Armani, Giorgio, 12, 161, 187, 189,
    220
Artificial neural networks, 281
Asset, information as, 346–47
Attitude formation, 42
Attitudes, Interests, and Opinions
    (AIO), 63
Attractiveness, and fashion change, 78
Automated replenishment
    systems, 284–85
Avant-garde concepts, 205–6
Awareness, 42

B

Baby boom generation, 62
Babybusters, 62–63
Backcast, 60
Bass model, 56
Bauer, Eddie, 222
Beene, Geoffrey, 161
Belgium individuality, 190
Benchmarking
    best practices, 371
    competitive, 371
Berardi, Antonio, 197
Best practices benchmarking, 371
Bias, handling, in qualitative
    techniques, 269–70
Biba, 189
Blend, 164
Bloomingdale's, 104
Blue-sky projects, 326
Boolean operators, 352
Boom and bust cycles, 166
Boutiques, 196–97

BP Style, 227
Brainstorming, 296
Brand image, 224
Branding, 224
Brands
    building, 225
    fashion, 222–26
    loyalty to, 224, 225
    names for, 163
    recognition, 225
    tiers in, 285
Branquinho, Veronique, 190
Bridge line, 220
British edge, 189
Bubble up, 92
Building blocks, in self-organizing
    systems, 321
Business consulting/marketing, 403
Business cycle, 275–79
Business news, 348
Business-to-business partners, 362
Butterfly effect, 320
Buzz, 9

C

Cardin, Pierre, 184, 206, 225
Carnaby Street, 189
Catalog 1, 228
Catalogs
    data mining by, 281
    emergence of, 227
    shopping in, 19
Category, organizing data by, 379
Category management, 285–86
Céline, 190
Census Bureau, 267

Chambre Syndicale, 189
Chanel, Coco, 101, 183, 184, 211, 328
Change agents, 44
    fashion, 44–52
    monitoring, 50–51
Chaos theory, 298
    insights from, 319–20
Chase and flight, 77
Chloé, 190
Chroma, 123, 153
Claiborne, Liz, 19, 222
Clanning, 295
Classics, 7, 25, 52–56, 54
Clicking, 293–96
Cluster filter, 354
Coattail effect, 53
Cocooning, 294–95
Cognitive innovators, 45
    strategy for, 51
Cognitive-sensory innovators, 45
Cohen, Jo, 170–71
Cohorts, 22
Collaborative forecasting, 346
    scan template for, 357–58
Collection selection, 67
Collections Premieren Dusseldorf (CPD), 197
Color
    in cars, 134
    in cosmetics, 135
    in interiors, 134–35
    language of, 123–26
    in marketing, 118–19, 144–45
    names for, 126–28
    psychology of, 120–22
    relationships across product categories in, 133–35
    sources for ideas and palettes in, 139–41
    specification systems for, 152–53
Color Association of the United States (CAUS), 117, 128, 145–47
Color cycles, 128–33
    and cultural shifts, 131–32
    forecasting with, 132
    long wave, 128–31
Color forecasting, 30, 115–54, 399–400
    organizations for professional, 144–48
Color Image Scale, 141

Color Key Program, 124–25, 132
Color Marketing Group (CMG), 145, 147–48
Color palette, 116
Color planning
    inside apparel industries, 148–53
    inside textile industries, 148–53
Color research, 133–44
Color story, 116
    dimensions of, 116–28
Color stylists, 139
Colorways, 148
Color wheel, 124
Compatibility, 40
Competitive advantage, 360
Competitive analysis, 23, 358–72
    benefits of, 359–60
    on career building, 374
    methods of data analysis in, 369–72
    question forming and information gathering in, 361–69
    steps in, 360
Competitive benchmarking, 371
Competitive environment scan, 363–64
Competitive intelligence, 358–59
Competitor profile, 365–67
Complementary colors, 124
Complexity, 40
Complexity theory, 324
Comprehension, 42
Computer-aided design (CAD) programs, 153, 340, 366, 396
Concept boards, 385–86
Concept garments, 168
Conspicuous consumption, 75
    quality issues in, 79–80
Conspicuous counterconsumption, 77
Conspicuous leisure, 75
Consumer adoption process, 39, 41–44
Consumer anthropology, 238–39
Consumer Behavior Odyssey, 307–8
Consumer cohorts, 312
Consumer confidence as indicator, 277–78
Consumer Expenditure Survey, 267
Consumer research, 219–53, 402–3
    and demand-activated product development, 220–22
    and fashion brands, 222–26

and listening to the consumer, 234–53
    and mass customization, 231–33
    and retail formats, 226–31
    and sales forecasting, 22–23
Consumers and psychology of color, 120–22
Consumer scan for shifts in preferences and lifestyles, 357
Consumer segmentation, 60–67, 213, 252–53
Consumer stylist, 91
Content analysis, 370
Context, cultural indicators for, 356
Continuum, 379
Convergent thinking, 377
Converters, 171–72
Corporate culture, 365
Correlation techniques, 264, 266–68
Cost/benefit analysis, 179
Cotton Incorporated, 144
COTTONWORKS® Fabric Library, 170–71
Counterfeit, 210
Counter-trends, 296
Courrèges, 206, 211
Couture, 194
Cross dyeing, 165
Cross-shoppers, 252
Cultural drift, 303–4
Cultural indicators, 23, 289–313
    changes in, 161
    implications for textile and apparel industries, 303–4
    and long-term forecasting, 291–99, 302, 304–13
    navigating change in, 290–91
Cultural indicators scans for context, 356
Cultural influence and color preference, 120–21
Cultural journalists, 93
Cultural news, 348
Cultural shifts and color cycles, 131–32
Cycles, 25
    boom and bust, 166
    business, 275–79
    color, 128–33
    fashion, 97–109, 110, 328
    long wave, 129–31

manufacturing, 29
product life, 273–75
Cyclical variations, 10

D
Daily News Record (DNR), 151, 162, 357
Daryl K, 197
Data
gathering, 377
government sources for, 267
methods of analysis, 369–72
organizational schemes for, 378
transforming, into information and knowledge, 378–81
Data mining, 279–86
Data warehouse, 280
Decision making on the edge, 324–26
Decision trees, 281
Decomposition, 275
de la Renta, Oscar, 190, 205
Delphi method, 269, 306–7
Demand, 275
Demand-activated product development, 220–22
Demeulemeester, Ann, 190, 211
Demi-couture, 194
Demimonde, 90
Demographics, 18, 44, 60–61, 245, 248–52
forecasts in, 331
and preferences, 249–52
Dennis, Pamela, 204
Depth interview, 236
Designer name brands, 222
Designer ready-to-wear, 193–94
Designer's designer, 211
Designers' signature collections, 12
Developmental fabrics, 168
Differentiation, 60
Diffusion curves, 39, 327
Diffusion of innovation, 38–60
Diffusion process, 39
visualizing, 56–60
Dior, Christian, 91, 129, 190, 194, 211
Direct competitors, 364
Direction, specificity versus, 334
Directional theories of fashion change, 94–97
Directional trend, 384
Discontinuity, 334

Disinformation, 370
Dissonance, 42
Distant opinion leader, 48
Divergent thinking, 377
Dolce, Dominico, 201
Dominating attitude, 69–70
Dominating events, 68–69
Dominating ideals, 69
Dominating social groups, 69
Dominating technology, 70
Double complements, 124
Dove Creek, 167
Drape, 164
Duck Head Apparel, 285
Dyeing fabric, innovation in, 165

E
Echo boomers, 63
Economic risk, 40
Edge of chaos, 322
Eiseman, Leatrice, 136–38
Electronic data interchange (EDI), 284
Embryonic trends, 384
Enjoyment risk, 40
Enterprise portals, 340
Environmental scanning, 304–5, 347, 351
Equipment management, 394–96
Ergonomics, 295
Erogenous zone, 98
Ethics in competitive analysis, 368–69
Ethnicity
and fashion change, 78
and preferences, 250–51
Ethnic sources, visual core concepts referencing, 204–5
European Textile Selection Show (ETS), 176
Evolution of a trend, 7
Executive committee, 269
Expofil, 173–74
Exponential smoothing, 266
Extranets, 284

F
Fabric
development of, 357
fashion in, 158–61
innovation in design, 166
innovation in structure, 164–65
Fabric councils and commissions, 167, 401–2

Fabric fairs, 172–76
Fabric finishing, 165
innovation in, 165–66
Fabric libraries, 168, 178
Fads, 7, 25, 52–56
future of, 55
versus trends, 334
Fantasy adventure, 295
Fashion(s), 52–56
as balancing act, 326–27
defining, 4–6
on the edge, 323–24
at end of 20th century, 10–20
first era of modern, 183
and gender differences, 6
pendulum of, 104–5
recycling ideas, 98–106
second era of modern, 184
third era of modern, 185–88
Fashion brands, 222–26
Fashion Center, 195
Fashion change
agents in, 44–52
interplay in directional theories of, 94–97
trickle-accross theory of, 83–88
trickle-down theory of, 75–83
trickle-up theory of, 88–94
Fashion Coterie, 197
Fashion counts, 108
Fashion cycles, 97–109, 110, 328
Fashion followers, 50
Fashion forecaster, 187–88
role of, 187
Fashion forecasting, 20–21, 24–27, 399–400
in apparel industry, 27–31
competititve analysis in, 23
consumer research in, 22–23
cultural indicators in, 23
defined, 24–27
future of, 317–42
integrated, 23–24
long-term, 28
and multimedia reporting, 340–41
short-term, 28
sources of information, 179
specialties in, 21–24
steps in developing, 25–26
as team effort, 335–42
in textile industry, 27–31
traps in, 328–35

Fashion geography, 189–93
Fashion Institute of Technology, 8
Fashion leaders, 46–48
Fashion map, 188–202
Fashion movement, 74
    direction of, 328
Fashion neighborhoods, 92
Fashion reporting, 401
Fashion scan for innovation, 356–57
Fashion scouts, 92–94
Fashion trends, 6–20, 7, 265
    avoiding traps in analysis, 332–34
    chasers, 2–20
    evolution of, 7–8
    identification, analysis, and
        synthesis in, 141–44, 202–14
    management in, 9–10
    movement in, 8
    reporting, 381–90, 395
    scouting for, 30–31
    watching, 74
Fashion weeks, 190–91
Fashion writers, 93
Federal Trade Commission (FTC), 163
Feedback filter, 354
FemaleThink, 295
Fibers
    fashion in, 158–61
    innovation in, 163–67
Fieldwork, 362
Filaments, 164
Findings, 166
    innovation in, 166–67
Fiorucci, 100
Fixed-model time-series (FMTS)
    techniques, 266
Flow, 212
Focus groups, 236, 305, 331
    moderator for, 237
    in research, 237–38
Ford, Tom, 190, 194
Forecasting bookmarks, 351
Fortuny, 184
French Luxe, 189
Fringe, 7
Future, probing, with media
    scans, 347–58
Futurists, 403–4

G
Gabbana, Stefano, 201
Galliano, John, 190, 194

The Gap, 14, 16, 222, 226
Garment dyeing, 165
Gatekeepers, 85, 212
Gaultier, Jean-Paul, 22, 96, 201, 202
Gender
    and fashion, 6
    and fashion change, 78
    and preferences, 251–52
Gender bending, 78
Gender blending, 78
Generational cohorts, 61–63, 333
Generation X, 62–63
Generation Y, 63
Generic name, 163
Genetic algorithms, 281
Geodemographics, 245, 248–49
Geographical area, sales volume
    by, 261
Gernreich, Rudi, 206
G.I. generation, 62
Girbaud, Francois, 285
Girbaud, Marithè, 285
Givenchy, 190, 194
Gordon, DeeDee, 246–48
Government sources for data, 267
Graphics, 396
Grunge look, 13
Gucci, 161, 187, 190, 194

H
Halston, 100
Hamnett, Katharine, 96
Hand, 164
Haute couture, 194
High culture, 293
Hilfiger, Tommy, 16, 19, 94, 119, 220,
    222, 225, 299
Historic continuity, 98
Hue, 123
Hype, 9

I
Iconoculture®, Inc., 7, 300–302
Ideabiella, 175
Idea chain, 96–97
Ideacomo, 175
Income and preferences, 252
In-depth interview, 306–7
Indirect competitors, 364
Industrial espionage, 368–69
Influentials, 44, 85
    celebrities as, 48–50

Information
    as asset, 346–47
    gathering, 361–69
    retrieval of, 352–53
    transforming data into,
        378–81
Information cascade, 55–56
Information design, 378
In-house expert, 268–69
In-house forecast, 150–51
Innovations
    characteristics of, 40–41
    diffusion of, 38–60
    in dyeing fabric, 165
    in fabric design, 166
    in fabric finishing, 165–66
    fashion scan for, 356–57
    in fibers, 163–67
    sizing up, 41
    timing of, 162–67
    in trims and findings, 166–67
    in yarns, 164
Innovators, 39, 45–46, 85
    celebrities as, 48–50
    cognitive, 45, 51
    cognitive-sensory, 45
    sensory, 45, 51
    targeting, 51
In-store testing, 243
Integrated forecasting, 23–24
Intensity, 123
Interaction design, 380–81
Internal models in self-organizing
    systems, 321
International Fashion Fabric
    Exhibition (IFFE), 176
International views, 348
International Wool Secretariat,
    167
Internet agents, 353
Interstoff Frankfurt, 176
Interviewing, 305–7
Intranets, 340
Intuition, 377
Italian ease, 189–90

J
Jacobs, Marc, 190
James, Charles, 209, 211
Japanese cut, 190
Johnson, Betsy, 159
Jones, Owen, 129

Jones New York, 162
Journal, keeping, 43
Just In Time (JIT), 258

K
Kamali, Norma, 159, 230
Karan, Donna, 2, 14, 19, 187, 192, 202, 225, 228
Kawakubo, Rei, 190
Kerrigan, Daryl, 211
Keyword filter, 354
Keyword searching, 357
Keywords scan, 350
Klein, Anne, 225
Klein, Calvin, 19, 119, 187, 192, 222, 225, 228
Knitting, 165
Knockoffs, 85, 96, 210–11
Knowledge, 378
    transforming data into, 378–81
Kors, Michael, 190

L
Labeling, 212
la Belle Époque, 75, 83, 189
Laboratory stores, 243
Labor Statistics, Bureau of (BLS), 267
Lacroix, Christian, 11, 22, 211
Lagerfeld, Karl, 12, 228
Land's End, 222, 229
Lang, Helmut, 192, 211
Lanvin couture, 190
Lauren, Ralph, 19, 204–5, 210, 220, 224, 225
Leaders, targeting, 51–52
Leading indicators, 278–79
Learning in self-organizing systems, 321
Lee Jeans, 2
Legal issues in competitive analysis, 368–69
Legitimation, 42
Level, 265
Levi's, 44, 222
Life stages, 64–65
Lifestyles, consumer scan for shifts in, 357
Lifestyle segments, 63–64
Linear, 298
Linear relationships, 319
Lombard, Carole, 205

Long-term forecasting, 28
    process of, 291–99, 302
    toolbox for, 304–13
Long-term trends, 10
Long wave cycles, 129–31
Long wave phenomenon, 25
Los Angeles International Textile Show, 176
Lost sales, 259
Low culture, 293
Lüscher Color test, 120

M
Madame Marguerite, 48
Madame Vionnet, 209
Mademoiselle, 13
Mainstream, 7
Major trends, 383
Mall intercept research, 241
Malls, research in, 240–42
Management profile, 367–68
Mandarina Duck, 303
Man-made fibers, 162, 163–64
Manufactured fibers, 162, 163–64
Manufacturing cycle, 29
Margiela, Martin, 190, 211
Markdowns, 259
Market information, media scans for, 358–72
Marketing
    color, 118–19, 144–45
    real-time, 258–59, 283–84
    relational, 239–40
    viral, 9
Market intelligence, 4
Market orientation, 4
Market reports, 365
Market scan, 364–65
Mass customization, 231–33
Mass market theory, 84
Mass production, efficiency of, 85
McCardell, Claire, 129, 189, 209, 328
McCartney, 190
McFadden, Mary, 159
McQueen, Alexander, 190, 194
Media analysis, 404
Media scans, 305
    for market information, 358–72
    probing future with, 347–58
Mega nichers, 19, 225
Megatrends, 15–16, 292–93
Memes, 8–9

Merry-Go-Round, 13
Metaphor, 379
Microfibers, 164
Microtrends, 7–8
Mid-range strategies, 359
Millennial generation, 63
Miller, Nicole, 11, 187, 204, 222
Mind map, 338
Minimalist scan, 350
Minor trends, 383
Mischka, Badgley, 205
Missoni, 189
Miyake, Issey, 190
Miyake, Issey, 161
Moda-In, 175
Model building, 281
Modernity, 206
Mods, 189
Montana, Claude, 22, 96
Moving average, 266
Mugler, Thierry, 96
Multimedia reporting, 340–41
Multiple time horizons, 327–28
Munsell Color System, 152–53
Muse, 204

N
Narrative drive, 391–92
National brands, 222
National Knitwear and Sportswear Association, 174
National news media, 347–51
Natural fibers, 162, 163
Nautica, 162, 220
New York Premier Collections, 197
The New York Times, 357
Niches in self-organizing systems, 321
Nike, 94, 222
Nippon Color and Design Research Institute (NCD), 141–43
Noise, 265
Nonlinear pattern, 320
Nonlinear relationships, 319
Nonlinear systems, 298
Normative forecasting, 332
Novelty fabrics, 165
Nygard International, 284–85

O
Observability, 40
Observation, 307–8
Obsolescence, 6

Oldham, Todd, 201
Omissions, 370
Online shopping, emergence of, 228–30
Open-model time-series (OMTS), 266
Outliers, 370

P
Panel studies, 244–45
PANTONE® Professional Color System, 152
Participant observer, 298
Past, visual core concepts referencing, 204
Patou, 184
Pattern recognition, 370, 377
Pendulum swing, 22
Perceived risk, 40
Performance fabrics, 161
Piece dyeing, 165
Pinpoint searches, 352
Pitti Filati, 174
Planned obsolescence, 6
Point-of-sale (POS) data, 23
Point-of-sale (POS) scanners, 259, 284
Poiret, Paul, 54, 129, 184, 211
Polling experts, 269
Polo, 162
Polyester Council, 167
Popular culture, 48, 293
Positioning strategy, 60, 225
Postmodern, 206
Potential Rating Index by Zip Market (PRIZM), 245, 248
Prada, Miuccia, 18, 161, 347
Pratoexpo, 175
Precursor media, 349
Preferences
    and age, 249–50
    consumer scan for shifts in, 357
    and demographics, 249–52
    and ethnicity, 250–51
    and gender, 251–52
    and income, 252
Première Vision, 140, 175, 176
Presentations, 177
    design as creative process in, 376–81
    techniques of, 391–97
PreTex, 174
Primary colors, 124
Primary sources, 7

Print, development of, 357
Print shows, 171–72
Private-label brands, 222
Problem perception, 42
Product categories, color relationships across, 133–35
Product life cycle, 273–75
Products, reverse engineering for, 371–72
Product segmentation, 253
PromoStyl, 177
Proximity operators, 352
Psychographics, 44, 61
Pull technology, 354
Purchase decisions, 54
Push technology, 354
Pyramid model, 44

Q
Qualitative method of research, 237
Qualitative techniques in sales forecasting, 264–65, 268–70
    blending with quantitative techniques, 272–73
    handling bias in, 269–70
Quality issues in conspicuous consumption, 79–80
Quant, Mary, 184, 189
Quantitative research, 240
Question forming, 361–69
Quick Response (QR), 258, 284–85

R
Rabanne, Paco, 206
Real-time marketing, 258–59
    and data mining, 279–86
    and strategic data partnerships, 283–84
Regional markets, 199
Regional media, 349
Regression techniques, 264, 266–68
Relational marketing, 239–40
Relative advantage, 40, 51
Reliability of information, 370
Retail anthropology, 238–39
Retail formats, 226–31
Retro fashion, 98, 99–100
Reverse engineering
    for products, 371–72
    for services, 372
Reverse ostentation, 77

Rifkind, Steven, 93–94
Rodriguez, Narciso, 197
Rogers model, 56
Rule induction, 281
Runway shows, 214

S
Saint Laurent, Yves, 12, 91, 184, 210, 211, 225
Sales channel, sales volume by, 261
Sales forecasting, 257–86, 259, 260
    in context, 273–79
    methods in, 261, 264–73
    understanding, 270–71
Sales plan, 260
Sales volume, 261
    by geographical area, 261
    by sales channel, 261
    by time period, 261
Sampling, 173
Sampling sources, 352
Sander, Jill, 161, 206
Satellite trade shows, 191
Saturation, 123
Scanning, technology tools for, 351–55
Scenario writing, 312–13
Schedule, 191–93
Schiaparelli, 184
Scope of trend, 385
S-curve, 57–59
Search engines, 352
Seasonal Color Analysis, 125–26
Seasonality, 265
Seasonal trends, researching, 168–78
Secondary colors, 124
Secret shopper, 363
Self-organized criticality, 323
Self-organizing systems, 320–22
Semiotics, 206
Sensitization, 371
Sensory design, 381
Sensory innovators, 45
    strategy for, 51
Services, reverse engineering for, 372
Sexuality, visual core concepts referencing, 205
Shade, 123
Shadow market planning, 371
Shifting erogenous zones, theory of, 98–99
Short-term forecasting, 28, 346
Short-term variations, 10

Showcase stores, 243
Showrooms, 195
Silent generation, 62
Simultaneous adoption theory, 84
Smith, Jaclyn, 222
Social risk, 40
Society of Competitive Intelligence
    Professionals (SCIP), 360, 369
Soft information, 362
Solution dyeing, 165
Specificity versus direction, 334
Spiegel, 2–3, 228
Split complements, 124
Sports, visual core concepts
    referencing, 205
Sprouse, Stephen, 128
*The Standard Color Reference of
    America,* 145
Staple length, 164
Static equilibrium, lack of, in self-
    organizing systems, 321
Statistic analysis, 332–33
Status float phenomenon, 89
Status markers, 77
    shifting power of, 79
Status symbols, and fashion change, 79
Stockouts, 259
Store brands, 222
Stores, research in, 240–42
Strange attractor, 320
Strategic data partnerships, 283–84
Strategic planning, 359
Strategic windows, 4
Strauss, Levi, 240
Street fashion, 200–202
Style testing, 242
Style tribes, 185–87
StyleWorks, 197
Subcultures, 90
Subject tree, 352
Sui, Anna, 187, 201, 202
Supply chain, 163
Survey research, 242
Surveys, 244–45
Syndicated surveys, 268
Synthesis, 213

T
Tactics, 359
Target (store), 3–4
Target audience, 9, 60, 179
    linking visible elite to, 81

Target markets
    color in, 119
    visualizing, 66–67
Technical fabrics, 161
Technology news, 348
Technology tools for scanning, 351–55
Techtextil, 176
Tertiary colors, 124
Test merchandise groups, 243–44
Test stores, 243
Textile Color Card Association of
    America (TCCA), 117, 145
Textile development, 30, 157–80
    fashion in fiber and fabric, 158–61
    researching seasonal trends
        in, 168–78
    sources of innovation in, 161–68
Textile Fibers Products Identification
    Act, 163
Textile forecasting, 399–400
Textile industry
    color planning inside, 148–53
    forecasting in, 27–31
    implications of cultural indicators
        in, 303–4
Textile specialization, 356
Textile Trend Watch, 158
Textile World, 162
Texture, 164
Thinking inside the box, 337
Thinking outside the box, 337
Thirteenth generation, 62–63
3-D brands, 225, 226
Time horizons, 331
Time lags, 95–96
Timeliness of information, 370
Time period, sales volume by, 261
Time-series forecasting, 264, 265–66
Time Warner, 228
Timing of trend, 385
Tint, 123
Tone, 123
Trade dress, 210
Trade media, 349
Trade organizations, 167
Trade shows, 172–76, 197, 199
Trend boards, 385–89, 392, 395
Trend contagion, 8–9
Trend dynamics, 212
Trend folders, reviewing, organizing,
    and editing, 308, 310
Trend map, 383–85

Trend multiplication, 182–88
Trends
    versus fads, 334
    offsetting, 334
    overlap in, 333
Trends Union, 177
Trendy, 7
Triads, 124
Trial, 42
Trialability, 40
Trial balloons, 211–12, 383–84
Trickle-across theory, 83–88
    in action, 87–88
    criticism of, 87
Trickle-down theory, 75–83
    in action, 78–80
    aggressive imitation, 81
    applying, in today's
        marketplace, 81–83
    criticism and revision of, 76–78
    fast-paced differentiation, 80–81
    origins of, 75–76
Trickle-up theory, 88–94
    applying in today's marketplace,
        94
Trims, 166
    innovation in, 166–67
Tully, Brian, 262–64
TV shopping, emergence of, 227–28
Two-step flow, 56
Tyler, Richard, 177

U
Unethical practices, 369
Utne Reader, 349

V
Valente, Sergio, 100
Value, 123, 153
Van Noten, Dries, 190
Versace, Gianni, 12, 96, 189
Vertical flow, 95
Vexed Generation, 93
VF Corporation, 285
Victoria's Secret, 222
Vintage fashion, 99–100, 201–2
Vionnet, 19, 211
Viral marketing, 9
Virtual dressing rooms, 228
Visual core concepts, 204–6
Visualization(s), 25, 59, 74, 319
    of target markets, 66–67

Visuals, 392–93
Vogue, 105
Vuitton, Louis, 190

W
Wall Street Journal, 350, 357
Wang, Vera, 177, 204
Wave dynamics, 106, 108–9

Weaving, 164–65
Wet Seal, Inc., 3
Wolfe, David, 207–9, 211
Women's Wear Daily (WWD), 16–18, 85, 151, 162, 357
Wool Bureau, 167
Word-of-mouth, 9
Worth, Charles Frederick, 182

Y
Yamamoto, Yohji, 190
Yarn Fair International, 174
Yarns, innovation in, 164
Yarn shows, 173–74

Z
Zeitgeist, 67–71, 209–10, 328, 384